THE
UNKNOWN
NAVY

To Wilma

THE UNKNOWN NAVY

CANADA'S WORLD WAR II MERCHANT NAVY

Robert G. Halford

Vanwell Publishing Limited

St Catharines, Ontario

Vanwell Publishing Limited
1 Northrup Crescent, Box 2131
St Catharines, Ontario L2M 6P5

First edition 1995
Printed in Canada
98 97 96 95   1 2 3 4 5

Design Linda Moroz

Canadian Cataloguing in Publication Data

Halford, Robert G.
The Unknown Navy: Canada's World War Two Merchant Navy

ISBN 1-55125-016-0

1. World War, 1939-1945 - Campaigns - Atlantic
Ocean. 2. World War, 1939-1945 - Transportation.
3. Merchant marine - Canada - History - 20th century.
4. Shipbuilding industry - Canada - History -
20th century. I. Title.

D9.C2H35 1994   940.54'5971   C94-931778-0

On the cover: A famous oft repeated wartime theme: convoy assembly in Bedford Basin, Halifax. According to their speed capability, merchant ships were assigned to fast or slow convoys. Those capable of at least 15 knots were allowed to sail independently (i.e., alone). *NAC PA112993*

CONTENTS

ACKNOWLEDGEMENTS

In the approximately six years representing the period of active research and writing that went into the preparation of this book, many individuals and organizations were called upon for assistance. The response to that call for information and memoirs was more than gratifying, probably reflecting a growing feeling that this was a story that finally should be told.

The Canadian Merchant Navy Association was the key to opening the door to contact with hundreds of wartime merchant seamen who had sailed on Canadian merchant ships. In letters, some hand-written, some typed, on tape and through personal interviews, scores of them answered with their recollections of life at sea during that hazardous time. There are too many of them to list individually here, but most of their names appear scattered throughout the following pages, and particularly in Part III, "In Their Own Words." For those who responded not in a manner lending itself to direct quotation, the insights and details they provided of their wartime experiences afloat, and ashore, nevertheless were of immeasurable value in the preparation of the manuscript and I am equally grateful for their contribution.

One whose name should be singled out here, however, is that of the late Roy Spry, a past president of the CMNA who in that role and then as the Association's membership chairman, played a central role in the growth and activities of the Association. His cooperation and assistance together were a significant factor in building the bank of information from which to draw, when the time to begin writing at last arrived.

The National Archives of Canada is a treasure trove of Canadian history, in this case, maritime history, but it requires the helping hand of the archivists to tap its riches. My first contact with that venerable repository was in 1989 when Archivist Glenn Wright was most generous in time and assistance in setting me on the right course at the start of my research. His interest in the project was ongoing and continued until he moved on to other archival duties, but when that happened Paul Marsden and Anne Martin proved to be equally helpful. Their willingness, indeed eagerness, to assist I discovered were the norm for the many other men and women employees of the National Archives who in myriad ways aided me in my searches, and convinced me that civil servants suffer from a bad press.

I wish also to acknowledge the assistance of Max Reid, author of *DEMS At War!*, which was the source of much of the information contained in the chapter on Defensively Equipped Merchant Ships. His suggested changes ensured an accurate description of the armaments package with which the Park ships were equipped, and of the branch of the Navy charged with the care and operation of that package. Similarly, I am grateful to Jim Green, author of *Against the Tide*, and the Canadian Seamen's Union History Project Committee, for allowing me to use that well-researched book as a major reference for my chapter on the Canadian Seamen's Union.

Others were generous with leads and suggestions as well as with offers to allow me to inspect their memorabilia. John H. Gill of Greenfield Park, Quebec, saved me a multitude of trips to the reference library stacks by providing me with a copy of Mitchell and Sawyer's incomparable *The Oceans, The Forts and the Parks*, without which no Canadian marine historian can possibly function. In a like vein, Michael D. Jackman of Burlington, Ontario, whose longstanding interest in the U-boat war traces back to his days as a very youthful Newfoundlander witnessing the Battle of Belle Isle, gave enthusiastic assistance and allowed me long-term access to his copy of Jürgen Rohwer's meticulous record of sinkings by axis submarines, *Die U-Boot-Erfolge der Achsenmächte 1939-1945*. Then there is Ken Macpherson of Port Hope, Ontario, naval historian and author, who unselfishly loaned his personal collection of merchant ship photos to help with the illustration of this work.

Finally, I wish to thank my wife, Wilma, for patiently awaiting the completion of the writing and then carefully proofing the entire manuscript of *The Unknown Navy*.

INTRODUCTION

"But I didn't know that."

The men who sailed on Canadian merchant ships during World War II, as well as those who built them, have grown accustomed to such a reaction from postwar generations to the news that during that mighty conflict of half a century ago Canada operated the wartime world's fourth[1] largest Merchant Navy, almost all of it built in Canadian shipyards. And the response to a personal claim of service in the wartime Merchant Navy is commonly, "You mean you were in the Navy?" Indeed, only with the mounting in the late 1980s of a campaign, ultimately successful in 1992, to gain official recognition for wartime merchant seamen as "Veterans," five decades after the fact, was some public attention focused on what was without question one of Canada's most important contributions to the success of the Allied cause.

It comes as a surprise to most that Canadian Government wartime expenditures, as well as the labour force involved, in the shipbuilding industry that supplied the fleet of preponderantly cargo vessels for the wartime Canadian Merchant Navy, were larger than those for the highly successful aircraft industry.[2] By war's end, Canada's merchant fleet, though substantially smaller than those of the Americans and British, trailed only those two among the western maritime powers. In construction of the 10,000 ton Park and Fort ships which became Canada's wartime standard ships, records in productivity were achieved but unfortunately were overshadowed by the better publicized though deservedly acclaimed United States Liberty ship program.[3] Despite this amazing achievement—Britain's Joint Parliamentary Secretary to the Ministry of War Transport, Sir Arthur Salter, described it as "magnificent" and "one of the most remarkable things in the history of the British Commonwealth"—it has received scant recognition in postwar overviews. The only two available biographies of the Hon. C. D. Howe, who was wartime Minister of Munitions and Supply responsible for shipbuilding, barely touch the subject. *C. D. Howe, A Biography*, by Robert Bothwell and William Kilbourn (McClelland & Stewart), offers scant detail, though it does boast that unit costs had been reduced to the point where ships built in Canadian yards were actually cheaper than their American counterparts built only a few hundred miles away. *C. D. Howe*, by John D. Harbron (part of The Canadians series published by Fitzhenry & Whiteside Ltd.), mentions shipbuilding only in the context of escort vessels for the Navy, and merchant ship construction not at all.

If Canada's shipbuilding effort could be praised as "magnificent" by Sir Arthur Salter, and the Canadian Merchant Navy described as a "fourth arm of the fighting forces" by the Hon. J. E. Michaud, Canada's wartime Transport Minister, and others prominent at the highest civil and military levels of government, how to explain this complete lack of present day public awareness? Compared to the plethora of reminders of the wartime achievements of the Navy, Army and Air Force that continues to this day, an ocean of silence surrounds the long gone Canadian Merchant Navy.

That it is long gone partially explains its present anonymity. Wartime secrecy, too, was a factor, but more important was the circumstance that at both the operational and administrative levels, the Canadian Merchant Navy involved relatively small numbers of personnel. Whereas the individual Armed Services each numbered in the hundreds of thousands, the Merchant Navy peaked at about twelve thousand. Whereas the military service establishments included almost as many administrative and support personnel as they placed on the front lines, the Canadian Merchant Navy had a single point man, Director of Merchant Seamen Arthur Randles, operating with a small staff from an Ottawa office. For the Merchant Navy, there was no equivalent to the Armed Services' platoons of Public Relations Officers to bombard the press and radio services daily with "hometowner" news releases about what the boys "somewhere overseas" were doing. Official casualty lists did not include merchant seamen, though their losses were disproportionately high vis-à-vis those for the Canadian Navy.

Postwar, the Army, Navy and Air Force carried on without loss of identity, albeit establishments much reduced. Despite these reduced circumstances, the three military services were still sufficiently active and in possession of the resources to continue publicizing their less glamourous peacetime roles, thus ensuring a place for themselves in the public consciousness on an on-going basis.

The Canadian Merchant Navy had no comparable infrastructure to ease the transition from war to peace. With the war's conclusion and the end of Government control, the Merchant Navy dissolved as a unified entity. For much of the war, the bulk of the merchant fleet was made up of the so-called Park ships, the Canadian-built 10,000 ton vessels operating under the flag of the Crown-owned Park Steamship Company Limited. While a minority of other Canadian ships were involved, it was the 176 Park ships with which the public generally identified the Canadian Merchant Navy, though they had no idea the fleet had grown to such a size. But with the end of the war, the Government moved quickly to sell off the ships. Many were bought by the Canadian shipping firms who had been managing them for Crown-owned Park Steamship Company on a contract basis, a term of the sale being that the new owners continue to operate the ships under Canadian registry with Canadian crews.

In this way, a much-reduced Canadian fleet remained in being for a few years after the war, though it no longer operated as a single entity. The ships, all having been renamed and dispersed under numerous house flags, had lost their common identity. Their Admiralty gray uniforms now discarded, they had taken on a variety of more colourful civvy garbs. Within a few years peacetime ship operating economics and the Canadian Government's Draconian union-busting reaction to an industry-wide strike of unlicensed sailors, combined effectively to sink what was left of the war-created Canadian Merchant Navy, something that U-boats and storms at sea had been unable to do. Obsessed with the "Communists under the bed" syndrome epidemic in the western world, the Canadian Government, with the whole-hearted support of the shipping industry, imported the infamous Hal Banks from the United States to lead the brutal no-holds-barred suppression of the Canadian Seamen's Union, whose leadership, though not its rank and file, was Red-tinged. Having successfully accomplished the destruction of the CSU, the Government then dropped its Canadian registration requirement for the taxpayer-financed ex-Park ships, which the new owners lost no time in transferring to low cost, less stringently regulated foreign registries. With that, whatever awareness still existed of a Canadian Merchant Navy, quickly faded from the Canadian public's perception.

Canadian seamen, licensed and unlicensed, turned their thoughts to other careers. Few in number, widely scattered and with no postwar support groups[4] or Government-sponsored rehabilitation programs such as those open to ex-Army, Navy and Air Force personnel, the ex-merchant seamen fell back on their own resources, learned new trades and professions and dispersed across the land. It would not be until forty years after the war that with reviving memories of what they had done and how it had been on those often dangerous seas, that the realization would grow among them that they had been ill-served by the nation. This realization would eventually coalesce into group action[5] which in 1992, too late for more than half their original numbers, finally brought a form of recognition to the seamen as "Veterans," eligible for associated Government benefits.

Meanwhile, the ship construction industry, which boomed during the war years producing 354[6] 10,000 ton and 43 4700 ton mostly cargo ships, plus 6 3600 ton tankers, as well as 487 escorts and minesweepers for the Royal Canadian Navy, shrank quickly with the cancellation of defence orders. The industry nevertheless was able to maintain some level of activity meeting foreign orders and supporting the surviving Canadian merchant fleet that steamed on for several postwar years. But the Government eventually ended subsidies for Canadian shipyards, without which they could not compete with low-cost foreign yards. So orders for new deep-sea construction dried up and the Canadian merchant fleet vanished to foreign registries, leaving Canadian shipbuilders to wither, some sustained by lake ship construction which, too, has become an industry teetering on the edge. Only a handful of merchant orders, such as for B.C. Government ferries, and the naval frigate and minesweeper construction programs, keep alive what remains of the industry that reached such an astonishing pinnacle of productivity during World War II.

PART ONE

Chapter One   **BACKGROUNDER**

The dream of a Canadian flag merchant marine—carrying Canadian trading goods in Canadian-built bottoms owned and operated by Canadian companies, and crewed by Canadians—has proved an elusive one, notwithstanding the nation's thousands of miles of coastline fronting on three oceans, and its long-established status as an important world trader. Occasional Government intervention, either in the form of subsidization of private companies or direct involvement in ship ownership and operation, the most recent example being the Crown-owned Park Steamship Company of World War II, has provided short-lived intervals during which Canadian flag ships became familiar sights in the seaports of the world. History has shown these occasional flag fleet appearances to be only temporary blips in an established pattern.

More typical of the century and a half since the sailing ship began slipping from pre-eminence, is the current situation with only a miniscule proportion—less than one percent according to some estimates—of Canadian deep-sea trade being carried in Canadian-registered ships. Ships flying such flags of convenience as Liberia and Panama alone account for the carriage of approximately one-third of Canadian exports and imports. The annual foreign exchange bill for this almost total reliance on foreign shipping has been estimated at over $5 billion. The other side of the coin, according to Canadian exporters and importers, is that their competitiveness would be seriously if not fatally wounded, were they forced to rely on Canadian-registered ships, which are burdened by high costs of operation as well as a lack of tax break incentives similar to those enjoyed by foreign ship owners. Subsidies as high as 17 percent have been projected as necessary to make Canadian-operated ships competitive.[1]

This is not to say that today Canadian shipping companies own no foreign-going ships. In the mid-1980s Montreal shipping analyst Kevin Griffin reported that there were no less than 114 vessels totalling 7.5 million tons deadweight[2] owned by Canadians but operating under foreign flags. There were also 82 Canadian-registered ships with deep-sea capability totalling over a million tons deadweight, though they were not necessarily in foreign trade.

The present state of Canadian shipping relative to other maritime nations contrasts sharply with that prevailing during the nineteenth century when Canada, particularly pre-Confederation Nova Scotia, was an important player in the maritime world. With the colony's ample forests, a rich source of construction materials and tall masts for the kinds of wooden sailing ships then dominating the ocean trade routes of the world, Halifax became the home of such ship builders and operators as Samuel Cunard.

Samuel Cunard was a descendant of a family of Prussian Quakers who in the late seventeenth century settled in what is now Pennsylvania. The family was headed by Cunard's great- great- grandfather, Thones Kunders, whose surname, through mispronunciations and misspellings over the years, eventually evolved into Cunard. Legend has it that Thones unearthed some buried pirate treasure and with this new-found fortune moved to Philadelphia where he purchased a coastal vessel, the start of a large and successful fleet. The family, loyal to the British Crown, moved to Halifax in 1780 after suffering the indignity of having had all their ships confiscated during the American Revolution. By that time the Cunards were headed by Abraham, great-grandson of Thones and father in 1787 of Samuel, the second son in a family of nine children. On Samuel's twenty-first birthday, his father took him into the increasingly affluent family business, now renamed A. Cunard and Son, simultaneously announcing that they had just acquired their first ship, the *Margaret*.

Following the 1812-14 war, during which the Cunard fleet grew to thirty vessels, Abraham turned the company over to Samuel and the name was changed to S. Cunard and Company, the "and Company" including two of Samuel's brothers, Joseph and Henry. By this time, the first marine applications of steam power had arrived on the scene, though initially these were confined to vessels operating on rivers and inland waterways. The conventional wisdom of the day was that the steamers' paddle wheels would not stand up to the batterings of open ocean voyaging.

While continuing to rely on the wind to power his company's ships, Samuel closely monitored steam developments. He became a major shareholder in the Quebec and Halifax Steam Navigation Company, which in 1830 ordered the construction of the *Royal William*, a ship that was to become an important symbol in the history of trans-Atlantic travel. This particular historical association notwithstanding, the *Royal William* was originally intended only for trade between Quebec and Halifax, its construction having been prompted by the promise of the Legislative Assembly of Lower Canada to provide £3,000 sterling to subsidize such a service for three years. Unfortunately, for reasons unrelated to the capabilities of the *Royal William*, the enterprise was not a success and the Quebec and Halifax Steam Navigation Company failed. In 1833, the ship was bought at auction by six former company shareholders who, after a short period of unprofitable operation, decided to sell her in England.

After taking on coal and passengers at Pictou, Nova Scotia, the *Royal William* began her historic twenty-five-day Atlantic crossing[3] on 17 August 1833, arriving in London on 14 September following a pause at the Isle of Wight for repairs and to be gussied up in preparation for inspection by potential buyers. Logged entries for the ocean crossing include notations of stops every four days en route to cleanse the boilers of salt deposits. Essentially a ferry operation with no aim other than to get to London where prospects for sale were greatest, the trans-Atlantic voyage of the *Royal William* under steam power nevertheless clearly, if unintentionally, demonstrated the feasibility of ocean steam navigation, and thus was an achievement that most certainly marked the beginning of the steam era of ocean travel.[4] Perhaps it was not immediately realized or admitted by contemporary shipping companies or mariners, but with the docking of the *Royal William* in London, the sailing ship had in effect been dispatched on a decades-long voyage to a permanent berth in the age of romance. Soon the black smudges of coal smoke from the funnels of the steamers would become a more familiar sight on the trade routes of the world than the white sails of the tall ships.

The *Royal William* is significant in Canadian maritime history, not only as the precursor of steam ocean navigation, but also because she was wholly the product of the Canadian shipbuilding industry. Built in Trois Rivières, Quebec, at the Campbell and Black shipyard, she was powered by twin 90 horsepower engines produced in Montreal by the foundry of Bennet and Henderson. Steam power was the high tech of the nineteenth century and Canada was not to be left behind.

While Samuel Cunard's direct involvement with the *Royal William* had ended with the demise of the Quebec and Halifax Steam Navigation Company, the ship marked the start of his interest in steam and he continued to maintain his careful watching brief on all developments relating to steam navigation. In 1838 he decided that the time was ripe to make the move into steam propulsion. One of the factors that prompted him was the knowledge that the British Post Office had introduced penny post, which was expected to lead to a large increase in the volume of mail moving across the Atlantic. Although Cunard yet had no steamers, when the Post Office issued a call for tenders for regular trans-Atlantic mail service, he outbid the competition, including an established steamship company which had been carrying the mail.

Awarded in 1839, the seven-year contract called for "twice-monthly service across the Atlantic, with branch lines to Quebec and Boston, at a cost of £55,000 sterling a year,"[5] subsequently increased to £60,000 sterling, the first of many such increases. To carry out the terms of the contract, Samuel Cunard organized the British and North American Royal Mail Steam Packet Company, with the principal backing being supplied by powerful British financial houses. Once regular service got underway with purpose-built ships from Clyde shipbuilder Robert Napier, the operating company's unwieldy name soon was to be found only on official documents and it became more familiarly known as the Cunard Line.

With the founding of this new enterprise, the centre of gravity of Samuel Cunard's operations shifted to Britain; not surprisingly, the man and his family followed that shift, settling in London. The Cunard Line's Canadian connection became tenuous. Halifax had dreamed that it would be the North American terminus for the new Atlantic steamer mail service, but it was deemed too small and, more importantly, it was isolated, with no rail connection to Montreal and Upper Canada. Although Halifax was briefly made a port of call, Boston became the designated terminus for Canadian as well as American mail. Eventually, New York replaced Boston as the Cunard Line's North American terminus for its ever-growing service. The company soon dropped Canadian feeder service linking Pictou, Nova Scotia, with Quebec City, completing the transition of the Britain/North America link into an exclusively Anglo-American route. With that, Cunard's original Canadian roots became primarily a historical reference. In a symbolic gesture signifying that Britain had fully adopted the Cunard Line as one of its own, the family patriarch was honoured with a baronetcy. Sir Samuel Cunard died in 1865.

The *Royal William* had been built in response to a Colonial Government initiative offering to subsidize service between Quebec and Halifax. The failure of that early experiment did not discourage the newly autonomous Canada Post Office from a much more ambitious plan in 1851 to subsidize nothing less than a Liverpool-Quebec-Montreal service. The Liverpool firm which initially won the £24,000 sterling contract proved unsatisfactory and in 1855 a new contract was signed with Hugh Allan's Montreal Ocean Steamship Company. The signing was an act of defiance by the Canadian Colonial Government, which was under pressure from Britain not to establish a competing Atlantic steamer service.

The Allan Line was operating on a weekly schedule by 1857 with the assistance of an annual subsidy of £55,000 sterling, an amount that proved insufficient in the face of the loss of nine ships through shipwreck. Nevertheless, the company's solid effort in maintaining the service over the demanding North Atlantic route despite these losses, had earned the trust of the Canadian Government, which not only continued to provide support but by 1860 had bumped up the subsidy to £104,000 sterling. By 1891 Allan boasted a fleet of no less than thirty-seven steamers and was operating eight different passenger services over the North Atlantic. Always in the van in the adoption of new technologies, in 1907 the company became the first to introduce steam turbine propelled passenger ships on the North Atlantic.[6] The Allan Line's service between Britain and Quebec/Montreal (using Halifax as its winter port) continued into the twentieth century, though in later years it was no longer the exclusive mail carrier. The company survived until 1916 when its by then eighteen vessels were taken over by Canadian Pacific Steamships.

* * *

The Canadian Government's next significant foray into merchant marine operations was very substantial and much more direct than its previous subsidizations of the shipping services of private companies. During and immediately after World War I, swollen wartime trans-Atlantic supply requirements, in combination with heavy losses of shipping to U-boats and surface raiders, severely strained Allied ocean shipping capacity, a scenario that was to be repeated during and after WW II. For the first time, the Canadian Government intervened directly, ordering a fleet of cargo vessels from Canadian shipyards.

"Early in 1918," the first annual report of the Canadian Government Merchant Marine, Limited explained, "the Dominion Government, owing to the serious shortage of world tonnage, realized the imperative need of Canada creating, owning and operating a strong merchant marine of her own." The report, which covered the year ended 31 December 1919, went on to say that the ships that were built "were intended primarily to cooperate with the British shipping in supplying the necessities of war, and in times of peace to provide the means of carrying abroad the products of Canada's farms, forests, mines and factories, without which Canada could not hope to take full advantage of the opportunity of expanding her export trade."

If the Canadian Government was serious in its expressed intention of helping British shipping in supplying the necessities of war, it seems strange that it waited until the waning days of World War I before acting. It was not until March 1918 that the first shipbuilding contract was placed, no more than eight months before the November Armistice, and no ships were delivered until early in 1919. Thus, the fleet of ships created by this ambitious but ultimately misguided program made no contribution to the 1914-18 war effort and in the event the smallest of them, which significantly made up over one-third of the fleet, proved unsuitable for competitive deep-sea peacetime operations.

Initially, sixty-two vessels, later increased to sixty-three, were ordered by the Department of Marine and Fisheries. Although sometimes compared to the "standard" ships of World War II, they were anything but, being a grab bag of sizes and design variations, ranging in tonnage from 2800 DWT to 10,500 DWT, with fully half falling into 5100 DWT and below categories.

One thing they did have in common was the prefix "Canadian" to their names, many of them apparently reflecting Canadian occupations, typically *Canadian Miner*, *Canadian Aviator*, *Canadian Harvester* among them, and strangest of all, *Canadian Skirmisher* and *Canadian Squatter*. They were steam-powered, mostly coal-fired, with a couple of exceptions among the larger vessels being oil burners. The fastest, the 10,500 tonners, were capable of about 11 knots, while the mid-size (8000 DWT) and smallest ships (up to 5100 DWT) laboured along at 9.5 and 8.5 knots respectively.

Contracts were placed with fourteen shipyards located on both coasts as well as along the inland waterways. Many of these same yards had previously been engaged in building a series of similar ships to the order of the Imperial Munitions Board, a British government agency. The vessels ordered by the Canadian Government for the CGMM were grouped in six classes based on size, ranging from Class 1, the largest at 10,500 DWT, to Class 6, the smallest at 2800 DWT. Just two Class 1 ships were built, the *Canadian Constructor* and the *Canadian Cruiser*, both at Halifax Shipyards. Class 2, 8300 DWT, was the largest in terms of numbers of ships with twenty-five. Class 5, comprising 3400-3900 DWT ships, was the only other class significantly represented, with seventeen vessels. The first ship completed, the *Canadian Voyageur*, of 4575 DWT, was handed over to the Canadian Government Merchant Marine on 22 February 1919 by its builder, Canadian Vickers Limited of Montreal. The sixty-third and final delivery, the 10,500 DWT Class 1 *Canadian Constructor*, took place 19 January 1922.

The sixty-three newly constructed ships represented an aggregate tonnage of 380,736 DWT, built at a carefully recorded total cost to the taxpayers of $79,521,932.32, or an average of an expensive $203 per DWT. The addition of the *Canadian Constructor* in early 1922 actually increased the CGMM roster to sixty-six, three existing Department of Railways and Canals ships—*Thomas J. Drummond, Sheba* and *J. A. McKee*, all approximately 3500 DWT—having been transferred to CGMM rolls in 1920.[7] With these three ships included, the aggregate tonnage of the CGMM fleet rose to 391,212 DWT.

Somebody had to be made responsible for the Canadian Government Merchant Marine, Limited, a war-conceived[8] waterbaby much in need of nurturing and guidance, and this foster parent role the Government assigned to the Canadian National Railway. It was a role that, CNR President Sir Henry Thornton regularly took great pains to stress, had no connection with the operations of the Railway company.

It soon became evident that the CGMM ships would be hard-pressed to turn a profit under the circumstances prevailing postwar. In its third annual report, the company was assessing 1921 as "the worst year in recent shipping experience. In addition to a general falling off in tonnage, ocean rates were reduced in some cases as much as 50 percent. Steamship rates that would bring in a proper return did not exist and the best rates would only pay operating expenses." It was a statement that would be repeated many times over the next decade or more, and would be echoed in 1949 by the private Canadian shipping concerns who had taken over the ships of CGMM's World War II created counterpart, Park Steamship Company.

The CGMM ships had been expensive to build under wartime and early postwar conditions, and shortages of materials and machinery at the time of their construction had made necessary frequent substitutions. This lack of standardization throughout the fleet of many items of equipment and auxiliary machinery contributed to increased maintenance costs. They were, in addition, general purpose cargo ships destined to come out second best against the purpose-designed vessels with which they were expected to compete postwar.

The smaller ships in particular were the most vulnerable to the criticism that they were uneconomic, so it is not surprising that by 1923 the directors of CGMM were recommending, and the Government approving, the sale of twenty-seven of the ships, mostly Class 5 and Class 6 vessels, on the grounds that they were so small that they could not compete in overseas trade with larger ships, and furthermore they were not suitable for inland trade because they were "too deep in draft and of the wrong type."[9] Also included in the twenty-seven ships recommended for disposal were six of the eight 5100 DWT Class 3 vessels built, because "they are too expensive to operate for their earning powers." Considering the purposes for which the ships had originally been intended, and the early discovery that they could not do any peacetime job, there is reason to question the wisdom of the 1918 decision makers who selected the types and sizes of the ships to be built. Moreover, even the largest of the ships laboured under a major disadvantage in the postwar sea trade, all them, large and small, having been built at the inflated wartime cost of an average $203 per DWT. By 1921, a survey of British and Canadian shipyards determined that the comparable peacetime construction cost had fallen to $75.[10] By May 1929 the Select Standing Committee on Railways and Shipping was advised, eighteen ships had been sold and two had been lost, reducing the CGMM fleet size to forty-six with a combined tonnage of 312,090 DWT. Reflecting a buyers' market, the sales were at bargain prices and often on easy terms. The average cost of each of the original sixty-three new construction ships was over $1 million, but the top individual price for the first eighteen sold was just $110,000, for a 3500 DWT vessel disposed of in August 1923. Six 2800-5100 DWT ships sold in 1925 went for a token $40,000 each. The Commons Select Standing Committee on Railways and Shipping was told that one sale in 1925 fetched $90,000, but the purchaser was given three years to pay.

In this way, ironically, ex-CGMM ships became the foundation for the sea empire of Aristotle Onassis when, according to popular biographies,[11] the shipping-magnate-to-be purchased six of them in the winter of 1933 at the price of $20,000 each, haggled down from $30,000. The Onassis biographers report that the Greek entrepreneur promptly renamed two of these first ships in his newborn fleet, as the *Onassis Socrates* (ex-*Canadian Spinner*) and the *Onassis Penelope* (ex-*Canadian Miller*), after his father and mother.

Notwithstanding that the end result was the same (although the deals finally made were even sweeter than described), the Onassis biographers' accounts of the acquisition of the ships by him appear to have been largely fanciful and no doubt based on Onassis' own self-serving memory of the events. As one biographer's version went, Onassis, accompanied by a marine engineer, spent three sub-zero mid-winter days inspecting the snow-covered vessels, which were laid up in the St. Lawrence.

He ostentatiously took copious notes while keeping an eye on the reaction of the Canadian officials following him around on his inspection tour, judging that they were desperate to sell. On the third day, standing on the deck of the *Canadian Miller*, he begrudgingly offered to take six of the vessels, but would pay only twenty thousand dollars each. According to this version, the grateful Canadians, painfully aware there was nobody else lined up for the ships, accepted the offer.[12]

Archival materials suggest less dramatic and much more protracted negotiations than in this colourful description. There is a memo dated 22 July 1932 from the CNS general manager[13] indicating that Onassis, dealing from Great Britain through a broker, had first bid earlier in the year on the *Canadian Miller* and five other ships sight unseen. The vessels were at the time laid up in Halifax, not in the St. Lawrence, and after the aspiring Greek shipowner finally had a chance to inspect them, he revised his offer, reducing it to $12,902.75 per ship. A statement of CGMM vessels sold between 17 March 1931 and 31 March 1932 lists the *Canadian Miller* as the only sale completed during that period to one A. Onassis, on 31 October 1932, for £3,775 sterling, approximately $15,430 at the mid-1932 rate of exchange. The dickering for the other ships went on not for three winter days, but for months extending into late summer 1933, with Onassis several times changing his mind about the ships he wanted, and the prices he was willing to pay. He refused to pay $20,000 for the *Canadian Britisher*, but instead offered $24,000 as a package deal for the *Canadian Conqueror* and the *Canadian Pioneer*, both Class 2 (8300 DWT) vessels.[14] The ultimate giveaway price of the latter was only $5,000, which was justified on the grounds that the ship had been out of service since 1929, was "in very bad condition" and would cost $23,500 just to be made seaworthy. Late in May, CNS was pressing the Government for a quick decision on this Onassis offer, before he left to return to London, otherwise the sale might be lost.[15] Earlier records show that approval was given to the sale of the *Canadian Spinner* f or $15,100 cash.

While the above facts hardly substantiate the Onassis biographical accounts of the transactions, it has to be conceded that the apocryphal version of the beginning of the Onassis shipping empire, in which the crafty Greek entrepreneur wrapped up a deal for his first six ships within three frigid days on the frozen St. Lawrence, made a much better story.

* * *

Out of the struggling Canadian Government Merchant Marine, Canadian National (West Indies) Steamships was born. For political reasons, in 1920 the Canadian Government agreed to sponsor a steamship service for passengers and cargo between Canada and the West Indies. Initially, this was operated with CGMM ships, some of them modified to provide accommodation for twenty-eight passengers, but they proved unsatisfactory, lacking facilities for perishable goods among their shortcomings. In 1925, a new agreement between the governments of the West Indies and of Canada was negotiated, a prominent feature of which was the Canadian commitment to provide vessels specially designed for the promised eastern (to British Guiana via various Caribbean Islands) and western (to Bermuda, Nassau, Jamaica and Belize) services.

To fulfill this commitment five new mixed passenger/cargo liners were ordered and Canadian National (West Indies) Steamships Limited was formed in 1928 to operate them. Built by Cammell Laird Shipyards of Birkenhead, England, the handsome 6370 DWT and 4665 DWT vessels were the famous white Lady Boats that became a familiar sight in West Indies and Canadian eastern ports from 1929 on. In the interim between the signing of the Canada-West Indies Trade Agreement of 1925 and the delivery of the Lady Boats, service was maintained with six improved CGMM ships. With the formation of Canadian National (West Indies) Steamships, title to these ships was transferred to the new company and their names were changed to reflect their new ownership. Still, although the new company had been formed to distinguish its operations from those of Canadian Government Merchant Marine, Limited, the antecedents of the new CNS were recognized by the adoption of the CGMM pennant as the CNS house flag. The red, white and blue pennant, emblazoned with a maple leaf in autumnal colors, continued to fly until CNS operations were closed down in 1958.

Meanwhile, the arrival of the Lady Boats in 1928 did not signal the end of the ex-CGMM vessels in CNS service. All six sailed on under their new names in their original freighter role (three also had some first-class passenger accommodation). They plied routes to the Caribbean and via the Panama Canal to Vancouver, as well as to Australia and New Zealand, throughout the 1930s and into WW II, when their area of operations expanded to even more distant waters. They suffered losses. One, the *Colborne* (ex-*Canadian Pathfinder*), was badly damaged when attacked at Penang by Japanese aircraft within a few days of the Pearl Harbor raid. She was not mortally wounded, however, and managed to return safely to Canada. Not so lucky was the *Cornwallis* (ex-*Canadian Transporter*). She was sunk by enemy action at

Bridgetown, Barbados, but was salvaged and returned to service only to be torpedoed by *U 1230* just south of the Bay of Fundy in the Gulf of Maine, 3 December 1944, sinking with the loss of forty-one of her crew of forty-six. This wartime service was the last time any CGMM ship sailed under the Canadian flag. Undoubtedly, however, many ex-CGMM ships continued to roam the world's oceans for years after they had vanished from Canadian registry.

Nothwithstanding Sir Henry Thornton's 1928 pronouncement that, "As from March 15 the title 'Canadian National Steamships' will be used in connection with operations of vessels controlled and operated in conjunction with the Canadian National Railroad and engaged in ocean and coastwise services," all of the ships other than those assigned to Canadian National (West Indies) Steamships continued generally to be known collectively as the Canadian Government Merchant Marine.

Uneconomic the operations of CGMM may have been,[16] its ships nevertheless ranged the Atlantic and the Pacific, regularly plying routes to the United Kingdom, the Continent, the Orient and Australia and New Zealand, as well providing services on both coasts of North America, along the St. Lawrence and even into the Great Lakes.

On a strictly commercial basis, both the Canadian Government Merchant Marine, Limited, and Canadian National (West Indies) Steamships Limited were chronic losers, reporting operating deficits, even before interest and depreciation, every year until 1935 when, for the first time both achieved respectable operating profits. Despite this dismal record, the glamourous image that the Lady Boats brought to their West Indies service seemed to assure it a favourable impression in both public and political circles. As Sir Henry Thornton said of his charge's white liners, "The only criticism I have heard of them is that they are rather too good for the trade, but I do not think they are." CGMM was not so fortunate. Projecting the mundane image of "rusty tramps" a pejorative which all freighters seem to acquire regardless of how shipshape they are kept, the blue-collar CGMM ships were hard pressed to justify their existence in response to the many critics of such Government ventures.

Nonetheless, Sir Henry defended, with qualification, his railway's maritime ward: "As far as the Canadian Government Merchant Marine is concerned," he told the Commons Select Standing Committee on Railways and Shipping,

> "in its services to the Dominion of Canada it furnishes services to certain trades and certain traffics, more particularly on the Pacific coast, which have been of considerable benefit to those who produce in Canada. It is a certain assurance against combinations and extortionate rates from private companies; it is a system which is constantly exploring and investigating new trade routes for the purpose of encouraging Canadian trade abroad.

If I were asked today should we as a nation embark upon the construction of a merchant fleet, I would say: "No, it is unwise to do it." But we have this fleet; it has been constructed at considerable expense, and we are using it as an instrument to promote Canadian trade, and I think it has fulfilled a distinctly useful purpose in that direction.[17]

In the end, it was the obsolescence of the ships that scuttled the Canadian Government Merchant Marine. By 1935, the fleet had been reduced to ten ships, all engaged in the Australia/New Zealand trade, and a buyer was being sought. An offer of $500,000 had been made, but refused, for apart from any consideration of whether or not the proposed purchase price was sufficient, the potential buyers would not guarantee how long the service would be maintained without subsidy, nor that after a few months they would not return seeking a subsidy.

Adding urgency to the situation was the fact that all of the ships were due for their second No. 1 Survey, a type of mandatory inspection imposed on all ships to guarantee their ongoing seaworthiness. To restore the ageing vessels to the standard required to pass this inspection, the CGMM management reported, would be so costly as to be unwarranted, leaving only the options of withdrawing the service or replacing the ships with new tonnage. The cost of new and faster replacement ships was estimated as $6.5 million, an amount that the then Conservative Government's Minister of Railways and Canals, Dr. H. J. Manion, found shocking.

CGMM management favoured building new ships, and in Canadian yards even though the cost would be 30 to 40 percent higher than if they came from British yards. The management argued[18] that Canadian construction would greatly ease the strain on the unemployment relief situation, then at a Great Depression high. Each ship built would mean shipyard employment for approximately 750, it was claimed, as well as work for additional numbers among supporting suppliers. Furthermore, if instead of revitalizing CGMM with new ships, the remaining Canada-Australasian service was turned over to private interests, it would probably have to be subsidized by the Canadian Government.

Then, the CGMM management reminded its political masters, there was the factor of Canadian employment for four hundred crewmen that would be lost if the ships were sold and the CGMM shut down. This particular argument did not carry much weight with members of the responsible Commons Standing Select Committee on Railways and Shipping, one of whom appeared to receive general agreement from fellow committee members when he sniffed disdainfully that, "They are all Englishmen on those boats now. I'll bet not ten percent of them are Canadian-born."

Though the Liberals swept the Conservatives from power in 1935, the problems confronting the CGMM were unchanged and the new Government was faced with the same choices. The new Minister of Railways and Canals (and, already wearing two hats, also Minister of Marine), C. D. Howe, like Dr. Manion before him, thought $6 million plus for ship replacement was too high a price to pay to keep CGMM on life-support. A new tender to purchase the last of the CGMM fleet was received, this time for only $240,000, but with the guarantee to maintain service without subsidy for five years. The offer, which was accepted, came from a consortium of three shipping firms comprising Ellerman, Bucknall Steamship Company, Commonwealth and Dominion Line, and New Zealand Shipping Company Limited. The troika planned to operate the trans-Pacific service jointly under the name, The Montreal, Australia, New Zealand Line Limited, which was soon given the acronym MANZI Line. As each ship returned to home port from its last voyage under the CGMM flag, it was delivered to its new owners and transferred to British registry. At the end of 1936, just prior to these final dispositions, the accumulated deficit of the ill-fated Canadian Government Merchant Marine was reported at $16,525,724.

The bitter and costly memory of the CGMM experience had barely started to fade when war was declared in September 1939. Within six years of CGMM's end, and again in response to war demands, the Canadian Government would launch an even more ambitious program to create a new Canadian Merchant Navy. This new Canadian Merchant Navy, like its departed predecessor, would also be equipped with ships destined for early postwar obsolescence.

Chapter Two   # VANGUARD

On 15 June 1940, Korvettenkapitän Liebe, commander of *U 38*, sent a torpedo crashing into the *Erik Boye*, in passage off Land's End (50:37N/08:44W) in eastbound convoy HX.48. The 2238 gross ton vessel thus became the very first Canadian-flagged[1] merchant ship to go down as a casualty of the Battle of the Atlantic. She would not be the last of the small Canadian fleet of pre-Park ships to suffer such a fate as they bore the brunt of the U-boat campaign in the early years of the war.

Although by 1944 most of the merchant ships flying the Canadian flag carried the Park name, there was certainly a vanguard of Canadian-owned or managed ships plying the world's oceans during the two years and eight months of war that had passed before the first Park ship was delivered. While true that the Canadian deep sea fleet in September 1939 was tiny by any standard, comprising, by contemporary assessments, a mere thirty-seven ships totalling 227,000 gross tons, it was engaged from day one and soon suffered grievous losses in ships and men.

It was reckoned that this handful of ships provided employment for only 1,450 Canadian seamen, though in fact there were many other Canadians sailing aboard ships of foreign registry. There were, for example, fourteen Standard Oil tankers under Panamanian registry which were for a period managed by Imperial Oil Limited and manned by Canadian or British officers and crews supplied by the Canadian company. The U.S., which was supportive of the Allied cause even before Pearl Harbor, permitted the arrangement in the early months of the war as a means of bypassing U.S. neutrality law, which forbade U.S.-registered ships or crews to trade with countries at war. The tankers were returned to U.S. management in 1940. In addition to these Panamanian tankers that were operated by Imperial Oil, the company's own fleet of Canadian-registered tankers plied their trade throughout the war. Three were torpedoed and lost while a fourth was captured.

Canadian National Steamships' Lady Boats and cargo vessels, eleven in number, and Imperial Oil's ten tankers represented over half of the prewar Canadian-registered tonnage which, in the months following the outbreak of hostilities was soon being supplemented by ships of occupied nations and prizes of war, as well as by Canadian coasters and Lake freighters. An early addition to the CNS fleet, for example, was the Danish-registered MV *Asbjorn*, which CNS managed throughout the war. Also under CNS management for the duration came ships of French, Finnish, Norwegian and even German and Italian registry. One of the latter, the *Bic Island*[2], was torpedoed and sunk on 29 October 1942 in mid-Atlantic (55:05N/23:27W) with the loss of its entire crew, all Canadians. On the other hand, CNS relinquished two of its ships for charter by the Department of National Defence, the *Lady Rodney* to serve as a troopship and the *Lady Nelson* as a hospital ship; a third, the *Lady Somers*, became a Royal Navy armed cruiser. Two of these three plus the *Lady Drake* and the *Lady Hawkins* were sunk by enemy action, though the *Lady Nelson* was salvaged to be converted for her later successful career in the role of hospital ship. The combined number of lives lost in the Lady Boat sinkings alone was 279. Three other large passenger ships attached to CN's west coast division were drafted into Naval service, the *Prince Henry* and the *Prince David* as RCN Armed Merchant Cruisers initially, and the *Prince Robert* as an anti-aircraft ship. The *Prince Henry* and the *Prince David* were later converted into Infantry Landing Craft carriers and participated in the Normandy invasion.

There were many of these early merchant draftees into the sea war that sank anonymously because of wartime censorship regulations. The *Cornwallis* was a Vancouver-registered CN freighter of 8390 DWT that was torpedoed in the Gulf of Maine, not far south of the Bay of Fundy (43:59N/68:20W) by *U 1230* on 3 December 1944. There were only five survivors from her forty-six mostly Canadian crew members. Typically, it was not until two months later that news of the sinking was released to the newspapers, and then only as one of several unidentified merchant ships that had fallen victim to U-boats around the same time in the same area. It was the second time the *Cornwallis* had been sunk, having been salvaged after an earlier torpedoing on 11 September 1942, while at anchor in harbour at Bridgetown, Barbados.

No target was too small to escape the attention of the *unterseeboot* prowlers. The crew of the *Lucille M.*, a motor trawler of a mere 54 tons, was forced to abandon ship and watch while their vessel, judged not worthy of an expensive torpedo by *U 89* commander Korvettenkapitän Dietrich Lohmann, was shelled and sunk not far off the southern tip of Nova Scotia (42:02N/65:38W) 25 July 1942.

Not among the thirty-seven vessels counted as making up the Canadian deep-sea fleet in September 1939 were most of those operated by Canadian Pacific. The company name notwithstanding, almost all of its mighty Empress and Duchess passenger liners, plus its Beaver cargo vessels, flew the Red Duster of the British Mercantile Marine, although Canadian seamen, officers and unlicensed personnel, comprised a portion of their crews. Two exceptions were the *Empress of Asia* and the *Empress of Russia*, which, though Canadian-registered, under a special arrangement were earmarked by the British Admiralty to be taken over from the onset of war for conversion as armed merchant cruisers. The *Empress of Asia* was bombed and sunk at Singapore by the Japanese on 2 February 1942, before it could be conscripted for its intended war role. Similarly, two of CP's Canadian-registered coastal fleet, the *Princess Marguerite* and the *Princess Kathleen*, were pressed into service as troopships in European waters. The *Princess Marguerite* was torpedoed and sunk in the Mediterranean (32:03N/32:47E) by *U 83*, 17 August 1942. Under the command of Capt. Richard A. Leicester of Vancouver, the ship was successfully abandoned with the loss of only 55 lives out of the 1,124 aboard. Captain Leicester was awarded the OBE for his leadership role in abandoning a stricken ship with such a minimal loss of life.

So desperate was the shortage of ocean vessels that Allied attention was not long in turning to the very large Canadian Lake fleet, which included many low-draft ships of 4000 tons gross or less. Among them were the canallers, so-called because they were small enough and of sufficiently shallow draft that they could make their way to the open sea via the existing lock system, at a time when the St. Lawrence Seaway was still only a dream for the future. In all, 133 lakers were eventually transferred from the relatively easy inland waterways for which they were specifically designed, to the rough and tumble of the open ocean ("Oh! how they could roll," remembers Ben Methot of Dalhousie, New Brunswick, who served as a deckhand on the SS *Ganandoc*). Initially, many of them—the first twenty-five made the Atlantic crossing in the spring of 1940[3]—were anxiously awaited as replacements for the British coastal vessels which were suffering heavy losses, particularly in Channel waters. Half a dozen of the lakers were almost immediately pressed into service in the great Dunkirk evacuation of the trapped British Army. Others typically spent most of their war service carrying bauxite ore from South America to Canada's aluminum smelters.

The lakers paid a heavy price for leaving their sheltered inland waterways to take a more direct role in the war. The Port Arthur (now Thunder Bay), Ontario, firm of N. M. Paterson & Sons Limited, for instance, lost ten ships to enemy action and marine disaster, half of its fleet of canallers that ventured into the dangerous seas. Down with them went fifty-eight crew members.

It is evident that though the Park ships eventually became overwhelmingly the dominant component of Canada's wartime Merchant Navy, their numerical impact did not peak until 1944, by which time the heterogeneous fleet of Canadian-registered and foreign-registered Canadian-managed merchant vessels flying the Canadian flag from the outbreak of war had already suffered the worst of the losses the Canadian Merchant Navy would be required to endure by August 1945. One list compiled from Department of National Defence and DEMS records indicates a total of sixty-seven Canadian flag vessels lost to enemy action 1939-45, of which only two were Canadian-registered Park ships (a third was torpedoed but didn't sink and was salvaged). Two other Park ships are also listed, the *Taber Park* and the *Avondale Park*, but despite their names they had been transferred to the British Ministry of War Transport in 1944 under Mutual Aid and were probably manned by British crews at the time of their sinkings. The inclusion in the DND/DEMS list of six Fort ships also appears questionable because though Canadian-built, vessels with that prefix to their names had been turned over to the British Ministry of War Transport under either Canadian Mutual Aid or through U.S. Lend-Lease. These and other possible exceptions aside, the list of Canadian flag ships lost—torpedoed, bombed, mined, or shelled—is still a high 56.[4]

Like all bookkeeping figures, that number in the account book of the war at sea takes on real meaning only when the loss of human life it represents is factored in. Behind it are slightly more than half of the 1,146[5] Canadian merchant seamen who died as a result of enemy action, according to the official casualty list compiled by the Registrar of Merchant Seamen. Of that total, 677 were lost while serving on ships of Canadian registry or under Canadian wartime management, while another 461 Canadian seamen were listed as missing or lost at sea while serving on ships of foreign registry (285 U.K., 27 Belgium, 48 Norway, 36 U.S., 13 Sweden, 36 Panama, 16 other). Sometimes in the records, a number loses its anonymity and a name surfaces to put a human face on the statistic. A list issued in 1942 by the Swedish Consul General in Montreal, of Canadian seamen lost at sea on Swedish ships to that wartime date, included George Finn Galbraith of Toronto, a member of the crew of the *Stüreholm*,[6] which was lost to *U 96* on 12 December 1940. Left behind by Galbraith were his widow and five children, whose compensation from the Swedish Government was the equivalent of Cdn.$2,356.04, plus Cdn.$298.07 from the ship owners for wages, compensation for lost effects and war bonus.

Account settled.

Other Canadians listed as lost on the *Stüreholm* were James Edward Evans of Brantford, Ontario, Reginald Trainor of Calgary, Charles Royal Hanely of Montreal, and Donald James McAllister of Sussex, New Brunswick.

The files of the National Archives contain poignant correspondence relating to lost or missing seamen. A letter from the mother of George Frederick Olsen, 31, of Halifax, lost at sea with the sinking of the *Cornwallis* in December 1944, seeks a confirming death certificate so that his Victory bonds may be cashed. There is an inquiry into the fate of Ernest Mason of Saint John, New Brunswick, a Canadian seaman who had signed on the Greek ship *Eugenie Livanos* and had not been heard of since sailing 23 September 1942. The Naval Service reported that the ship was apparently sunk by a raider in the Indian Ocean, 7 December 1942; one survivor, not identified in the Naval

Service report, was a POW in Japan and had communicated with his next of kin. There was no knowledge of any other survivors[7].

There were in all, 198 Canadian seamen taken as prisoners of war when their ships were captured or sunk, often in the very early years of the war, so that their terms of internment were long. Eight of them died while POWs or during repatriation. One wonders if the Government was successful in collecting from their estates the Income Tax for which POW merchant seamen were liable, on basic detention allowance accumulated during their period of internment.

As can be seen, the brunt of the losses were borne by the Canadian vessels and their crews which were going about their business through dangerous waters for nearly three years before the Park ships began arriving on the scene in numbers. Indeed it has been estimated that 88 percent of the casualties suffered by Canadian merchant seamen had occurred by the end of 1942.[8] Only two Parks were sunk by enemy action with a loss of thirteen lives. Another, the *Nipawin Park*, was torpedoed but did not sink though two crewmen died. Of course enemy action was not necessarily the only hazard or the only cause of loss of life; two crewmen and six longshoremen died when the *Green Hill Park* blew up while loading cargo in Vancouver, and fifteen crewmen and one DEMS gunner were killed when the *Silver Star Park* collided with another ship off New Bedford, Massachusetts. Storms at sea and shipwrecks also took their toll, but then these are normal hazards of seafaring, equally in peace as in war.

Chapter Three

THE PARK LINE

In October 1940 the war was barely twelve months old but all was going badly for the Allies, who, with the fall of France in June had been reduced to Britain and its Commonwealth partners. Reports of the many setbacks and disasters, strictly rationed by the censorship bureaucracy in an attempt to make the situation palatable to the public, were the daily news serving.

In no area of the seemingly hopeless struggle were the disasters more despairing than in the Battle of the Atlantic.

Ships carrying war supplies to rebuild the British forces shattered at Dunkirk, as well as cargoes of barely sufficient food to separate the walls of the beleaguered Island's stomach, were being sunk at a faster rate than they could be replaced by shipyards in Britain, which in any case were much preoccupied with a sweeping Naval construction program.

Germany's rapidly expanding submarine fleet prowled the shipping lanes, picking off their fat prey with, it seemed to the convoys' Naval escorts, frustrating ease. Lumbering along at the often slow convoy[1] speed of an agonizingly languid seven or eight knots, the plump merchant vessels were easy targets for an enemy that the Naval escorts rarely saw and only occasionally heard by straining their imperfect ASDIC ears[2]. Aerial reconnaissance forces on both sides of the Atlantic were being developed that could aid in protective coverage for several hundred miles offshore, but the aircraft available at that stage of the war were still too short in the legs to close the vast hole in the middle of the deep. The well-trained, skilled and highly motivated U-boat crews, the elite of the German Navy, lead by daring commanders and enjoying the advantage of stealth, surprise and opportunity, comprised a formidable foe who was parried and finally defeated only after a deadly struggle of several years, eventually requiring a major commitment of resources by the Naval forces of Canada, Britain and the United States.

The shipping losses were staggering and with British shipyards heavily committed to demanding naval construction, there was insufficient capacity in the Island kingdom for production also of new merchant ships at the pace needed to transfuse the hemorrhaging trans-Atlantic artery.

It was at this point in the war that Britain looked to the shipyards of, initially, the United States, a sympathizer but still a non-combatant, and Canada. Subsequently, a British shipbuilding mission came to North America in October 1940 to explore the possibility of replacement tonnage being supplied by the shipbuilders of the great western continent. Existing Canadian capacity was modest to say the least. What had been a thriving shipbuilding industry in the early 1920s, had been reduced by two decades on a starvation diet of orders to the point of acute malnutrition. The surviving yards were being barely sustained by the trickle of ship repair work for the tiny fleet of Canadian merchant vessels existent at the start of the war. Although by the time of the arrival of the British shipbuilding mission, the Canadian yards were beginning to hum with orders for convoy escorts and other Naval vessels, in all of Canada there were still only nine ways suitable for construction of cargo vessels of the optimum size required for the Atlantic lifeline.

It was against this backdrop of urgent need that Canada took the first steps to, yet again, build and operate a deep-sea merchant fleet. An order to Canadian shipyards for first 20, later increased to 26 10,000 ton class dry cargo vessels which followed the North American visit of the British shipbuilding mission, provided the leaven for a massive Canadian shipbuilding enterprise. The British contract triggered a decision by the Canadian Government to order additional ships for its own account, initially 88 10,000 ton and 5 4700 ton vessels. At first there were some who thought that the additional ships, like those for the British order, might be manned by British seamen, but as Merchant Navy casualties mounted to near disastrous proportions (reaching 25,000, mostly British, within the first two years of the war), thinking then turned to the possibility of crewing at least some of them with Canadian seamen.

Such a combination of Canadian-built ships with Canadian crews was nothing less than the first step toward the creation of a new Canadian Merchant Navy. What could more logically follow than the setting up of a formal organization, Park Steamship Company Limited, to administer this embryo fleet? The ghost of the only recently deceased Canadian Government Merchant Marine, Limited[3], must have been looking on with a bemused smile as the Park Steamship Company Limited was officially born with its incorporation on 8 April 1942. Two weeks later R. B. Teakle, General Manager of Canadian National (West Indies) Steamships, was appointed first President of the new Crown company which, having set up headquarters in Montreal, on 30 June took delivery of the *Prince Albert Park*, the first of 5 10,000 ton ships it would receive from Canadian shipyards by year's end 1942. They were the beginning of a fleet that would grow to 176 ships, all but two[4] named after Canadian national, provincial and municipal parks.

* * *

Park Steamship Company Limited was a strange creature. It was a Crown company created to act as a holding company to which would be assigned title to the ships that had been ordered by the Government from Canadian shipyards for operation by Canada, but it did not itself operate any of the ships in the large fleet that eventually came under its house flag. Instead, it contracted this task to an array of existing private steamship companies and shipping agents, who for a management fee plus a percentage of cargo earnings assumed responsibility for the care of the vessels, furnishing the crews, payment of all expenses and collection of revenues. How the ships were used and where they would sail did not come up in the contractual arrangement, this being at the dictates of such wartime bodies as the Admiralty and the Ministry of War Transport in London, the Canadian Shipping Board in Ottawa and the Allied Shipping Pool in Washington.

For Park Steamship Company and the managing operators it seemed a simple and straightforward arrangement, but in practice complications arose, most importantly in the matter of crewing. In the beginning, the first managing operators to take over Park ships, most of them Canadian subsidiaries of British shipping firms, did proceed to hire crews in the same way they had always done for their own ships. But with the introduction of the Government-operated manning pool system under the authority of the Director of Merchant Seamen, the managing operators' control over what individuals were selected to work aboard the ships for which they were responsible was very much reduced. The situation was further complicated when increasing union activity lead to the signing of a working agreement between Park Steamship Company and the Canadian Seamen's Union under which wage rates were standardized throughout the Park fleet. The managing operators, who were not signers of the agreement (applicable first on the East Coast and later on the West Coast) and possibly were not even part of the discussions leading up to it, were nevertheless responsible for complying with it.

The Union agreement also had an impact on the managing operators' contractual requirement making them responsible for care of the vessels they controlled. With their new-found Union clout, crews began seeking accommodation amenities that might involve mechanical installation or minor structural modification. These were matters that most often could have been easily and quickly settled by the managing operator, but Park Steamship Company insisted that they be referred to head office in Montreal. So, the Park Line, as it came to be widely known, evolved as a combined operation with overlapping input from three organizations or groups, viz., Park Steamship Company, the managing operators, and the Director of Merchant Seamen's manning pools and training schools. Sometimes the overlap could blur the dividing lines between the areas of responsibility.

In short, the new Canadian Merchant Navy was soon suffering from a severe case of growing pains. An Interdepartmental Committee on Merchant Seamen memorandum of 3 November 1943 signed by Arthur Randles, Director of Merchant Seamen, as chairman of the committee, attempted to diagnose what ailed the hastily assembled fleet. The memo is only partially successful in straightening out the confusion with its explanation that,

"An anomaly in the Canadian position exists and that is the Crown company (Park Steamship Company), while holding title to the Government-owned ships, is actually not a direct employer of seamen labour. At the present time each individual ship is entrusted to different companies or shipping agents . . . [so] each of these companies or agents is in effect the employer of the crew, but while the Park Company as owners of ships can stipulate the conditions [under which the seamen serve], each company has practices different from the other.

The method chosen to operate the new Canadian ships has the effect of establishing a number of "one-ship" companies, leaving thereby no facility for the interchange of crews or for the promotion in rank which is possible in "multi-ship" owning companies. Without a common employer, organized arrangements for leave or relief are absent. There is no pension scheme or other form of security offered to encourage men to remain in sea employment.

The lack of such facilities eliminates any possible "esprit de corps" which is so evident and so valuable in other shipowning enterprises. Our seamen can best be described as "Nobody's children," except that the Manning Pools form a kind of "melting pot.""

From an organizational, management and operational standpoint it was an untidy arrangement, but the ships sailed where and when they were supposed to. In the final analysis that was really all that mattered in the context of the Allied cause that the Park fleet had been created to support.

* * *

The Park ships that began arriving in 1942 may not have marked the beginning of Canadian Merchant Navy participation in the war, they nevertheless quickly became the dominant element of the wartime fleet. The five deliveries of 1942 were just a start; in 1943, 50 ships were handed over to Park Steamship Company by Canadian shipyards, including 36, 10,000 tonners (32 dry cargo, 4 tankers), and 13, 4700-ton dry cargo vessels. Among the 50 was also an ancient, vintage 1905, dredger (ex-*W. S. Fielding*) which had been converted into a 2000 DWT tanker and gloriously renamed *Riding Mountain Park*.

Park deliveries from the booming Canadian yards accelerated rapidly, peaking in 1944 at 94—almost 2 a week— with 63, 10,000 ton and 17, 4700 ton dry cargo ships, plus 8 10,000 ton and 6 3600 ton tankers being taken on strength by the Crown company. The next year, 1945, brought the surrender of Germany early in May followed by that of Japan in August. With the collapse of these two once formidable enemies, all contracts for construction of the wartime standard ships were cancelled, but not before a further 15 10,000 ton and 12 4700 ton dry cargo ships had been delivered, bringing to 176 (175 new construction) the number to hoist the Park house flag at one time or another.

Extraordinary as was the production delivery record of Park ships, it represented less than half the number of merchant ships that poured from Canadian shipyards from the start of the program in April 1941, when the first keel was laid, until shortly after the end of hostilities in August 1945. What makes this record even more impressive is that it was carried out in parallel to an equally impressive Naval construction program which produced nearly five hundred escort vessels, including destroyers, frigates, corvettes and minesweepers.

* * *

It was all very well to send merchant ships down the ways on almost an assembly-line basis to hand them over to Park Steamship Company, but where was Canada to find the men to take them to sea? In 1942, there were few if any unemployed experienced seamen on the loose. The Royal Canadian Navy, in the throes of its own enormous wartime expansion, had already recruited every civilian who had ever set foot on a moving deck; most importantly, those with watchkeeping or navigational skills. The very people donning Navy uniforms were equally in demand to man the new merchant ships. The Army and the RCAF were similarly chasing the fit to meet their burgeoning needs, and those whose bodies weren't quite warm enough to meet even the Services' minimum standards were quickly absorbed into the mushrooming armaments manufacturing industry where their jobs were declared "essential" by Canada's Selective Service organization.

It was a predicament well summed up by William Hutcherson of Richmond, British Columbia, who first went to sea in 1944 as third Sparks on the *Crystal Park*:

> You've got to remember that at the start of the war Canada had only thirty-seven ocean-going ships. Now during the three-year period from 1942 to 1945, manpower had to be enlisted and/or trained to at least the following numbers: over 175 Master Mariners, 530 deck officers, a like number of radio officers, 900 engine room officers, 6,000 seamen and engine room ratings, 700 stewards, cooks and mess boys, 350 officer cadets, 350 bosuns and carpenters and a whole assortment of ships' mascots! [These figures] represent the operational requirements to man all the ships,

but in addition, many more men were held in reserve and resided in all the Manning Pools located in each of the Canadian ports.

The Royal Canadian Navy, of course, also managed to provide another 2,500 DEMS[5] ratings for the gunnery defences of the vessels.

Our Merchant Navy was formed with its [manpower] nucleus coming from coastal steamers, ships of the Great Lakes, tugboats of both coasts, Canadian Pacific Empress ships—[by then] nearly all gone to different seas—Imperial Oil tankers and from the fishing fleets of the Maritimes, Newfoundland and British Columbia. It was fleshed out by an assortment from every walk of life, among them the stubble-jumpers, and kids who had never before seen or smelled salt water, guys who washed dishes in the greasy-spoon restaurants, hoboes from the jungles, beer-slingers and guzzlers from the waterfront bars, tinkers, tailors, goofballs and sailors and ically from every conceivable corner of the country. Most were good to excellent, adapting to the deep-sea life as if they were born to it. A few served and suffered each voyage but would never earn the designation of a bonafide sailor. There were also the characters and we ended up with a goodly share of these!"

Somehow, enough were found, approximately twelve thousand by war's end, to take the ships to sea.[*] Some were too young to be soldiers, but sixteen was considered an ideal age for a Cadet Officer to begin his apprenticeship. And age didn't seem to be an obstacle for a fifteen-year-old bent on the adventurous life of a sailor, so there were many who started their sea career as a baby-faced Peggy (messboy) in a seamen's or a firemen's mess. Then there was Joseph Wood, now of St. Thomas, Ontario, whose height made it easy to pass for something more than his fourteen years to get a messboy's job aboard the Imperial tanker *Rideaulite*.

There were others who were too old for the Armed Services; over fifties were common and occasionally a seventy-year-old retread Master Mariner or mate would appear on a Park bridge. Reporting on an inspection of the *Kootenay Park* in

---

* Canada's wartime Merchant Navy was almost exclusively a male affair, but there were some exceptions on other than the Park ships. CNS Lady Boats, for example, normally carried two stewardesses and this would have continued until at least such time as the ships were conscripted for service away from their West Indies runs. As a hospital ship, *Lady Nelson* carried nursing sisters as well as Red Cross workers. In a less traditional role, a handful of Canadian women served as radio operators on ships of the Norwegian merchant navy. Fern Blodgett of Cobourg, Ontario, at twenty-two became the first of eight Canadian women Sparks to sign on Norwegian ships. She joined the 15 knot 3000-ton cargo/passenger *Mosdale* in Montreal mid-June 1941. A year later, while continuing as the ship's Sparks, she added the role of Captain's wife, becoming Mrs. Gerner Sunde. She made an incredible seventy-eight wartime Atlantic crossings. Six months after the war ended she came ashore in Norway to make her home and raise two daughters. Fern Blodgett Sunde, 74, died at Farsund, Norway, 19 September 1991.

Vancouver in the spring of 1944, a Naval Boarding Service officer noted that the ship's new Captain, who was seventy, hadn't been to sea for seven years and his most recent previous employment had been as a security guard for new ships constructed in Victoria! The NBS report concludes cryptically: "Lost his previous source of income due to occupation of Hong Kong. Seemed rather pleased to be going back to sea." Another NBS report lists the age of the skipper of the *Winona Park* as being seventy-three.

In between these extremes of youth and age were the thousands who might be within the age limits for service enlistment but had been rejected for some minor physical shortcoming, or had served and been discharged for various reasons. Then there were those who simply wanted no part of service life and saw the Merchant Navy as their preferred way to do their bit. Unfortunately, a few misguided elements of the civilian population linked service in the Merchant Navy with draft dodging. There were, sad to say, even some service personnel who took the same view, as postwar comments have indicated.

To go voluntarily to sea in wartime with no say in your ship's destination was indeed a strange way to avoid being drafted into the Army's "zombie" units. To be drafted was, in fact, almost a guarantee of safe passage through the war years because draftees were limited to home service, at least until late in the war.

There were, on the other hand, no safe waters for merchant seamen. The hazard of enemy attack was most intense along the convoy routes of the North Atlantic and on the notorious Murmansk Run, to be sure, but there were no safe havens anywhere. Ships were torpedoed in the St. Lawrence River and the Gulf of St. Lawrence, just outside Halifax Harbour and even right in the harbour of St. Lucia (CN Steamships' *Lady Nelson*) in the West Indies. The Nova Scotia-Newfoundland ferry *Caribou* was torpedoed by *U 69* while in night passage across the Gulf of St. Lawrence. One hundred and thirty-seven perished, including thirty-one of the crew of forty-six; among the crew losses were the Captain, Benjamin Taverner, and his two sons, Stanley and Harold. Whether the coastal waters of North America, the North or South Atlantic, the Mediterranean, the Indian Ocean or the Pacific, all the waters were dangerous and Canadian ships with Canadian crews travelled them all. Not even in the waters off the west coast of North America was the undersea threat entirely absent. Where the German Navy could not easily reach, at least one far-ranging Japanese submarine did. On 20 June 1942, the Canadian-built *Fort Camosun* was torpedoed and shelled not far beyond Cape Flattery, which marks the entrance to the Strait of Juan de Fuca, the channel that divides lower Vancouver Island from the mainland. The vessel, fortunately, did not sink and was towed to Esquimalt for repairs.[6] And torpedoes were not the only unpleasant surprise awaiting the merchant mariner; mines of both contact and magnetic varieties were an ever-present hazard, even in eastern coastal Canadian waters. The approaches to Halifax had to be swept regularly to clear mines laid by U-boats.

Captain David G. Martin-Smith of Victoria, B.C., a Canadian who began his sea career aboard a British tramp as a shilling-a-month "dogsbody," a junior deck boy, expresses the frustration of many merchant seamen over postwar reluctance to recognize their wartime service in dangerous waters:

> I was under age and employed at sea on September 3, 1939, and continued at sea in dangerous waters thereafter for most of the next six years. I was simply "there" so not really a volunteer, except that I could have sought out a billet ashore were any offering—and they were later on. Like many seamen, I just stayed with my calling. In 1944, in Simonstown, South Africa, I took a gunnery course after being a member of the guns crew on two previous ships and nominally in charge of the British DEMS gunners on one of them, and continued as gunnery officer/navigator after completing the short course. I was in charge of eleven RCN DEMS gunners before and after that point, yet I was not allowed to wear the Volunteer Service Medal. Those eleven gunners were awarded the medal, and I was in charge and denied it. They went off after one voyage and were given a spell of base time. I went right back to sea and into dangerous waters.

* * *

The ship that became the backbone of the Park fleet and was also supplied in large numbers to the British was known as the North Sands type, a design developed at the North Sands yard of the British firm of J. L. Thompson & Sons Limited of Sunderland, on England's north-east coast. Even by the standards of 1940, when the British Technical Merchant Shipbuilding Mission came to North America on its shopping spree, the North Sands ship was definitely low-tech. Chosen by the British Ministry of Transport for its simple design and ease of construction, it was powered by a triple expansion steam engine (a type of marine propulsion machinery the Americans considered antiquated) with coal-fired Scotch marine boilers. These features not only made rapid construction possible but also ensured simplicity of operation, both of vital importance at a time when experienced shipyard workers as well as experienced seamen were in increasingly short supply. They also ensured almost instant obsolescence the day the war ended.

As time went on and experience was gained, improvements to the basic North Sands design by its Canadian builders lead to the introduction of the Victory variant, a major feature of which was the installation of two oil-fired water tube boilers, replacing the three Scotch marine boilers required in the coal burners. This new variant was more economical to operate, fuel cost being less and fewer firemen (and no trimmers) being required. However, because of heavy wartime demand on oil supplies, a further development was the Canadian type, which could be adapted to burn either oil or coal. This further design variation entailed the re-introduction of Scotch marine fire tube boilers as being more suitable for the optional fuel role.

By shortly after war's end, Park Steamship Company had taken delivery of 44 North Sands coal burners, 45 Victory oil burners and 28 Canadian coal/oil burners.

One odd variant was the tanker version, which externally appeared no different to the standard Park dry cargo 10,000 tonner. The prototype conversion, the *Point Pelee Park*, was the second of the five ships delivered to Park Steamship Company in 1942. This curious hybrid, a North Sands type which, though converted to carry bulk petroleum products, was fuelled by coal. It had been all but completed as a dry cargo vessel in the Montreal yard of Canadian Vickers Limited when the heavy toll of tankers being lost to enemy action at that time prompted a decision to convert it into a bulk oil carrier. Twelve other Park tanker versions followed the anomaly that was the *Point Pelee Park*, but all were of the oil-burning Victory type.

The Park tanker conversions, though less efficient than conventional design purpose-built tankers, brought with them an unforeseen benefit. Tankers were then right at the top of the German Navy's hit list, but the *Point Pelee Park* and her kind looked like any other general cargo ship, thereby increasing their chances of being ranked as lower priority targets by U-boat commanders intent on conserving their precious torpedoes for ships with the distinctive conventional tanker profile.

Though the 10,000 tonners may have been the workhorses of the Park fleet, the smaller Gray class of 4700 ton cargo vessels was also an important component. The role of these coal-fired 4700 ton steamers, built in Canadian yards to a design of William Gray & Company of West Hartlepoole, England, was to ply lower volume trade routes servicing coastal and shallow water ports. The 42[7] operated under the Park name became a familiar sight in the Canadian coastwise trade as well as in Labrador, Newfoundland and West Indies harbours. But their sphere of operation was not always confined to the waters of the Western Ocean. In 1944 Park Steamship Company responded to a call from the Washington, D.C.-based Allied Shipping Pool for the supply of all available 4700 ton vessels to transport troops and material in support of the Normandy landings, a task for which their size and shallow draft made them well suited. Fourteen were sent.

The third type of ship operated under the Park flag was a 3600 ton Canadian designed tanker, only six of which were built. These diesel-powered twin screw vessels, all delivered in 1944, were intended primarily to transport high octane aviation gasoline, particularly to Newfoundland to meet the huge fuel demands of the streams of aircraft by then being ferried to bases in the U.K.

* * *

The manning demands of the rapidly expanding Park fleet meant that some very raw human material had to be converted almost overnight into knowledgeable and experienced ships crews, a process in which a doctorate in alchemy would have been an advantage. Yet somehow each ship delivered to Park Steamship Company did manage to put to sea with a full complement of navigating officers, engineers, radio officers, stewards, cooks, deckhands and firemen.[8] And in spite of the widely diversified practices and methods of management of ship operations followed by the thirty or more independent shipping companies and agents who actually operated the Park ships under contract, huge tonnages of war materials as well as more peaceable cargoes were successfully delivered to ports all over the world.

But initially, Park Line operations scarcely caused a ripple. After all, the company did not receive its first ship, the 10,000 ton *Prince Albert Park*, until 30 June 1942, and by year's end still had only five, one of which was the tanker conversion, the *Point Pelee Park*. Park Steamship estimates of tonnages carried, based on voyages from east coast ports completed in 1942, show only 18,000 tons of cargo to the U.K. and 45,000 tons under tanker time charter. From the west coast, just one round trip to Australia/New Zealand was completed. Given the average loading of 9,000 tons, these estimates indicate only eight completed voyages in the company's first six months of operation.

In 1943, with the pace of ship deliveries stepping up to a total of 50 for the year, 36 of them 10,000 tonners (including four of the tanker versions), the Park workload increased rapidly. Cargo tonnages on voyages from east coast ports jumped to 161,000 and India and the West Indies were added to the U.K. as destinations served. From the west coast, another 36,000 tons went to Australia/New Zealand ports.

On 6 July 1943, the *Jasper Park* became the first Park ship to be lost to enemy action when it was torpedoed and sunk in the Indian Ocean (32:52S/42:15E) by *U177*. Four of the crew lost their lives.

By 1944, Canadian shipyards were completing vessels at a rate of more than 2 per week and 94 of them—71 10,000 tonners (including 8 tanker versions), 17 4700 ton cargo ships and 6 3600 ton tankers—joined the Park fleet during the year. Tonnage carried soared to some 2.5 million, with east coast sailings accounting for 1.9 million of this total and the west coast for the balance. Park ships were by now becoming a common sight in U.K. ports, particularly along the Manchester ship canal and the Thames River, both under frequent aerial bombardment and with heavily damaged dock facilities. The Canadian-built ships had expanded their area of operations to include the Mediterranean, Africa, and the grimly perilous Murmansk Run. It was at this time that the Park company also responded to a call from the Allied Shipping Pool for all available 4700 ton vessels to support the Allied landings on the Normandy beaches. This call to the action scene notwithstanding, the only Park casualty during the year was the 4700 ton *Kelowna Park*, which ran aground without loss of life at Chicoutimi, Quebec, on 8 August 1944; it was salvaged and later returned to service after repair.

The war ended two-thirds of the way through 1945, but the demand for ocean shipping continued to grow beyond the suspension of hostilities, a trend that was reflected in, compared to 1944, an almost doubling of Park tonnage carried to 4.9 million, nearly three-quarters of it being by ships with east coast home ports. By this time, Italy and France had been added to the Park boats' world-ranging list of destinations.

If 1945 was a banner year for delivering the goods, it was the worst year for Park ship losses. The first bad news came right after the New Year when on 4 January 1945, the *Nipiwan Park*, a 3600 ton tanker, was torpedoed by *U 1232* only seventeen miles off Halifax (44:30N/63:00W). Two members of the crew lost their lives in the explosion, which blew off the forward half of the ship. The stern section was towed into Halifax where it was sold by War Assets Corporation and after reconstruction re-emerged as the privately owned *Irvinglake*. The *Nipiwan Park* was not the only Park ship to come under the enemy hammer. In the distant South Atlantic some five hundred miles off (29:42S/09:58E) the west coast of South Africa, the *Point Pleasant Park* was torpedoed and shelled by *U 510* on 23 February 1945, sinking with a loss of nine crew.

The survivors escaped in three lifeboats and after being questioned by the U-boat captain, Kapitänleutnant Alfred Eick, they were left to their own devices. After seven days, one of the lifeboats made a safe landing on the African coast and the seventeen men aboard were taken by fishing boat to the Southwest African port of Luderitz. Two days later, the other two lifeboats with a total of thirty-three aboard, some of them injured, were picked up by the South African Navy trawler *Africana*.[*]

Two 4700 ton ships bearing Park names, the *Taber Park* and the *Avondale Park*, also became casualties before German resistance collapsed, albeit at the time they were probably British manned and were sailing under the British Red Duster,

---

[*] In 1967, a cairn was dedicated in Halifax's Point Pleasant Park to the memory of the nine men who died when the park's namesake ship was sunk by enemy action. The cairn was erected through the efforts of Canadian Coast Guard Captain Paul Tooke, who had been third officer aboard the *Point Pleasant Park* and officer-in-charge of one of the lifeboats picked up by the *Africana*. The cairn bears a plaque listing the names of the nine casualties: Joseph Bayless, Fred Breen, George Edwards, Patrick Guthrie, Robert Hallahan, Alfred Malmberg, Robert Munro, Leslie Toth and Louis Wilkinon. During a Remembrance Day service in 1967, one of the wreaths placed on the cairn was from the crew of the *U510*.

having been two of the ships turned over to the U.K. to support the 1944 Normandy landings. The *Taber Park* succumbed to a torpedo in the North Sea, reportedly from a midget submarine, though German records show no claim for this sinking[9]. The *Avondale Park* also went down in the North Sea after being torpedoed by *U 2336*, thereby winning the dubious distinction of being the last "British" merchant ship to be sunk by enemy action before the end of the war, in fact just hours before the cease-fire officially came into effect. Park Steamship Company records of the two sinkings say only that "the loss of life was limited."

Three other Park ships were damaged or lost during the year, though not as the result of enemy action. On 6 March, the *Green Hill Park* exploded and burned at dockside in Vancouver with two crewmen and six longshoremen being killed in the accident. The badly damaged ship was sold by War Assets to Greek interests who had her rebuilt to sail again as the *Phaeax II*.

Barely a month later, on 12 April, the 10,000 ton tanker *Silver Star Park* collided with another vessel off New Bedford, Massachusetts, the collision and subsequent fire causing serious damage to the ship and bringing death to fifteen crewmen and one DEMS gunner. The hulk was towed to New York where it was sold. The final loss of the year occurred when the 10,000 ton cargo ship *Westbank Park* was driven ashore by a hurricane in Magdalena Bay, on the coast of Southern California. There was no loss of life but the ship was a total write-off.

In the context of overall wartime sinkings it has to be said that the Park fleet emerged relatively unscathed, unlike the many other ships of Canadian registry that were exposed to war hazards from 1939 on. That the Parks did so while continuing to sail through dangerous waters, in convoy and independently, can be attributed partly to luck but largely to the fact that the fleet did not reach its peak strength until 1944-45, when the Allied Naval forces were turning the tables on the German Navy in the struggle that was the Battle of the Atlantic. U-boats did nonetheless roam the shipping lanes right up to the day of Germany's surrender. It is perhaps worth noting that all of the Park ships to be singled out for enemy attack were travelling independently, i.e., unescorted, at the time.

* * *

The surrender of Japan in August 1945 brought an end to World War II and with it the cancellation of all ship construction contracts. Though the cancellation orders were effective immediately, they came too late to prevent the completion and delivery of a further 15, 10,000 ton and 12, 4700 ton dry cargo vessels to Park Steamship Company. The last Park ship to be delivered before war's end was the 10,000 ton Canadian type *Gaspesian Park*, on 22 July 1945. But the *Gaspesian* was not the very last Park delivery, that distinction going to the 4700 ton *Shakespeare*

Park, months after war's end, on 14 November 1945. These final additions raised to 176 the number of ships that had been registered under the Park name in just over three years, a phenomenal rate of growth by any standard.

No sooner had plans been set in motion in the early years of the war to build a Canadian Merchant Navy, than discussions were begun on its future dismemberment. Before the last shot was fired, the decision had been taken. With the end of the war the Government moved promptly to either sell or charter the vessels of the Park fleet to private shipping companies. Although the move was not unexpected, there had been much debate over the future of the ships in the previous two years when it became evident that Canada was in the process of accumulating a merchant fleet of such a size as to rank the country high among the world's major merchant marine powers. In the spring of 1943, Munitions and Supply Minister C. D. Howe forecast in the House of Commons that an all-Canadian merchant fleet numbering over two hundred ships would emerge postwar. He predicted that the ships would be a "substantial source of employment in the postwar years and will be a real benefit to Canadian postwar commerce." The Minister's vision of an ongoing Merchant Navy was no doubt influenced by the widely held view that war's end, with unemployed ranks being swelled by discharged servicemen and released war industry workers, would be shortly followed by a renewal of the prewar depression. A postwar Merchant Navy was seen by many as a source of employment for ex-Navy personnel.

What happened, of course, was that there was a postwar boom rather than a depression; RCN veterans, their enthusiasm for the sea life having doubtless been bounced out of them in the crowded messdecks of Canada's corvette Navy, and presented with the opportunity to better their educations under the Government's generous rehabilitation program for service personnel, for the most part showed little interest in Merchant Navy careers. On the other hand, similar educational benefits were not offered to merchant seamen, on the grounds that they would be encouraged to abandon the sea life at a time when it was thought their services were still needed and would continue to be for the foreseeable future.[10] Just in case anybody had interpreted Mr. Howe's remarks to mean that there would be a second coming of the Canadian Government Merchant Marine after the war, Transport Minister J. E. Michaud in a pre-Christmas 1943 address indicated that nobody should plan on a Canadian Merchant Marine beyond the end of hostilities. What followed was, in effect, a compromise whereby the Park ships were to be sold or chartered to private interests with the covenant that they maintain Canadian registry, a requirement that ensured the continued employment of Canadian unionized crews. When it came to the crunch in Cabinet discussions about a postwar Government Merchant Marine, the Hon. Mr. Howe probably did not hesitate in agreeing with Mr. Michaud. In 1936, Mr. Howe was the Minister of Transport in the recently elected Liberal Government when he was called on to play the role of undertaker at the demise of the Canadian Government Merchant Marine.

On the one hand, the sell-off of the Park ships started almost immediately after the decision was taken not to retain the fleet under Government ownership and by the end of 1945, 5 3600 DWT tankers and 14 4700 DWT dry cargo ships, as well as the *Riding Mountain Park* (the dredge that had been converted into a 2000 DWT tanker) had new owners. On the other hand, all the while the sell-off was proceeding, Park ship operations were ongoing through 1945 and into 1946. In many cases, a ship would be at sea when its sale was arranged so that the formal handover to its new owner did not take place until it returned to its home port on completion of its voyage, often a period of several months. In addition, most of the ex-Parks under their new ownership continued to find the heavy immediate postwar demand for shipping services kept them busy on the same trade routes they had been plying in wartime. Consequently, during this period of disposal being overseen by the Park Steamship Company, the Montreal-based holding company carried on tracking the performance of the fleet-in-transition.

The 1946 combined total for both east and west coast sailings was reported as 4.7 million tons (about 2.2 million of which was by vessels still under Park Steamship Company ownership), just short of the record 1945 year. The accumulated total tonnage sealifted by Park ships throughout the 1942-46 period was 12.4 million, the Park company calculated. Emphasizing the value to the national economy of a Canadian Merchant Navy, the company stated in its final review of operations that, "Assuming the Park Steamship vessels carried 80 percent of Canadian Exports to all countries (excluding the U.S.A.) during the years 1944-46, the approximate value of tonnage carried would be $4.46 billion."

But for Park Steamship Company Limited, its real role ended once the war had been brought to a satisfactory conclusion, and the one that thenceforth commanded most of its management's attention became that of a ship broker, a seller of ships. Around this time, direction of the company was taken over by H. J. Rahlves, a former Imperial Oil Marine Superintendent who succeeded E. F. Riddle as President. Mr. Riddle, who had served as Park President from 27 October 1943 until 13 July 1946, had come to the crown company from Canada Shipping Company Limited, Vancouver, of which he was an owner and director.

For the merchandise it was purveying, Park Steamship Company found a ready market. That merchandise included not only 176 Park ships (less those lost to enemy action and other mishaps) and tens of millions of dollars worth of supporting equipment and machinery, but also scores of Canadian-built Fort ships which had been Mutual-Aided to Britain for the duration and were now being returned. First choice for the ex-Parks went to the companies who were prepared to operate the ships under Canadian registry. With the high postwar demand for shipping to support the rebuilding of shattered nations, there was no lack of willing Canadian buyers, principally the companies who had been wartime managing operators under Park Steamship Company agreements. But foreign interests were quick to line up as well; in 1946 War Asset's sales book listed buyers from French Indo-China, Brazil, Sweden, France, Norway and Newfoundland (at that time still three years away from becoming Canada's tenth province).

The 11 knot ships, built for wartime service (they were, in fact, classed as "munitions") to standards of performance that for competitive peacetime commercial operations were obsolete and uneconomic, were nevertheless ready-to-go bargains capable of filling a pressing need that simply could not wait a year or two for more efficient, and expensive, new construction. And what irresistible bargain prices and what appealingly never-never easy terms! The 10,000 DWT vessels were offered at one quarter to one third their original cost (with reductions for buys of three or more); 10 percent down on signing of purchase order, 15 percent more on delivery, and the balance over fifteen years at 3.5 percent. For the 4700 DWT ships, the deals were only slightly less sweet, with the price tag being approximately half the original cost.

By May 1947, Park Steamship Company was reporting 182 vessels of all sizes sold at an average price of $470,527, for a total of just under $72 million. Some of the sales from 1 December 1946 on involved the survivors of the 104 Fort ships,[11] which, having originally been delivered to Britain mostly under Mutual Aid, had since war's end been operated under bareboat charter to the British Ministry of Transport. Following the signing of an agreement with the Ministry on 1 December, tem ships were sold immediately on an "as-is-where-is" basis for cash; twenty were scheduled to be returned to Canada in 1948 and the balance in 1950.

Meanwhile, what was the effect on the Park ship crews of this transition from a single wartime Government-controlled fleet to a diversified multi-private company operation? The Government had declared the official termination of the war to be 31 December 1945, and with it the end of all benefits associated with seamen's wartime agreements, such as reduced rail fares and special payments in case of sickness. Though the Manning Pools were kept open for nearly a year after the suspension of hostilities in August 1945, the Canadian Seamen's Union was moving quickly to consolidate its position and to ensure that the gains that had been enshrined in the agreement signed with Park Steamship Company remained in place with the new private owners, who had themselves organized an industry-wide shipping federation to represent their interests vis-à-vis the Union and the

Government. The Union became a very prominent fact of life for both the seamen and the ship owners,[12] and one of its first moves was to insist successfully that the War Risk Bonus of $44.50 per month be incorporated into the seamen's basic wage structure. Officially the bonus had been danger pay, but in effect it had served as a Government subsidy for what was little more than a subsistence level of pay scales for both unlicensed and licensed personnel, higher than British rates to be sure but far below those paid on American ships.

In March 1946, Transport Minister Lionel Chevrier had recommended that the manning pools remain open until 30 September 1946, but by Order In Council P.C. 3396, the Cabinet set 31 July 1946 as the closing date. The manning pool system had provided the seamen on the two-year agreement with a "between ships" source of meals and lodging as well as basic pay (sans War Risk Bonus), a guarantee of a steady job, so to speak, a guarantee that loomed large in minds still fresh with memories of the dirty thirties depression. To compensate somewhat for the loss of this support system, which effectively provided continuous employment whether ashore or afloat, the Government acted to bring the seamen into the Unemployment Insurance Scheme, even though hitherto neither the seamen nor the managing operators had been paying into the fund. There was also the Special Bonus, under which a seaman who had signed a Two-Year Manning Pool Agreement was eligible for a bonus payment amounting to 10 percent of his gross earnings, of which the War Risk Bonus of $44.50 was considered part.

For all the complaints that the crews may have had about Park Steamship Company's ships and the manning pools, their existence had provided a sense of unity and of belonging to the entity that was the Canadian Merchant Navy. After all, hadn't wartime Transport Minister J. E. Michaud labelled the Merchant Navy as virtually a "Fourth Arm of the Fighting Forces?" Now, with the dismantling of the Park Line and the dispersal of the renamed ships among three dozen private shipping lines, that sense of being part of a common enterprise with a common purpose had vanished and no Union could replace it. Also soon to be forgotten were the virtuous proclamations of the Government which, within a few years would turn on the Union of the very seamen it had so recently lavishly praised as heroes.

Jack Stewart of Burlington, Ontario, remembers what it was like when he arrived back in Victoria after eleven months away as an oiler on the *Tantara* (ex-*Whiterock Park*). When he had signed on through the Vancouver Manning Pool for what was supposed to be only a two- or three-month "back home for Christmas" voyage to Formosa and China, the pool and all seamen support services were still functioning, but by the time he returned many changes had taken place:

That trip lasted eleven months! [When we finally arrived back] at Victoria
... they let us off on the shore, if you like. We were paid off in the ship's saloon
and caught the midnight ferry for Vancouver. The next day I went to the
manning pool on Dunsmuir Street to find it had been changed into a
rehabilitation centre. The Navy League's Seamen's Club had gone. To me it
had all changed overnight. Then I came home with a feeling I'd been had.

Chapter Four   # THEM AND US

Sometimes Park ships were not happy ships. Among the growing pains experienced by the swiftly expanding wartime Canadian Merchant Navy was the problem of crew disaffection. The reasons for this were explored in 1943 by a Government interdepartmental committee[1] which found one explanation, simply stated, to be that the new-to-the-life Canadian seamen didn't quite know, or didn't readily accept their place in the traditional shipboard hierarchy. "It is evident," reported a committee memorandum of its findings,

> that the essential customs and traditions of the sea, evolved from experience to contribute to the general safety, are unknown to our new Canadian seamen. Those from the Lakes and Home Trades are acccustomed to an absence of caste barriers as between officers and men and submit very unreadily to such conditions as are common and necessary on foreign-going vessels. Other seamen now recruited have learned their trade on American-owned ships where Trade Union control has reached the point of absurdity, such as the appointment of Union delegates from among the ranks of each department on board, who interfere in many cases with the operation of the vessel and its internal economy. The new recruits (trainees) quickly follow the undesirable practices.
>
> Experienced ship's officers in many cases find it difficult to reconcile themselves to the crew's outlook, and in the absence of any set rules or agreements, distrust and antagonisms continually arise. This is especially true where United Kingdom officers and Canadian seamen are serving together.

Not mentioned in the memorandum was the fact that there were also shortcomings in crew living conditions which, perhaps in the rush to get the Park ships into service, had not been given too much thought. As they gained experience, however, Canadian shipyards made progressive design improvements and these were not necessarily confined only to the ships' construction and equipment features. Crew accommodation and amenities were slowly upgraded. For unlicensed personnel in particular these were initially spartan by any standard, a reflection of the British antecedents of the ship design, not to mention the very British cast of the methods of operation and amenity standards adopted for the Park Steamship Company vessels.

Technically, crew amenities were not the responsibility of the Park company, the corporation being simply the owner of the ships, not the operator. This management task was assigned to existing private shipping companies which chartered the ships from the Crown holding company. As previously explained, under the terms of their contracts[2] with Park Steamship Company, these managing operators were responsible for the care of the vessels, furnishing the crews, payment of all expenses and collection of revenues. In return, they were paid a management fee plus a percentage of cargo earnings.

In practice, the Park company was not, as ostensibly intended by its explicit arrangement with the managing operators, able to maintain a completely arm's length relationship with ship operations, especially with reference to crew conditions. The Canadian Seamen's Union (CSU), which at the start of the war had been exclusively a Great Lakes shipping union with a fractious relationship with the inland ship owners, soon acquired the ambition to go deep-sea and began aggressively making its presence felt among the rank-and-file seamen shipping out of eastern ports. The Government, determined to maintain the national war effort at maximum tempo, was anxious to keep the peace on the labour front and so, eventually, reluctantly granted recognition to the CSU. More than a little of this reluctance was attributable to the unabashed Communist leanings of the CSU leaders, several of whom because of those leanings had indeed been interned from June 1940 until March 1942, nine months after the Soviet Union had earned automatic membership in the Allied camp through being invaded by Nazi Germany in June 1941.

A working agreement contract with the Union was signed in 1943 covering unlicensed seamen sailing from east coast ports, and later in 1944 the same coverage was extended to west coast port sailors after they had indicated their preference for the CSU in a Government-supervised vote. The contract was, however, between Park Steamship Company and the CSU, and not between the Union and the individual shipping companies who were the actual operators of the Park ships. Thus the shipping companies lost whatever control they had originally enjoyed over rates of pay, which became standardized throughout the Park fleet. The operators of non-Park Canadian-registered ships also found themselves compelled to fall in line in order to keep crews.

Furthermore, the shipping companies found themselves playing a diminishing role in the selection of crews for their ships. But the companies' loss in this respect was not necessarily the CSU's gain; the Union, too, failed in its objective to be the main supplier of unlicensed crewmen. Because ship crewing is synonymous with

Union power, the CSU desperately wanted to control this critical function through Union hiring halls, but it was largely frustrated in this ambition by the Canadian Government, which was intent on denying the Union any leverage to interfere in any meaningful way with the operation of the Park fleet. The wartime powers of the Government were awesome and it never hesitated using them to achieve its desired ends. The Union in any case had committed itself to a "no-strike-for-the-duration" policy in its contract with Park Steamship Company.

The Government effectively exercised power over crewing through its Directorate of Merchant Seamen, which was established within the Department of Transport in May 1941 and charged with manning and training. Under the newly appointed Director of Merchant Seamen, Arthur Randles, the new Directorate moved quickly to establish a system of manning pools, first taking over the existing British-operated Place Viger Manning Pool[3] in Montreal and then following up with the establishment of additional pools in Vancouver, Halifax and Sydney, Nova Scotia, and Saint John, New Brunswick. With the exception of the Sydney Pool, all continued in operation until closed on 31 July 1946.

Through the manning pools, the Government successfully thwarted CSU attempts to play a more meaningful part in the crewing of the Park fleet. Even such Park ship operating companies as CNS and Imperial Oil, which were accustomed to hiring crewmen for their own ships in just the same way as they hired any other employees, found themselves being nudged into using the services of the manning pools. They were unenthusiastic participants.

"CNS used this source of personnel reluctantly as it felt the pools were a training ground for trade unionists," according to *The Lady Boats*[4]:

> Shortly thereafter the Canadian Seamen's Union began to gain strength. It was the first maritime union in Canada and there was some concern that the Communist Party was backing the Union. CNS subsequently refused to have anything to do with the Union but the CSU was successful in obtaining a contract with Park Steamships.

* * *

Because the Park ships were entering service so rapidly, the training of Canadian deck and engineering officers to licensed standards, which in any case entailed several years of sea experience, could not keep pace with the requirement for licensed personnel. The solution was to import experienced officers from the U.K., and these Britishers also found it strange to be presented by the manning pools with a packaged crew in whose selection they had played no part.

Capt. John M. Mann of Oakville, Ontario, was a second mate when he was sent to Canada early in 1944 along with several other British ships' officers, including the Captain, to join a new ship, the *Belwoods Park*, which their employer, Manchester Liners Limited, was to manage for Park Steamship Company. They joined her at Sorel, Quebec, where she was still receiving the finishing touches by the builder, Marine Industries Limited.

"Eventually the *Belwoods* was ready for her trials," Captain Mann recalls,

> and the first of our surprises regarding the crew was when we were told that we would have no choice of men. All hands would be sent down from Montreal by bus . . . . We of course had never experienced this before, having always been able to pick what we considered the best men for the job. Anyhow, our crew arrived and sorted themselves out to which department they belonged and we proceeded up the river to Montreal to load a general cargo for the U.K.

The manning pool system came to dominate the crewing of the Park ships because it was attractive even to individual CSU members. A seaman on joining the manning pool was assured of food and lodging and regular pay (not including War Risk Bonus) while ashore between ships. In exchange, he was required to accept whatever ship he was assigned to, when his name was posted. The Union could not compete with such a deal. It was also refused, despite many representations, participation in any of the training programs the Director of Merchant Seamen, Arthur Randles, established for deck and engine room personnel, navigating officers, wireless operators and even cooks.

These training programs, most importantly St. Margaret's Sea Training School for Ordinary Seamen and Cadet Officers, and the Prescott Marine Engineering Instruction School for engine room personnel, served to strengthen the Director of Merchant Seamen's position in the control of manpower for the Merchant Navy. From first contact, the young men who became trainees at these schools were Arthur Randles' "boys." He was responsible for recruiting them, supplying them with transportation from wherever their homes were in Canada to Hubbards, Nova Scotia, or Prescott, Ontario, housing, boarding and training them for several weeks and then, on graduation, feeding them directly into his manning pool system. By the end of 1944, it was common for a new Park ship setting out on its first voyage to have signed on two or three newly minted Ordinary Seamen and two Cadet Officers fresh from St. Margaret's, as well as two or three firemen/trimmers from Prescott, altogether representing over 15 percent of the normal complement of a Park coal burner. By war's end, graduates of Randles' two schools for unlicensed deck and engine room personnel numbered an estimated two thousand,[5] nearly 17 percent of the approximately twelve thousand merchant seamen that were reckoned to have served in Canada's wartime Merchant Navy. Little wonder that the Director of Merchant Seamen's authority over both the training establishments and the manning pools gave him an iron (and autocratic) grip on crewing that no Union could break under wartime controls.

* * *

The CSU, frustrated in its hope of gaining control of manning (which of course it did soon after the war ended), turned its attention to winning the hearts and minds of the seamen by providing them with a voice to speak to management, gradually gaining improvements in shipboard living and working conditions for its members. The managing operators and Park Steamship Company had to be prodded and nagged to provide even such low-cost comforts as cooling fans for crew cabins (which were stifling when travelling in the tropics under wartime blackout) and water coolers for the crew pantry. There was much room for such improvements to crew living conditions and in this area the Union proved very effective over time.

The early Park ships provided the most basic of accommodation for unlicensed personnel. Typically, on the *Nemiskam Park*, delivered in July 1943, crew members, four to a cabin, slept in open bunk beds in which thin mattresses, little more than pads, rested on an unsprung latticework of flat metal strips. By the time the *Green Hill Park* entered service early in 1944, it had been recognized that even lowly sailors were entitled to some comfort and privacy. The bunks now came with thick spring mattresses and were fitted with draw curtains, though it wasn't until the ship's second voyage in the tropics that fans were introduced.

The CSU was successful in exploiting to its advantage this seeming reluctance on the part of the Park company and the Park ship managing operators to provide what they viewed as extras, failing to appreciate the pay-off in crew morale and contentment that would naturally follow. Low morale and discontent were crucial elements that could quickly sour relations between the two solitudes of foc's'le and bridge, raising the risk of confrontations. Situations often arose that were complicated by the insistence of Park Steamship Company that it approve from Montreal head office even the most minor of modifications that an improvement might entail.

A threatened strike in Vancouver in February 1944 by the crew of the first *Mohawk Park*, a North Sands type coal burner under the management of the Canadian Australasian Line, serves to illustrate how stubborn the Montreal-based Park Steamship head office could be in making even the most modest of concessions to the seamen. It also demonstrates the shortcomings of the contractual arrangement between Park Steamship Company and its managing operators in that it should have been possible for the Canadian Australasian Line to handle what was really a trivial problem on the spot rather than having to refer it to Montreal. The Naval Boarding Service[6] report of the incident explains that on 3 February, the crew had complained to the Captain that the seamen's and the firemen's messes had only a single-burner hotplate each and so could make only one pot of coffee at a time, not enough to serve all hands. They requested installation of a steam-heated percolator in each mess.

While awaiting action on their apparently simple request, the crew became aware of another irritating problem. The domestic water supply serving the thirty-five men living in the seamen's, firemen's and DEMS ratings' quarters was stored in a header tank which had to be constantly replenished from a main tank by means of a hand pump. The crew claimed the header tank was empty most of the time. It was the utility boy's task to keep the tank topped up, but he also had to do double duty as a trimmer in the stokehold. He frequently had to be rousted from his bunk to pump water. Water supply was important at any time, but doubly so on coal burners, which were notoriously dirty.

By 8 February, on the eve of sailing, there had been no response to the request for steam percolators and at 10:30 a.m. the crew threatened to strike at 1:00 p.m. unless the coffee makers were supplied, now adding the demand that a steam-powered pump be installed to rectify the water supply problem.

Although the Captain, Second Engineer and the Naval Boarding Service rep thought the crewmen had reasonable grounds, the Park head office in Montreal refused permission to rectify their complaints. Finally, Park Steamship Company conceded that it would install the power pump and steam percolators when the ship returned from its voyage, later modifying its stand to say the pump would be installed at the first port of call, Auckland, New Zealand, and the coffee urns on return to Vancouver. The crew eventually agreed to this; surprisingly, because by doing so they would still have to put up with the water supply problem for the approximately three weeks that it would take to get to New Zealand, and the insufficient coffee-making capacity for the entire voyage, probably three months. Given that many of the crew would in all likelihood sign off on return to Vancouver, the only real satisfaction gained was that things would be better for the next crew.

The Naval Boarding Service rep, while criticizing the crew for acting without consulting their Union first, and for giving the Captain only two and a half hours notice of their intention to strike, was also critical of Park Steamship, pointing out that company could have given permission for the work easily within two and a half hours. "But no, it has taken them three to four days to make up their mind." The NBS report noted as well that midships, where the officers were quartered, enjoyed the convenience of a steam pump for water supply; also that the installation of the coffee urns would not have been precedent-setting as at least one other Park ship under Canadian Australasian Line management already had them.

* * *

This management reluctance to make concessions possibly owed less to the common them and us labour/management relationship than it did to the already mentioned very British cast of the instant Merchant Navy that Canada had created. The prewar British Mercantile Marine, archetype of the new CMN, was infused with centuries of tradition in which life in the foc's'le was seen as, on at least one level, a sort of a tough prep school for future officers. The thinking seemed to be that poor living conditions and often even worse food would bring to the brightest among the sailors the realization that the only way to escape to the better life midships was to serve their time, study, write their exams and thereby work their way up to the licensed glory of a deck or engineer officer. For those not thus inspired, or incapable, well, they deserved the misery of foc's'le life.

That the wartime Canadian Merchant Navy would have a decidedly British stamp should not be surprising although in this case, unlike that of the Canadian Armed Services,[7] there does not appear to have been any overt attempt from London to tell the Canadians how to go about their business. In point of fact, such an attempt was hardly necessary. The unconscious British influence was pervasive throughout the equipping, development, manning and operation of the Park fleet from the very start. Even when it came to planning a training institution for seamen, the Director of Merchant Seamen took as his prototype the well-known British sea training school at Gravesend, England. This adoption of the British model in all respects for Canada's embryonic Merchant Navy was perfectly understandable and certainly not necessarily bad. After all, who knew more about ships and shipping than the British? At the beginning of the War, the United Kingdom was the world's leading maritime nation, with an ocean merchant fleet of 16,643,904 gross tonnage, nearly double that of its closest maritime rival, the United States.

Canada, with its tiny thirty-seven-ship fleet totalling 227,000 gross tons, was effectively invisible as a maritime nation in September 1939, so it is hardly surprising that unconsciously it should look to No. 1 for an example to follow. Then, too, this was a time when Canadians generally, Quebec excepted, still referred to Britain as the "Mother Country" or the "Old Country," sang "God Save the King" with fervour, and when, on the threshold of war King George VI and Queen Elizabeth toured Canada, cheered them because they were our King and Queen and not because they were media celebrities. And it was only a couple of years past the time when teachers in Canadian schools were, in sepulchral tones suggesting the death of a beloved parent, breaking the news to their students that King Edward VIII was exchanging his crown for a duke's coronet so he could marry *that* Mrs. Simpson. At the same time, though these old links persisted, Canadian attitudes toward the British were changing, an evolutionary process that had started during the prematurely designated "war to end wars" Great War of 1914-18. The young people entering the Canadian Forces in World War II, whether of British or European stock, were two and sometimes three generations removed from their antecedents. To them the "Old Country" was simply a nostalgic figure of speech used by their parents or grandparents. And when French Canadians joined the Canadian Forces, it was certainly not for any attachment to Britain, or even France. It was a factor that would affect the way Canadian Park ships were operated. It soon became clear that, even outside the obvious relative inexperience of Canadian crews, they were very different from their British counterparts.

* * *

As junior partners to the larger, more experienced British Services, the Canadian Armed Forces had been put under overall British leadership, so for the very practical reason of commonality, they looked to British models for their own equipment. Thus the Canadian Navy found itself at sea in British designed corvettes, the Canadian Army was firing British-designed 25-pounder field artillery pieces and the RCAF was flying British-designed Lancaster bombers, all of which were, however, produced in Canada by a mushrooming domestic munitions industry. It was only natural then that a British merchant ship design should be adopted to equip the nascent Canadian Merchant Navy. It was a decision made especially easy by the fact that production of the ship in question, the 10,000 DWT North Sands type cargo vessel, was already underway in Canadian shipyards, having been sparked by a straight commercial order from the British Purchasing Mission for twenty-six.

The ship was so very British in layout, most significantly in the separation of the quarters for the deck and engine room hands (and DEMS ratings) from those for the officers. The latter were located midships, in what might in relative terms be described as the comfort zone, where the effect of a ship's motion is least felt, whereas the former were tucked away in the stern, where even a modestly heavy sea could provide a nonstop roller coaster ride to the accompaniment of the rattling cacophony of the steering machinery's backlashing gears. The thrashing of the huge propeller was also a noisy presence, but somehow it was more reassuring than annoying.

To these accommodation shortcomings were added the messing arrangement whereby the crew's food had to be transported from the galley, which was midships, aft to the seamen's and firemen's messes. Winter and summer, fair weather and foul, the meals were carried in stacked uninsulated metal containers called kids. The load could be awkward and heavy, especially if the Peggy was a very young teenager as was often the case; and the travelling time from midships to stern could be long and slow if the seas were rough and a high deckload had to be negotiated. Cold fried eggs for breakfast were standard fare. It was a poor arrangement in all respects, but that was the way the British had been doing it for years and Canada had adopted a British ship design, unmodified in layout, so there was no choice but that the same routine should be followed on the Park ships. At least it was an improvement on what had been a British practice of only a ship generation or two earlier, that of locating the crew's quarters forward in the pinched space of the forecastle, where the ship met the sea head on and the motion could be at its most violent. When the foredeck was taking seas in heavy weather, a Peggy bringing his load of mess kids (one hand for the kids, one hand for himself) from galley to foc's'le was truly risking his life.

This "two-different-worlds" separation of quarters, with its perception of privilege for those midships that was the nurturing bed for many of the "crew troubles" which plagued the Park fleet throughout its life, was avoided by the more egalitarian Americans when they metamorphosed the same basic North Sands design into the famed Liberty ship. On the Liberties, a single large midships superstructure combined the bridge with all living accommodation and messing facilities for both licensed and unlicensed personnel. The one exception to this arrangement was that quarters for some of the Armed Guard (the USN counterpart of DEMS) were located in the stern.

At the outset, the pervasiveness of the British ingredient was heightened by the fact that up to mid-1943 most of the new Park vessels had been allocated for management by Canadian branches of British-controlled steamship companies who drew on their own reserves of deck officers and engineers in the U.K. to operate the Canadian vessels. Not unnaturally, these officers joined their new ships with the mindset that they were working for their U.K. parent company, not Park Steamship Company. It would take some time for them to adapt and some of them never did.

The Canadian Government was also quick to adopt the British fixed rate War Risk Bonus of £10 Sterling per month for Canadian seamen, which at the pegged wartime exchange rate of one pound Sterling equalling $4.45 Canadian, worked out to $44.50 per month. The Canadian merchant seamen regarded with envy, and the Director of Merchant Seamen with horror, the lavish union-driven system of bonuses and danger pay provided for American seamen. Unlike the British-style one bonus for all occasions, the U.S. National Maritime Union had negotiated a schedule of extra payments to suit every degree of risk, real or imagined. These included a 100 percent Voyage bonus that in effect doubled the basic wage. Little wonder that Canadian merchant seamen were constantly contriving ways to gain berths on American ships; little wonder that Director of Merchant Seamen Arthur Randles was ever vigilant in his efforts to thwart such ambitions, regularly calling on Immigration and wartime manpower authorities for assistance in preventing "his" seamen from quietly slipping across the border.

It is perhaps of significance that Arthur Randles, fair and concerned about his charges as he most often was, was solidly British (though a longtime resident of Canada) and steeped in the traditions of the Cunard White Star Line, for which he had been Canadian passenger agent before being recruited by the Canadian Government for the pivotal position of Director of Merchant Seamen. He was also determined to keep the brakes on Union influence.

* * *

For the most part, when the Captain and the majority of the officers on a Park ship were Canadians, the relationship between midships and foc's'le (most seamen continued to use the term even though their quarters were now in the stern) was relatively relaxed. But when the officers were predominantly British, the gap between the two solitudes could sometimes be measured in light years. This was not always the case, to be sure, and on many ships Canadian crewmen and British officers adapted to each other's strange ways with a minimum of difficulty. But with insufficient numbers of native Canadian officers and engineers to meet the manning quotas of the ships that were being added to the Park fleet weekly, Arthur Randles had little choice but to turn to the U.K. By 1944, the British component amounted to 40 percent of all navigating officers and marine engineers serving aboard Park ships.

All of these things, the design of the ships, the presence of many British officers, frequently lead to the Parks being mistaken for British ships, an error of considerable annoyance to the Canadian crews. This possibility of mistaken identity was reinforced by the standard practice of flying the national flag while in foreign port. The Canadian flag at the time differed from the Red Duster of the British Mercantile Marine only in that the Canadian coat-of-arms had been added to the fly. Consequently, should the ensign be hanging limply while in port, as it was wont to do, the Canadian coat-of-arms vanished in the folds, making it very difficult not to mistake what the eye was observing for the Red Duster, thereby identifying the ship as British to the casual onlooker. "One of the things that bothered us," recalled Alex White of Regina, Saskatchewan, a Sparks on the *Green Gables Park*,

> was when our ship went into port and the flag hanging, as flags do when there's no wind, and no one knew us from a British ship, and that bothered us. We were Canadian and God, we wanted people to know we were Canadian.

As if this didn't present enough of a national identity crisis for the Park ships and their crews, the Canadian media sometimes referred in general terms to the Canadian-built North Sands type vessels as Liberty ships.

* * *

There is an appendix to the Merchant Seamen Committee memorandum of 3 June 1943 that provides examples of the frequent crew troubles on Park ships, culled from reports of the Naval Boarding Service, and in which it is commented that "the . . . reports of trouble all deal with friction between officers and men and general discontents with food and accommodation. This mutual suspicion and hostility between officers and men is evident in nearly all reports. In the *Dartmouth Park* the Seamen's Union delegate stated bluntly that British officers were not suitable to handle Canadian crews. The Mate of the *High Park*, interviewed at Montreal 12 July 1943, complained that Canadian deckhands were undisciplined, inefficient and ignorant of ordinary marine language (the language difficulty for new hands may be increased by having to take orders given in unfamiliar accents) and the officers of the same ship repeat this complaint at Sydney on 24 July, giving a very exaggerated estimate of the number of 'first trippers' on board.

"The 'unhappiness' of Park Line ships cannot be entirely due to labour agitators, 'sea lawyers' among the crew, or poor calibre of officers, as all ships must suffer from these evils occasionally." The commentator discounted the combination of British officers and Canadian crews as being responsible for the problem, noting that there were "more happy than unhappy" mixed crews.

> There does, however, seem to be a touchy and suspicious attitude among the crews and even the Officers of Park Line ships. The men seem to feel that there is continual unjust resistance to what they regard as rightful claims; feel that they have to fight for each and every minor concession. In instances where their claims have been promptly and adequately settled, crew trouble has disappeared.
>
> Obviously, if crew trouble is to be stopped, it is necessary to convince crews that there is no reason for their suspicious, hostile attitude towards their officers and employers. Crews are not likely to cause trouble if they can feel sure that their reasonable demands will be met, and the experience of the happier Park ships is a clear indication of this.

Although complaints of crew trouble were usually associated by management and the Director of Merchant Seamen with unlicensed hands, the officers were not always paragons, as the Naval Boarding Service summary makes clear:

> In three cases, trouble was caused directly by officers. The Master of the *Dufferin Park* drank heavily and on one occasion threatened a member of his crew with a revolver before he was arrested and removed at Halifax in August 1942. U.S. authorities considered second and third officers largely

to blame for crew trouble on the *Port Royal Park* at Bahia prior to 24 April 1943, and a further report on 31 August indicates the trouble of an unspecified nature continues. On the *Stanley Park* at Montreal, 4 September 1943, serious trouble was caused by the second and third engineers who refused to sail unless certain comforts (e.g., hot drinks at 11 a.m. each day) were provided.

A reading of Naval Boarding Service reports of Park ship boardings leaves at least some feeling that any action that brought management authority into question was automatically and conveniently categorized as crew trouble. For example: "The deckhands and firemen of the *Gatineau Park* went on strike about 21 November 1942, when they were refused cash advances on their wages. This difficulty was ended by arbitration and a compromise." And:

> A firemen's strike occurred on the *Rockcliffe Park* in Tampa, August 1943, when stokehold temperatures became hard to endure in hot weather with inadequate ventilation. This was remedied when the owners consented to extending the ventilator cowls enough to catch sufficient air.

Viewed through the lens of five decades of time, it becomes clear that a significant proportion of the NBS-reported incidents categorized as crew troubles (the term nearly always appeared bracketed in quotation marks) could just as easily have been classified as management troubles, a term embracing everything from a managing operator scrimping on provisioning to the bad attitude of a bloody-minded shipmaster. A minor confrontation observed by Gilbert O. L. Tate of Halifax, Nova Scotia, a cadet officer on the *Stanley Park*, serves to illustrate how a penny-pinching managing operator might thoughtlessly plant the seed for crew dissatisfaction months hence. "We were to sail from Saint John to Cape Town via Trinidad," Tate remembers:

> A little incident happened while taking on stores; the [shipping company] agent asked the Chief Steward what the forty pounds of fruit cake was for. The Steward replied that we may be away for Christmas; it may be nice for the approximately forty crew, counting DEMS gunners. "Send it back," was the agent's reply.

In the bloody-minded Master category there was the sad incident reported to the Security Control Officer at Cape Town (the equivalent of the RCN's Naval Boarding Service) involving the *Winona Park* while enroute from Colombo, Ceylon, to Bombay. The Captain was alleged by five crew complainants to have refused requests that proper medical care be sought by putting into the nearest port when several members of the crew began exhibiting symptoms of cholera. The crew were said to have forced his hand when the engine room department, represented by the Second Engineer, advised that they would stop engines unless he altered course to Madras.

In the event, despite altering course to Madras, two of the sick men died (in all, twenty-one of the crew contracted the disease). The boarding report describes what was claimed to have followed:

> The first, [Tom] Mullins the donkeyman, was buried outside the three mile limit after the "briefest and most insincere" ceremony ever conducted by a Master. The Master [was] alleged to have read a verse from the Bible and said, "Toss him over the side." Only six or eight members of the crew were present at the "Service," the Master refusing to wait for them to muster. The other man who died was given a decent funeral ashore by the [Shipping] Agents after the crew complained to them.

George Byrnell of Victoria, B.C., who was an AB on the Winona Park at the time of this incident, remembers it in not quite such dramatic terms though with the recollection that there was considerable crew unhappiness typical of a ship that had been long away from home and was enduring the miserable heat of a tropical summer.

> We had a crew made up . . . of a cross section of Canadians from Cornerbrook to Prince Rupert. We had fighters, especially when on the sauce, we had philosophers after a fashion, we had hot heads and cool heads and by the time we reached Cape Town there were few cool heads. The report from [the Security Control Officer] states that we were on our way from Colombo to Bombay when cholera broke out. My recollection is that this occurred after we left Calcutta. However, whichever is correct we pulled into Madras after a meeting of the crew and lay outside the breakwater until the Port Doctor came aboard and had the sick men removed ashore and the crew vaccinated. We buried Tom Mullins also before we were allowed inside the breakwater where we dropped the hook. The old man . . . slowed the vessel down but to my memory I don't believe we were stopped when we were told to commit the body to the deep. Where it is said in the Cape Town report that [the Captain] said, "toss him over the side," well, that's forty-seven years ago and I can't honestly say that I remember what he said. However, I was present and I do remember that haste seemed to be important to the skipper. We had very little time to assemble. Some of the gunners were there and I remember Donovan Terry, the chief gunlayer, and some of the gunners had their uniforms on. It was over very quickly and aft there was anger at the seeming lack of respect. It was still a time of war and I can't pretend to know what was going on the mind of [the Captain]."

THE UNKNOWN NAVY ■

THE UNKNOWN NAVY ■

It is not surprising that relations between the foc's'le and the bridge on the Park ships should have so often been troubled. They were crewed largely by men who arrived aboard not only with little experience but with no background of maritime tradition. In their naiveté they failed to appreciate the importance of the caste barrier between officers and seamen that was characteristic of the British Mercantile Marine after which the Canadian Merchant Navy had been patterned. Unwilling to accept the status quo, they brought sea change to the relationship and in the end it was the bridge that, not without reluctance, did most of the adapting.

In the *Winona Park* incident, George Byrnell perceived the growing signs of change:

> The crew were mostly a good bunch, one or two rang-a-tangs, mostly when drinking. However, there were a few who were constant complainers but would never accept any responsibility when it came to representing the crew. So we had anger, frustration, and a new breed of cat. Where for many years the Old Man's word was law, now we had some questions and we asked them. I was [union] secretary on the *Mission Park* with old Buck Buchanan in command; he was a former China Coaster and felt that his word was the final word. I had occasion to challenge him on a matter of importance to the crew. When he met with me and the other reps, his first question was, "What makes you think that I am going to listen to you?" As spokesperson my reply was: "Well, Captain, it's either here or with the shore delegates when we arrive in Vancouver." He looked at us for a moment and then invited us into his cabin.
>
> So there was change in the offing.

Chapter Five # MANNING THE SHIPS

Hard to endure as the massive loss of ships and their precious cargoes was during the first years of the war, there was always the knowledge, buoyed by eternal hope and optimism, that ships and cargoes could somehow be replaced by industry. Much more painful and not replaceable in any factory, was the frightful loss of life among the merchant seamen who crewed the sunken vessels. The casualty rate for civilian sailors was far higher than that for all of the Armed Services combined. In the first two years of the war, merchant seamen deaths attributed to enemy action reached a staggering twenty-five thousand mostly British but including significant numbers of the citizens of other anti-Nazi nations, Canada among them.

As has been seen, in 1942 the Canadian Government decided that, in addition to the ships being built in Canadian shipyards for the British account, others would be ordered for Canadian operation. This significant step was taken, apparently, without much thought being given to how these Park ships, as they became known, would be manned. Many of the experienced seamen, particularly licensed personnel, who had been working the tiny Canadian prewar deep-sea merchant fleet, had been taken into the RCN, which had expanded tenfold since the onset of hostilities. And because of the prewar lack of job opportunities on Canadian deep-sea ships, there were other Canadians sailing on ships of foreign registry, British, Danish, Dutch, Norwegian among them, and, most desirable for pay reasons, United States. Still, all in all, the combined number of active Canadian seamen employed on deep-sea ships of all registries at the outbreak of war, was probably no more than four thousand and, as already noted, many of them were quickly recruited into the Canadian Navy.

As outlined in an earlier chapter, the manning demands for the new ships grew rapidly and placed great pressure on Canada's already strained manpower resources. It was bad enough that due to the urgency of the situation ships were sailing with many first trippers who often had no or at best, limited related experience. If complements of inexperienced first trippers were unavoidable, and they were, then something had to be done to apply a veneer of training in seamanship fundamentals to them so they would board their first ship at least knowing port from starboard.[1]

Little wonder that in March 1941, Cdr. J. A. Heenan, RCNR, wrote to L. D. Wilgress, Chairman of the Canadian Shipping Board, Ottawa, expressing concern that the Canadian Government's decision "to adopt a policy of 'all out' merchant ship construction carries with it the vital necessity for providing personnel for those vessels, a problem which appears to have been overlooked or perhaps just taken for granted." Commander Heenan pointed to the British example of mercantile training establishments, suggesting something similar be set up without delay on both Canadian coasts for the training of officers, seamen and marine engineers.

The very next day, Wilgress forwarded with his endorsement copies of Heenan's letter to Lt. Col. K. C. Maclachlan, Acting Deputy Minister, Department of National Defence, Naval Service (DND/NS), and to the Deputy Minister of Transport, Cdr. C. P. Edwards.

Though Heenan's idea was well received by the Naval Service, the question was raised as to whether the training of merchant seamen was really a naval matter at all. Capt. H. T. W. Grant, Director of Naval Personnel, was enthusiastic but begged off any Navy involvement, saying the RCN was already stretched beyond capacity with its training centres overcrowded and inadequately equipped to train its own men. He cited a shortage of experienced instructors and a lack of training ships. The Chief of the Naval Staff, VAdm. Percy W. Nelles, was similarly enthusiastic but prepared to offer only moral support, telling Heenan that, "Our own problem is of such magnitude now that it is literally impossible with our present resources to take on further commitments at this time."

Despite this refusal to get involved in the training of merchant seamen, Naval Service HQ did consider undertaking the provision of canteen and recreation services in all Canadian ports for all seamen. Naval Service told the Shipping Board's Wilgress that

> a very great strain is now being put upon the morale of merchant seamen. This strain is not at present met or compensated for upon the same lines as it is done in the case of the regular fighting forces. On the other hand, the successful prosecution of the war is entirely dependent upon the upkeep of the morale of the merchant seamen of all nations who are working for the Allies.

Early in April, Cdr. C. P. Edwards, Deputy Minister of Transport, suggested following the British example whereby Merchant Navy recruits would train alongside RCN recruits for three months at RCN rates of pay before transferring to the Merchant Navy at civilian rates of pay. This proposal, too, was rejected by the Navy for already stated reasons of lack of capacity and facilities.

Capt. E. S. Brand, Director of Naval Intelligence (DNI), a Royal Navy Officer who had been seconded to the RCN prior to the start of the war and who was destined to play an influential role in the evolution of Canada's wartime Merchant Navy, said that Commander Heenan's merchant seamen training proposal was really a matter for a new section that had been proposed for the Department of Transport.

This new section, as described in the Department of Transport proposal, would deal with all merchant seamen matters, including the organization and development of manning pools, general control of Merchant Navy canteens and other welfare arrangements, as well as training. This proposal received general approval, including that of the Shipping Board's Wilgress, who suggested that training establishments be set up in Halifax, Montreal and Vancouver.

Within weeks, the Transport Department proposal had cleared its way through to Cabinet and on 19 May 1941, Order In Council P.C. 14/1550 was promulgated, authorizing the establishment of a special branch of the Department of Transport under a "Director of Merchant Seamen," to be responsible for the creation and operation of manning pools and welfare facilities for merchant seamen; also for the extension and operation of existing nautical schools for the training of merchant seamen, marine engineers and officers.

The man chosen to fill the post of Director of Merchant Seamen was Arthur Randles, a veteran executive of the Cunard White Star Line who was to prove indefatigable in fulfillment of his new mandate. Though his appointment did not become official until several weeks after the creation of the new Transport Department branch, Randles was quickly at work making plans for the establishment of manning pools and the drawing up of a training proposal.

Despite the passing of Order In Council P.C. 14/1550 and the activities of the energetic Randles, it still remained the feeling of some, within the Navy itself, that the RCN should be involved in the training of merchant seamen. Early in September 1941, in a letter to Captain Brand, DNI, Commander B. L. Johnson, RCNR, Merchant Seamen Liaison Officer, outlined in some detail a plan for Navy participation. Commander Johnson noted that Canada's shipbuilding plans included the construction of 110 cargo ships which would have a crewing requirement of about 5,000 licensed and unlicensed personnel. He ostensibly felt that with the example of the heavy Allied merchant seaman casualty rate, 25,000 in the first two years of the war, along with the manning requirements of the new Canadian-built ships, the scale of the Canadian training and manning program being envisaged would be inadequate.

In a memo to Brand on 16 September, Johnson reported that the building and preparations for operating manning pools and welfare centres were well in hand and being vigorously pursued by Randles. Two days later, following an exploratory visit to Kingston, Brockville and Prescott, all in Ontario, Johnson wrote to Randles to advise the new Director of Merchant Seamen that Kingston would be the ideal location for a marine engineering school. He pointed out that it was already the location of an RCNVR barracks where LCdr. (E) J. L. Dunn, RCNR, had been operating an engineering school for the preceding nineteen years, and was currently operating the naval school for entries in the Engine Room branch.

The Kingston site recommendation was a neat fit with Commander Johnson's position that the Navy should at least play some part in the merchant seaman training program. In a memo to the Deputy Minister, Naval Service, just one day after his report to Randles, Johnson continued to press for Navy involvement, while acknowledging that his naval superiors considered this inadvisable. He again raised the matter of heavy merchant seamen casualties, stressing that while seamen's morale continued high, the quality of replacements was diminishing. He said ratings as young as fifteen and as old as sixty-seven had been noted.

"The interested Canadian Government departments have been discussing training for the past six months," Johnson concluded, "but none is yet directly charged with the responsibility. The Director of Merchant Seamen is pressing for a decision. Consensus of opinion is that training should be commenced immediately."

If, to Commander Johnson's disappointment, the Canadian Navy was reluctant to become involved in the training of merchant seamen, the same could not be said of the Canadian Seamen's Union (CSU). Although the Union eventually played no part in the training of recruits for the wartime Park fleet, it was not for want of trying. An early proposal called for the Union to be the recruiting agency for seamen, and that a minimum of ten schools be established, turning out five hundred men every six-to-eight-week term. This ambitious proposal was ignored by the Government, which opted for a much more modest program.

Though Commander Johnson's wish for Navy participation was never realized, it became evident in the later years of the war that Arthur Randles would have appreciated an injection of Navy discipline as he considered frequent reports of the unruly behavior in ports abroad of his growing number of charges.

Commander Johnson's assertion notwithstanding that no one had yet been charged with training, Arthur Randles had been very busy, and on 19 September he was ready with a comprehensive and detailed program for training merchant seamen in Canada, including estimated costs, which he presented to Deputy Transport Minister Edwards.

The training proposal conceived by the office of the Director of Merchant Seamen called for the provision of a school for the training of Ordinary Seamen (OS) at St. Margaret's Bay, Hubbards, Nova Scotia, with an initial capacity of 100 men, and an Engineering School at Kingston with a capacity of 50 engineer officers and 50 men. Provision was also to be made for officers taking navigation courses and for additions to existing schools. Estimated cost for the first year was $584,100, made up of a $250,000 founding charge and $334,100 operating cost. It was further suggested that an additional $175,000 be provided for a second training establishment on the west coast, which would have brought the total for the first year to $759,100.

The Randles program was based on having to supply crews for at least 36 10,000 ton class ships then being built in Canada for Canadian registry, plus an additional 7 4700 tonners that might be built in the same period. The Canadian manpower requirement for the 36 large ships was estimated at 1,800 plus a reserve of 20 percent, for a total of 2,260 required by September 1942. An additional 300 would be required if construction of the 7 4700 ton vessels were to proceed.

The St. Margaret's school, offering a twelve-week course (later expanded to thirteen weeks), would start with an initial intake of 50 trainees in November 1941, building to a capacity of 150. The engine room ratings school at Kingston, which would be run by the same Lieutenant Commander Dunn recommended by Commander Johnson, the Navy's Merchant Seamen Liaison Officer, would also start up in November with an intake of 50 for six weeks of training, building to 150. This school would also provide instruction for the certification of engineer officers.

Existing navigational instruction schools at Vancouver and Halifax for deck officers preparing for the second mate's certificate would be augmented immediately. The possibility was also held out that eventually additional navigation schools would be established at Queens University, Kingston, Ontario, and at Quebec City. For radio operators, reliance would be on graduates of established commercial schools such as those operated by Marconi, and on recruiting ham operators as well as candidates from broadcasting companies.

The catering department came in for special attention, particularly the central role of cook, for which a requirement of fifty per annum was foreseen. It was proposed that an arrangement be made with existing military cooking schools to train cooks for Merchant Navy service. In the event, the manning pool kitchens became the training centres for ships' cooks. Recognizing that happy ships were well-fed ships, the Randles proposal described the catering department as the most important branch of the Merchant Navy, noting that the reports of the Naval Boarding Service, which was responsible for ensuring that merchant vessels were ready for sea, "frequently drew attention to dissatisfaction of the crew with the cook."

The rate of output of the training program as proposed obviously could not meet an almost immediate manpower requirement that numbered in the thousands. It was acknowledged that the injection into a crew complement of a large component of first trippers would be setting a course for disaster, so it made no sense to produce more trainees than could be safely absorbed by each crew. Thus, in the deck crew establishment of nine for a 10,000 ton cargo vessel, comprising five Able Seamen (AB) and four Ordinary Seamen (OS), only two or three of the latter could be newly assigned from St. Margaret's. One of the two cadet officers or apprentices carried by each ship could also be a newly-minted St. Margaret's alumnus. Similarly, just two or three new graduates from the Engineering School could be worked into a ship's engine room department without unduly jeopardizing safety or efficiency.

Rates of pay suggested for the periods of training were $100 per month for all officers (with dependents), with a subsistence allowance of $1.50 per day to married men if away from home. Alternatively, if convenient, the latter were to be accommodated and fed in manning pool. Wireless operators were to get $50 per month and the same subsistence allowance as the officers. The St. Margaret's and Kingston school trainees would get, if with dependents, $50 per month; without dependents, $21. Because room and board would be provided for these trainees, no subsistence allowance would be paid. Trainee cooks would receive the same rates as the St. Margaret's and Kingston recruits.

Although the Randles proposal had set a target date of November for the first intake of trainees at St. Margaret's and Kingston, approval to proceed in the form of P.C. 148/9130 was not given until 22 November 1941. Furthermore, the authorized expenditure was restricted to a maximum of $500,000, to come from the 1941-42 War Appropriations, short of the $584,100 that had been estimated as necessary for the first year. No funding provision was made for the suggested additional school on the west coast at a cost of a further $175,000. Eventually, the idea of a west coast school would be dropped.

In fact, anticipating that official Cabinet approval would be forthcoming, Randles had been busy with his preparations for several weeks. By 27 November he was able to report that the Gainsborough Hotel, a former tourist hostelry at Hubbards on St. Margaret's Bay, thirty miles south of Halifax, had been taken over to serve as the administrative headquarters of the sea training school.

Meanwhile, despite the momentum that the Randles training program had acquired with its acceptance by the Government, Commander Johnson was not yet ready to give up his push for Navy involvement. A request to borrow officers and seamen from the "hard pressed" British merchant service to man ships of CN Steamships as well as one owned by the Canadian Government, because no Canadian crews were available, was seized on by Johnson as proof that the efforts to recruit and train Canadian seamen were inadequate. On 20 December 1941, he memoed Randles to this effect and early in January 1942 followed up with a memo to Captain Brand criticizing the training scheme because it would produce only five to six hundred junior ratings per annum, saying this would not meet even the expected casualty rate, based on experience to date. Possibly perturbed because his expressed concerns were not producing any modification of the program, Johnson at this point questioned whether it was in the best interests of the Naval Service to continue the office of Merchant Seamen Liaison Officer.

In the same memo he told Brand that the welfare needs of merchant seamen were being adequately met through the efforts, coordinated by the Director of Merchant Seamen, of such organizations as the Navy League of Canada, the Seamen's Mission, the British and Foreign Seamen's Guild, the Catholic Seamen's Club, and various Women's Auxiliary clubs.

He also reported that training was scheduled to begin at Kingston on January 15 with the arrival of the first class of engine room ratings. Despite the frequent references to Kingston as the site of the Marine Engineering Instructional School, ultimately all its activities became centred at Prescott, sixty miles downriver.

The Marine Engineering Instructional School was able to swing into action so quickly because LCdr. (E) J. L Dunn, RCNR, who had been running such an operation for the Navy at Kingston for two decades, was appointed, as suggested earlier by Commander Johnson, as commandant of the training institution.

At St. Margaret's, where construction of the dormitory and instructional buildings had proceeded rapidly, seventy-five youths were to begin training in April, some five months later than Randles' optimistic start-up date of November 1941. Various Navy shore establishments had been canvassed for retired or unfit-for-sea-duty petty officers to join the St. Margaret's instructional staff, but in the event Capt. T. P. Wilson, who had been appointed commandant of the school and was himself a veteran merchant seaman, turned to the British merchant service for instructors with the necessary background and experience.

In addition to his shore-based training schools, Randles was exploring on-the-job training possibilities. He had received information from the British Ministry of War Transport's New York office that consideration was being given to the installation of an extra bunk in each of three crew cabins aboard the ships being built in Canada for the British account. The supposed motivation for this extra accommodation was that so few experienced firemen were currently available that it was expected twelve would be required to do the work normally performed by nine. However, it was hoped this situation would quickly change, with the result the extra firemen would no longer be necessary. Randles wanted to know, in that event, if the three bunks thus no longer required for an enlarged engine room complement could now be used for three of his Canadian trainees. The Ministry of War Transport's response was that actually, no request had been made to expand crew accommodation, and in any event it was "definitely undesirable to house boys individually with the average run of grown seamen."

Captain Brand, who by this time had added the hat of Director of Trade (DTD) to the one he already wore as Director of Naval Intelligence (DNI), reported on 3 November

1942, that he had visited St. Margaret's where he was impressed by what Captain Wilson had done in setting up and equipping the school. He suggested that the Navy could do more to help, saying that he had discussed the matter with Commander H. Pullen, Superintendent of Naval Armament Depot (SNAD), who had advised that, with authorization, there would be no problem supplying some Naval weaponry for familiarization purposes, including a 12-pounder L/A gun and a 20-mm Oerlikon.

The Navy was highly cooperative in meeting the St. Margaret's requests for instructional and demonstration equipment, but a request for the loan of some DEMS weaponry provoked a good deal of controversy and aggravation reaching right up into the highest levels of Naval command, which included the Commander-in-Chief, Northwest Atlantic, Adm. L. W. Murray. Wars are fought not only in the combat arenas of sea, land and air, as we shall see from what might be called the guns of St. Margaret's affair.

* * *

At the root of the problems that were encountered was confusion on the part of Naval DEMS personnel in Halifax as to why the weapons were wanted at the school at all. The Navy already operated a DEMS school in Halifax where two-day courses, including weapons firing, were provided for merchant seamen, and all St. Margaret's graduates were supposed to be sent to this school following completion of their sea training course. So why did St. Margaret's want the guns at Hubbards? Did they want a DEMS course provided on site? Impractical and unnecessary in the eyes of the DEMS Officer East Coast.

The fact of the matter was that familiarization only was the original simple intent of the suggestion that guns be positioned at the school. It was known that when the St. Margaret's graduates were posted to ships, they, along with other members of the crews, would be expected to assist in manning the ships' defensive armament. Thus, it was reasoned, if there were some typical DEMS weapons in place at Hubbards, the trainees would have the opportunity for hands-on familiarization with their components and controls, as a lead-in to the later formal DEMS course, and for this purpose, unserviceable weapons would have been suitable.

Initially, the weapons loan proceeded without a hitch. Shortly after Captain Brand had discussed the matter with Commander Pullen in November 1942, the transfer was approved, on December 11, of a 12-pounder L/A gun, a 20-mm Oerlikon, a pair of Colt .50 machine guns, a PAC^2 rocket projector and a stripped Lewis gun. In keeping with the familiarization-only concept, which seems to have been understood by all concerned up to this point, Captain Brand suggested that the St. Margaret's chief officer be sent for the intensive two-week DEMS course provided for Navy DEMS ratings, with the idea that the chief officer would then be capable of answering any questions about the guns that the St. Margaret's trainees might have. Practical though this proposal seemed to be, it was turned down by Randles on 13 January 1943 on the grounds that the school was so short staffed nobody could be spared for two weeks.

There the matter stood until 24 May 1943 when a memo from the Secretary of the Naval Board in Ottawa to the Commander-in-Chief Northwest Atlantic, RAdm. L. W. Murray, advised that Captain Wilson of St. Margaret's had called at Naval Service HQ to report that though the ordnance had been delivered to the school late in 1942, it had not been set up and was still laying about. Furthermore, no DEMS representative had visited the school as instructed. Meanwhile, two courses of trainees had been passed out without benefiting from the presence of the weaponry.

"It is directed," the memo sternly instructed, "that immediate measures are to be taken by the DEMS staff to have the equipment set up and functioning as intended, and periodical visits made." The memo concluded with the order that "a report to the effect that the matter is in hand be made."

This missive to Admiral Murray was no doubt passed on with pointed comment to the DEMS Officer East Coast, Cdr. A. E. Woodward (T), who, after an apparently unheralded visit to St. Margaret's on 5 June, reported back, outlining with some asperity a host of problems surrounding the guns. Not only had he found Captain Wilson, the school commandant, indisposed and unable to see him, but the chief officer, second in command, whom he did see, had no information to pass along. Commander Woodward advised the Admiral that there was no building in which to house the equipment and the 12-pounder and the Oerlikon were at present sitting across the road from the school, an unsuitable location because the guns were serviceable, a factor that under Naval regulations called for the mounting of a guard at all times. The memo concluded by saying there was such a variety of views in Ottawa and Hubbards that the only way to arrive at a consensus was that all too familiar solution—convene a committee.

Meantime, the Naval Board in Ottawa, having still had no report from Admiral Murray in response to its memo of 24 May, sent a rocket on 26 June demanding the report it had called for, saying it "is awaited and is to be forwarded without further delay."

This brought a response, though not quite the one expected. Admiral Murray, no doubt thinking that his recently acquired responsibilities in connection with the anti-submarine war in the Northwest Atlantic sector were of somewhat higher priority than the guns of St. Margaret's, forwarded a copy of Commander Woodward's report with a cryptic covering letter, stating that no action should be taken until a gunnery training program had been formulated. He was of the opinion that the existing practice of giving all DEMS training at HMCS Stadacona in Halifax should be continued.

Furthermore, Admiral Murray recommended the return of the 12-pounder and the Oerlikon to the Armament Depot in Halifax until it was deemed advisable to organize a DEMS gunner school at St. Margaret's.

Anxious by this time to stem the rising tide of misunderstanding, the Naval Board advised Admiral Murray on 6 July that the Director of Merchant Seamen, Arthur Randles, was going to St. Margaret's to sort things out. In the meantime, the guns were to stay where they were, though DEMS staff should be responsible for keeping them in condition.

Following his visit to St. Margaret's, Randles reported to Captain Brand on 21 July that the DEMS officer who had visited Hubbards had evidently been under the impression that what was wanted was to start a full-fledged gunnery school there, which was never intended and could not in any event be worked into an already strained syllabus. Insofar as the guns were concerned, it was expected that they would be more or less "museum pieces" suitable for familiarization only, "so that the boys could study and handle them during their free hours." Randles went on to tell Brand that another location behind the administration building had been found for the 12-pounder and the Oerlikon, and the Twin Browning could be erected in an equipment room. Much of the ancillary equipment supplied by the Navy was superfluous, Randles said, and he was planning to have it returned. This applied particularly to the supply of live ammunition, about which Randles commented: "I am very anxious not to have any live ammunition on the premises for either small arms or the larger guns, as boys are naturally mischievous and accidents might occur." The remark was a telling reflection of the paternal attitude he held toward his St. Margaret's "boys," which he maintained even after they had left the school and were serving at sea.

Finally, Randles complained, the Navy had billed the school for everything. Pleading too poor to pay on his present budget, he said special authorization would have to be obtained to purchase the equipment and "I cannot imagine Treasury allowing me to buy a 12-pounder gun for example. As a matter of fact, I find it difficult to buy anything at the moment on my present budget."

The Randles visit to St. Margaret's and subsequent report seems to have achieved the desired result in smoothing ruffled Naval feathers in the office of the DEMS Officer East Coast, and in clarifying the situation to the satisfaction of the Naval Board in Ottawa. The Board followed up on 26 July 1943 with a memo to the C-in-C NW Atlantic stressing that the ordnance equipment was to be on loan only, "as clearly stated in instructions to SNAD[3] on 11 December 1942." It ordered that the weapons be mounted on sites satisfactory to the school, and moreover, a DEMS officer was to make periodic visits to advise and help, but in no way was any attempt to be made to set up classes. In conclusion, the Naval Board directive said that superfluous equipment, such as spare parts, was to be returned to the Superintendent Naval Armament Deport (SNAD).

C-in-C NW Atlantic had one last question before getting on with the Battle of the Atlantic. Responding to the Naval Board message of 26 July 1943, he reported that a quote for the mounting of three guns at St. Margaret's had been received from Foundation Maritime. He insisted on written authority to proceed and wanted to know "to what account [should] this contract be charged?" No record has been uncovered to reveal the Naval Board's response to the Admiral's query.

By September Commander Woodward was able to report to Captain Brand that a DEMS gunnery instructor and one ordnance artificer had spent four days at St. Margaret's, with results that were pleasing to Captain Wilson, the school commandant. Captain Wilson had subsequently requested that an instructor come to the school once a week and Commander Woodward told Brand he was prepared to do that, if approved, plus a visit by a DEMS officer once a month. To the relief of all, this seemingly concluded to everyone's satisfaction the affair of the guns of St. Margaret's and both school and Navy were able to return their attentions to their more important respective tasks at hand.

* * *

If archival records of the Merchant Navy training program may be taken as a measure, the Director of Merchant Seamen was much preoccupied with St. Margaret's Sea Training School, a preoccupation that did not extend to the Marine Engineering Instructional School. In seeming contrast with his ongoing concerns about St. Margaret's, his role in the Prescott school, once it was up and running, was that of recruitment. To a degree, this was probably because the task of organizing and operating the school was entrusted to an experienced RCNR engineering officer, LCdr. (E) J. L. Dunn, himself a marine engineer who for twenty years had been running just such a school at Kingston for Naval engine room ratings. Once accommodation for the school had been arranged at Prescott—an existing building was taken over and extended with add-ons—it was second nature for the well-connected Lieutenant Commander Dunn to line up instructional staff and establish a curriculum. The Prescott training establishment was in operation by mid-January of 1942, several months before St. Margaret's, where entirely new buildings had to be constructed for accommodation and instructional purposes.

Both schools were intended to teach the rudiments of their respective disciplines, but with the St. Margaret's syllabus requiring thirteen weeks of training compared with six weeks for Prescott, the implication seems to have been that there were more rudiments to be passed on to an aspiring ordinary seaman or cadet officer than to an engine room trainee. Indeed, more than one recruit was attracted to Prescott by the school's name, which gave the impression that some form of advanced technical training was being offered. Its high sounding name notwithstanding, Prescott's simple task was to turn out, as quickly as possible, trimmers-cum-firemen for the growing Canadian fleet of hand-fired coal burners then under construction. One graduate described it as "a low-cost holding tank for merchant sailors destined for the 'black gang'."[4] A Prescott graduate could count on at least one voyage being spent as a trimmer, in the age of coal probably seafaring's most physically demanding job.[5] In an acknowledgement of this, the recruiting for the school was directed at the more physically mature age group of nineteen to thirty, compared to St. Margaret's, which favoured youths at the lower (and more malleable) end of the seventeen to twenty-two bracket.

Although the Prescott school's main purpose was to turn out trimmers/firemen at a rate of some fifty every six weeks, it also provided training for engineer officers whereby candidates with sea as well as workshop experience could be tutored for examination for all classes of certificates of marine engineering competency. Plans for the school had called for an initial intake of fifty engineer officers, but it seems doubtful that there were ever more than a handful of certificate of competency candidates in house at any one time.

Located on Prescott's waterfront, the Marine Engineering Instructional School was housed in an old two-storeyed brick building which under one roof accommodated classrooms, sleeping quarters and messing facilities. The sleeping quarters were partitioned off into rooms with two double-tiered bunks for four trainees, unlike St. Margaret's where the trainees were quartered in dormitories each sleeping about thirty, also in the ubiquitous double bunks.

The location in small-town Prescott of the Marine Engineering school ensured that its trainees, unlike those at isolated St. Margaret's, had access to a range of recreational and entertainment pastimes. There were even opportunities for spare time jobs with which to supplement a trainee's standard $21 per month training allowance, and many took advantage.

During the standard six-week stay at Prescott, the trainee was exposed to classroom sessions familiarizing him with engine room machinery and terminology, as well as steam engine and boiler theory. Much of his classroom time was spent absorbing lectures and sketching equipment and identifying its component parts. The classroom sessions were backed up by hands-on practical training in the *Joseph Dubrule*, an ancient ferry moored nearby and permanently assigned to the school. The *Dubrule* was also used to introduce the budding "marine engineers" to the rigors of lifeboat training. On this aspect of the syllabus, the Director of Merchant Seamen's promotional brochure, *Training for the Merchant Navy,* describes the open stretch of the St. Lawrence River at Prescott, with its strong currents and long sweep of wind, as providing "ample experience in the vagaries of the weather under all conditions," followed by the dubious claim that, "A stiff row in the lifeboats provides one of the most popular means of recreation."

Chapter Six   # THE PAY MYTH

The casualty rate for merchant seamen was disproportionately high compared to the Navy, yet the civilian seamen had to suffer the myth that they were extravagantly paid. In his postwar book, *On the Triangle Run*, author James B. Lamb states flatly that in the merchant service, "Pay was vastly higher than in the naval service." More recently, a serving Canadian Navy Lieutenant Commander[1] attached to National Defence Headquarters in a 1991 newspaper interview used the pejorative, "mercenaries," in a reference to wartime merchant seamen. And a Toronto newspaper reader expressing opposition to the notion of Veteran status for wartime merchant seamen reasoned that "These men were highly paid and not subject to military discipline. They could quit whenever they liked."[2] And so the myth of high pay while enjoying the freedom to leave at will was perpetuated and continues to be perpetuated.

Many wartime merchant seamen at one time or another were exposed to raw threats of military force should they not attend to their duties, so the suggestion that they were not subject to military discipline is palpably wrong. Typically, the velvet glove came off when some crew complaint threatened to delay a sailing, as in an incident recalled by Captain David G. Martin-Smith of Victoria, B.C.:

> A breakdown in discipline occurred on the SS *Beaton Park* in 1944, my first Canadian Park ship where I was her proud second mate, in Port of Spain, Trinidad. The men refused to sail because of what they perceived as food disparities and tainted fresh water. The British Minister of War Shipping's representative there boarded us—back up by a U.S. Navy armed guard under an officer—and read a sort of riot act (sail or jail), after which we hove anchor and joined the convoy going to Recife, and thence on to South Africa.

That he could quit at any time would also have come as a surprise to the seventeen-year-old galley boy who received two weeks at hard labour in tough Oakalla Prison Farm in September 1944, for causing a sailing delay of several hours when he deserted his ship just before sailing time.[3]

Neither could the myth of being highly paid been further from the truth, as the Canadian Shipping Board made clear in a 15 July 1943 submission on Merchant Navy manning to the Minister of Trade and Commerce, James A. MacKinnon. "The present rates of pay on Canadian merchant vessels," the Board concluded, "are not considered equivalent to the remuneration granted to no more sustained and no more dangerous work of a similar character in the Canadian Navy." And further: "Merchant seamen are not granted the same exemption from income tax as is granted members of the Naval service. With income tax at present rates, this exemption is very important." In a 1945 pamphlet issued under the imprint of Transport Minister Lionel Chevrier, the Minister reported that in 1940 the average basic monthly wage for an AB was $52.50 plus a War Risk Bonus of $13.12. By 1944, this had risen to $89.93 plus War Risk Bonus of $44.50. Cadet Officers (Apprentices), Ordinary Seamen and messboys earned even less.

To John Covan of Markdale, Ontario, who began his seagoing career in 1942 as a Cadet Officer on the *Green Gables Park*, the idea that he was highly paid is laughable:

> One of the things I remember [is that] when we went to the recruiting office in Windsor, there were two or three other young people there making inquiries, and one of the fellows asked the Navy recruiter what the pay was, and he said, "Oh, sometimes you get in off a voyage and pay off with a thousand dollars." You know, to a seventeen-year-old in 1942, a thousand dollars was an unheard of sum. They forgot to tell you that you had to be out five years at least, 'cause I can remember at the end of our first voyage—it was five months and twenty-two days—and I paid off with $42. It was raining and I went out and bought a Burberry and it cost me $35. I had seven dollars left after five months and twenty-two days. This publicity of a Navy lieutenant or lieutenant commander in Halifax who referred to us as mercenaries! Well, as a cadet, my total pay, that included basic pay, war bonus and cost-of-living bonus, came to $32.70 a month. That's some mercenary!
>
> Our basic pay was based on the British apprentices' first year pay, which was two pounds a month, or approximately $9.00 Canadian, [plus] $22.25 per month for war bonus and $1.00 cost-of-living. The old chief officer we had worked it so that the other Cadet and myself could earn Ordinary Seaman's overtime from time to time, and if my memory serves me right that was $.25 per hour. We had two deck boys . . . two kids about sixteen years old . . . their basic pay was $30.00 per month and the thing I really resent to this day was that the war bonus was $44.50, but if you were under twenty-one, you got $22.25. It wasn't until 1944 that the award was equalized and all crew members got the same war bonus.
>
> Toward the middle of 1944, I remember when we came back we were ordered to go up to Park Steamship's office in the Marine Building. We

went up there and they presented us with this set of indentures. We were going to be apprentice officers instead of cadets, which was more the British style. We weren't quite sure [about] these indentures because I remember reading: "You shall not frequent ale houses, houses of ill repute, etc., etc.!" And what was that about going anywhere, anytime? Captain Clark, I think it was, looked at it and said, "It's not much of a document, is it?" The thing was, this came into effect while we were at sea and if we signed all these papers, it was retroactive. If we didn't, we were finished right then. Whether this was fact or not, it was fairly effective blackmail because we signed right on the dotted line and they gave us all that back pay, probably $99 or whatever it was. I remember I went out and bought a suit."

The Canadian Shipping Board submission of July 1943 comparing RCN and Merchant Navy rates of pay (see Appendix 1) shows that commissioned Naval officers were faring substantially better than their equivalent numbers on the 10,000 ton Park ships (on 4700 tonners, the rates were lower for licensed personnel). A Navy Commander, for example, was paid $415.50 per month, tax free; his merchant service opposite number, a ship Captain (Master), on the other hand, received $330.92 per month gross, comprising basic wage plus War Risk Bonus[4] and $18.42 Cost-of-Living Bonus, subject to Income Tax of $68.30 (married, one dependent). Similar pay comparisons heavily favouring RCN officers over MN officers appear all the way down the hierarchy of rank. A Lieutenant Commander's monthly pay was $331.50 tax free vs. $212.92 (less $25.90 Income Tax) for a Chief Officer. Even a lowly MN Third Officer's gross pay was approximately $80.00 shy of that for a Navy Lieutenant. The Naval pay scale, the CSB submission explained, included "Command Money, Senior Officers Allowance (Marriage Allowance), [and] Entertaining for Commander Allowance," no equivalent of which was available to MN officers, except possibly the latter for a Captain. Furthermore, the Naval officers received a clothing allowance, whereas the MN officers paid out-of-pocket for their uniforms.

Below officer rank, merchant seamen fared slightly better than their RCN opposites. A Bosun, equal to a Naval Chief Petty Officer, grossed $127.42, bettering the CPO by only $6.00. That Everyman of the sea, the ubiquitous Able Seaman, was paid $119.12[5] per month in Merchant service but only $90.00 in Naval service. The RCN AB, however, was issued free clothing, a benefit not available to the merchant sailor. Moreover, the Naval rating received his full pay and room and board whether ashore or afloat; the merchant seaman was paid and received room and board while ashore only if enrolled in a manning pool. While in the pool he did not receive the $44.50 War Risk Bonus, which was paid only when on ship's articles. Those merchant seamen who had not signed a Two-Year Manning Pool Agreement, and chose to take some time off between ships, received neither shore pay nor any other benefit in terms of food and lodging. For the most part, the level of earnings of unlicensed personnel was too low to attract Income Tax, which applied only to the basic wage. Conversely, most deck and engineering officers were sufficiently well paid to make them subject to the tax. Were any of them unfortunate enough to become prisoners of war, the Government made it known that the long arm of its Revenue Minister reached even behind enemy lines, insisting that MN POWs were liable for tax on basic pay in the form of detention allowances accumulated during the period of internment. The official stance was that the Government had to draw the line somewhere between military personnel and civilians because if merchant seamen POWs were exempted, it would set such a precedent that similar exemption would be sought by other civilian groups whose "callings became more arduous or more dangerous as a result of the war."[6]

On the handful of 10,000 ton Park tankers, thirteen in number, the licensed officers and engineers enjoyed higher monthly rates of pay than their opposite numbers on the dry cargo vessels, in terms of both basic salary and War Risk Bonus. Under the pay schedule, which became effective 1 November 1943, a Park tanker Master received a basic $340 plus a War Risk Bonus of $119, which, along with cost-of-living bonus provided him with a total of $469.40, subject to Income Tax. Inexplicably, the Master's cost-of-living allowance amounted to only $10.40; for all other tanker ranks, licensed and unlicensed, the standard payment was $19.94.

The Chief, Second and Third Mates, as well as all the Engineers on the tankers also received both higher base rates and War Risk Bonuses than those on the dry cargo ships. Curiously, though the level of War Risk was evidently considered higher on tankers than on cargo ships for the licensed officers, this concern did not extend to tanker unlicensed personnel, all of whom received the standard $44.50 and for the most part were paid at the same or similar base rates for dry cargo vessels (e.g., the basic rate for a cargo AB was $70.00, one dollar less than that for his tanker opposite).

As a postwar sweetener, all Canadian seamen who had entered the standard Two-Year Manning Pool Agreement became eligible for a Special Bonus amounting to 10 percent of total annual earnings, including War Risk Bonus. To qualify, the seaman must have served at least six months in "dangerous waters." Also eligible for the Special Bonus were permanent seagoing employees of the shipping companies, Canadian merchant seamen POWs, and U.K. contract officers and ratings. Those who had not signed a two-year agreement, though they may have spent many wartime years as seamen, were out of luck for the Special Bonus. In the postwar payout of the Bonus, the Government anticipated some six thousand claims qualifying for an average payout of $400. It was also promised that "Facilities for courses of instruction will be provided for men otherwise suitable to enable advancement in the profession of Seaman." These offerings, combined with eligibility for Unemployment Insurance, were to comprise the Canadian merchant seamen's pale version of the generous rehabilitation program established for Service personnel regardless of where they had served.

The Government's official position on postwar benefits for merchant seamen was set out by Transport Minister Lionel Chevrier in a pamphlet published in 1945:

> The Government has studied the possiblity of extending rehabilitation benefits to Canadian Merchant Seamen. While it is not considered justifiable, having regard to the terms of employment and remuneration of Merchant Seamen, to make available to them benefits on the scale provided members of the Naval, Military and Air Forces, it is deemed advisable and equitable, in consideration of the essential services rendered by them, involving hardships and risks in many respects comparable to those met by members of the Forces, to offer certain additional benefits to those who have served in dangerous waters and are prepared to serve for the duration of the war if required. *Such benefits should not be of a nature which would encourage Seamen to leave the industry at the end of the war to seek employment in other fields as the services of many skilled Seamen will be required if Canada is to maintain a Merchant Marine after the war.* (Author's italics)

There is little doubt the notion that Canadian merchant seamen were extravagantly paid came about because they became confused in the public mind with seamen of the U.S. Merchant Marine, who were, indeed, extremely well paid (see Appendix 2). On Park ship mess decks Canadian seamen would often enviously repeat tales, possibly apocryphal, they had heard of American deckhands who had earned as much as $1,000 in a single month, an astonishing amount for the period.

True or not, under the complicated but lavish U.S. system of war risk bonuses, such earnings seemed at least within the realm of possibility. Under this system, for the purposes of assessing degree of risk, the world was divided into three classifications: High bonus, Low bonus, and No bonus, based on degree of hazard assessed. A High bonus would be 100 percent of compensation (base wage), but not less than $100 per month, which would be applicable to both trans-Atlantic and trans-Pacific voyages and extensions thereof. A Low bonus would be 40 percent of compensation but not less than $40 per month, applicable to voyages between Pacific ports in the U.S., Canada and Alaska, while east of 136 degrees W. Long.

In addition to these basic "voyage" bonuses, $125 would be paid for one or more calls in an area designated as High risk, such as the U.K. and Northern Ireland, Australian ports north of 20 degrees S. Lat.; $100 for ports in New Zealand or New

Caledonia; $60 for Iceland, Persian Gulf, Eire. In its comparison of Canadian and U.S. pay scales, the Canadian Shipping Board reckoned that an American AB would average earnings of $300 per month,[7] aided by the described bonuses and such others as a $25 per month Port Attack and Area Bonus, and payment to each individual crew member of $125 each individual time a ship experienced enemy action, "as well as an additional danger area bonus of $5 per day."

In their idle moments, the Canadian seamen may have envied their well-paid American counterparts and some actively worked to get signed on U.S. ships (and occasionally succeeded), but for most of the thousands of young first-time voyagers the uniqueness of their sea-going experience kept them sufficiently distracted that, to the frustration of their Union, they did not dwell on whether or not they might be getting short-changed. Typical was the youthful attitude of Donald F. Patterson of Hamilton, Ontario, a twenty-year-old Ordinary Seaman fresh out of St. Margaret's Sea Training School when he joined the new *Mount Revelstoke Park* in Montreal for a voyage that took him halfway across the world to India with many exotic ports of call en route. He returned home eight months later, thrilled with his adventure. "When we signed off I received about $35 pay—not much after eight months of service, my first trip. But what an experience and being paid for it!"

Chapter Seven　　　　　　　　　**MOVERS AND SHAKERS**

In Canada's attic that is the National Archives, there are hundreds of cardboard boxes wherein are stored in mostly random order the files of Canada's wartime Merchant Navy—memos, reports, studies, letters, minutes, hand-scribbled notes by authors long gone. In a very real sense this administrative flotsam and jetsam of a nation's things past tell the story of the organization that sent the ships to sea and of the crews who manned them. The files are full of officialdom's names—ministers, deputies, administrators, directors, officers and gentlemen—but no names appear more frequently than those of Arthur Randles, Director of Merchant Seamen, and Captain Eric S. Brand, RN, the RCN's Director of Trade.

It is not without reason that these two vigorous Britishers, both middle-aged but manifestly at the height of their powers of intellect and energy, should figure so prominently in the record of success achieved by the Canadian merchant service during World War II. They did not create the huge merchant fleet that mushroomed from the handful of ships flying the Canadian flag in September 1939, nor did they have any direct responsibility for its management, yet indisputably, through their activities, reaching into and influencing almost every aspect of operations, it was made to work.

Captain Brand was a career Royal Navy officer who wore the 1914 Star and held the rank of Commander when he arrived in Ottawa on 17 July 1939. He had been seconded to the still tiny Royal Canadian Navy[1] as Director of Naval Intelligence (DNI), taking up his new posting in Ottawa scant weeks before the Navy would find itself embarking on a program of unprecedented expansion. A no-nonsense individual described by contemporaries as having a British reserve, being brusque in manner and dry of wit, and possessing a willingness to accept unorthodox ideas, Brand ran, it was said, a happy ship but a tight one.[2]

He was also self-effacing, as he demonstrated in a 1967 interview[3] in which he described the career path that led him to Ottawa. Late in 1937, he explained, he was close to the end of the promotion zone for Captain and he was just one of fifteen RN commanders eligible for only three openings available at the higher rank. In the event, along with eleven other Commanders he was passed over, but he received such "a blaze of sympathy" that he was able to capitalize by being allowed to indicate a preference for his next job. So he and his wife looked at the Navy list. "We turned it over. We said, this DNI Ottawa looks a damned good place and [we] have always wanted to see North America."

But the Ottawa job would not be vacant until July 1939 and for a while, Brand's quiet campaigning nothwithstanding, it appeared another officer had the inside track. Even when this competitor indicated he was not interested after all, another obstacle arose when the Canadian Chief of Naval Staff (CNS), Rear Admiral, soon to be VAdm. Percy W. Nelles, let it be known that he was tired of the Admiralty sending him passed-over commanders to be the RCN's DNI. Fortunately for Brand's chances, Admiral Nelles expressed this opinion to a visiting RN officer who happened to be a friend of Brand and told the Canadian CNS he would be lucky to get Brand. "So . . . that's why I came and that's how I got here!" On the evidence of his wartime record as both Director of Naval Intelligence and Director of Trade (he held both positions simultaneously for a time), the Canadian Navy was indeed lucky. And Brand got his captaincy after all.

The practice of having the RCN's Director of Naval Intelligence slot filled by a Royal Navy officer dated back to World War I. Though to some the idea of an RN officer in such a key Canadian position smacked of colonialism, it was done for the good practical reason that in an unofficial way it bypassed much communications red tape between NSHQ in Ottawa and the Admiralty in London. The Ottawa DNI, by virtue of his being a serving RN officer, could legitimately correspond directly with DNI Admiralty in London, and the correspondence was not necessarily restricted to Intelligence matters. On the other hand, should CNS be forced to use official Canadian channels to contact the Admiralty, he had to place his request with DND's Deputy Minister, who in turn went to External Affairs who contacted the Dominion Office in London who applied to the Admiralty. The response backtracked along the same torturous route.

On the outbreak of war in Europe, Brand's Canadian role was quickly enlarged with the addition of the important Trade file. In his two-hat position of Director of Naval Intelligence and Trade his responsibilities included the maintenance of normal seagoing trade in wartime, insofar as that was possible, and most particularly for the transocean delivery of munitions and supplies essential to the war effort, as well as for troop transport. In that capacity on 10 September, when Canada was officially declared at war, he was already centre stage putting into action plans for the inception of the convoy system. Within a week, on 17 September, the first convoy had sailed from Halifax for the United Kingdom.[4]

The absence of public acclaim for Navy administrators and planners such as Captain Brand, working mostly anonymously out of Naval Service Headquarters in Ottawa, is no measure of the significance of their contributions to success in the struggle for control of the sea lanes, as Cdr. F. B. Watt, RCN(R), (Ret'd), made clear in his assessment of his wartime boss:

My stint in Ottawa was giving me some idea of Brand's full stature and the scope and significance of the organization he had created. [RN] Rear Admiral Manisty, organizing genius of the convoys of World War I, and originator of the system for their control in World War II, visited North American ports in 1943. He reported to Admiralty that "Naval Service HQ, Ottawa, has been the basis of the organization [of merchant shipping control in North America] and has been the source from which the whole mechanism derived its impetus. This mechanism seems to have worked so smoothly it has been accepted as being almost automatic."[5]

Brand was the father of that mechanism.

* * *

By the Spring of 1941 it had become recognized by Brand and others that more would have to be done to counter the crew troubles that were hampering convoy sailings from east coast ports. Attempts to intimidate recalcitrant or reluctant merchant seamen through such draconian measures as the Canadian Cabinet's notorious "sail or jail" Order in Council P.C. 4751 of 12 September 1940, and its successor Merchant Seamen Order, 1941,[6] might have provided immediate solutions, but the long-term effect of their ruthless imposition was to undermine even further the morale of seamen whose nerves were already battered and bruised by sinkings and storms. At this point in the war, the crew survival rate of a ship sinking was only 50 percent. These non-judicial Cabinet edicts did indeed have the desired instant advantage of getting ships to sea, but the resentment their application kindled only exacerbated the feeling of the seamen that the day of the press gang had not yet passed by.

A perceptive and sympathetic Naval Boarding Service Lieutenant (later Commander), Frederick B. (Ted) Watt, soon discerned from his own observations and those of his small crew of Reservists, many of whom had themselves been merchant seamen in civilian life, that poor shipboard conditions, lack of amenities, autocratic old school shipmasters, themselves strained to the limit, and a host of essentially petty aggravations were among the root causes of many of the crew troubles which periodically threatened to delay ship sailings. Though their primary designated task was to search for evidence of sabotage and generally to ensure that ship was "in all respects ready" to sail, the NBS crews more and more often found themselves providing a sympathetic ear to the complaints of unhappy merchant seamen and acting as intermediaries to the higher powers that could provide solutions. While their sympathy was genuine, their motives were not entirely altruistic for in the final analysis their job was to see that no ship missed or delayed a convoy sailing.

Stated briefly, crew troubles were to a considerable extent a morale problem. It was noted that even such a simple gesture as the NBS crew arriving aboard a ship with a supply of magazines for the merchant seamen, paid dividends in crew morale out of all proportion to the relatively small effort required from the boarding crews. And it was not lost on the seamen that there were also many shore people with concerns for their welfare, for not only was the Naval Boarding Service reaching out by distributing the magazines, but making it possible for them to do so was a group of hard-working Halifax women volunteers who were the operators of the magazine collection system, which was the supplier of the periodicals. Lieutenant Watt reported these observations to his Halifax Naval Control Service Office (NCSO) boss, Cdr. Richard H. Oland, who forwarded them with his enthusiastic endorsement to Captain Brand at Naval Services HQ in Ottawa. Increasingly, the role of the NBS took on a diplomatic aspect, diminishing fears, soothing aggravations, satisfying complaints, and generally smoothing the course of relationships between crews, bridge and shore management.

But when these well-meant tactics didn't work, there was always the drastic P.C. 4751, which gave Canadian authorities the power to remove rebellious foreign seamen nationals from foreign-registered ships in Canadian ports and imprison them without trial until they saw the error of their ways. The Order In Council, which came into effect 12 September 1940, was apparently inspired by Captain Brand who likely had no problem convincing Cabinet that desperate times required desperate measures. His tough uncompromising job was to see that the convoys sailed, and on schedule. It was the tenor of the times that few would disagree with him.

The only problem was that P.C. 4751 applied only to foreign seamen, who had been the source of most of the crew troubles up to this point in the war, Canadian ships and crews still being relatively few in number. This oversight was rectified within the year by the passage on 4 April 1941 of P.C. 2385, The Merchant Seamen Order, 1941, under which a troublesome (or even considered likely to be troublesome) seaman, licensed or unlicensed, Canadian or otherwise, could be removed from a ship of any registry in a Canadian port, detained, and within forty-eight hours brought before a Board of Inquiry comprising three officials from DND (Naval Service), the Department of Transport, and the Immigration Branch, who had the power to jail the offender for up to three months. If, after the three months was up, the offending seaman still wasn't prepared to fall in line, his confinement could be extended by a further six months. Clinching the unforgiving powers of P.C. 2385 was the clause, "There shall be no appeal to any court or tribunal from an order of the board, which order shall be final." P.C. 2385 also applied to seamen in manning pools.

* * *

Meanwhile, other wheels had been turning in Ottawa. Plans were already afoot to build a fleet of merchant ships to be manned and operated by Canada. How to forestall potential crew troubles on these Canadian ships was much on the minds of the members of the recently formed Interdepartmental Committee on Questions of Discipline and Treatment of Merchant Seamen[7] when it met in Ottawa early in March 1941. Up for discussion and approval was a proposed plan to establish within the Department of Transport a new branch headed by a Director of Merchant Seamen. Already lined up to fill the newly created position was Arthur Randles, a veteran of the shipping industry based in Montreal, where he had been General Passenger Traffic Manager for Cunard White Star since 1926.

Born at the start of the final decade of the nineteenth century, Randles was already over fifty at the time of taking up his new post, though the evidence of archival records is that his energy level belied his age. Indeed, he had attempted to join the Forces but having been turned down because of over-age, he was eager to serve when the Government requested the loan of his services from Cunard White Star to fill what became the pivotal post of Director of Merchant Seamen. Until just before taking on his new job, he had been busy at Cunard White Star on projects to adapt luxury liners as troop carriers, as well as assisting in organizing the overseas movement of troops.

Randles' prewar management position with Cunard White Star may have coloured him as just another businessman, but his background was that of an adventurous man of action never reluctant to get into the thick of the fray. A Yorkshireman by birth, educated in Liverpool, he was already working in the shipping industry on the day war was declared in 1914, an event that promptly sent him into the Royal Navy as an Admiral's Secretary. In search of a more active role, he succeeded in transferring to the Army and was sent to France in 1915. A later attempt to switch to the Intelligence Corps, where he thought his knowledge of languages would be useful, lead instead to his becoming a leader of guerillas on the Murmansk and Archangel fronts, in support of the White Russian forces during the Russian revolution. He was one of the last of the Allied contingent out of Archangel in 1919.

Postwar, he rejoined the shipping industry as Cunard's man in Central Europe, where he was deeply involved in shipping arrangements for the mass transocean migrations to North America that occurred in the early 1920s. It was in 1926 that Cunard White Star sent him to Montreal to represent the company as its General Passenger Traffic Manager, the position he left behind to become Director of Merchant Seamen.[8] His long association with such a tradition-oriented company as Cunard White Star was to be reflected in his handling of his new assignment.

* * *

Though authorization for the new Department of Transport branch, and for Arthur Randles' appointment, took until May 1941 to wend its way through Government channels, he was not one to waste time waiting for the official stamp of approval. As Director of Merchant Seamen, he was to be responsible for the "organization and development of proposed Manning Pools; General Control of Proposed Merchant Navy Canteens and other Welfare Arrangements; Training of Canadian Seamen."[9] At the time, few of these things existed in any form, with the exception of the single Place Viger Manning Pool in Montreal, which was being operated by the British at their expense to house British seamen awaiting completion of ships being built in the U.S.A. and Canada to British order.

That measures to bolster and maintain the morale of merchant seamen would have to be of high priority for the new Director of Merchant Seaman was made clear in a letter of 5 April 1941 to L. D. Wilgress, Chairman of the Canadian Shipping Board, from the Acting Deputy Minister, Naval Services, who wrote:

> As you are well aware, a very great strain is now being put upon the morale of merchant seamen. This strain is not at present met or compensated for upon the same lines as it is done in the case of the regular fighting forces. On the other hand, the successful prosecution of the war is entirely dependent upon the upkeep of morale of the merchant seamen of all nations who are working for the allies.

Randles tackled the morale problem by appealing to civilian volunteer organizations for help in providing shore-based support for his merchant seamen charges. He found no lack of willing hands. The Navy League of Canada, the Red Cross, the Seamen's Mission, the British and Foreign Seamen's Guild, the Catholic Seamen's Club, the Knights of Columbus and countless women's auxiliary groups were eager to participate in meaningful ways, giving generously in both time and facilities to provide support in one form or another in all Canadian ports.

The Navy League, for example, operated the Allied Merchant Seamen's Club in Halifax, which as well as being a drop-in centre providing social activities and entertainment, also boasted a twenty-six-bed sick bay for convalescent seamen of all nationalities. The facility, staffed by two nurses under a club doctor, included a free medical clinic that was open two hours a day. St. John's Ambulance provided volunteers who assisted the nurses.

In Vancouver the Navy League operated a Seamen's Club in a two-storeyed building that had been purchased and equipped with funds raised by the Vancouver area public and shipyard workers. The Club, which boasted a swimming pool among its amenities, maintained a busy schedule of social and entertainment activities, providing stage shows, concerts, boxing and wrestling matches, dances and Christmas parties, with most of the burden of the organizational and staffing work being carried out by an active and tireless Women's Auxiliary.

By 16 September 1941, Cdr. B. L. Johnson, the Navy's Merchant Seamen Liaison Officer, was able to report to Captain Brand that building and preparations for operating manning pools and welfare centres were well in hand and being vigorously hastened by Randles.

But Randles could not call on volunteers to establish manning pools or develop a training program, although the Canadian Seamen's Union, by now dabbling its toes in salt water, was only too eager to relieve him of the responsibility in both areas. At this point in time, however, the CSU was being dismissed as being only a lake union with no relevance to deep-sea shipping.[10] Its overtures were peremptorily rebuffed.

As a first step in the setting up of a Canadian manning pool system, arrangements were made at a 17 October 1941 meeting in Ottawa with several representatives of the British Ministry of War Transport for Canada to take over the Place Viger Manning Pool in Montreal, provided accommodation was guaranteed on an ongoing basis for up to nine hundred British seamen awaiting ships. Initially, it was expected that places for only one hundred Canadian seamen would be required, a number that would quickly expand with the beginning of Park ship deliveries in 1942. In Halifax, there was no suitable hotel type accommodation available for acquisition so buildings had to be constructed on North Street Hill. Other secondary pools were established at Sydney, Nova Scotia, and Saint John, New Brunswick. In Vancouver, where it was expected that housing for about four hundred seamen would be required, the multi-storeyed down-at-the-heels Dunsmuir Hotel was taken over for unlicensed personnel while the tonier Sylvia Court apartment hotel near Stanley Park was acquired for the officers.

While all this was going on, the industrious Director of Merchant Seamen was also heading up sessions to devise a training scheme to turn out merchant seamen to fill the various seagoing trades. By 23 September 1941, Randles was ready with a comprehensive training program proposal, including cost estimates, for C. P. Edwards, Deputy Minister of Transport. Though Treasury Board did not signal a green light for the proposal until 22 November 1941, it was evident that Randles had during the interim been acting in anticipation because in a letter of 27 November he reported that Hubbards, Nova Scotia, thirty miles south of Halifax, had been selected as the site of the seamen's training school, and further, that the Gainsborough Hotel in Hubbards had been taken over as headquarters for the school, already being referred to as "St. Margaret's Sea Training School," the name reflecting site location on the shores of St. Margaret's Bay. At the same time, Randles was lining up a site at Prescott,

Ontario, for the Marine Engineering Instructional School that was the other major component of his training program proposal.

For both schools, accommodation had to be acquired or constructed, instructional and housekeeping staff hired, and curricula drafted. Most importantly, a national recruiting system had to be established to ensure a steady flow of trainees, ultimately to be about 150 per thirteen-week course at St. Margaret's and 90 per six-week course at Prescott. News items and advertisements in newspapers across the country publicized the courses and Navy League offices and RCN recruiting centres cooperated by acting as sources of information and application forms.

Arthur Randles was a busy man indeed.

His task may have been demanding but the Treasury Board did not make it easy by unlocking the national vault for him. He had originally estimated the cost of setting up and operating the schools for the first year at $584,100 with an additional $175,000 necessary should it be decided to proceed with a second training centre on the Pacific Coast. In approving the training plan, the Treasury Board cut the requested allotment to just $500,000, a shortfall that soon found the Director of Merchant Seamen scrounging for equipment that could be used in the training syllabi.

Enter Captain Brand, who prodded the Naval Dockyard at Halifax to see what spare gear might be found that would be useful at St. Margaret's. The Navy was happy to cooperate, "finding somewhere in the yard" a variety of items, including a Kelvin sounding machine, a patent log, a merchant ship's telegraph, pinions for the construction of a steering teacher, charts, tide tables and a steering wheel.

There was much more to come from the eager-to-help Navy. In a memo [11] dated 23 December 1942 to Captain Brand, Cdr. W. B. Armit, A/Director of Naval Stores, reporting on a visit to St. Margaret's, was high in his praise of the school. He advised that in addition to the equipment already supplied, other items on the way included twenty-four Duffel coats with seventy more to follow. There were also coils of old wire for splicing, rope and canvas, sets of illustrated instructions and regulations for ships lights and markings. Much of this assortment simply comprised surplus equipment, but the Navy effort went well beyond searching the Halifax dockyard for such odds and ends, including, as it did, the making by dockyard shipwrights of a complete set of ship models and lights for demonstration of the Rules of the Road.

There were nonmilitary sources prepared to help get the school up and running as well. For example, at one point the school's commandant, Captain Wilson, seeking a replica of a ship's bridge, evidently sent out feelers to his many merchant shipping contacts, resulting in a letter to Captain Brand from C. E. Bryant, Halifax-based Deputy Representative of the British Ministry of War Transport, advising that "our people [in British shipping circles] have been asked to look around to see what they have available." However, when Randles got wind of this request, he scotched the idea because it would involve a donation by a commercial organization, i.e., a shipping company, to a Government department, which was contrary to policy. He said that a model bridge was being built for the school by his department.

Throughout the war Randles and Brand were indefatigable, there seeming to be no detail of Merchant Navy operations that escaped their attention and action. In 1939, Captain Brand's mandate had embraced Intelligence as well as Trade but by 1943 the growth of the Canadian merchant fleet dictated that the Trade Division was accounting for 80 percent of his time so the two files were split with another officer taking on the Intelligence assignment.[12]

* * *

One of the problems that constantly exercised Randles was the cross-boarder leakage of Canadian seamen, drawn to American ships by the lure of big money. While the wayward (in Randles' eyes) seamen were attracted mainly to U.S.-registered ships and U.S.-owned ships sailing under such flags of convenience as Panama and the Honduras, there were other foreign vessels, the Greeks and the Norwegians among them, that, particularly during the first years of the war, offered higher wages than their Canadian counterparts. Canadian seamen could be hired in Canadian ports for these non-U.S.-affiliated foreign vessels without passing through a Manning Pool, a loophole that irritated Randles though he was forced to concede that a Manning Pool couldn't really refuse a request from a foreign master for a hand, "the Manning Pool system... having originally been designed to avoid ships missing convoy through being deficient of crew." This admission nothwithstanding, as the Park fleet began to expand exponentially, Randles wanted the services of Canadian seamen reserved to meet the growing manning requirements of the Canadian-built ships.

The magnitude of border leakage loomed large for the Director of Merchant Seamen, who in a 25 March 1943 memo to the Consul General Designate in New York worried that "some 2,000 experienced Canadian seamen were procured by certain agencies in Canada and sent over the border within a 12-month period." In his attempts to stem the cross-border leakage, U.S. officialdom was not much help, what with the U.S. War Shipping Administration advertising on Canadian radio and in Canadian newspapers for recruits for the U.S. Merchant Marine. They were doing this in contradiction of the fact, Randles complained, that it was against their own rules set in 1942, restricting employment on U.S. vessels to American nationals, and on Panamanian and Honduran vessels to American, Panamanian and Honduran nationals.

The Director of Merchant Seamen left no possible regulation unturned as he tried to fence in Canadian seamen seeking the greener seas that the Yankee dollar promised. He called on the Passport Office to refuse to issue a passport to any seaman, licensed or unlicensed, unless he had a Labour Export Permit which, of course, would have to be obtained from the Director of Merchant Seamen. He called on Canadian Immigration but he was told that their interest was restricted to people entering the country; they had nothing to do with those leaving the country. He called on the U.S. government, which at first agreed not to issue a visa to an applicant unless he had a Labour Export Permit, but then backtracked and told U.S. consuls that they were not to demand the Permits, nor were they required to ask that authorization from the Director of Merchant Seamen be displayed. He even tried to enlist the aid of the Foreign Exchange Control Board, but the Board told him it was interested only in controlling foreign exchange for travel and didn't want to get involved in the reasons for the travel.

Adding to Randles' frustration were the several seamen employment agencies set up in Canada to recruit, for a fee, seamen for foreign ship assignments. One of the best known of these was the grandly named National Shipping Federation, of which Capt. H. N. McMaster was the self-styled president. Operating out of a tiny office in Montreal, McMaster had a chequered history dating back to the 1930s as the creator and sole executive of several seamen's associations, all of which were sponsored by lake shipping companies and all of which were, in effect, despised company unions. The Canadian Seamen's Union came into being in the mid-1930s largely in reaction to McMaster's activities and his close links with the shipping companies, which backed all his no-holds-barred attempts to undermine any movement to form an independent seamen-controlled union, most specifically the CSU.

But from the time the Director of Merchant Seamen was made responsible for the manning of Canadian ships, McMaster was equally a thorn in the side of Arthur Randles, clandestinely channeling Canadian sailors across the border for ship assignments in the U.S. Randles, determined to scuttle McMaster and his ilk, on 12 February 1943 advised the Directors of the manning pools at Halifax, Montreal and Vancouver that,

> I must emphasize again that no experienced Canadian seaman shall be allowed to leave Canada. If the authority extended to me and through me to you is not carefully controlled, the smuggling of men across the border will lead to an open door for draft dodgers and we will be subject to criticism if the necessary safeguards . . . are not taken.

But McMaster, the hardened veteran of maritime labour-management wars, was not easily intimidated by bureaucratic manoeuvrings to cut him off at the border. Now identifying himself as President of the National Maritime Federation, he fired off a telegram to Prime Minister Mackenzie King complaining that the Director of

Merchant Seamen had set up regulations "which make practical manning of existing Canadian ships impossible." The telegram went on to claim that a Canadian ship had been delayed in a U.S. port by current regulations preventing prompt replacement of crew members.

Doubtless unaware that the National Maritime Federation was a front for a one-man employment agency, the Prime Minister passed the McMaster missive on for action to the Minister of Transport, to whom Randles had to explain that McMaster's National Maritime Federation was engaged in the recruitment of seamen, generally for ships of foreign registry, and that he was causing the Director of Merchant Seamen many problems. The seamen, too, were often victimized, Randles indicated. He said several Canadian seamen had been recruited by McMaster as ABs for a ship in New York, but on arrival there, "they found the agreement they had signed had been altered to the effect that they were offered positions as messmen." When the seamen balked at the downgraded positions, they were left stranded in New York. Randles went on to accuse McMaster of deliberately evading the Exit Permit Order.

In April 1944, Canada Customs agreed to cooperate in controlling the exit of merchant seamen but not until January 1945 was it announced that Customs had been instructed not to allow any man of callable age group to leave Canada unless he had permission from the mobilization board. Meantime, late in 1944 McMaster was still trying to get permission to send Canadians to the U.S. for service on ships there. In spite of Randles best efforts, some Canadian merchant seamen continued throughout the war to find ways, either on their own or through the likes of McMaster, to join foreign flag ships.

Curiously, as late as September 1946, the Government was apparently still trying to control the cross-border movement of Canadian seamen with Labour Export Permits. In a 7 September 1946 memo to C. P. Edwards, Deputy Minister of Transport, the Department's Supervisor of Nautical Services, J. W. Kerr, stressed that "the effort made to control the exit of seamen from Canada to the United States or elsewhere during the war, was not a success." How then, he questioned, could better results be expected in peacetime. He focused on the obvious injustice of attempting to impose movement control on a specific occupational group:

> Trained Canadian personnel leave Canada in considerable number to seek employment in many forms of occupation in the United States. There appears to be little difficulty in such persons leaving Canada and entering the United States to take up positions in large United States industrial corporations. If restraint is placed upon Canadian seamen by which they

have less freedom than other nationals, objection may arise requiring the close attention of the Department.

* * *

The stubborn attempts of the National Selective Service to corral merchant seamen for military service posed another difficulty with which Randles had to contend. In mid-1941 he was successful in getting agreement from Maj. Gen. L. R. Lafleche, Associate Deputy Minister, Department of War Services, that qualified seamen called up under National Selective Service for military service would be considered to be employed in an "essential" service and exempted.

Major General Lafleche's assurances notwithstanding, in August 1941 he had to order C. G. Pennock, Vancouver National War Services divisional registrar, to back off from calling up deck and engineer officers for military training. Pennock was insisting that the draft board had no authority to exempt merchant seamen, except where they were serving on armed merchant vessels. Lafleche pointedly told Pennock that, "The Department of Naval Services and Mr. Arthur Randles, Director of Merchant Seamen . . . leave no doubt in my mind as to the absolute necessity of postponing such men." Despite this seemingly unequivocal declaration by Lafleche, difficulties persisted in getting seamen exempted from military service throughout 1942 and beyond. Both deep-sea and coastal services were affected to the extent that Randles was moved to describe the situation as "critical," with sailings being delayed because of crew losses. Draft board Notices of Call would be sent to the home addresses of merchant seamen while they were at sea, and by the time they returned they would be told that it was too late to apply for deferment.

Many merchant seamen, being civilian volunteers, themselves often made it difficult to justify deferment because of their predilection for heading for home on signing off at the completion of a voyage and not checking back into the manning pool until their money ran out. Sometimes they simply took a shore job and did not return to sea. One-trippers were common. The problem for Randles was to keep them coming back, either by re-signing on the same ship or checking into the manning pool within a reasonable period.

In a 2 December 1942 letter to S. T. Garside of the National Selective Service, Randles expressed doubt that his department had any right to force or coerce a seaman to re-sign, "because that would be regarded as equivalent to conscription for foreign service, which would be a greater measure of compulsion than the Armed Forces are as yet legally entitled to enforce."

The proposal was made that on signing off, a seaman be told that he must obtain a "Seaman's Employment Card," then National Selective Service and Unemployment Insurance Commission offices would be instructed that any seaman presenting such a card should be directed to return to his sea trade. If necessary, he could be advised to report to the nearest manning pool.

Although the riddle of how to keep the seamen tied to the system challenged Randles as long as he was Director of Merchant Seamen, the introduction of the Two-Year Manning Pool Agreement on 1 April 1944 did go a long way toward resolving the problem. Under the agreement, which was for the shorter of two years or the duration of the war, the between-ships seaman was effectively assured of continuous employment. He had his job-rated pay, sans War Risk Bonus, and room and board in the manning pool. It was an offer difficult to refuse. In return, the seaman had to register in the pool within forty-eight hours of signing off his last ship, thereby making himself available for re-assignment as soon as required by the pool. For those who were reluctant to commit for two years, there was still the option of registering with the pool for individual voyages without the obligation of re-entering the pool on return, but foregoing the benefits of the two-year agreement. Then there were some, particularly those with strong Union ties, who avoided the manning pools as a matter of principle and found other ways to obtain berths aboard the ships.

* * *

Randles see-sawed between paternalism and exasperation in his treatment of his sometimes recalcitrant charges. On the one hand, the Interdepartmental Committee on Merchant Seamen, of which Randles was chairman, worked hard and successfully to get transportation privileges for merchant seamen, argued in favour of income tax concessions and sick benefits, improvements in shipboard conditions and increased chances for promotion so that the seamen would come to regard the sea as a career opportunity. Randles and the other members of the Committee, Brand prominent among them, recognized that if the Merchant Navy were to survive in the postwar years it would require a stable workforce that could be ensured only if such social programs as pension plans were eventually introduced.

Discussions were held by Randles with the Deputy Minister of Veterans Affairs and the Chairman of the Canada Pension Commission regarding war gratuities and rehabilitation credits for merchant seamen similar to those extended to the Armed Services. He reported that the discussions had been favourable. In the event, however, the Government excluded the seamen from the postwar benefits, the Minister of Transport, Lionel Chevrier, explaining that such concessions would only encourage the men to abandon their seagoing careers.

Randles took great pride in the graduates of the training schools he had established, typically circulating a letter to all the manning pools, Captain Brand, and Captain T. P. Wilson, commandant of St. Margaret's, in which the Master of the *Algonquin Park* had good things to say about his new crew members:

Sailors engaged through the Canadian Manning Pool, for this ship, have all turned out very well indeed. They are willing, obedient and at all times on the job, both at sea and in port. The boys from St. Margaret's have all turned out very well indeed; this includes the two cadets.

On the other hand, frequent reports of crew troubles aboard ships and unruly behaviour ashore (where ship masters had no authority) provoked him to regard with favour reports of stern measures used in other countries to keep seamen in line. In a letter to the Judge Advocate General, Naval Services, he quotes approvingly a British news report describing punishment meted out following a U.K. incident. Three British crew members of a British ship were described as being a bad example to their ship's crew because on different occasions they had been so drunk as to have been unable to perform their duties. Two of them were fined ten pounds and the other five pounds, considerable sums at the time for low-paid British seamen. Randles applauded the punishment as an example of how unmanageable seamen were treated in the United Kingdom, and went on to suggest wishfully to the Judge Advocate General that, "It would be most helpful to us if similar severe penalties could be meted out to our Canadian seamen who veer off the straight and narrow path."

Captain Brand was equally concerned when seamen behaviour affected ship operations. When Park Steamship Marine Superintendent J. S. Thomson complained that seven days in jail was too light a sentence for a seventeen-year-old galley boy who by jumping ship had delayed sailing by several hours, Brand explained that to the Judge Advocate General the case appeared to be that of a young seaman with little or no experience, leaving a ship without realizing the consequences. When, however, the same youth repeated the offence on another ship (and Thomson wanted him drafted into the Army or the Navy, or at least debarred from the Merchant Navy), Brand was able to report that the Merchant Seaman Order Board had given the offender two weeks at hard labour at Oakalla Prison Farm in British Columbia. Said Brand: "The Board advises that . . . he obviously has no sense of responsibility. So long as boys of seventeen and eighteen are given what would normally be a man's wages, there are bound to be cases of this sort."

* * *

Nothing seemed to escape the attention of the two apparently tireless men. At one point, Randles' penchant for detail steered him into an uncomfortable position between two powerful volunteer organizations, each jealously guarding its self-perceived prerogatives and determined to be the one to fulfill a requirement he had identified. Somewhere Randles had learned that Vaseline-impregnated woollen socks were supposed to prevent "immersion foot," an affliction caused by long exposure to wet feet in, for example, a lifeboat. To supply the socks would be an ideal undertaking for Randles' team of volunteer organizations providing welfare services for his merchant seamen. Because the requirement could eventually run into tens of thousands of pairs of the socks,[13] he thought the task would be too much for any single organization. The Navy League and the Red Cross, both of which commanded nation-wide resources and volunteers, were naturals for the undertaking, but neither wanted to share the project with the other.

The Red Cross was the first to respond to Randles' call for volunteers in August 1943, saying that it would be pleased to supply the socks, of which it was assumed only a few thousand would be required, and that a large heating vat would be necessary to liquify the Vaseline. P. H. Gordon, Chairman of the Red Cross Executive Committee, said the organization would go ahead as soon as the number required was known, and that delivery would be at the earliest possible moment.

Within days the Navy League had also expressed willingness to supply the socks, but wanted to take on the job all by itself, because, it was said, when it divided work with the Red Cross in the past, competition developed and confusion and trouble sometimes resulted. Randles replied by suggesting that the Navy League supply an initial five thousand pairs of the Vaseline-impregnated woollen socks, which he reckoned to be enough for fifty to sixty ships.

Gordon of the Red Cross, which had heard from Randles at the same time, responded promptly saying that while it would be okay for the Navy League to supply the initial five thousand pairs of socks, he, Gordon, had talked to Surgeon Captain C. H. Best (of Banting and Best fame), who said there was a possibility of sixty thousand pairs being required very soon. Gordon went on to add that while the Red Cross worked in perfect harmony with the Navy League, women of the Red Cross Work Committee

> dislike very much the Navy League undertaking to do certain things and then ask various other organizations to come in and do the work for them. We have labour to burn, and if the material is made available the Red Cross could turn out the required quantities in a very much shorter time than any other combination of Societies.

While this jockeying for position was going on, there were attempts to discourage the project. Park Steamship President R. B. Teakle suggested that nothing be done until it was certain the Transport Department's Board of Steamship Inspection would allow the additional equipment in the lifeboats. F. A. Willsher, Chairman of the Board of Steamship Inspection wrote to Randles trying gently to dissuade him from pressing on, noting that the socks, which were bulky, would present a problem of stowage, and pointing out that the lifeboats were already required to carry protective clothing in the form of a two-piece suit which had proven "most satisfactory" for the purpose intended.

I appreciate the [ship] owners may not voluntarily furnish this equipment but as it appears, in a measure, an article whose function is already being performed by existing equipment, I hesitate to agree to any duplication, especially now, as more additional equipment is being recommended which ultimately must have a serious effect on the number of persons carried on lifeboats and the necessity to increase the capacity to accommodate them.

This was followed in mid-September by a letter from the U.K. Ministry of War Transport advising that experiments by the British Medical Research Committee had determined that after one-half to one hour, there was no material subjective difference between the bared leg and one protected by grease-covered trousers and socks.

These discouraging words nonetheless, Randles told the Navy League to go ahead with the supply of five thousand pairs of socks, which were to be delivered each pair separately wrapped so they could accompany the individual immersion suits in the lifeboats. By year's end the socks were ready and the Navy League was told to deliver them to the various managing operators for distribution to their ships. But the matter didn't end there. A member of the Navy League's executive committee, Eric Reford of Cunard White Star, protested that the Navy League should not be supplying the socks as freebies to the shipping companies, including his own. He was adamant that the arrangement was improper and that the companies should at least reimburse the Navy League the cost of $1.41 per pair of socks of impregnation, plus express charges. Randles' suggestion that Cunard White Star pay the equivalent amount as a donation to the Navy League's general fund was rejected by Reford, who insisted that an invoice be issued by the Navy League stating the charges.

How the matter was finally resolved and if any additional pairs of Vaseline-soaked socks were ever supplied is unknown, but the well-intended undertaking was typical of the minutiae with which the diligent Randles often became involved in the fulfillment of his demanding job. Whether dealing with his seamen charges, eager-to-help volunteers, or civil and military officials in Canada and abroad, his diplomatic and negotiating skills were put to the test on an almost daily basis.

In July 1943 he was advising the Deputy Minister of Transport that a proposed Order In Council did not adequately deal with the problem of repatriation of Canadian seamen stranded abroad when paid off in foreign lands by the foreign-registered ships on which they had been serving. While the seamen had sometimes signed on the ships of their own volition, just as often they had been assigned to them under manning pool direction. The problem was a serious one because the involuntarily beached seamen would be without funds or means of transportation back to Canada.

The 26 July 1944 found him writing to the British Ministry of War Transport advising that Canada would demand compensation for Canadian seamen lost or injured while serving on Allied ships of foreign registry in an amount not less than that demanded by the U.K., that is, £1,500 Sterling for each officer lost or permanently injured; £1,000 Sterling for each seaman. He was at his desk on Boxing Day 1944 dictating correspondence to R. G. Greene of Furness, Withy & Co. who had complained about the medical fitness, or lack of it, of many crewmen being supplied by the manning pool. Randles reply was tactful, but in effect: "Don't you know there's a war on?" Nevertheless, it was a matter that concerned him and at a meeting in February 1945 of the Interdepartmental Committee on Matters Relating to Merchant Seamen, he said he had decided to have all seamen serving under the Two-Year Manning Pool Agreement undergo a thorough medical inspection. At the same time he anticipated difficulty in carrying out such a plan due to the shortage of doctors and the length of time, two days, each full examination would require. Later in 1945, after the war had ended, he had to deal with complaints from the Canadian Merchant Service Guild, representing ships' officers, that U.K. and other non-Canadian officers were "ousting Canadians from Canadian Government-owned ships." On 26 October 1945, it was a meeting of the Sub-Committee on Awards to Merchant Seamen, of which both he and Captain Brand were members. The Sub-Committee recommended the awarding of eleven OBEs, seven MBEs and seven BEMs. Five of the awards were in connection with the sinking of the torpedoed *Point Pleasant Park*. Just a few months later, at the end of February 1946, Arthur Randles ended his service as Director of Merchant Seamen and returned to his management position with Cunard White Star in Montreal.

Meanwhile, with the end of Naval involvement in ship movements, the RCN's Trade and Intelligence Divisions had been recombined under Captain Brand. It would be expected that once the need for convoys had ceased, his links with merchant ship operations would be of a nature more theoretical than functional. Nevertheless, after he had taken retirement from the Navy, he was called on by the Canadian Government to take over and operate twenty-nine lake shipping companies strikebound by the CSU. His appointment, with full powers over the companies' assets and operations, reflected the high regard with which he was held in both Government and shipping circles. Even the Union, which had good reason to be suspicious of any Government appointee, appreciated his even-handed management of the ticklish situation. Said CSU historian Jim Green: "Brand worked to ease tensions in an effort to achieve a settlement. He persuaded the companies to drop 274 charges of desertion against seamen who had struck their vessels."[14]

To most wartime seamen, whether serving in the foc's'le, on the bridge or in the engine room, Captain Brand and Arthur Randles were remote, even unknown figures, but without question, Canada's WW II Merchant Navy bore their indelible stamp.

Chapter Eight   # THE UNION

In its short, stormy life, the Canadian Seamen's Union enjoyed only one relatively peaceful interlude, and that was, paradoxically, during those war years when Park Steamship Company became the dominant maritime employer. To be sure, it didn't start out that way.

The years between 23 July 1936, when two nascent seamen's organizations merged to form what eventually became the CSU, and the first wartime Spring, were a time of almost unbroken waterfront warfare between fiercely implacable enemies. Initially, the battlefield encompassed only the Great Lakes, for there was then no deep-sea shipping industry of note and what there was, was thinly scattered between the east coast and the St. Lawrence on the one hand, and the west coast on the other.

Simultaneously but independently in the spring of 1936, the Marine Workers Union of the Great Lakes and the National Seamen's Union had sprung to life in Toronto and Montreal respectively. The move to organize by the lake sailors should have come as no surprise to anybody, least of all the shipping companies who provided working and living conditions that were steaming fertile beds for labour unrest. For deckhands, it was take it or leave it servitude. Wages had dropped from $60 a month in 1929 to $40 in 1935, a level that has to be considered in perspective with the fact that the working day was unlimited. Once aboard ship, the seaman was effectively on call twenty-four hours a day, a condition of which he was acutely aware when traversing the lock system along the St. Lawrence and through the Welland Canal. As remembered for CSU historian Jim Green by one Thirties lake sailor, David Crain, it was hard and dangerous work:

> From Montreal to Cardinal [at the west end of the St. Lawrence system near Cornwall] there are twenty-six locks. That's the lower canal. There would be three deckhands on each laker. Two of them would go ashore on a landing boom and one guy would stay and run the aft winch. A landing boom was a swinging boom that was used to put you ashore. There was a bosun's chair or a man rope—a rope with knots—on the end of the boom. The reason the guys are ashore is to get the lines, haul the wires on and put them on the bitts.

You are kind of pulling yourself along the canal and into the locks. You were walking from Montreal to Prescott. That's really what it was on the lower canal. Depending on how much traffic there was it would take you maybe three days to get through the twenty-six locks. It was okay in the summer because you could always jump in the river or the lake, wherever you were, and kind of refresh, but you never got much sleep. You'd get intermittent sleep, but there would never be any time when you got eight hours sleep.

There had been some instances when people going out on a landing boom ended up between the ship's side and the canal and were squashed to death. There were a fair number of deckhands running around with two or three fingers off . . . . There were also a couple of instances that I knew about where people were down [in the hold] sweeping off ledges and things like that when they were unloading grain and they would fall in. They never got them out alive. They would suffocate.[1]

Vessels of no more than 5000 tons were not required to carry a radio so a sailor on a smaller lake ship in peril on stormy seas could not expect any help to come from shore. The owners opposed any regulation mandating the addition of wireless, less due to the cost of the equipment itself but more because it would mean the addition of a wireless operator's wages to their operating costs. Not even passenger vessels seemed sacrosanct when it came to the owners' reluctance to include all possible safety measures. The union pointed to two Canadian National Steamship lake ships operating between Toronto and Port Dalhousie, *Dalhousie* and *Northumberland*, each of which, it claimed, carried approximately 1,000 passengers plus crew, but had lifeboat and life raft seating capacity for only 224 people.[2]

* * *

The Canadian Seamen's Union had a difficult birth. To be born in a time of hostile anti-unionism was disadvantage enough, but to be conceived and lead by admitted Communists only added to the problems the CSU faced in achieving its central goal of a better deal for the sailors. It was not only shipping companies and government that emphasized the Red label in their attempts to discredit the CSU, but within many other Canadian unions as well there were right wing elements as strongly anti-Communist as were to be found at any level of society. McCarthyism may not have reached full flower until the early 1950s, but, as yet unbranded in the 1930s, it was alive and well.

Before the CSU, the only organization purporting to represent the sailors' interests was the National Seamen's Association which, to the extent that it resembled a union at all, answered to the labour epithet of "company," as in company union. The NSA was the creature of Capt. H. N. McMaster, a former operating manager for Canada

Steamship Lines before he concluded that there was more profit in representing the seamen. In his self-appointed task he was assisted by his daughter as secretary-treasurer of the NSA. The Association was in fact, little more than a recruiting service for the ship owners. A sailor in search of a job would go to Captain McMaster, pay $5.00—a considerable sum in those days—and the Captain would place him on a ship. He had a network of ship captains so that if a sailor had been able to get a job independently, he would be told by his captain that he had to sign one of McMaster's union cards. In the midst of the job-starved depression, it was an offer no seaman could refuse. It also, by no coincidence, created the illusion of a closed shop.

During periods of unemployment, particularly the long closed season of winter, the shorebound seamen, often destitute, hung out at the facilities of, typically, the Single Men's Unemployed Association in Toronto. Here, they came into contact with experienced trade unionists and, being at loose ends, they assisted by taking on such routine union tasks as the distribution of leaflets. The unionists reciprocated by teaching the sailors how to use united action to improve their lot. That the seeds of dissatisfaction were being sown was no doubt perceived by McMaster who, in order to protect his territory, decided he had to make a show of actually appearing to do something more tangible for the "members" of his association. Under pressure from the newly aware seamen, he advised the shipowners that they should raise wages or face the possibility of a general strike on 1 August, at the height of the 1935 shipping season. Much to McMaster's consternation, when the deadline came and went without the desired result, the seamen did walk off the ships. The ship owners, believing that McMaster had switched allegiance, publicly denounced his association as not being a legitimate union. McMaster claimed the walkout was all a mistake, and he had in fact called it off but somehow the seamen hadn't received the message.

In terms of immediate benefit, the strike proved a failure, with the strikers facing blacklisting. It was, however, the starting point for what was soon to become the Canadian Seamen's Union. The sailors, seemingly abandoned on their picket lines by McMaster's NSA and without visible means of support, in their plight attracted the attention of the Workers Unity League, a creation of the Communist Party of Canada. Neither of the major Canadian union organizations of the day, the Trades and Labour Congress of Canada (TLC) and the All-Canadian Congress of Labour (ACCL), showed much sympathy. Only affiliates of the American Federation of Labor qualified for membership in the TLC and the ACCL accepted only Canadian unions. Whatever it was that the striking seamen represented, it did not qualify under either criterion. It did not help either that not only did both the TLC and ACCL have a strong right wing bias, they both also believed that no strike could succeed in the depths of the depression.

There was a vacuum and the Workers Unity League rushed in to fill it. One of the striking seamen who emerged as a leader in Toronto was Dewar Ferguson. So impressed was he by the dedication to working class issues of the Communist unionists and party members he now found himself working with, that he hesitated not when invited to join the Party.

* * *

Despite losing the first round in their fight with the ship owners, the seamen were determined to organize an effective union. They appointed Dewar Ferguson and Joe Turnbull—both of whom had been blacklisted by the ship owners—to establish a Toronto office in space provided by the Union of the Unemployed, from where they could sign up new members and coordinate the activities of the committees that the sailors were setting up on the ships. These recruiting activities were so successful that by April 1936, just prior to the opening of the shipping season, more than two hundred employed seamen were attracted to a meeting which saw formation of the Marine Workers Union of the Great Lakes and the election of Dewar Ferguson as its president.

Meanwhile, in Montreal, in a similar rebellion against the activities of McMaster's NSA, the National Seamen's Union had been brought into being under the leadership of J. A. (Pat) Sullivan, a ship's cook, and chartered as a Canadian union by the All-Canadian Congress of Labour (ACCL). As in Toronto, the Union of the Unemployed had assisted at the birth. When the two rudimentary seamen's organizations became aware of each other's existence and mutual aims, they lost no time in amalgamating, with Ferguson as president and Sullivan as secretary-treasurer. Initially named the National Seamen's Union, in September 1936 the amalgamated union officially became the Canadian Seamen's Union, and established headquarters in Montreal.

In what seemed like a good idea at the time, the affiliation with the ACCL was retained, a decision that was soon to prove troublesome. With both Ferguson and Sullivan Communist Party members, it was not surprising that they should soon clash with right wing elements of the ACCL leadership. Using as an excuse the cash-strapped CSU's failure to meet its financial obligations to ACCL, the right wingers attempted to assume control, charging financial mismanagement. For the CSU, it was time to leave and seek affiliation with the Trades and Labour Congress of Canada, a difficult process because the TLC was made up mostly of international unions affiliated with the American Federation of Labor, but made possible when the CSU sought and gained a charter with the U.S.-based AFL-affiliated International Seamen's Union.

Given that the Red tint of its leadership, and of a few of its members, made the CSU a nettlesome embrace for most other Canadian unions, the question arises as to why there was never any move to downplay the association. Danny Daniels, who became an editor of *Searchlight*, the CSU newspaper, put it bluntly:

> The seamen looked around and said, 'These guys [the Communist Party members] are going out of their way to help us. They are on our side. They talk our language. They put out for us, put us up in their homes, they lay out bread for us. Hell, we'll look into their ideas." And that's exactly what happened. The Communist Party became the most influential organization of shoreside people on the ships.[3]

* * *

The CSU grew rapidly. By the time of its first annual convention in March 1937 it was claiming a membership of 1,200. When delegates gathered for the second convention one year later, it was reported in the press that this number had climbed to 5,000 and that twelve locals were operating along the inland waterway. The office of president, to which Pat Sullivan was elected, became a full-time paid position. In 1937, the union had achieved a major breakthrough when it won recognition as the seamen's representative from Canada Steamship Lines, the largest shipping company on the Great Lakes. Other companies followed the CSL, but many of them regarded their move as only a temporary expediency to gain time while they marshalled forces to sink the CSU. They again threw their support behind Captain McMaster, who by this time had set up three organizations claiming to represent the engineers and the deck officers as well as the seamen. The shipping companies were confident that with the compliance of McMaster's three associations they had the strength to challenge the CSU. They made membership in a McMaster union a condition of employment and at the same time refused to hire known CSU members. The companies justified their preference for McMaster's union on the grounds that it was a Canadian organization, whereas they claimed the CSU was controlled by "outside interests" and was a "foreign union," an allusion to the CSU's American Federation of Labor affiliation that had been used to gain admittance to the Trades and Labour Congress of Canada. Ironically, a few years after the end of World War II, in their ultimately successful campaign to eliminate the CSU, the same companies would be instrumental in the importation from the United States of the Seafarers International Union and the notorious Hal Banks.

It was a make or break situation for the CSU. A strike date was set to coincide with the official opening of the 1938 shipping season, midnight, 15 April. The confident shipowners refused to bargain and the seamen walked ashore. Many of the strikers did in fact carry McMaster's National Seamen's Association membership cards to comply with the ship owners' condition of employment, but their hearts were with the CSU. By 17 April, not a ship was moving. The shipping companies signed. It was a landmark victory for the CSU. A significant battle had been won but the war between union and management would go on for many years before it ran its course.

Apart from a number of skirmishes that followed as a handful of the shipping companies tried to end run the agreement that had been reached with the CSU, the union was faced with no further major challenges from the ship owners until the spring of 1940, when the 1938 agreement was due to expire. By then, Canada was at war and the War Measures Act had been invoked, giving the Federal Government sweeping powers to control all aspects of Canadian life.

* * *

In August 1939, Germany and the U.S.S.R. signed the Soviet-German Pact, the terms of which included collaboration of the Soviets in the German conquest of Poland and agreement on the division of the resulting geographic spoils. On 1 September, Germany invaded Poland from the west; on 3 September, Great Britain declared war on Germany with Canada following suit on 10 September. On 17 September, the Soviet Army crossed Poland's eastern frontier.

This unholy alliance of German Fascism and Soviet Communism brought mental confusion for Communist sympathizers in western nations, the CSU leadership among them. The fount of Communist inspiration and principle was now linked in common cause with Fascism at its most bestial. Nevertheless, the CSU adhered to the line that it was passionately anti-Fascist and pledged to support the Canadian war effort provided the Government would not use its wartime powers as an excuse to suppress unionism.

It looked to Union eyes, however, that such an aim was exactly what Ottawa had in mind when, in the midst of CSU attempts to get the lake shipping companies to the negotiating table to renew the 1938 agreement before the new shipping season opened on 15 April 1940, the Federal Deputy Minister of Labour announced that the Government would not allow a strike to happen. This announcement cut the feet from under the Union's bargaining position and the companies promptly withdrew from all negotiations, confident that with the CSU stripped of its principal weapon, it could be easily crushed. Shocked and angered, the Union challenged the Government's opinion that a strike would be illegal under the Industrial Disputes Act, arguing that the new lake shipping season had not yet opened, and the seamen were therefore not at that particular time employees of the shipping companies. As it digested this argument, the Government vacillated and turned to the Justice Department for a ruling. The Union leadership, sensing that it was now or never, announced that its membership, by now claimed to number 6,500, would not permit any ships to sail if agreements had not been signed by the official opening of navigation season at midnight, 14 April. On 15 April, the picket lines went up on the docks and some 285 lakers remained at their moorings. With the support on both sides of the lakes of longshoremen who refused to load the struck ships, the CSU stood fast in the face of a Government threat that if the union did not agree to binding arbitration, the Government would side with the shipowners to break the strike. Knowing that it would be difficult to withstand the Government's formidable wartime powers indefinitely, the CSU proposed as an alternative to binding arbitration, a conciliation board with non-binding powers and recognition of the Union as the legitimate representative of the seamen. This proposal was accepted and on 20 April the pickets were removed.

Through the conciliation process that followed, the Union won recognition from the majority of the lake shipping companies as sole bargaining agent for unlicensed seamen, as well as other concessions. Not so successful was a later attempt to strike ships of two holdout companies. By that time, the CSU leadership had been interned along with other known Communists and the Government had demonstrated that it was prepared to deal harshly with any further attempts to prevent ships from sailing.[4] The ships of the maverick shipping companies were reluctantly allowed to sail on. Nonetheless, when the conciliation board made its final report to the Government in January 1941, it came down solidly on the side of Union, recommending that any holdout companies should join in the recognition by the majority of the shipping industry of the rights of the seamen to organize and bargain.

* * *

Now firmly established as an element of the lake shipping industry, the CSU turned its attention to the deep sea industry. Tiny though the Canadian foreign-going merchant marine was in 1940, there was about to be a rebirth of shipbuilding in Canada and with it a Government-sponsored wartime Merchant Navy. When what were to be the Park ships sailed, the CSU was determined to be aboard. Though the Union had hitherto focused on building its strength on the Great Lakes, the extension of its sphere of influence to include deep-sea had long been in its plans. Indeed, with exactly that in mind it had established a one-man office in Halifax late in 1938. That one man was Charlie Murray, who was, like others leading the CSU, a Communist Party member.

When the U.S.S.R. joined Germany in the invasion of Poland, it became inevitable that the Canadian Government would act to restrain Communist Party activities. In the suspicious wartime milieu ("even the walls have ears!") individuals whose political leanings were considered too far left— or for that matter, too far right— were quickly classed *persona non grata*. In June 1940 Ottawa cast its net. Caught and herded into internment camp at Petawawa, Ontario, on 15 June 1940, possibly for the duration,[5] was Pat Sullivan, CSU president, who was joined a month later by Jack Chapman, national secretary-treasurer, Charlie Murray, vice-president, and Dave Sinclair, editor of the *Searchlight*, the union's mouthpiece publication.

Despite the CSU executive's being in the bag, so to speak, the organization's voice was hardly muffled. The interned national officers continued to plot union strategy and to formulate plans. Union activity carried on virtually unhampered under the guidance of Dewar Ferguson—inexplicably not caught in the round-up of Party members—who was appointed acting president and along with other acting officers became the collective alter ego of the insiders.

Undeterred by the internment of four of its top executives, the Union lost no time in proclaiming its ambition to extend its activities to foreign-going ships. It was a subject to which, Acting President Dewar Ferguson proclaimed to the CSU's national executive meeting in Montreal on 22 December 1941, "the Union has not paid sufficient attention." In a lengthy report, Dewar made it clear that the CSU wanted to be fully involved in recruiting and training seamen for deep-sea requirements.

Early in January 1942, the Union organized a meeting with representatives of the Canadian Navigators Federation and the National Asssociation of Marine Engineers, the avowed purpose of which was to formulate proposals for presentation to the Canadian Government, "aimed at supplying adequately trained crews for ships of both salt water and inland waterways."

Following the meeting, the Canadian Press reported on 6 January 1942, "that the organizations involved will present proposals to the Government for training seamen and will also offer a plan whereby the organizations are prepared to undertake large-scale recruiting of seamen and prospective seamen in Canada." Subsequently, this joint group submitted a memorandum of "Proposals for mobilization of the marine transport industry," calling for the establishment of a joint commission to carry out a plan to supply adequate and trained crews for all shipping, including the Great Lakes. As perceived by the three organizations involved in the drafting of the proposal, this joint commission would comprise the Government, shipping companies, and organizations of officers and men.

In the same month the CSU followed up independently with a brief prepared by its interned executive officers. This brief proposed that the Union be the recruiting agency for seamen, and that a minimum of ten schools be established at coastal and inland ports, training a minimum of five hundred men during each six-to-eight-week term, a program far more ambitious than the Government's plan for two, possibly three schools.

Initially, Ottawa countered by downplaying the Union and its proposals. With the recent history of hostile union/management relations on the Great Lakes, the Government saw only the possibility of disruption of its soon-to-be Merchant Navy.

* * *

The ink was barely dry on the appointment of Arthur Randles as Director of Merchant Seamen in the Spring of 1941 when he had to deal with an early feeler from the CSU, albeit an indirect one. R. B. Teakle, then general manager of CN Steamships[6], reported to Randles that he had received an offer from the Union to supply Lakes seamen for the merchant service, claiming at least two hundred of its members were anxious to go. Teakle suggested that Randles might want to make a deal to enrol the proffered men in the new Canadian Manning Pool, a suggestion with which Randles agreed while expressing the need for caution in dealing with the Union. He proposed that Teakle "hint" to the Union that the two hundred men would be welcome in the Manning Pool provided they were experienced. He stressed he did not want the CSU to get the idea that the Government recognized it as the medium through which employment and conditions were to be regulated.

Early in 1941, the Union tried another approach in its attempts to become a significant player in the manning of the deep sea ships. Fred T. Hackett, CSU port organizer in Toronto, forwarded nine applications for the Manning Pool in Halifax, saying that the men were all experienced and had passed their medical exams. He requested that rail warrants for transportation to Halifax be sent to him for distribution to the men concerned. Randles returned the applications, coolly dismissing them as lacking references or evidence of experience. He suggested that in future medical exams not be taken until, "I have identified whether the applicant is suitable from the point of view of his experience, and whether or not a pool vacancy exists." He went on to note that rail warrants could be sent only by registered mail direct to the person intended at his home address.

In an interdepartmental memo of 10 January 1942, C. P. Edwards, Deputy Minister of Transport, dismissed the CSU as "a Great Lakes Union and does not touch deep-sea operations." And in a letter of 12 February 1942, Arthur Randles, the Director of Merchant Seamen, to J. W. Sutherland, Regional Director, Manning Pool, Halifax:

> I do not want the CSU interfering in any way with the manning of foreign-going ships, and on no account are you to encourage them or let them believe their services are necessary. The CSU have never had any stake or interest in sailing on foreign articles. They are endeavoring now to get into that line and there is no particular service they can render to the Canadian Government.

Randles was reacting to a report from Sutherland that an offer had been received from the CSU's Halifax business agent to ship men on Allied vessels through the CSU Halifax office. Sutherland had rejected the offer, advising the CSU agent that all the crewmen had to go through the Manning Pool, which had been established for that purpose.[7]

Despite the Government's efforts at this stage to discourage the CSU, the Union remained determined and continued to press for full involvement in the manning and training programs for the still embryonic merchant fleet. A *Toronto Star* report on 15 April 1942 said the CSU was calling for a distinctive and effective Canadian Merchant Marine and "The CSU will supply the men required and every union office will become a recruiting centre."

But Arthur Randles was adamant that the CSU should be kept at arm's length. To the Deputy Minister of Transport, C. P. Edwards, he said,

> I must definitely state to you that the Canadian Seamen's Union are not capable of handling either the recruitment of seamen or their training. This Union only represents a small section of seamen and is not representative enough to be used by the Government in the manner suggested.

He rejected as not feasible a CSU proposal that a recruiting campaign, sponsored by the Government, should be undertaken by two or three officers of the Union. He was disdainful of the Union executive, telling Edwards that,

> it is staffed by men who are not practical seamen. For instance, the President was a cook on a lake boat for a short time and none of the others, so far as I know, have had any service on the ocean. The Union itself can be of practically no assistance to the manning problem and while the scheme they mentioned is so sketchy, whatever it is, it cannot offer any advantage commensurate with that offered through our own system of Training Schools, Manning Pools, etc., all of which are in full and effective operation.[8]

In support of his position, vis-à-vis Union proposals, Randles cited arguments that while technically correct at the moment, covered situations that were soon to change. He quoted Federal statute requiring a seaman to have three years of foreign-going service before qualifying as an Able Seaman. In practice, as manning needs rapidly became more pressing, sailors were soon being promoted to AB after one short voyage as an Ordinary Seamen. Accelerated promotions were common all along the line and more than one unlicensed third mate was created prematurely, by measure of prewar standards, out of raw but apparently promising deckhand material.

Randles' response to a CSU suggestion regarding the setting of wages on foreign-going ships was that the matter was of no concern to the Government, "as the Government is not an employer of sea-going labour." Again, only technically was this true, the shipping companies who contracted as managing operators of Park ships initially having been charged with responsibility for crewing them. But the eventual setting of a standard scale of wages by the Crown-owned Park Steamship Company, combined with the introduction of the Department of Transport-operated manning pool system, did in fact make the Government an employer of sea-going labour.

In a letter intended for the CSU, which Randles apparently drafted for signature by C. D. Howe,[9] the Director of Merchant Seamen continued to cite the same argument, explaining that Park Steamship Company had been formed to operate the new vessels being built, but that it had in turn entrusted the management of them to private shipping companies. "The arrangements for manning the ships and operating them are entirely in the hands of the individual Managing Operators, who in setting the scale of wages are, of course, governed by those prevailing in the shipping industry. No wage scales are set by the government itself." This draft letter was dated 11 September 1942; one month earlier, Park Steamship Company had published a standard Scale of Wages, War Risk Bonus and Cost-of-Living Bonus[10] for Park ships, covering all positions from master to pantry boy. Ready or not, these were the wages that the managing operators were required to pay.

Like all successful executives, the pragmatic Arthur Randles was flexible, some might say cynical, adapting to changing circumstances as necessary. On 24 November 1943 he telegraphed Captain G. L. C. Johnson, Regional Director, Vancouver Manning Pool, advising that Dewar Ferguson, CSU secretary-treasurer, was coming to Vancouver for the purpose of setting up a CSU West Coast organization. Randles instructed Johnson to extend Ferguson every courtesy, "especially in view of the fact that the CSU have now concluded a collective bargaining agreement with Park Steamship Company." Randles added that both he and E. F. Riddle, Park Steamship Company General Manager,[11] approved of Ferguson's mission.

In another goodwill (but tongue-in-cheek) gesture, he fired off a telegram to the CSU in convention in 1944: "Heartiest good wishes to delegates attending the 5th Annual Convention of the Canadian Seamen's Union."

* * *

In the event, though the CSU was soon successful in intensifying union activity, particularly on the East Coast, and eventually gained recognition as the official seamen's bargaining agent on both coasts, it never succeeded in its wartime attempts to short-circuit the Government-operated manning pool system, and had no input whatsoever in the training program.

This lack of success in those two areas nothwithstanding, the Union accepted that while not ideal, the manning pool system provided the seamen with hitherto unknown security and adequate shoreside living conditions. Aboard the ships, the CSU won higher wages and many improvements in accommodation comforts and victualling. Compared to earlier experience with the private sector shipping companies, it found Park Steamship Company a reasonable employer.

"The CSU," relates Jim Green in *Against the Tide*, his history of the Union,

> had always been forced to fight to the last bell to be recognized by any company as the legitimate union of the seamen. Finally, on the government-owned vessels, the union was recognized without even a shrug.

There was no work stoppage or unrest because 'the CSU was an established organization and the Park Steamship Company took a very realistic attitude toward the democratic rights of their employees. This company,' the union felt, 'has not attempted in any way to impede our organizational work, either ashore or aboard ship'."[12]

The wartime years for the CSU were a period of growth, consolidation and increasing influence in maritime circles. It emerged from the war strong and well positioned to maintain status in the postwar years. Its aim then was to fight for the maintenance of a Canadian Merchant Marine to guarantee jobs for its members, and to continue to improve their lot. The years following war's end may have been much-welcomed peacetime for Canada at large, but for the CSU it was anything but a period of peace. It was soon to be in the fight of its life, for its life.

It lost.

It could be argued that the turmoil of this turbulent postwar period of marine labor relations and the antagonism that was generated in all quarters, may have established such an enduring climate of hostility, particularly in Government political and bureaucratic circles, as to have been an influential factor in the long delay in granting wartime merchant seamen something approaching "Veteran" status. Nearly half a century would pass, and many changes of government occur, before the official stamp of approval would be bestowed on the survivors of the 7,705[13] who were later reckoned by the Department of Transport to have sailed in "dangerous waters," and who, in wartime, had been praised by the Government of the day as the "Fourth Arm of the Services."

Chapter Nine   # THE SHIPS

You could hardly describe them as beautiful, those plodding, flat-bottomed, slab-sided, mass-produced, Canadian-built vessels that became known in the marine community as the Park boats. If ships have a personality, as sailors are wont to believe, then the drab wartime dress of basic Admiralty gray worn by the Parks and their identical twins, the Forts, was a most appropriate choice. In the hostile environment in which they were built to serve, anonymity and inconspicuity were in. Flair was out.

The Parks may not have had lines of the kind that would inspire the lyricism of a John Masefield, but viewed with a not-too-critical eye, with their raked stem and cruiser stern they could be seen as having some esthetically pleasing features. Unladen, high in the water, they appeared bulky and awkward, which, of course they were. But when loaded to the Plimsoll mark, with freeboard reduced to an allowable minimum, they acquired a certain fineness of line that gave them a much more pleasing profile than that presented by their American cousin, the Liberty, with its high chunky superstructure. Such a flattering way of looking at the Park's very plain-Jane design may at first seem strange, but it was not uncommon among crews who, on arrival in a foreign port, would find symptoms surfacing of national pride for their ship.

The Park ships did not have the glamour of a *Queen Mary* and other like troop-carrying mighties crossing the seas at a blistering 25 to 30 knots. The relationship was as a Rolls-Royce to a one-ton truck, but when all was said and done, the contribution of the utilitarian 11-knot Parks (named after Canadian parks) and Forts (named after historic Canadian forts) and Liberties to the winning of the war ranked right alongside all the armies and all the navies and all the air forces of the Allied nations.

There were in fact three types of Park ships, the most significant of these being the 10,000 deadweight ton class, both in terms of numbers built and in their total contribution to the war effort. They were identical to and interchangeable with the Fort ships being launched from Canadian shipyards for delivery to the British Ministry of War Transport under either Canada's Mutual Aid program or United States' Lend-Lease. It was not unusual for a ship to be launched as a Fort, or vice versa, only to be reassigned to meet the constantly shifting priorities of the moment, and renamed according to whether it ultimately landed on the roll of the Park Steamship Company Limited, or that of the Ministry of War Transport.

The Park/Fort 10,000 tonners were, in turn, almost identical to the Oceans being built to British order in the United States, the major differences springing from the fact that the Canadian-built Park/Fort ships were of almost entirely riveted construction whereas the American-built Oceans were all-welded. All of them shared a high degree of commonality with the famous Liberty ship: same dimensions, same basic closed shelter deck hull design, same engines, same deck machinery. Their familial resemblance was hardly surprising given that all were based on the *Empire Liberty*, a ship designed and built in the North Sands shipyard of Joseph L. Thompson & Sons Limited of Sunderland, England. Indeed, the prototypical *Empire Liberty* was still abuilding when the British orders were placed in the U.S. for sixty Oceans, and was not launched until after the first, the *Ocean Vanguard*, had slid down the ways.

To distinguish the Canadian-built 10,000 tonners from the lookalike Oceans being built in the U.S., they were given the designation "North Sands," after the shipyard that had produced the design. The original design was of 9300 DWT capacity, but for North American production it was changed from open to closed shelter deck, and length between perpendiculars (BP) was increased from 416 feet to 425 feet, increasing DWT to 10,350. Later, as further modifications were introduced to meet the dictates of changing requirements, two additional variations emerged and these were identified as the Victory and the Canadian types. All were built to the same basic dimensions (which were essentially the same or similar to those for the Oceans and the Liberties): 425 ft. BP, 441 ft. overall (OA), 57 ft. breadth, 27 ft. draft fully loaded. There were minor specifications variations, particularly in terms of overall length, which could be as short as 438.5 ft. and as long as 441.5 ft. for the double-bottomed hulls. On average, their gross registered tonnage (GRT) was 7130 and their deadweight tonnage, which in effect is payload rating, was generally listed as 10,000, although the official figure was, as noted, actually 10,350.[1]

For the public at large, 10,000 tons was an abstract figure difficult to visualize in material form, so wartime publicists were pleased to provide a more tangible picture of a typical cargo that could be transported by a single Park ship. Such a representative manifest listing of an all-in-one load never failed to impress: enough flour, cheese, bacon, ham, canned and dried goods to feed 225,000 persons in the U.K. for a week; more than 2,000 tons of steel bars and slabs; gun carriers, trucks and motorcycles sufficient to motorize an entire infantry battalion; bombs to load 950 medium or 225 heavy bombers; timber and plywood, wallboard and nails to build 94 four-room cottages; space on the afterdeck for 2 bombers and room in the hold for enough aluminum to build 310 medium bombers or 740 fighters.[2] Put another way by the Americans, the capacity of the similar Liberty was equivalent to that of 300 freight cars. The conventional wisdom was that a Park ship paid for itself if it delivered just one cargo.[3]

Huge deckloads were the norm. From eastern ports these might be tanks, locomotives or crated aircraft; from the west coast they were commonly timber, covering every available inch of deck space and spilling over the covered hatches to a height of approximately eight feet. Precarious catwalks would be built over these deckloads by Chips, the ship's carpenter, to make it possible for the crew to traverse the ship.

The 10,000 DWT Parks may have been classed as ll-knot ships, but under ideal conditions of wind, current and sea state another knot or so of speed could be cranked out of the oil burner variant. For reasons of fuel economy, however, this was rarely done and in any case, ll-knot capability was sufficient to qualify for inclusion in a so-called fast convoy.[4] Probably the highest speed recorded by a Park 10,000 tonner in other than a brief sprint during acceptance trials, was 12.6 knots averaged over an 8,910 mile voyage by *Dunlop Park* under Capt. John A. Wright, late in 1945. As described in a news report,[5] the ship travelled from Glasgow, Scotland, to Vancouver via the Panama Canal in thirty days elapsed time, one and a half days of which were spent tied up in ports of call. Normal time for such a crossing by a Park ship was put at thirty-five days.

Propulsion for the 10,000 tonners was provided by triple-expansion reciprocating steam engines, 135-ton monsters that, installed, towered approximately thirteen feet above the engine room deck. Rated at 2500 International Horsepower (IHP) at a nominal 76 rpm, they had three cylinders: a high-pressure cylinder of 24.5 in. bore, intermediate pressure of 37 in. and low pressure of 70 in. Stroke was 48 in. Steam from boilers redlined at 220 PSI (three Scotch marine boilers for coal burners, or, alternatively two water tube boilers for oil burners) first entered the high-pressure cylinder, then passed on to the intermediate- and low-pressure cylinders before exhausting into a condenser and eventual return to the feedwater supply. It was not only for propulsion that steam supplied the ship with muscle power; all deck machinery, including cargo winches and mooring and anchor windlasses, derived their motive force from the same source, which also drove the electrical generators and other ancillary equipment, as well as supplying heat for the living quarters.[6]

Although for reasons of wartime expediency the U.S. chose an adaptation of the North Sands design for its mass-produced Liberty ship program, the U.S. Maritime Commission (USMC) regarded the triple-expansion steam engines and coal-fired Scotch marine boilers as antiquated and would have preferred turbine or diesel power. Indeed the triple-expansion engine would not, even then, have looked out of place in the steam exhibit at London's Kensington Science Museum. No wonder, it was said to be based on an 1895 version of the type, which was first introduced between 1870 and 1880.[7] Antique the triple-expansion engine may have been, it was still USMC's compromise choice when combined with oil-fired water tube boilers. High among the engine's attractions was that being simple to build it was ideal for mass production (and was in fact already in production for the British-ordered Oceans). Furthermore, U.S. manufacturing capacity was by then fully occupied turning out other more modern and more complex types of marine propulsion equipment.[8] Another significant virtue was simplicity of operation, important in engine rooms where there were almost always sure to be at least one or two inexperienced first-trippers. Being simple, the engines were also extremely reliable.

Such considerations, although equally applicable to the Canadian ships, did not enter into the Government's selection of the North Sands design for the Crown-owned Park fleet, this choice being dictated by the circumstance that the ships and their triple-expansion engines were already in production in Canada to British (and later U.S. Lend-Lease) order at the time the decision was taken to equip and man a Canadian Merchant Navy.

* * *

In general arrangement,[9] the 10,000 DWT Park ship was internally divided into five cavernous cargo holds, numbered from fore to aft, three of them forward of the engine and boiler rooms and two of them aft. No. 4 hold below the 'tween deck had a further subdivision in the form of a deep tank which could be used for liquid cargo or water ballast. Forward of No. 1 was the forepeak where below deck there were compartments for the anchor chain locker and for what was sometimes known as the bosun's locker, where such maintenance and replacement items as paint and spare rope were stowed. Just ahead of the No. 1 hatch coaming was the burly anchor windlass, which doubled as the forward warping winch during mooring operations. The stern warping winch was located immediately aft of No. 5 hatch coaming.

At each of the five hatches were two winches and two 5-ton capacity wooden derricks for working cargo. In addition, there were heavy lift jumbo booms to service holds Nos. 2 and 4. When not in use, these were stowed vertically against, respectively, the foremast and the mainmast. The foremast boom had a lift capacity of 30 tons and the mainmast, 50 tons.

Above weather deck level, between the hatches for No. 2 and No. 3 holds was a three-level deck house, which at its lowest level housed the deck officers' accommodation, officers' dining saloon and pantry. The second level comprised the bridge deck, which was given over principally to the Captain's living quarters. On the North Sands and Canadian versions, there was one lifeboat port and one lifeboat starboard on this bridge deck. The third level was the navigating bridge with enclosed wheelhouse, radio room, and chartroom, in which was installed the Sperry gyroscopic compass for ships so equipped. In the open air atop the navigating bridge was the so-called monkey island which was complete with duplicates of the wheelhouse's helm, magnetic compass binnacle, gyro compass repeater and engine room telegraph. From this lofty perch the ship could be steered in good weather.

In the North Sands coal burners, required bunker space reduced the cargo capacity of No. 3 hold significantly. The Canadian version had to provide stowage for both types of fuel, bunkers for coal and tanks for fuel oil. The Victory oil burners required fuel oil tanks only.

In the 'tween deck at No. 3 hold, in the area generally immediately beneath the lowest level of the bridge deckhouse, were located the ship's food storage and refrigeration rooms. Aft of No. 3 hatch was a deckhouse that surrounded the casing for the engine and boiler room. Arranged down each side at weather deck level were the quarters for the engineering officers and the catering staff. The ship's hospital was also accommodated here. Across the forward end was the galley.

Atop this accommodation was the boat deck where, on the North Sands and the Canadian types were mounted single lifeboats, port and starboard. On the Victory models, there were no lifeboats on the bridge deck, but the boat deck was extended to make room for two lifeboats on each of the port and starboard sides.[10] On this same boat deck level, at the aft end, was accommodation for the petty officers (i.e., the bosun and the carpenter). Topping it all off were the fiddleys for engine room ventilation, and of course, the funnel.

At the stern was a smallish deckhouse housing the seamen's and the firemen's messes, their shared pantry, and their washrooms. Living quarters for the crewmen, as well as for the DEMS gunners, were located below deck with access from the mess deck. Being below deck, the crew cabins were fitted with portholes, which during daylight when the weather was fine and the sailing smooth, could be left open to supply a measure of ventilation. But while blackout was in effect between nightfall and sunup, or when the sea was rough, the porthole deadlights had to be lugged down. The atmosphere, especially in the tropics, could become stifling. It wasn't only in stormy seas that portholes could become submerged. Sometimes, though the sea surface might otherwise be smooth, but with a heavy swell running, the ship would roll and pitch so vigorously that water would be taken forcefully through the open portholes and it would become necessary to keep them closed even in daylight.[11]

* * *

A major incentive in the development of the Victory variant was the Department of Munitions and Supply's belief that the U.S. was going to continue to be a principal purchaser of Canadian-built cargo ships.[12] On the basis of this belief the decision was then made to introduce certain modifications to bring the ships in line with American requirements. This entailed the adoption of some features of the USMC's EC2-S-C1 (Liberty ship), specification, principally two oil-fired water tube boilers in place of three coal-fired Scotch marine boilers. The Victory also complied with American rather than British statutory and naval requirements, had more elaborate fittings and provided more comfortable crew accommodation.

The new variant, the first of which entered Park service in August 1943, also incorporated all the improvements that had evolved while the shipbuilders' learning curve was climbing steeply. The contrast between the early production ships of 1942 and those of two years later brought the Naval Boarding Service to comment on the old *Kootenay Park* that the

> ship is over two years old, being one of the first Park ships built on this coast. Changes made in new construction during this period are very noticeable and this vessel lacks many of the improvements featured in more recent products of the local [west coast] yards.[13]

It was October 1944 and the old *Kootenay Park*, a North Sands coal burner, was about to be transferred to the British Ministry of War Transport as the *Fort Nisqually*. The replacement to which it was being compared was the new *Kootenay Park*, a Burrard-built Victory fresh from the yard. The crews certainly found the newer ships a marked improvement, but more significant were the economies of operation that the Victory offered. Not only were fewer firemen and no trimmers necessary, but bunker fuel oil required much less stowage space than bulky coal and could be stowed in the ship's double-bottom, thereby freeing more space for revenue-producing cargo. Weight was saved by the elimination of one boiler, further increasing cargo capacity. Refuelling was also speeded up thereby cutting turnaround time. Given availability, oil was in all respects, the preferred fuel. It was cleaner and offered greater efficiency, permitting the maintaining of constant steam pressures and consequently steadier steaming.

As it developed, the U.S. capped its orders for Canadian cargo ships at ninety of the 10,000 tonners, all of them North Sands coal burners. The U.S. Maritime Commission had originally contracted for one hundred ships, ten of them to be 4700 DWT Gray types, but it cancelled the order for the smaller ships. According to the Department of Munitions and Supply the change in U.S. policy vis-à-vis purchase of Canadian ships was associated with the exchange of the two national currencies. It is possible also that Liberty ships were streaming out of American shipyards at such a rate that some of them could be, and were, diverted to the British Ministry of War Transport. The closing of the U.S. order book led to a further development in the form of the Canadian variant of the basic North Sands design. The Canadian was a convertible that was adaptable to being fired by either coal or oil. While retaining most other features of the Victory, the new type reverted to Scotch marine boilers, which were considered more suitable for the dual role. Provision for both coal bunkers and fuel oil tanks also had to be made. The advantages of oil over coal notwithstanding, coal remained the fuel of choice for the British because of its ample availability in the home islands. In the event, ironically, all the Canadian convertibles were assigned to Park Steamship Company, and it appears that most of them were operated as oil burners.

The second type of Canadian-built dry cargo vessel to carry the Park name was the 4700 DWT Gray ship. Like the larger North Sands ships, the Grays were of British origin, based on a design by William Gray & Company of West Hartlepool, England. They were selected principally to meet the requirements of coastwise service. Of three-island layout, they had an overall length of 328 ft., a breadth of 46.5 ft., and draft of just under 21 ft., were powered by triple expansion engines of 1176 IHP with coal-fired Scotch marine boilers and were capable of 10 knots. After twenty-seven had been built, some changes were made to the cargo derrick arrangements and accommodation, the ten ships so altered being designated the Revised type. A further modification of the final half dozen saw the introduction of a 'tween deck with this variant becoming known as the Dominion type.[14]

* * *

One of the North Sands ships and twelve of the Victory ships were built as tankers. The North Sands tanker, the *Point Pelee Park*, was almost ready to go as a dry cargo vessel when it was decided to convert it into an oil tanker. The conversion, which necessitated the installation of oil tanks and pumping equipment, was accomplished in two and a half months and resulted in something of a marine anomaly in the form of a coal-fired oil tanker. The twelve oil-burner Victory tankers which followed the *Point Pelee Park* were, unlike her, all laid down as tankers.

These Park tanker variants, while lacking the efficiency of regular purpose-designed tankers, filled a vital need at a time when conventional tanker capacity was at a premium. In their appearance they enjoyed a natural camouflage that made them a less attractive target for an enemy. Externally, they appeared to differ little from the dry cargo vessels, an important consideration because the unmistakable profile of conventional tankers made them targets of first choice for the German Navy.

Also sailing under the Park flag were six smaller Canadian-designed and -built tankers of 3600 DWT. Powered by aft-mounted Diesel engines, these twin screw vessels had a length overall of 259 ft. and breadth of 44 ft. A critical design specification was that they have a length one foot less than that of the shortest lock in the St. Lawrence canal system. Because of their size they could serve in the Great Lakes as well as coastal waters. One of their main cargoes was aviation fuel to Newfoundland, to meet the demands of thirsty bombers about to be ferried overseas.

Yet another Park tanker was the *Riding Mountain Park*, an ancient vessel of pre-World War I vintage that had been a dredge before being converted into a 2000 DWT tanker by Wartime Merchant Shipping. Diesel-powered, she measured 245 ft. between perpendiculars and 43 ft. in breadth.

* * *

The Park ships, built to meet a wartime emergency, did what they were intended to do in war, and more, carrying on for many years of peacetime service. Nevertheless, they had their faults and no lack of critics to point them out. A Naval Boarding Service report of 4 November 1943 on the *High Park*, docked in Saint John, N.B., quoted the Chief Officer as stating that there was no comparison between his former ship, the *Carnesk*, and the Park boats. The Parks were poor sea boats, according to this officer, as they had not enough freeboard (about 10 ft.) when fully loaded. A related criticism may be that of Captain John M. Mann of Oakville, Ontario, who served as Second Officer on the *Belwoods Park*, and says he found it,

> and I suppose other Park ships very dirty [wet] when in a following sea.
> Even in the slightest sea they would without warning ship water amidships
> and frequently flood the officers' accommodation.

On the other hand, Joseph Wood of St. Thomas, Ontario, who served as a messman aboard the *Belwoods Park* and whose duties included housekeeping the officers' cabins, refutes the suggestion that they were ever flooded, at least during his time of service.

In yet another Naval Boarding Service report the unsubstantiated claim was made that Park boats were not suitable for the North Atlantic trade. The author of that opinion was unidentified, fortunately for his credibility, given that several hundred Parks/Forts/Oceans and thousands of their first cousins, the Liberties, made tens of thousands of safe crossings of that recalcitrant body of water, both during the war and in decades following.

One Park characteristic that was apparently more disconcerting than dangerous was referred to in a west coast 1944 Naval Boarding Service report where it was noted that during bunkering of the *Mohawk Park*, which had a deck load of lumber, she took a list of eight degrees in still water: "She is obviously 'tender' as other Parks similarly loaded have been." The sudden listing was possibly more indicative of inexperienced engineers acquainting themselves with unfamiliar valves than it was with any inherent instability in the ship design. A similar incident is recalled on the *Green Hill Park* during loading for her maiden voyage. While taking on a deckload of timber dockside at Port Alberni on Vancouver Island, the ship suddenly listed heavily to port. During the next several days of loading, she was gradually righted, only to assume a lesser starboard list which was not eliminated until after the ship departed Port Alberni, B.C., for San Pedro, California. Albeit a solution had seemingly been found for the listing inclination, word of the Port Alberni incident preceded the *Green Hill Park* across the wide Pacific Ocean to Brisbane, Australia, its first port of call after San Pedro. Here the ship was forced to remain at anchor in Brisbane Roads for nine days before being allowed to proceed upriver to the Port of Brisbane for discharge of cargo. The delay, it was said, was because the local pilots feared the *Green Hill Park* might capsize in the river and block the channel. While their fears were groundless, their caution was understandable in that Brisbane was then a major staging port for support of American military operations in the South Pacific. A blocking of the river would have caused serious supply problems.

One criticism made of the basic North Sands ship was that it lacked input from ship operators in its design. The members of the British Technical Merchant Shipbuilding Mission included "not one shipowner," it was stressed by Thomas C. Steven, editor of *Canadian Shipping and Marine Engineering News*,[15] who contended that this led to shortcomings in the ship's ability to accommodate the vast and varied conglomeration of goods and materials the publicists were boasting could be carried in its spacious holds. According to Mr. Steven,

> The stowage plan of a vessel loaded with this cargo would certainly be a most enlightening and welcome document to anyone who has had any experience on loading operations on a vessel of this type. It is to be feared that many of the suppliers of this diversified cargo would receive notification that a large part of their consignment had had to be shortshipped for want of suitable stowage space.

Mr. Steven's criticism notwithstanding, it is difficult to see how it would have been possible, even with shipowners' input, to arrive at a design more versatile and adaptable in meeting the incredibly diverse demands of wartime merchant shipping. To be fair to Mr. Steven, his concerns were largely focused on the fact that the Parks, with their built-in obsolescence, would not be able to compete in postwar shipping with, in particular, the fleet of state-of-the-art American Victory class ships (not to be confused with the Victory version of the Canadian-built North Sands ship) that were being built by the U.S. Maritime Commission in a program paralleling that for the Liberty ships.

The Canadian-built 10,000 tonners, it appears, did not encounter structural problems to the same degree as the U.S. Liberty ships. Their tried-and-true riveted construction, though slower than welding, proved advantageous in respect of hull strength. A disadvantage was that it added considerable weight not only in the form of the 400,000 rivets[16] but also the extra steel necessary for the overlap of the plates, neither of which were required for the seam-welded Liberty ship hulls.

In terms of comparative strength, there was nothing inherently wrong with welding, as was ultimately proven, but at the time it was still considered to be in its infancy[17] in its application to ship construction. And as practiced in the hurry-up of Liberty ship construction it was sometimes below acceptable standard due to low welder skills level, carelessness and poor supervision, all the by-products of the pressures of an emergency-fuelled mass production program.18 The welding also set up stresses that did not occur with riveting, particularly in the case of the Liberty, which was a welded adaptation of a riveted design. The combination of welding and mild steel, the standard material of merchant ship construction for the period, set up or exaggerated stress concentrations that were not critical in riveted construction. In the welded Liberties, this led to a spate of so-called brittle fractures, especially at low temperatures. Eventually the causes of these and other structural problems were pinpointed and corrected,[19] but not before there were numerous well-publicized Liberty ship failures. At one point the U.S. Army ruled that Liberty ships could not be used as troop carriers.[20] The records that were set in the production of the all-welded Liberty ships came at a price.

Although the riveted construction of the Canadian Parks and Forts fortuitously kept them mostly free of catastrophic breakups, that is not to say that they were without structural fault, as one Park crew learned to their alarm. Travelling light westbound in a violent Atlantic gale in January 1947, the *Tecumseh Park* had her main deck plates split almost two-thirds of the way across, with a sound like a cannon shot (characteristic of a brittle fracture). As described by Basil Charman of Whitehorse, Yukon Territory, the ship's bosun at the time, the fracture occurred between the galley bulkhead and the rear coaming of No. 3 hatch. To prevent further progression of the split, the ship was quite literally lashed together by heavy steel cable stretched around the superstructure and tensioned. Fortunately, the storm abated and the ship was able to make way at five knots though her troubles were far from over. With fuel running short, she had to call for a tow by the U.S. rescue tug *Mesopelia* to complete the run into Bermuda for repairs.

In a postwar incident recalled by Jack Stewart of Burlington, Ontario, a fireman on the *Tantara* (ex-*Whiterock Park*), his ship suffered damage similar to the *Tecumseh Park* when it encountered violent typhoons while en route to Shanghai:

> We lost part of our deck load, ventilators sheared off. When we did arrive in Shanghai we had to have some plates repaired midship. They were damaged when the ship tried to sit on a sea midship and nothing at either end, and then tried to sit on a sea at each end with nothing midship! You had to be there!

Such conditions, known respectively as hogging and sagging, subject a ship's hull to enormous structural stress.

On balance the Parks and Forts proved to be sturdy, reliable ships that in just doing their job played a key war role. "These vessels are very capable," said Captain John A. Wright, Master of the *Green Hill Park*, "well-found and well-equipped and handle extremely well. I am very glad to have command of a vessel of this type and hope I will be able to keep her in good shape."[21]

Chapter Ten # SHIPS OF WAR

"**A**s fast as Park Steamship Ltd. freighters come into this port," began a Vancouver datelined news story in the January 1946 edition of a Canadian trade magazine,[1] "they are being shorn of their defensive guns, armour and their wartime equipment, to form a mountain of steel on Granville Island." The report went on to say that in the shearing process each 10,000 ton ship was being relieved of between seventy-five and one hundred tons of metal comprising guns, rocket weapons and such equipment as minesweeping paravanes, torpedo nets and booms and AA automatic weapons "tubs" (armour-protected gun pits) as well as degaussing equipment, ammunition magazines and the built-in quarters for the Navy gun crews.

With fifty-four of the Park ships scheduled to be stripped in Vancouver of their Defensively Equipped Merchant Ship (DEMS) state, that mountain of now unneeded steel was expected to reach about 5,000 tons of mostly scrap for disposal by War Assets Corporation; only the guns would be salvaged and sent to the Naval Armament Depot in Esquimalt on Vancouver Island. But the Vancouver pile represented the discards from only about one-third of the 10,000 ton Park ships that were produced and sent to sea by Canada during WW II; the two-thirds balance of the fleet was similarly being disarmed and returned to civilian mufti at Halifax. It may have been that some of the vessels completed in the fading months of the war, or in the immediate postwar period, never received any DEMS armaments, nevertheless, it is obvious that from the 10,000 ton freighters alone, the overall amount of related equipment removed on both coasts would have weighed in at well in excess of 10,000 tons. And then there were the 4700 ton Park ships, some forty in all, as well as a similar number of deep-sea ships already in the Canadian merchant fleet at outbreak of war, or acquired during the war, all mounting a variety of DEMS weapons and equipment which they now surrendered without protest.

It was no wonder that the DEMS scrap pile should be so enormous. The 12-pounder forward gun standard on the 10,000 DWT Parks alone weighed 7,000 pounds with mounting. Max Reid, chronicler of the WW II DEMS organization,[2] makes the point that a Park ship was more heavily armed than a naval frigate, so each one clearly had a lot of suddenly superfluous metal to give up. The 75 to 100 tons of deadweight this DEMS equipment represented could now make way for an additional 75 to 100 tons of payload capacity.

* * *

The practice of arming merchant ships goes back centuries to early in the age of sail. Indeed, the first warships were simply merchant ships on which guns had been mounted; naval ships designed specifically for an offensive role followed later. In the more modern context of the age of steam and ships of steel, however, the mounting of defensive weaponry on merchant vessels was first introduced on an extensive scale during World War I, and even then not until after Germany had adopted a policy of unrestricted submarine warfare.

Mindful of the heavy losses attributed to submarine attacks of more than two decades earlier, Canadian Naval planners were in 1938 already discussing what had to be done to give Canadian deep-sea ships some measure of defensive capability. In May of that year, an RCN Committee produced a report[3] outlining a policy for the Canadian Government with regard to defensive measures, beginning with the recommendation that Canadian-registered ships should be "stiffened" (i.e., structurally reinforced to withstand the shock of heavy weapons firing, enabling the quick mounting of defensive armament in time of war). The report said there were thirty-eight vessels of Canadian registry that might be candidates for stiffening, but these did not include Canadian Pacific's liners and Beaver class cargo ships, almost all of which were of British registry. Two exceptions were the *Empress of Russia* and the *Empress of Asia*, both of which, though on the Canadian registry, were tagged under a special RN arrangement for conversion into Armed Merchant Cruisers.

Of the thirty-eight Canadian-registered vessels under consideration for stiffening, Canadian National Steamships' Lady boats were described as the most important. The Naval Service Committee recommended that each of the five Lady boats should be stiffened at Government expense to permit the mounting of a 4-inch anti-sub gun, with provision for an ammunition magazine. Anti-aircraft protection would be in the form of machine guns, for which no stiffening was necessary. In a telling reflection of the state of Canada's preparedness a little more than a year before the country would go to war, the Committee took note of the fact that, "At present the Canadian Government does not possess guns and mountings," but that, "A number of guns and suitable mountings are stored at Esquimalt on Imperial account." It was hoped that Britain would make these available.

Additional recommendations were that the Lady boats should be fitted with paravanes for minesweeping and that a Merchant Navy defence course patterned on those existing in the U.K. should be instituted at Halifax. The order of priority for stiffening was set out, large cargo ships leading off, followed by intermediate passenger/cargo ships, large passenger ships, and, at the bottom of the list, tankers. The logic for the low priority assigned to the deep-sea tankers, in the Committee's opinion (which was soon to be proved faulty in the extreme), was that those of

Canadian registry were not of major importance to Canada because it was possible to import oil by other means—pipeline, lake and coastal shipping, and rail tank cars. It was noted that there were seven Canadian tankers on the east coast and one on the west coast, "however, both on the east coast and to a lesser extent on the west coast, movement of crude oil is effected by U.S. tankers."

In a 4 February 1939 memo to the Deputy Minister of National Defence, RAdm. (later VAdm.) Percy Nelles, RCN Chief of Naval Staff, agreed with the Naval Service Committee's recommendations, with the exception that he was in favour of arming oil tankers. He also reported that provision had been made in the 1939-40 estimates for the purchase of guns and ammunition, and that Naval Service would provide technical members of gun crews for the armed merchant vessels.

Late in August, when it was clear that war was imminent, the British Secretary of State for Dominion Affairs advised Canada's Secretary of State for External Affairs that the U.K. was proceeding with the mounting of defensive armaments and the carrying of munitions in merchant ships in peacetime. On the day the world went to war once again, 3 September 1939, Germany countered with the declaration that every vessel of the British Merchant Navy was to be regarded as a warship. On 25 September 1939, an Order In Council authorized the defensive arming of fifteen Canadian-registered merchant ships.[4]

With the alignment of Canada beside Britain as a fellow belligerent (after delaying a week to demonstrate independent initiative), the Canadian Minister of National Defence reported that a stiffening program was underway for all ships of 500 tons gross or over then under construction or to be built in Canada. Those up to 1,000 tons were to be stiffened to allow one gun to be mounted in a position well aft, while for those over 1,000 tons the reinforcing was to be for one low angle gun aft and one high angle gun in any suitable position. The British offered to loan, without charge, guns and mountings for ships operated by the Dominions and Colonies in trade with the U.K. The offer did not include the cost of stiffening or ammunition. Paravanes for minesweeping were also to be provided under a similar arrangement. Later, the British loan offer was expanded to include anti-magnetic mine degaussing equipment, with the requisite special insulated cable to be supplied by Canada at its own expense.

Initially, the work did not exactly proceed swiftly; by the end of January 1940, only one 6-inch gun, five 4-inch guns, and one HA 3-inch gun had been fitted to Canadian merchant vessels.

Meanwhile, there was a great deal of discussion going on about how DEMS personnel should be signed on ship's articles, the consensus being that they should be designated "deck hands" rather than "supernumeraries" or "supplementaries." The explanation for this apparent nitpicking was to be found in the legal definition of a defensively equipped merchant ship, in which it was stated that such a ship was to carry a "normal complement" of crew. Presumably the presence of Naval personnel would make it offensively equipped and therefore by definition a warship. The debate seems to have been academic, considering that Germany had declared from the outset that every vessel of the British Merchant Navy was to be regarded as a warship. The Germans certainly were not about to differentiate Canadian from British.

At this early stage, for all practical purposes there were no DEMS training facilities in Canada for naval personnel, much less for the merchant seamen who were to be assigned the role of supporting cast. For the latter, any training initially had to be of the on-the-job variety, though even this was not immediately accessible because of the time it was taking to install weapons aboard the small number of Canadian merchant ships operating in September 1939. For the naval personnel, the solution was to send them off to established RN gunnery training establishments in the U.K., and it is estimated about two hundred earned their DEMS rating this way.[5] Naval personnel assigned to DEMS were normally already trained as Anti-Aircraft Lewis Gunners (AALGs) or other gunnery rates such as Quarters Rating (QRs) or Layer Rating (LRs).

Unlike WW I, when the threat to merchant shipping came only from surface raiders, submarines and mines, attack from the sky now posed a new and added deadly element of danger. Accordingly, emerging WW II DEMS courses for both Naval ratings and merchant seamen gave equal weight to training on active defence measures against air attacks and attacks from surfaced vessels. With firing ranges already existent, the RCN was better positioned and equipped to quickly establish anti-surface training than it was for an anti-aircraft program, though active live AA weapons firing practices could be carried out from Navy training vessels. To organize a comprehensive AA course required time, seemed to be what was being said by the Canadian response[6] to a late 1941 British request for a progress report. It had taken nearly a month for the response to be forthcoming, possibly because its authors were exercising their creative writing skills in an attempt to put the best face on a program that, lacking training equipment and facilities, was still lagging. Nevertheless, it was reported optimistically to the British that AA weapons training was now being provided by DEMS staffs, as well as RCAF instructors, at Halifax, Sydney, Nova Scotia, Montreal, Saint John, New Brunswick, and Esquimalt and Vancouver in British Columbia, with facilities "which are not as yet completely adequate."

Among the essential aids slow to arrive were instructional eye shooting films and most importantly, Dome Teachers, five of which were to be erected, at Halifax,

Sydney, Saint John, Montreal and Esquimalt. The Domes were large hemispheres (about 20 ft. radius) which, by means of a combination of special interior lighting giving the illusion of infinite sky, and the projection on a Dome's interior surface of moving images of aircraft in various modes of attack, were used to instruct in such basic aiming techniques as leading the target. Duck hunters usually performed well in the Domes.

* * *

That in late 1941 the setting up of the Canadian DEMS operation might seem to be proceeding at a snail's pace should be no cause for surprise. DEMS was just one relatively small component of a mushrooming RCN that was agonizing its way through the early stages of an unprecedented program of expansion, the Royal Navy had its hands full at home so could no longer be entirely relied on as an ever-ready provider of equipment and experienced training personnel, and Canada's still tiny manufacturing sector had to be mobilized to provide domestic sources of supply. There was much to be done.

Fortunately, the demand for DEMS personnel and DEMS training for Canadian merchant seamen did not reach significant proportions until 1942, the year deliveries of the Park ships began, growing rapidly in 1943 and peaking in 1944. With this speedy build-up of the well-armed Park fleet, the urgency of the requirement for DEMS Naval ratings lead Cdr. A. E. Woodward, RCN(T), DEMS Officer East Coast, to instigate a recruiting campaign directed at RCNVR Divisions across the country, citing an early need for three hundred men for the east coast and one hundred for the west coast.

In a promotional message to Divisional COs, Commander Woodward described DEMS career opportunities in glowing terms. He depicted DEMS as a very special service offering

> vast opportunities for the rating to do big things for the cause of humanity in general, and for this service only the best type of man will do. He is specially selected and trained in all the newest weapons of attack and defence, and technical machines and instruments. Each man has to be self confident, capable of making quick decisions and acting upon them, beating the split second, upon which so much depends when attacked by airplanes with speeds of over 300 mph.
>
> An individualist in every respect, the Senior Layer Rating is practically the Gunnery Officer of the merchant vessel on which he is serving, and the Advisory Counsel to the Master for all the defensive armament aboard. He has no Gunnery Officer or Gunner's Mate to get him out of trouble. And above all, the DEMS Ratings have to be diplomatic to get the best [out] of the ships' crews who will help him to man and fight the many weapons

supplied. His personality and leadership must be of the highest order and his conduct exceptional at all times. He will travel to the uttermost corners of the earth, and in doing so will expand his wisdom, meeting exceptionally fine men, and people of both sexes, in his journeyings.

Whether or not Commander Woodward's evangelistic testimonial in praise of DEMS service was responsible, recruits were won and the organization grew.[*] The Domes were built, the instructional films produced, teaching aids of all kinds obtained and instructors trained. By July 1944, Captain E. S. Brand, Director of Trade Division, reported that approximately thirteen hundred of the authorized DEMS complement of fifteen hundred had already been obtained. With an intake of eighty per month, he expected the full complement to be reached by October.

That, however, would provide an insufficient number of ratings to man the 222 Canadian merchant ships Brand expected would be in service by the end of 1944. With the per ship complements ranging from a high of ten for the 10,000 ton Parks, of which he foresaw 104 by year end, to two for the less heavily armed mixed fleet of 71 lakers and coasters, plus allowances for base administrative and training staff (80), personnel under training to higher rating (50), and leave and illness at 11 per cent (166), Brand estimated a more realistic complement would be nearly 1700.

He observed that the 10,000 ton Park complement had originally been fourteen[**] but due to changes involving armament this had been reduced to ten, a number that he did not consider excessive to fight and maintain a typical array of weapons comprising one 4-inch high angle/low angle (HA/LA) gun, one 12-pounder HA/LA gun, seven 20-mm Oerlikons and two twin .50s. It is apparent that Naval Staff was contemplating further reductions in DEMS complement, and Brand was trying to forestall this. He argued that most of the ships were employed in long voyages to Australia, India, South Africa, etc., that the majority of the ratings were inexperienced, that cooperation from the merchant crews was not always adequate, and that DEMS ratings gave a steadying effect to the assisting merchant seamen, whose weapons training was to a lower standard. It was also noted that a complement of twenty-four USN personnel was assigned to similarly armed U.S. ships.[7]

Brand's criticism suggesting that merchant crews were uncooperative with DEMS must have penetrated Park Steamship's Montreal headquarters, prompting a memo

---

[*] Max Reid, author of *DEMS At War! Defensively Equipped Merchant Ships and the Battle of the Atlantic 1939-1945*: "Up until at least 1944, DEMS were Volunteers from General Service. In my case, May 1943, sixty volunteers were asked for during Divisions, Ship's company fallen in at HMCS *York*. There was no screening process. If you volunteered, you were in."

[**] Sometimes the number was even higher (e.g., in 1944, the *Dunlop Park* had fifteen, compared to only seven on the *Beaton Park* in 1943).

to all Managing Operators from J. S. Thomson, the company's Marine Superintendent, complaining that some ship masters were not cooperating with DEMS by allowing merchant seamen to assist in gun shoots and drills. He urged more cooperation and encouraged ships' officers to take DEMS gunnery courses when in Vancouver, Halifax or Montreal. The memo also noted that increasingly DEMS ratings were being required to perform ship's duties, including stoking. That practice, Thomson allowed, was to be discouraged because it lowered the efficiency of the DEMS ratings to perform their primary duties. Although Thomson's memo implied that the ratings were being "required" to perform merchant seaman duties, in fact their participation was voluntary except in an emergency, and they were paid at merchant service rates of pay.

Despite Brand's arguments in favour of holding the 10,000 ton DEMS complement to no less than ten, there was further slippage to nine, which he attributed to the fact that deliveries of Oerlikon guns from the munitions industry were slow, so that ships were going to sea with less than their assigned number of these particular weapons. By September 1944, he was fighting a further drastic reduction to five, such as had been introduced on British ships.[8] "Owing to only moderate cooperation of Canadian merchant crews, this reduction cannot be recommended for Canadian registered ships." His objections to no avail, Naval Staff approved a cut to five in DEMS complement on Canadian ships sailing exclusively on the North Atlantic run. The rationale was that the likelihood of air attack on the North Atlantic had become negligible, justifying a cut in the manning scale for the light AA weapons. On other Park ship trade routes, the DEMS complement remained at the higher levels.

* * *

The question raised by Captain Brand of poor cooperation of merchant crews could often be traced to the ship masters, some of whom, considerations of self-preservation notwithstanding, were reluctant to allow seamen to leave their normal duties to participate in gun drills, live ammunition practice "shoots," or the standing of gun watches. For the seamen's part, deckhands in particular, DEMS activity was a welcome break in sea routine and a chance to escape for a while from the all too common but seemingly fruitless chipping and scraping of rust, and the endless painting of acres of steel.

"Gunnery practice at sea was fun," recalls Kelso S. Whyte of Charlottetown, P.E.I., a *Runnymede Park* Ordinary Seaman. "The DEMS gunners got to show off and it broke the routine for a day." Others, like Brock Cummings of Prescott, Ontario, participated in DEMS activity with even greater enthusiasm. "I was chumming around with a Newfoundlander," says Cummings, who was an AB on the *Riverdale Park* at the time:

I believe I was the trainer on the 12-pounder and he was the layer, or vice versa. We were quite interested in these guns, and of course the Oerlikons. We took every gunnery course we possibly could. One morning we went over to the firing range at West Saint John, with the big guns and everything. They were amazed at what we could do. We knocked everything. We fired at a sock towed along by an airplane. They used to say the safest place was the sock, but it wasn't with Newfie and me.

Gunnery practice could also be dangerous to your health. When Murray Sommerville of Toronto was a radio operator on the *Whiteshell Park*, the ship's Chief Engineer had a close call:

This trip they decided they were going to have a gunnery practice. They had a corvette drop a smoke float off the starboard bow and they fired at it with the 12-pounder forward gun and the 4-inch aft gun. Nobody comes close, of course. After everything was over and secured, the kid in a midship Oerlikon turret decided to get himself out. He reaches up and goes to swing himself out, grabs the trigger, lets off a blast of the Oerlikon gun, shoots the stern out of the lifeboat about six feet above the Chief Engineer's head. The Chief was out on deck there with his handgun taking target practice or something. Anyway, he came within a few feet of being splattered.

Only the ships on the outside of the convoy were supposed to be firing at the smoke float. Actually, we were supposed to be the only one firing at it. An American about the third column in hears the gunfire. He says, "Oh, there's a smoke target there, let's go!" He starts shooting damn shells over our head, like a bloody fool.

Shortly after this, as soon as we got to port, they had railings put around the gun turrets, soft iron rolled bars with hills and valleys so that the gun barrels couldn't point at any part of the ship. Seemed like a reasonable idea. Couldn't point at Chief Engineers either.

* * *

Captain Brand's assertion, in his arguments for a higher DEMS complement, that the weapons training of merchant crews was of a lower standard than that for DEMS service personnel, was a statement of fact, not a criticism. How could it be otherwise? The course for Navy DEMS gunners was an intensive one of up to eight weeks in duration. As described by Max Reid,[9] the graduates emerged from their training with detailed knowledge of the mechanics of the many weapons they were expected to use, as well as skill in their operation and maintenance.

With regard to the gunnery training, the examinations were based on two aspects: memorizing the "idle movement" of the breech mechanisms of the larger guns and the ability to assemble the automatic weapons while blindfolded. The former to ensure that we could fix any of our automatic machine guns in the heat of battle and in extenuating circumstances. However, all this was for naught if we failed to pass the ability to take charge of a squad on a parade square. The idea was that if we could not command a group on a parade square, then we could certainly not command a gun's crew, made up mainly of merchant seamen, in a gun battle in the heat of the night.

The training received by the merchant seamen, on the other hand, was in the form of quickie two-day courses that varied in their degree of effectiveness on the size of the class that had to be passed through in the two days. A small group, for example, meant that each individual could have more time in the Dome Teacher, or on the firing range. The time for hands-on activity for individuals in a large group was correspondingly lower. At the completion of a course the seaman could typically find himself in possession of a Merchant Navy A/A Gunnery Course Certificate of Proficiency stating a mite optimistically that he was "qualified in the firing, cleaning and lubrication of Lewis, Oerlikon and Browning."

* * *

The array of weapons and passive defence devices with which the *Green Hill Park* was equipped, was typical for the 10,000 ton Park ships joining the fleet in 1944. A brand-new Victory class from Burrard Dry Dock Company of Vancouver, she fairly bristled with armaments to defend against both surface and air attacks. At the bow was a 12-pounder HA/LA gun intended primarily for use against surface vessels or surfaced submarines. At the stern, mounted atop the deckhouse for the seamen's/firemen's messes was a 4-inch HA/LA gun that could be equally effective against surface or air attacks. Also atop the same deckhouse, on an elevated mounting immediately behind the 4-inch gun, was a Pillar Box,[10] an anti-aircraft rocket weapon which was armed with twenty rail-launched 2-inch high explosive rockets in racks, ten on each side. On some ships, a 40-mm Bofors AA gun or an Oerlikon was an alternative for this position.

Between the bow and stern extremities of the ship where the heavy weapons were spotted, were no less than eight armoured gun tubs for light automatic weapons, primarily AA. On the *Green Hill Park*, in only four of these tubs were there weapons mounted, 20-mm Oerlikons in all cases. Two gun tubs were located port and starboard at the aft end of the boat deck; two were port and starboard on the wings of the upper bridge. Two further tubs intended for, but lacking Oerlikons, were situated port and starboard of the foremast deckhouse. The remaining two tubs were port and starboard immediately ahead of the forward extremities of the captain's bridge deck. These were intended for Twin .50 machine guns,[*] which were also conspicuous by their absence. That the *Green Hill Park* had only half the number of light automatic weapons for which it had positions possibly could be attributed, in the case of the Oerlikons at least, to the fact that deliveries from industry were tardy.[11] Another consideration may have been that the hazard from air attack was much diminished in the area, the South Pacific, into which the *Green Hill Park* was shortly to venture.

The "armour" that afforded a measure of protection against shrapnel and small arms fire for the gun tubs was a sandwich of steel plate with a thick asphaltic filling. A similar shielding also covered the front of the navigating bridge, the ship's command centre.

The ship's anti-aircraft weaponry was rounded out with two Fast Aerial Mines (FAM) mounted port and starboard near the funnel. The FAM was a strange device which one could imagine had been conceived in a small dark room by two consenting boffins. It comprised a propelling rocket and some one thousand feet of light wire cable at the end of which was afixed an explosive device, or mine. When fired, the rocket trailed the wire cable into the air in front of an attacking aircraft. On reaching optimum altitude, two parachutes were automatically deployed, a large one at top of the cable and a smaller one at the lower end. The concept was that a strafing aircraft would fly into the trailing wire as it slowly descended. Once snagged, the wire would be dragged by the larger parachute until the mine made contact with the aircraft's structure with, it was hoped, satisfactorily destructive results. The mental picture of the FAM's trailing wire cable uncoiling at lightning speed from its metal basket, hissing like some berserk snake with a very lethal sting in its tail, inspired as least as much fear in the ship's crew as it was supposed to do in an enemy.

Most ships also carried a poor man's version of the FAM, the PAC (Parachute And Cable), which was sans bomb and trailed only some four hundred feet of cable, less than half the length of that for the FAM. Perhaps it was hoped that the cable would entangle a propeller.

The *Green Hill Park*, like other well-equipped Park ships, also went to sea with several passive DEMS devices. On either side of the foredeck were stowed the minesweeping paravanes, which looked rather like small unmanned aircraft. Their purpose was to be towed by cables attached to the large A-frame projecting from the ship's bow. When the anchor cable of a submerged mine was snagged by a paravane tow cable, it was diverted along the cable by the ship's forward motion

*These were to counter attacks by E-boats, the German Navy's speedy torpedo boats.

into the paravane's cutting jaws. Released from its anchor, the severed mine then popped to the surface where attempts would be made to explode it, usually by small arms fire.

A prominent recognition feature of the 10,000 ton Park ships was the towering (about 75 feet above deck level) booms for their torpedo nets[12]—known in navalese as Admiralty Net Defences (AND). Normally stowed in the vertical position against the ends of the mast crosstrees, the booms pivoted from base attachments on each side of the fore and aft masthouses. Deployment involved lowering the booms and winching the nets forward from the after booms. It was a sight to behold, the drawing of Brobdingnagian steel mesh curtains, their function being to entangle or divert attacking torpedoes. When in position, to increase the spread of the nets the foremast booms were swept forward while the mainmast booms were swept aft. The protection they afforded, probably as much psychological as real, covered approximately four-fifths of the ship's length. This included the vital engine room and most if not all of the living quarters for the crew.

How effective the nets were can never be known with exactness. While the reason for their being was appreciated as a morale booster, when the order came to stream them the ship's deckhands were sometimes less than enthusiastic. To deploy or stow the clumsy gear could be hard, dangerous work, even in the best of sea conditions. The nets also affected ship performance. When stowed, their weight added an element of top-heaviness, increasing rolling propensity. When deployed, the added drag reduced speed by about 2 knots, a significant slowing for a vessel that under ideal conditions was good for only 11 knots.

AND-equipped Park ships were usually positioned in the outside columns of convoys because their nets theoretically made them less vulnerable to submarine attack. Alex White of Regina, a radio operator on the *Green Gables Park*, recounts the comedy of errors that went on when his ship, positioned in the Coffin Corner (the last ship in an outside column), was ordered by the convoy commodore to lower its nets:

> They wanted us to put the nets down and we would tell them that if we put the nets down then we couldn't keep up with the convoy. Then the Commodore's vessel would come back: "*Green Gables*, why can't you keep up convoy speed?" And we'd come back: "We can keep up convoy speed if we don't have to put the nets down." You've got to picture this convoy—ten miles wide and three miles deep—the messages being relayed through several ships, all communicating by flashing Aldis signal lamps—the ships rolling and sometimes not getting the message through.
>
> Forty-eight hours later we were still sending the same messages back and forth. Finally, I'll never forget this Canadian corvette roaring over with

a loud hailer on: "What Goddamn problem do you have! Put the damn nets down!" And our reply: "We can't keep up [if we put the nets down], but if we leave them this way, fine." He roared off, just roared off through the convoy, going here, there and everywhere. If this damned corvette had come by in the first place, there never would have been a problem. It took forty-eight hours to solve that thing.

In contrast to the obviousness of the torpedo nets was the virtual invisibility of the degaussing equipment, basically a closed loop electrical cable completely encircling the interior of the hull below deck. It was a countermeasure to the magnetic mine, which the Germans had designed to be triggered by the magnetic field of a passing steel ship. By sending a current through the degaussing cable, the ship's magnetic field was effectively counteracted or reversed and thus should not activate a magnetic mine.

* * *

The Canadian ships that were already in service when the war began, and even the first Park deliveries, did not enjoy the built-in range of weaponry and passive defence equipment characteristic of the 10,000 ton Park ships joining the fleet by 1944. In the earlier years, weapons were in short supply and what was available was not always very formidable. "When I first went on the *Riverdale Park*," says Brock Cummings of his ship, a September 1943 delivery,

> we had very poor armament. We had a single Oerlikon on each side of the wing of the bridge, and we had a 12-pounder aft and a single Bofors above that. And on our boat deck, where the lifeboats were, we had twin Marlins on each side. They were a wonderful thing; you couldn't even shoot a seagull with them. I believe they were .30 calibre and they were belt-fed. They consisted of two little barrels about two and a half feet long. I was on the starboard Marlins and when we'd go on alert, you took along a hammer and a screw driver and a pair of pliers to the gun pit, because you might get off five or six rounds and then they would jam up.
>
> But afterwards, we went in drydock and they put Oerlikons on each side of the bridge. They switched our 12-pounder to the bow, put a 4-inch back aft, and we had Oerlikons on the boat deck, and so on.

Arthur Lockerbie of Sydney, Nova Scotia, recalls his time as a radio operator on the *SS Randa*, a ship which had a DEMS complement totalling one.

> In January 1942 I joined the *SS Randa*, a little old ex-Danish freighter flying the Canadian flag for the duration and run by the CNS. A new DEMS gunner signed on the same day and he had problems. His main anti-aircraft

gear was a Hotchkiss machine gun in a mount on monkey island, just forward of the funnel. Since aircraft dived from astern, he would not see anything until the plane had dropped the bomb and appeared over the stack. However, he had two stripped Lewis guns and he figured he could fire one until it got hot from out on the wing of the bridge, drop that and grab the other. The 6-inch gun on the stern was a relic from the first World War, so loose on the mount that if it was fired while the stern was rising on a wave the shell would hit about two miles beyond where he was aiming, and if the stern was dropping, the opposite would happen.

One day we had firing practice. They dropped a barrel over the stern and got ready to blast it. The gunner yelled "Pull!" with the stern rising, but the AB pulled the lanyard when the stern was dropping. The shell hit just astern of the ship, again miles short of the target. One of the ABs with a Scandinavian singsong said: "Gonner, are you not afraid you will sh*ooo*t the ship?"

Many Park ships were at sea when the last shot was fired in anger in August 1945. Some MN veterans remember that their ships were given permission to jettison their torpedo nets. *Tuxedo Park* radio operator Bill Hutcherson of Richmond, British Columbia, recalls that they had a celebratory fireworks display:

With the war now over and us on our way home to Vancouver, the DEMS approached Captain Stewart and asked if they couldn't dispose of some of the ammunition we had on board by shooting it off. Stewart felt this might be a good idea so we spent about three hours shooting our 4-inch gun, the 12-pounder, Oerlikons, Brownings—just having a field day getting rid of the ammunition. The empty cartridges were hoarded by many of the crew members and from there up to Vancouver, several brass ash trays, letter openers, you name it, were formed out of the resulting scrap that came from the spent shells.

Chapter Eleven **THE SHIPBUILDERS**

Canada's shipbuilding effort since the start of the war was described as "one of the most remarkable things in the history of the British Commonwealth" during a general debate in the House of Commons in London recently on wartime and postwar merchant shipping. Sir Arthur Salter, Joint Parliamentary Secretary to the Ministry of War Transport, said Canada is now building approximately the same tonnage of merchant ships as Great Britain, in addition to corvettes and other protective naval craft. Only the United States has a greater merchant shipbuilding program. "Canada has shown an astonishing power of adaptation in industrial capacity to the development of production of what is most needed in every war sphere," said Sir Arthur. Her shipbuilding effort was "magnificent."

News Report[1]

In the high international councils of war planning, the Parks and other wartime standard ships like them, were not thought of as ships at all. They were classed as "munitions," just another entry in the shopping list for war matériel, appearing somewhere after "bullets and corvettes" but before "tanks and trucks." And with all munitions, they shared the common characteristic of being expendable, just another of the consumables of war.

So thought the Allied joint planners, whose acquisitions and disposals of warriors and weapons had to be carried out with the cool detachment of a good accountant analyzing a financial statement. Not so detached were the shipyard workers, who could be forgiven for having difficulty thinking of the mountains of steel they were proudly sending down the slipways as consumable munitions. And certainly for the crews who took the ships to sea, any thought that they were aboard a consumable of war, if it had ever entered their minds, was quickly banished.

The utilitarian Park boats were just one part of the mighty wartime shipbuilding effort mounted by Canadian industry, accounting for less than half the immense merchant ship output that poured from east and west coast yards in less than four years. It was quite appropriate that a parliamentary secretary to the British Ministry of War Transport should all in one statement describe Canada's record of ship production as "remarkable," "astonishing," and "magnificent." How else could be described the delivery of 354[2] 10,000 DWT, 43 4700 DWT and 6 3600 DWT class ships in the brief timespan between the first delivery in December 1941 and shortly after the end of the war in August 1945? And all the while the shipbuilding industry was simultaneously turning out equally remarkable, astonishing and magnificent numbers of Naval vessels: 281 escort ships (destroyers, corvettes, frigates), 206 minesweepers, 254 tugs and 3,302 landing craft.

That shipbuilding emerged as Canada's largest single wartime industrial program does not seem to have left any lasting impression on the public mind. The achievements and scope of the aircraft manufacturing industry are well remembered but, in terms of both value of production ($900,000,000 plus) and peak numbers employed (116,000), it was outranked by shipbuilding where total payments to the yards and component manufacturers reached $1,185,000,000 by the end of 1945, and employment topped 126,000 in 1943, the year in which 150 cargo ships were delivered.[3] The value of cargo ships delivered alone, most of them 10,000 tonners, was $692,000,000. Salvage and ship repairs were responsible for another $206,000,000 value added to the work performed under the mantle of the shipbuilding industry.

One reason that in the 1990s there is a relatively low level of public appreciation of the record wartime shipbuilding program may be because the shipyards declined very rapidly after enjoying a brief postwar flurry of commercial orders. Out of sight, out of mind. What remains of the industry today has but a fingertip hold on life, survival depending almost entirely on existing Defence Department contracts for naval patrol frigates and minesweepers, plus B.C. government orders for ferries. The aircraft industry, by way of contrast, has continued to flourish with varying degrees of ongoing activity in both the military and commercial sectors, thereby maintaining a high public profile to the present day.

Yet, by any yardstick, past or present, Canada's wartime standard ships production program was of mega project rank, though its inauspicious beginning was certainly no harbinger of things to come. A measure of the task about to be undertaken is that at outbreak of war, Canadian shipyard employment was estimated to be as low as two thousand, all engaged in repair work. Moreover, no large deep-water ship had been launched in Canada since shortly after the First World War.[4] How the industrial transformation that took place was accomplished by a country that in 1939 was little more than an industrial toddler is remarkable indeed.

* * *

In the "Phony War" interval between the German invasion of Poland and the disastrous three-month period of 1940 that began with the German occupation of Norway in April and ended with the fall of France in June, it was, in London's mind, business as usual insofar as Britain's relationship with the Commonwealth countries was concerned. That is, in the war scenario as it seemed to be perceived by London, the Commonwealth countries would supply men and raw materials, the men to fight

THE SHIPBUILDERS

under British leadership, and the raw materials to be turned into tools of war by British industry. That was, after all, how the British Empire had once become mighty, not to mention wealthy.

By 1939, however, when a finally awakened British government realized it had run out of choices and was forced reluctantly to declare war, the leader of the Commonwealth was much reduced in terms of both might and wealth. It did not want—really could not afford—to expend scarce foreign reserves on purchases of munitions from abroad, and already looking ahead to postwar, London had no intention of nurturing industries in Canada or Australia that might compete with British industry. The status quo would do just nicely, thank you. For the first ten months of the war, Canadian industry waited in vain for meaningful war orders from the British. Indeed, not even Canada's own armed services seemed to be able to decide what their own immediate needs were, apart from, perhaps, boots and uniforms.

The series of military disasters that culminated in the evacuation of the British Army from Dunkirk, sans weapons, brought swift changes in attitude. The British Isles—in fact the very ideal of western democracy—faced peril of never previously encountered dimensions. Bottom-line concerns were thrust away to beyond infinity. Isolated, disarmed, Britain needed all manner of war supplies from wherever they could be obtained. Moreover, the need was immediate. The ocean supply lines bringing not only the new arms but also the foodstuffs and fuel to sustain the crowded island, had to be maintained despite the blockade being mounted by the growing U-boat fleet. Even at this early stage, the German Navy's strategy was showing the distinct possiblity of success. U-boats were sinking merchant ships faster than they could be replaced and would continue to do so well into the future. In October 1940 alone, long before the U-boat fleet reached peak operational strength in the North Atlantic, sixty-six merchant vessels went down[5] with their precious cargoes of weapons, fuel and bodily sustenance.

It was in this atmosphere of imminent danger that the Admiralty despatched a Technical Merchant Shipbuilding Mission to North America in September 1940. Lead by Robert C. Thompson, with Harry Hunter as the Marine Engineer member, the Mission also included representatives of Lloyd's and the Admiralty.[6] Mr. Thompson was head of the British shipbuilding firm of Joseph L. Thompson & Sons Ltd., Sunderland, England, which was the source of the cargo vessel design that became the basis for the Canadian-built Park and Fort ships, as well as for the similar American-built Ocean ships and eventually, the most famous of them all, the Liberty. Mr. Hunter was Technical Director of North Eastern Marine Engineering Co. Ltd., where the main engine design had originated. As described by Mr. Thompson, the Mission's mandate stated:[7]

The object of the Mission was to endeavour to obtain, at the earliest possible moment, the delivery of merchant tonnage from U.S.A. shipyards at the rate per annum of about sixty vessels of the tramp type of about 10,000 tons deadweight. Before leaving, we were also informed that it was hoped that it would be found possible to arrange for the Mission to investigate possibilities of merchant shipbuilding in Canada.

One of the Mission's early contacts in the U.S. was Todd Shipyards Inc. who, it emerged, was a joint owner of Seattle-Tacoma Shipyard, in partnership with a consortium of west coast civil engineering contractors known as Six Services Inc. The consortium was headed by Henry J. Kaiser, a builder of giant construction projects, the Grand Coulee Dam for one, but a neophyte in ship construction who was soon to be seen as the revolutionary who turned traditional shipbuilding on its ear. When the British Mission met with this group, Thompson recalled,

They produced a nicely coloured drawing of a modern British tramp steamer, and offered to build ships for us, providing they had reciprocating engines and water tube boilers—Scotch boilers might be possible—and a specification generally to meet the special conditions.

Brochuremanship was alive and well even in 1940. The Americans regarded as antiquated the triple expansion steam engine/coal-fired boilers combination specified, but the British choice was on the practical ground that they had ample domestic stocks of coal whereas fuel oil would have to be imported and should be conserved for military needs.

The Mission then travelled to Ottawa to call on C. D. Howe, Canada's recently appointed Minister of Munitions and Supply, and David B. Carswell, the department's Director General of Shipbuilding. The word again was that choice was limited to reciprocating engines, and Scotch boilers could be produced. On-site examinations of Canadian shipbuilding facilities in eastern Canada and on the west coast revealed that there were just four shipyards with a total of nine berths capable of handling ships of the 10,000 DWT category. They were: in the east, Canadian Vickers Limited, Montreal, with three berths; Davie Shipbuilding and Repairing Company Limited, Lauzon, Quebec, with two berths; and in the west, Burrard Dry Dock, Vancouver, with two berths, and Prince Rupert Dry Dock with two berths.

Subsequently, orders were placed on a cash basis in December 1940 for the first twenty, later increased to twenty-six 10,000 DWT ships, divided among the two eastern yards and Burrard in Vancouver. At the same time sixty similar ships were ordered in the U.S. from the Todd/Kaiser syndicate on the west coast, and from Todd-Bath Ironworks Corp. on the east coast. At both the U.S. locations the British financed the construction of new shipyards specifically designed for the production of the Ocean class vessels.[8]

Although the ships to be produced on both sides of the international boundary were based on a parent Joseph L. Thompson & Sons Limited ship identified as the *Empire Liberty*, there were sufficient differences, principally in methods of construction, that it was considered desirable to make type distinctions. Thus the American-built ships became known as the Oceans, all of them bearing that family surname— *Ocean Liberty*, *Ocean Peace*, etc. The Canadian ships, on the other hand, were designated as the North Sands type (after the Thompson North Sands yard where the *Empire Liberty* had been designed and built), but were named after Canadian parks and historic forts.

Essentially, all the differences between the types sprang from the very significant fact that the Oceans were of all-welded construction while the Canadian North Sands vessels were 90 percent riveted. Because welded construction had been widely adopted by U.S. yards, the British structural plans had to be reworked to conform with American practice. The few Canadian yards, however, still practiced traditional riveted construction methods, combined with a limited amount of welding. The reworked American welded plans would have been readily available, but conversion by the Canadian yards to all-welded construction could only have meant unaffordable delays while the ship berths underwent the necessary extensive modification, while the required welding equipment was obtained from the U.S., and while the workforce was retrained. For this reason of unacceptable delay, when the first keel under the Canadian program was laid in April 1941, the commitment was for close adherence to the riveted design working from original British plans. In the event, as the program expanded and Canadian experience grew, the amount of welding increased substantially, though riveted construction always remained as the dominant form.

One drawback to riveted construction was that, because of the physical strength associated with heavy rivet guns, the participation of women was limited. As welders, however, they were under no such handicap and demonstrated excellent skills. Consequently, the number of women employed on Liberty ship all-welded construction in U.S. west coast yards at one point exceeded 30 percent of the workforce, compared with, at the most, 7 percent in Canadian west coast yards. Although women filled a wide range of shipyard jobs other than welding, Canadian shipbuilders were never able to tap this very large pool of potential workers to the same extent as could their U.S. counterparts, even at a time when there was a desperate shortage of manpower in Canada. That having been said, the numbers of women employed in Canadian shipyards were still significant. At the Foundation Maritime Pictou, Nova Scotia, yard alone, some six hundred women worked at what had hitherto been considered exclusively male tasks. That yard would eventually account for over half of all Canadian launchings of the 4700 DWT Gray ships.

* * *

By the time the keel was laid by Canadian Vickers in Montreal for the hull that was to become the *Fort Ville Marie*, the first ship to be delivered under the British order, the losses in the North Atlantic had risen to crisis proportions. In March 1941, 119 ships totalling 489,299 tons gross fell victim, a figure estimated to be equal to one quarter of Britain's annual building capacity, and more than half of all the tonnage on order in the U.S. and Canada. "In these critical circumstances," John deN. Kennedy of the Department of Munitions and Supply recorded, "an urgent call came to Canada to build as many cargo ships as possible."[9]

The initial response was to approve a program to build to Canadian account, 88 North Sands class 10,000 DWT vessels and 5 4700 DWT Gray ships. The smaller Grays, also a British design, were intended to provide coastal services where many of the ports of call were not capable of accommodating deep draft vessels. That initial Canadian order was just a start. Shortly after the Hyde Park Agreement was reached on 20 April 1941 by Prime Minister Mackenzie King and U.S. President Franklin D. Roosevelt, the U.S began ordering 10,000 ton ships from Canada, initially on a one-by-one basis. However, on 15 June 1942, a contract was signed by the U.S. consolidating all the orders to a total of 100, including 10 4700 DWT Gray ships. In the event, the Gray component of the order was not exercised and only the 90 10,000 DWT vessels, all bearing Fort names, were acquired by the U.S. Maritime Commission to be handed over to the British under the terms of Lend-Lease. Almost month by month the order book was expanded by additions for both Canadian and U.S. accounts until by July 1943 the number of ships delivered and on order had reached 366 of the 10,000 ton class and 36 4700 tonners.

It was clear that if results were to be achieved within the crisis timeframe prevailing, there would have to be not only a substantial expansion of shipyard capacity but also a central organization to administer and coordinate all aspects of the program to which Canada was now committed. To do otherwise would leave individual contractors competing among themselves for scarce materials, supplies and labour. The answer was the creation in April 1941 of Wartime Merchant Shipping Limited, with components of the Shipbuilding Branch of the Department of Munitions and Supply being spun off to form the nucleus of the new Crown company.[10] Headed by Harvey R. MacMillan, the powerful high-profile B.C. industrialist who was one of C. D. Howe's dollar-a-year men, the company was soon up and running. One of MacMillan's first acts was to call a conference of the shipbuilding companies. He painted a there-is-no-tomorrow picture and asked the shipbuilders for their most optimistic estimates of what they could produce, given the desperate war situation. Thus prompted, so bullish were the projections of the builders that one British expert pronounced them as rash, beyond any hope of realization.[11] Yet within a year, those supposedly unrealistic estimates had been consigned to the waste basket because they had been outstripped by actual accomplishment.

Wartime Merchant Shipping became a formidable enterprise with sweeping dictatorial powers. It was, in effect, master shipbuilder to the Canadian Government, with the relationship of the shipbuilding companies to it being akin to that of subcontractors. From its headquarters in Montreal, the Crown company controlled all aspects of the program. It fostered the industrial infrastructure to provide the big triple-expansion steam engines for the ships, the boilers, the propellers, the stern frames, the steering engines, cargo-handling winches, windlasses, compasses, the burly anchors with their hefty chain cables, and the literally thousands of other components, items and materials needed to build and equip a new ship to make it ready for sea.

In the operational plan it had adopted, the Crown company was simply following the pattern established by its parent, the Department of Munitions and Supply. In the U.S. and Britain, all of the various military services jealously guarded the right to manage their own procurement branches, with consequent fierce competition for scarce equipment and supplies. Alone among the western Allies, Canada centralized all procurement of war matériel under a single agency, DMS, thereby eliminating interservice competition and its handmaidens—sometimes a shortage here, sometimes a surplus there, and sometimes inflated prices.

As the offspring of DMS, Wartime Merchant Shipping established itself as the purchasing agent for all major ship components, ordering in quantity to reduce costs and scheduling deliveries to the yards only when they were needed and only in the quantities needed. Half a century later, such a system would be hailed as a forward-thinking manufacturing innovation dubbed "Just In Time" delivery. Competition for components with the associated possibility of stockpiling by individual yards, to the detriment of other yards, was thereby avoided.

Among the major items that Wartime Merchant Shipping undertook to supply to the shipyards were the main propulsion engines. Eventually, there were four builders of the big 135-ton triple expansion 2500 IHP steam engines: Canadian Vickers Limited, Montreal; Canadian Allis-Chalmers Limited, Montreal; Dominion Engineering Works Limited, Montreal; John Inglis Company Limited, Toronto. So successful was the powerplant production record that in 1942 Wartime Merchant Shipping was able to permit diversion of 23 engines surplus to immediate Canadian requirements to the U.S. Maritime Commission for Liberty ship installation.[12] In addition to the engines, 65 stern frames and 6 winches as well as 34 sets of anchor chain cable were shipped to the U.S. to help prevent a delay in the American program through temporary component shortages. Canadian suppliers were able to meet the demand without triggering any delays in Canadian ship deliveries.

The boilermakers were Dominion Bridge Company with plants in Montreal and Vancouver, John Inglis Company of Toronto, and Vancouver Iron Works. Their product, though demanding of the highest manufacturing and safety standards, was by its nature one that rarely received the recognition it deserved as possibly a ship's most vital single component. Only other boilermakers and the ship's engineers could love the hulking steam generators that were the heart of the ship's power.

The Canadian single source for the 18 ft. 6 in. diameter propellers for the 10,000 ton ships was William Kennedy & Sons Limited, an Owen Sound, Ontario, firm that had been in business since before Confederation. Its choice was a natural one, given that an estimated 90 percent of the ships plying the Great Lakes were already fitted with Kennedy propellers. Massive the 14 ton, four-bladed bronze propellers may have been, their size belied the metallurgical, casting and machining precision that went into their manufacture. The Kennedy firm was also the supplier of propellers for all the destroyers, corvettes, minesweepers, Fairmiles, frigates and motor torpedo boats manufactured in Canada for the Navy.

* * *

Where there was no established Canadian supplier of an item of equipment, Wartime Merchant Shipping sought out manufacturers in unrelated industries who might have machine shop or some other fabricating capacity that could be utilized. Thus the machine shops of thirty-two pulp and paper companies and sixteen mining companies were recruited to manufacture the thousands of valves needed for the hundreds of cargo ships and naval vessels abuilding. Where there were shortages of some materials, such as steel, the company found new suppliers, or alternatives in the form of less critical products. Thus wood was substituted for steel for the ships' cargo handling derricks. In the expanding shipyards themselves new facilities which would normally have been of steel were constructed of wood, including gantry cranes. Eventually, over three hundred Canadian firms were involved in the program, pushing the Canadian content of the North Sands and Gray ships to 95 percent.[13]

Wartime Merchant Shipping's umbrella covered much more than the nuts and bolts of shipbuilding. Labour supply and training, yard organization, supervising personnel, and incentive systems and plans all felt the authoritative influence of the company's Shipyard Organization and Personnel Department. Little escaped its notice. "On a regular basis," wrote departmental historian John deN. Kennedy,

It dealt with labour relations, including such problems as absenteeism, safety, industrial health, military service deferments, housing, feeding and recreational facilities. It promoted the formation of Labour-Management Production Committees and Foremen's Clubs, and acted as a liaison between the shipyards, the Department of Munitions and Supply, and the Department of Labour.

None of this is to say that in the overseeing of the Canadian program by the all-embracing Wartime Merchant Shipping Limited there were not glitches. One critic[14] cited two for-want-of-a-nail examples. Somebody forgot to include manilla rope in the specification for the ships, an oversight that created a critical situation in 1942 as the first ships were being handed over to their managing operators, at a time when manilla rope was in very short supply. Similarly, ships' chronometers, once the navigator's basic tools, had not been specified with the result that a frantic newspaper advertising campaign had to be mounted begging retired mariners who owned chronometers and binoculars to donate or sell them.

And there were shipyard practices for which Wartime Merchant Shipping could hardly be held responsible. Capt. John M. Mann of Oakville, Ontario, remembers being charged as Second Officer with responsibility for checking out all miscellaneous equipment being placed aboard during the fitting out of the new *Belwoods Park* at Sorel, P.Q:

> One of these was the auxiliary fire pump, which when it became time to test it worked perfectly, throwing a good stream of water clear across the deck. However, I noticed when it became time to sign the receipts, that as far as the fire pump was concerned the serial number was not the same as that on the pump that had been tested. They assured me that it was just as efficient. When I insisted that I would sign only for the original pump they were most disappointed but finally complied. I was told afterwards by one of the foremen in the Yard that the pump we had on board had been used for demonstrating for several months!

* * *

The nine berths in existence when the original British order for twenty-six ships was placed were obviously inadequate to cope with the suddenly added task of meeting the Canadian order for eighty-eight of the 10,000 ton cargo vessels along with the U.S. order for ninety.[15] Munitions and Supply financial incentives encouraged existing shipbuilders to add berths; in other cases, the department directly financed the construction of new berths. In Montreal, six Government-funded 10,000 ton berths were constructed and placed under a newly formed Crown company, United Shipyards Limited, with Dominion Bridge Company Limited and Fraser, Brace Limited being assigned the task of operating the enterprise. In Pictou, Nova Scotia, the Government constructed four 4700 ton berths for which Foundation Maritime Limited was made the managing operator.

The United Shipyards operation became one of the most efficient in Canada, several times boasting same-day double launchings of 10,000 ton hulls and once achieving a triple launching, on 19 August 1943. One of this trio, the *Fort Romaine*, was being sent down the ways in record time, just 38 days from keel-laying to launching. Twenty days later, 8 September 1943, 58 days[16] after keel-laying, also a Canadian record, she was ready for delivery. The *Fort Romaine* was the two hundredth ship to be launched in the less than two and a half years since the keel for the first Canadian completion had been laid in spring 1941. That first completion, the *Fort Ville Marie*, had by comparison required 210 days from keel-laying to acceptance on 21 December 1941. Hurried through by Canadian Vickers to avoid being trapped by the St. Lawrence freeze-up, it was also the only cargo ship to be delivered under the Canadian program in 1941.

In Vancouver, shortly after it became evident that the Government was embarking on a major shipbuilding program, a group of businessmen organized a new company, West Coast Shipbuilders Limited, adding four 10,000 ton berths. Capacity on the west coast built up rapidly as Burrard's South Yard, North Van Ship Repairs, Victoria Machinery Depot Company Limited, and Yarrows Limited, joined the list of yards operating 10,000 ton berths. Prince Rupert Dry Dock & Shipyard with two berths, which had not received an order under the original British purchase of twenty-six ships, was brought into the larger Canadian program. Meanwhile, back in eastern Canada, Marine Industries Limited of Sorel, Quebec, joined Canadian Vickers and United Shipyards as a builder of the 10,000 ton ships. By the end of 1943 when the production of ships was nearing its peak, the number of berths engaged in 10,000 ton construction had grown to thirty-eight operated by ten yards.[17]

Shipyards in the Maritime Provinces, meantime, were almost totally occupied with Naval construction programs, exceptions being Saint John Dry Dock & Shipbuilding which, along with the Government-funded shipyard at Pictou, Nova Scotia, operated by Foundation Maritime Limited, became two of the four builders of the 4700 ton Gray type cargo ships. The others were George T. Davie & Sons Limited of Lauzon, Quebec, and Morton Engineering & Dry Dock Company Limited of Quebec City. When in July 1943 poor labour/management relations threatened the performance of these two companies, which were also involved in Naval construction programs, they were placed under the stewardship of Quebec Shipyards Limited, a Crown company specially formed for that purpose.

The west coast yards, which eventually accounted for some 71 percent of the output of the 10,000 ton vessels, operated under the clear advantage of year-round mild weather working conditions. Rainy winters prevented neither outdoor construction work nor launchings (at Prince Rupert, the winter rains were almost nonstop). The yards on the St. Lawrence River, on the other hand, were severely inhibited by the frigid December-March temperatures characteristic of the region. Not only was it difficult for the workers to handle cold steel with frost-stiffened fingers, but many productive hours would be lost whenever hundreds of hands had to be assigned to digging out equipment and materials following one of the frequent heavy snowfalls. And ships not complete enough to move downstream before freeze-up would remain icebound until spring breakup.

The detrimental effect of working under such hostile weather conditions became apparent very quickly. Though Canadian Vickers was the first to deliver a 10,000 ton ship, and was the only yard to do so in 1941, this was made possible only by moving the hull from Montreal, with shipyard workers aboard, for further work at Quebec City where freeze-up would not arrive until two weeks later. In fact, detail work was still going on in Halifax right up to sailing time for the *Fort Ville Marie* and was not finally completed until the ship was docked in Britain. On the west coast, Burrard Dry Dock did not make its first delivery until 29 January 1942, the *Fort St. James*, but had made two more by the time Canadian Vickers was able to make its second.

Canadian Vickers did enjoy some advantage over other yards on the St. Lawrence in that its berths were covered, making it possible for work to go on regardless of weather conditions. The long-established yard was fully integrated, with the capability to produce most major components, including the big engines and rudders. Nonetheless, the Canadian Vickers production of 10,000 ton ships and their engines was stopped at six, with the company's facilities thereafter being dedicated principally to more complex Naval construction programs.

The Marine Industries yard at Sorel was unique among those building 10,000 ton ships in that its launchings were by marine railway, a procedure made necessary because the confinement of the Sorel site made it impossible to launch ships by traditional methods. On each side of the marine railway and parallel to it were three building slips which were used to lay keels and build up the hulls. As construction progressed, the hulls were winched sideways[18] in assembly-line fashion, each one in turn replacing its predecessor on the marine railway for completion to launch stage. Unlike ships built on the more common inclined slipways, throughout this method of construction and launching the hulls remained in a level position. This simplified construction, making it faster and reducing costs.

The unique installation was developed by Marine Industries and was ready for the first keel-laying within six months of start of construction in July 1941. It launched its first 10,000 ton ship in July 1942. With a 5000 ton handling capacity (a ready-to-launch 10,000 DWT vessel would weigh about 3500 tons), the marine railway had a launch capability for ships of up to about the 20,000 DWT category. Motive power was supplied by 250 hp motors. The massive chain required to move the cradle on which a ship was launched, was over a mile long and was the thickest ever manufactured in Canada. The only two American companies capable of manufacturing it could not guarantee delivery within the required time frame, so Marine Industries awarded the contract to an associated company, Sorel Steel Foundries Limited, which delivered on time.[19]

It was not surprising that Marine Industries should be so innovative. Even in the years leading up to WW II, the company had demonstrated an advanced technological capability, being extensively equipped for and experienced in welded ship construction methods. In the mid-1930s it built an aluminum coast guard vessel, *l'Interceptor*, for the Canadian Government; it was the first ship of aluminum to be constructed in Canada and was believed to be the largest in the world at the time.

* * *

With the eastern shipyards being more heavily focused on Naval construction and support programs, as well as, for those along the St. Lawrence, being inhibited by long periods of hostile weather conditions, the main burden of 10,000 ton ship production fell on the west coast yards. Concentrated mostly on both sides of Vancouver Harbour and in False Creek, but also including the yards at Prince Rupert and in the Victoria area, they responded to the challenge with an astounding outpouring. Lead by Burrard Dry Dock, the west coast yards turned out 224 of the 10,000 ton merchant vessels plus, based on the same hulls, 9 stores ships and 21 maintenance ships for the Royal Navy. In twenty-nine months from first delivery, the *Fort St. James* in January 1942, until the end of the war, the western companies maintained a better than 2-per-week average in deliveries of 10,000 ton merchant vessels. In some months during the program's peak year of 1943, Burrard alone was delivering one per week.

Canada-wide, the delivery rate by mid-1943 was even more impressive, averaging 3 per week for 10,000 ton vessels and when the smaller 4700 DWT and 3600 ton vessels were factored in the average rose to almost 3.5 merchant ships per week, or one every 2.5 days.

Like most of the yards, east and west, engaged in merchant ship construction, Burrard also carried a substantial workload of naval construction including, besides the RN stores and maintenance ships already noted, ten corvettes and minesweepers and the conversion of nineteen new escort aircraft carriers from U.S. to British Navy specifications.

The conversion of the carriers was one of those seemingly inexplicable paradoxes that are rife in war. Delivered spanking new to Vancouver from the Tacoma, Washington, shipyard of Seattle-Tacoma Shipbuilding Corp., where they had been built for the USN but then redirected to the British under Lend-Lease, the vessels arrived with systems and installations designed to USN requirements. The decision to modify them so extensively raised a few eyebrows, but the Royal Navy's explanation was that as they were to be manned by British and Canadian crews accustomed to RN-style systems and equipment, it was easier and faster to alter the ships than it was to retrain thousands of crewmen.[20]

Late in the war years there were other British orders to Canadian shipyards for both RN and Ministry of War Transport accounts. For the most part these were related to the planned step-up of British participation in the Pacific war, but with the sudden Japanese surrender, the orders that were for special landing support vessels were scaled back sharply.

In 1944, the British Admiralty Technical Mission had placed orders with shipyards in eastern and western Canada for seventy-one so-called transport ferries, Pacific islands invasion vessels purpose designed to carry tanks, armoured vehicles and trucks, as well as personnel. Fitted with bow opening doors, the 4000 DTW Diesel-powered, twin-screw, low-draft ferries measured 345 ft. in length and 54 ft. in breadth. Depth amidships was 27 ft. All bridge and accommodation superstructure was located aft, as was the engine room.

Only fifteen ferries had been delivered when the Pacific war ended and by then thirteen of the original order had been cancelled because they had not progressed even as far as keel-laying. The British Admiralty agreed to accept an additional eleven provided they could be completed by the end of October 1945, but the remaining thirty-two were to be cancelled.[21] Some of these ferries were later declared surplus and were turned over to War Assets Corporation, which in 1946 offered seven for sale, declaring them suitable for conversion into general cargo or pulp wood carriers.[22]

Meanwhile, the British Ministry of War Transport scattered orders among eastern and western Canadian yards for a total of thirty-five British-designed small coastal ships for service in Far East and South Pacific waters following the restoration of peacetime shipping. The orders were not placed until early in 1945 and consequently deliveries did not commence until 1946 and were completed only in January 1947.

Two types of coaster were involved, the 1250 DWT "B" type, colloquially known as China Coasters, and the tiny 300 DWT "C" type. Orders for 15 of the larger China Coasters were placed with western yards: Burrard Dry Dock (6), Pacific Drydock (3), Prince Rupert Dry Dock (2), and Victoria Machinery Depot (4). Five eastern yards shared the 20 C type orders: Collingwood Shipbuilding (4), Davie Shipbuilding (5), Morton Engineering (5), Port Arthur Shipbuilding (3), and Saint John Dry Dock (3). All of both types were originally given names beginning with the prefix "Ottawa."

The 9-10 knot B coaster measured 224 ft. overall in length and 37 ft. in breadth, whereas the 9 knot C type was 151 ft. overall and 27 ft. in breadth. Both types had aft-mounted engines.

On completion, the thirty-five coasters were turned over to the War Assets Corporation, which seemed to have no problem finding ready buyers. The sale of all fifteen of the China Coasters was reported by mid-1946, at prices of $300,000 and $400,000 each. Seven were bought by Chinese interests in a deal worth a reported $2,500,000, which followed the earlier sale of eight, five of them to Canadian buyers.[23] The B coasters were fetching prices almost as high as those for the surplus 10,000 ton freighters. The smaller C types were also quickly disposed of to buyers in Canada and abroad.

* * *

How good were the ships produced by the Canadian yards? By their operational record, they were very good indeed. Sailing through the stormiest of seas all over the world, they proved tough and durable, encountering few structural problems. Considering that they were built as expendables, which needed only to deliver one cargo to justify their existence, they more than met that specification. After wartime service hundreds of them soldiered on for years under Canadian and foreign flags. As late as 1966, more than twenty years after the last launching, there were still some 155 ex-Parks and ex-Forts of the 10,000 ton class in service with many nations.[24] Of the smaller former Park ships, 27 of the 4700 tonners and 4 of the 3600 ton tankers continued to sail under various house flags. Regrettably, few if any of the Canadian-built ships were by that time listed on the Canadian registry, the dream of a Canadian Merchant Marine having died by 1950 following the crushing of the Canadian Seamen's Union, and the reversal of Government policy that had required the Canadian-built ships sold to Canadian shipping companies be manned only by Canadian crews.

More recent evidence of the durability of the Canadian constructions is to be found in a 1992 Vancouver newspaper report[25] of several west coast built ships that were only then being sent to the shipbreakers, almost half a century after they first went to sea. One of these was the ex-*Mount Royal Park*, launched by Victoria Machinery Depot Company Limited in September 1943 as a tanker and sold in 1946 to Norwegian interests who converted her to cargo configuration. She later served British and Yugoslav shipping companies, and was last on the registry of the Republic of Somalia. Right to the end, she worked her way, carrying a cargo from the Continent to Shanghai before being dispatched to a shipbreaker's yard on mainland China. Others listed in the same report as having avoided until 1992 being sentenced to the shipbreaker's hammer and torch were the ex-*Windermere Park* and the ex-*Tuxedo Park*, 1943 and 1944 launchings of West Coast Shipbuilders, Vancouver, and the Burrard-built ex-*Fort Brisebois*, launched in 1944.

As late as 1993, HMS *Rame Head*,[26] one of the much modified Burrard-built Royal Navy Escort Maintenance Ships which were based on the same hulls as the Parks and Forts, remained on the Navy's lists. Delivered in August 1945, a few days after war's end, HMS *Rame Head* underwent a refit in 1990 preparatory to being sold to the Greek Navy. There was, however, a change of plans that saw her being taken over by the RN's Special Boat Squadron as a training ship[27] based at Portland.

Also still in existence in 1994, though mothballed at Esquimalt, was HMCS *Cape Breton*. Delivered by Burrard to the Royal Navy in 1945 as an escort maintenance ship and named HMS *Flamborough Head*, she was acquired by the Royal Canadian Navy in 1953 and renamed. As HMCS *Cape Breton* she saw service in a variety of maintenance roles, including that of mobile repair ship. Her expected fate is a date with the shipbreakers, though there had been some talk of preserving her as a marine museum.

By 1994, HMS *Rame Head* and HMCS *Cape Breton* were the only two surviving examples of the 354, 10,000 ton hulls produced almost five decades earlier under Canada's wartime shipbuilding program.

The explanation for the remarkably successful Canadian shipbuilding record is to be found in the revealing comment[28] of the vice chairman of the U.S. Maritime Commission, RAdm Howard L. Vickery, that whereas in Britain ships were still being "built," in the United States they were being "manufactured." What the Admiral meant by the distinction, applicable to standard ship production in Canadian as well as U.S. yards, was that in Britain shipbuilding continued on traditional lines by fully integrated yards offering both design and construction capacity and often capable of fabricating almost all the ancillary machinery and equipment that went into a ship, as well as the hull itself. In effect, following this established practice, each British ship might be likened to a one-off, often designed and constructed to the special order of a particular shipping company. In the early stages of the war, this practice was maintained even though the customer was usually the Ministry of War Transport. The British yards quickly became so stretched by Naval construction that there was no capacity available to make possible introduction of mass production of a standard ship design, the very concept that was about to be adopted in North America. The British yards were largely staffed by experienced workers capable of interpreting and carrying out job requirements from general plans. Conversely, the Canadian yards had to contend with a mushrooming labour force most of whom had never been in a shipyard previously. Jobs had to be broken down into more easily understood segments, with more detailed working plans than were required in the British yards.

It would be an overstatement to say that the Canadian "manufactured" ships were produced on an assembly-line basis. Nonetheless, their construction in such large numbers in such a short time was possible only because many yards, coordinated by a central agency with virtually dictatorial powers, were simultaneously engaged in building the same standard design using many common construction methods, including extensive prefabrication of major hull and superstructure components. Regardless of the building shipyard, engines and other auxiliary machinery, which themselves were of standard designs, all manufactured in production runs by specialized contractors, were fully interchangeable with those on ships built in any other yard. Thus it was possible to install main engines built in Canada in some U.S. Liberty ships, though the engines and stern frames and such deck machinery as cargo winches were about the only items that were interchangeable between the Liberties and the Canadian-built Forts and Parks.

The Canadian yards were never able to match the degree of prefabrication practiced by the U.S. yards, where indeed the building of Liberty ships did come close to being an assembly-line type operation. The American genius for mass production was never better demonstrated than in its Liberty program, which saw 2,710 ships delivered within the same time frame as Canada delivered 354 similar mostly Forts and Parks and at competitive cost (average per 10,000 ton ship, CDN$1,700,000 vs. US$1,780,000). The tight financial supervision maintained by Wartime Merchant Shipping through its system of centralized control was the key to keeping Canadian costs in line. For example, once the program had become established and Wartime Merchant Shipping had a more exact measure of costs, contracts were changed from a fixed-price basis to cost-plus-management-fee contracts. Depending on the yard, the management fee for a 10,000 DWT Victory ship could be as low as a minimum $30,000 to, with the aid of an incentive bonus system, as high as $50,000.[29] In the U.S. and Britain the prevailing management fee was $100,000 for a 10,000 ton cargo vessel.

Though comparison with the American production record was inevitable, Canada had no need to be modest. The country had entered the war under the enormous handicap of being rated on the international industrial scale as a backwoodsy hewer of wood and drawer of water. Within three years a transformation had taken place; the hewer of wood and drawer of water had become one of the Western Allies' leading industrial powers. A measure of its new status as a builder of ships is that by 1942 it was estimated that in completions of ocean-going vessels by all British Commonwealth countries combined (including the U.K.), the Canadian program was responsible for 47 percent.[30] It was that record the British Government was later moved to describe in superlatives, "magnificent" among them. Even the sceptics would have to say, for a nation of a mere twelve million, Canada's achievements as a wartime builder of ships were not bad.

Not bad at all.

SS *Algonquin Park* departing Baltimore 2 February 1944 bound for India via the Suez Canal. A North Sands coal burner launched 2 October 1942 by Marine Industries Ltd., she lacks the 12-pounder bow gun that was typical of the armament of later 10,000 tonners. *United States Navy, photo via Frank Seems*

3600 DWT tanker MV *John Irwin*, in peacetime colours of postwar owner Canadian Oil Cos., was the wartime *Eglinton Park*, one of six Canadian-designed tankers ordered for Park Steamship Co. Delivered 10 June 1944, she was one of three from Marine Industries Ltd. Collingwood Shipyards built the other three. *Photo via George C. Fleming*

Steaming off B.C. coast in July 1944, SS *Green Hill Park* was probably enroute to a Vancouver Island port for additional Australia-destined cargo, as suggested by elevated loading derricks at holds 1, 4 and 5. A 10,000 DWT Victory type oil burner, she blew up in Vancouver harbour 6 March 1945. *DND/National Archives of Canada/PA112311*

Australia-bound from B.C. via San Pedro for bunkers, SS *Bowness Park* has been topped off with a deckload of timber. A Victory type dry cargo vessel she sports a full suit of DEMS weaponry that made her more heavily armed than a Canadian Navy frigate. *DND/NAC/PA187471*

No mistaking the coal-burning North Sands class 10,000 tonners, as SS *Nemiskam Park* illustrates. Delivered 7 July 1943 by Prince Rupert Drydock & Shipyard, she lacks a bow gun and an A-frame for towing minesweeping gear, both features of later Park ships. *DND/NAC/C35481*

At anchor, probably in the St. Lawrence, unladen North Sands SS *Elk Island Park* awaits loading orders. Delivered 6 June 1943 by Montreal-based United Shipyards, like all Park vessels she was equipped with torpedo nets, apparent here secured to the tall booms vertically stowed against the mainmast aft. *DND/NAC/PA147981*

Dead slow ahead, SS *Mount Maxwell Park* is caught in the act of deploying her torpedo nets. When fully deployed the net booms would be horizontal. Lack of cargo-handling derricks indicates that *Mount Maxwell* was one of the thirteen 10,000 DWT vessels built as tankers, all but one of them being of the Victory type.
DND/NAC/PA187472

SS *Fairmount Park*, a Canadian type convertible coal/oil burner was delivered by Burrard Dry Dock 31 January 1945. She has no forward gun, torpedo nets or A-frame at her bow for towing minesweeping paravanes, possibly none of this DEMS equipment being installed because the sea war was close to winding down.
DND/NAC/PA181330

Lying quietly at anchor, SS *Crescent Park* bears the marks of recent exposure to vigorous Atlantic weather. One of forty-three 4700 DWT British-designed dry cargo coal burners produced by Canadian yards for coastal service, she and twenty-three others were built in Pictou, N.S., by Foundation Maritime Ltd.
DND/NAC/PA147983

Transport Ferry No. 3504, built by Canadian Vickers Ltd., Montreal, one of seventy-one ordered by the Royal Navy from Canadian shipyards late in the war in anticipation of an expanded British role in the Pacific theatre. In the event, only twenty-six of the 4000 DWT diesel-powered invasion vessels were completed. *DND/NAC/C32120*

HMCS *Cape Breton*, now de-commissioned Canadian Navy maintenance ship awaiting her fate at Esquimalt. A conversion of a 10,000 DWT Victory type cargo ship hull, she is believed to be one of possibly only two examples remaining of Canada's wartime output of 354 10,000 ton hulls. Attempts are being made to save her from the shipbreakers for preservation as a maritime museum.
National Defence Canada/E53746

A famous oft repeated wartime scene: convoy assembly in Bedford Basin, Halifax. According to their speed capability, merchant ships were assigned to fast or slow convoys. Those capable of at least 15 knots were allowed to sail independently (i.e., alone).
NAC/PA112993

Hull No. 130, the soon to be SS *Windermere Park*, nearing completion, looking forward from abaft the mainmast. The 10,000 DWT Victory type dry cargo vessel was delivered by West Coast Shipbuilders Ltd., Vancouver, to Park Steamship Co., 12 November 1943.
NAC/PA187475

Bow-on view of Hulls 131 (left) and 130 being completed dockside at West Coast Shipbuilders' yard, Vancouver. Both were 10,000 DWT Victory types but Hull 130 was a dry cargo vessel whereas Hull 131 was a tanker version. Hull 130 became the *Windermere Park* and Hull 131 the *Mount Bruce Park*. *NAC/PA187474*

Looking aft, Hull No. 133 under construction at North Van Ship Repairs Ltd. (a unit of Burrard Dry Dock) with second deck beams in place. Openings provide access to holds Nos. 4 and 5. A Victory type dry cargo vessel, Hull 133 became the *Dundurn Park*. *DND/NAC/PA187473*

Crankshaft of 2500 IHP triple expansion steam engine being lowered into its bearings during engine assembly at Canadian Vickers Ltd., Montreal. Canadian production of the 135 ton engines for 10,000 DWT merchant vessels was so advanced that twenty-three were supplied for the U.S. Liberty ship program.
NAC/C32783

2500 IHP triple expansion steam engine in final assembly at Canadian Vickers Ltd., Montreal. The big cylinder visible at top is the engine's 70-inch bore low pressure cylinder. The engines for the 10,000 DWT merchant ships operated at a nominal 76 RPM.
NAC/C32081

Workmen fitting out North Sands type cargo ship *Fort Nipigon* at Canadian Vickers yard, Montreal. *Fort Nipigon* was the second of the 10,000 DWT vessels built by Canadian Vickers and only the fourth under the Canada-wide shipbuilding program. Completed 8 April 1942, she was the first of ninety built in Canadian yards for purchase by the U.S. Maritime Commission to be turned over to the British Ministry of War Transport under U.S. Lend-Lease. *NAC/C32850*

Torpedo explosion damage to port lower side of hull of SS *Fort Camosun*. Built by Victoria Machinery Depot under U.S. Maritime Commission order for Lend-Lease to the British Ministry of War Transport, she had barely cleared the Strait of Juan de Fuca on her first voyage after loading in British Columbia when torpedoed by a Japanese submarine 20 June 1942. *Fort Camosun* did not sink and was towed back to Esquimalt for repairs to sail another day. *NAC/PA190186*

SS *Green Hill Park* burns dockside at CPR Pier B in Vancouver. Ship was heavily damaged by a cargo explosion 6 March 1945 which shook the city's downtown. Two seamen and six longshoremen were killed. Salvaged, sold to Greek interests who had her rebuilt, she survived to sail again as the *Phaeax II*.
Steffens-Colmer Photo

The power of the cargo explosion that blew up the *Green Hill Park* at Pier B in
Vancouver 6 March 1945 is evident in this starboard side view. No. 3 hold has been
blasted open and the ship's bridge has collapsed into the gaping hole. Half-inch steel
hull plates were torn like paper.
Steffens-Colmer Photo

One of Canadian National Steamships Lady Boats, SS *Lady Nelson* was torpedoed and
sunk at dock in St. Lucia Harbour by *U 161* with the loss of seventeen lives, 22 March
1942. She was salvaged and converted into a hospital ship, a role in which she
completed thirty-one voyages transporting 25,000 wounded back from the war zones.
Canadian Forces Photo

North Sands type *Mount Robson Park* was delivered by North Van Ship Repairs 27 August 1942, sailing under that name until September 1944 when turned over to the British Ministry of War Transport and renamed *Fort Miami*. Simultaneously a new Victory from West Coast Shipbuilders became the new *Mount Robson Park*.
Canadian Forces Photo

Heavily laden *Fort Dauphin* heading south by southwest out of British Columbia topped off with a deckload of raw timber. Typical of many British-operated Fort ships, she had no bow gun. When challenged by patrolling aircraft, a merchant ship was required to display coded signal flags and her name, as *Fort Dauphin* is doing here (name, normally covered, may be seen high on the bridge).
Canadian Forces Photo

SS *Mohawk Park* was the first Burrard-built North Sands type to be delivered to Park Steamship Co., sailing under that name for about a year before being turned over to Britain under Canada's Mutual Aid program and renamed *Fort Spokane*. Although the ship has provision for a bow gun, none has been installed.
Canadian Forces Photo

Canadian-built SS *Fort Stikine* won unwanted wartime notoriety 14 April 1944 when she caught fire in Bombay igniting 1400 tons of explosives aboard. Two subsequent massive blasts destroyed much of the Indian port city, causing thousands of casualties, killed and injured. The explosion also destroyed ten other ships.
Canadian Forces Photo

MV *Ontariolite*, an Imperial Oil tanker, spent much of its wartime service running between Caribbean oil ports and Portland, Maine, terminus of the Portland-Montreal pipeline. All of the twin diesel-powered *Ontariolite*'s equipment was marked in German, reflecting the fact that she was a prize of war.
Canadian Forces Photo

There was no place to hide from German submarines, even in the St. Lawrence. The British SS *Essex Lance* (left) and the Greek SS *Joannis* (right) were both torpedoed just off the Gaspé coast by *U 165*, 16 September 1942. *Joannis* sank in ten minutes but *Essex Lance* was towed into Quebec City. All crew members took to lifeboats, seen here, and survived. Later the same day *U 165* struck the American SS *Pan York*, which also survived the attack.
Dave Wright Photo

Lightly armed Imperial Oil tanker *Albertolite* brought crude from Pacific oil ports in South America and California to Imperial's terminus at Ioco, B.C. IOL's fleet of ten tankers comprised almost half of Canada's deep-sea fleet at war's outbreak. Three were lost to German U-boats and one was captured.
Canadian Forces Photo

Heavy weather scenes like this one from the bridge of SS *Lake Sicamous* are simply a commonplace part of the seascape, in war or peace. *Lake Sicamous* was originally *Weston Park*, delivered to Park Steamship Co. 3 October 1944. She went through several postwar ownerships and finally came to grief in March 1963 when she ran aground in Portugal and broke in two.
W. Hutcherson Photo

Trainees at wartime St. Margaret's Sea Training School for aspiring merchant seamen often found their first attempts at handling a lifeboat somewhat difficult. Perhaps this session was a lesson in repelling boarders. Before closing in 1946, the school produced over eight hundred graduates for Canada's Merchant Navy.
James Boughner Photo

On 11 November 1994, in a ceremony headed by Governor General Ramon Hnatyshyn, the national Merchant Navy Book of Remembrance was officially installed in the Memorial Chamber of the Peace Tower in Ottawa. At present the Book lists the names of 2040 Canadian Merchant Seamen known to have been lost to enemy action during WW I (573) and WW II (1467). Shown displaying the Book at the installation ceremony are Merchant Navy Veteran Osborne MacLean (L) of Westfield, N.B., and Don Ives of Veterans Affairs.
Veterans Affairs Canada

DEMS Gunner John (Chris) Christie of St. Catharines, Ontario, and the author absorb a little R&R in San Francisco, January 1945, on the last leg of a round-the-world voyage in the *Green Hill Park* that covered some thirty-one thousand miles.

Green Hill Park deck crew members take a break from their never-ending painting duties while docked in Port Lincoln, South Australia, taking on a cargo of wheat for India, September 1944. Left to right, front: Art Bourgeois, St. Boniface, Manitoba; the author, Winnipeg, Manitoba; Earl Jackson, Vancouver, B.C. Second row: Ken Bannister, Toronto, Ontario; "Aussie"; Ray Campbell, Vancouver, B.C.; Don Harrett, Fruitvale, B.C. At rear: Bosun Ron Mitchell, New Zealand.

Chapter Twelve

LAISSEZ-FAIRE SOLUTION

If any one person could be said to be responsible for what finally was established as Canada's postwar shipping policy, and with it the scuttling of the concept of a Canadian flag merchant marine, that person would be J. V. (Jack) Clyne, first chairman of the Canadian Maritime Commission (CMC). A prominent tough-minded Vancouver lawyer specializing in marine law, future British Columbia Supreme Court judge, future Chairman and CEO of multi-national forest products giant MacMillan Bloedel, forty-five-year-old Clyne was the Mackenzie King cabinet's first choice to head the new Commission. Staunchly Canadian, Clyne had accepted the appointment out of a strong sense of public duty and at some financial sacrifice as well as over the objections of his law partners.

The Government hoped the Commission would solve the conundrum posed by the very existence of the huge fleet of wartime-built ships. Up to that point, the future of the fleet was being decided piecemeal, most of the decisions originating with C. D. Howe, by now Minister of Reconstruction and Supply. Many of the ships had been sold to Canadian shipping companies with the proviso that they remain under the Canadian flag, thus ensuring jobs for Canadian seamen. Others were on bareboat charter to the British Ministry of Transport, to be returned to the Canadian registry in 1950. With the passing in July 1947 of the Maritime Commission Act, further dispositions were put on hold pending the outcome of the new Commission's findings.

There were many who thought that for strategic reasons, Canada should maintain a merchant fleet, which would mean not only ship operations but also the shipbuilding and repair infrastructure required to support a merchant marine. It seemed clear to many others that such a course could lead but to subsidization of private commercial interests, because the idea of bringing forth a reincarnation of the between-wars Canadian Government Merchant Marine was not even to be contemplated. Once burned, twice shy. The Canadian Seamen's Union of course favoured maintaining a substantial merchant fleet and with it seamen's jobs, by whatever means necessary. If government subsidies were required, the CSU reasoned, then so be it.

J. V. Clyne came from a family of modest financial means, though with good connections, but through merit and ability he had risen to prominence as a successful

Vancouver lawyer, enjoying the high regard of his peers in the legal community. He moved easily in business and industry circles and his capabilities had obviously come to the attention of faraway Ottawa. It could be fairly said that he had a management mindset and was not sympathetic to labour ideals and unionism. He was, in a word, solidly establishment. At the same time he was not entirely unfamiliar with the life of the so-called working man, having spent part of his British Columbia youth as a working cowboy and at manual labour in a hydraulic gold mine project, as well as having worked his passage to England in 1925 as a foc's'le hand in order to take up a position as an articled clerk in a London firm of solicitors.

In 1926 while Clyne was still in London, a clash between mining unions and mine owners over a proposal to cut wages and increase working hours, lead to the calling of a general strike by the Trades Union Council with the aim of shutting London down. Clyne had no trouble deciding where his sympathies lay, quickly volunteering to become a member of the Metropolitan Special Constabulary Reserve's flying squads, whose job it was to help the police keep the strikers in line and quell riots. On the other side, working in the office of the Trades Union Council, was a friend from University of British Columbia days and now a Rhodes Scholar at Oxford, Norman Robertson, whom Clyne said had still not overcome the socialist tendencies he had shown at UBC. Norman Robertson later went on to become one of the Federal civil service's top mandarins.

The point having been made that Clyne's thought processes were of a conservative bent, the poor and getting worse labour/management relations in the Canadian shipping industry that existed when he took up his new post as Canadian Maritime Commission chairman on 1 November 1947,* appear to have been only one of many factors, and not a decisive one, that had to be considered in developing a policy for the future. The legal mind that was to find a home on the B.C. Supreme Court for seven future years was not one to arrive at a decision without careful examination of all the evidence. That said, Clyne and his fellow commissioners soon concluded the economic reality to be that Canadian flag ships were costly to operate compared to those of most other maritime nations, only the U.S. being higher.

Canadian seamen's wages were not out of line by domestic shoreside norms, but did exceed international shipping standards, a situation impossible to ignore when more and more ships of all nations were being transferred to flags of convenience. Furthermore the Canadian war-built ships were obsolete, too small and too slow to compete with the larger,

---

* Shortly thereafter, he also took over the presidency of Park Steamship Company Limited and moved its head office and remaining staff of nineteen from Montreal to the Ottawa headquarters offices of the Canadian Maritime Commission.

more modern and therefore more efficient equipment being introduced by other nations.

As chairman of the Canadian Maritime Commission, Clyne ran a tight ship. When the legislation authorizing the establishment of the commission had been passed earlier in the year, a senior civil servant had estimated that a staff of two hundred would be required. Clyne set up an organization that, in addition to himself and two fellow commissioners, numbered only twenty-three exclusive of clerical help. They set to work to study all aspects of shipping and shipbuilding. The Commission was assisted in its studies by a network of volunteer committees and these included, according to Clyne's account, not only representatives of the shipping and shipbuilding industries, but also just about anybody concerned with Canadian shipping, among them seafaring personnel and shipyard labour as well as importers and exporters.

One of the authorities Clyne consulted was his American counterpart, RAdm. Emory S. Land, Chairman of the U.S. Maritime Commission. Clyne said he was appalled by the cost to the U.S. taxpayers of subsidizing U.S. ship operations, as cited to him by Admiral Land. This information probably only further strengthened his belief in the *laissez-faire* creed espoused in the eighteenth century by Adam Smith that free market forces should always prevail. As Clyne was to say some years later in a speech when he was Chairman and CEO of MacMillan Bloedel: "State control and state socialism, either directly or through Crown corporations, represent the complete antithesis of Adam Smith's doctrine."[1] When he was CMC Chairman, Clyne acknowledged the existence of strong feeling in Canada that there should always be a Canadian flag fleet, but on the strength of the Commission's studies he came to regard this view as "ill-informed."[2]

By 1948, problems for Canadian ships were increasing, aggravated by falling freight rates and devaluation of the pound. Furthermore, they could not benefit from the Marshall Plan which the U.S. had established to aid European recovery because carriage of the related shipments of cargoes, massive in quantity, was restricted to either U.S. bottoms or those of the aid recipient countries.

There had been a change in policy in 1948 permitting the Canadian owners of the ex-Park/Fort ships to sell them to foreign flag buyers, provided the proceeds of the sales were put in an escrow fund for modernization of the Canadian flag deep-sea fleet. Up-to-date replacement tonnage had to be acquired within five years (with a two-year extension possible). By 1949 some $27 million had been accumulated under this scheme, but it was ineffective in its stated aim because when the shipping companies ordered new ships, they were being built for the Great Lakes or coastal trade. Though a clear breach of stated policy, this diversion was excused by Clyne on the ground that, given it was not possible for the owners to make money with deep-sea ships, they were justified in using the escrow money for ships of types with profit potential.

It had been expected that it would take the Commission five years or more to make its recommendations, but barely two years had elapsed before Transport Minister Lionel Chevrier received the CMC's memorandum outlining the state of the Canadian shipping industry and offering the Minister five possible courses of action. In the event, the fifth proposal that "transfer of flag to an agreed number of vessels to foreign registry upon agreement to re-transfer at the request of the Canadian Government and to assist owners of ships remaining under Canadian flag" was the one favoured by Mr. Chevrier and adopted by Cabinet. The details of this proposal, which became the blueprint for Government policy, were as follows:

PROPOSAL NO. 5[3]

To permit transfer of flag of an agreed number of vessels to foreign registry upon agreement to re-transfer at the request of the Canadian Government and to assist owners of ships remaining under Canadian flag.

The implications of this proposal are:

(a) Ownership of all vessels would be retained in Canada either directly or through wholly-owned subsidiaries. The Canadian shipowning industry would be maintained irrespective of the flag under which vessels are operated. The revenues of Canadian shipowners would be subject to Canadian income tax and their foreign flag operations should show a profit especially when rates improve.

(b) All vessels whether operated under Canadian or foreign flag would still remain subject to the present replacement plan. Thus owners who bought ships from the government on favourable terms on the implied understanding that they would remain in the shipping business would still be bound to keep the capital investment in the business.

(c) It would be desirable to restrict transfers to flags of Commonwealth nations but some bargaining discretion should be retained in case sterling bloc areas should seek to impound dollar freight earnings thus disabling operators from meeting their commitments to the Canadian Government. The Greek and Italian flags have some attraction as they are E.C.A. dollar earners.

(d) The cost differential between Canadian and United Kingdom ships is about $400 per diem. The actual operating deficit of Canadian flag ships is on the average about $300 per diem. It is estimated that government aid of $200 per diem should be sufficient to encourage operation of Canadian flag vessels.

(e) It is further estimated that owners of between 30 and 40 vessels would be prepared to operate with assistance amounting to $75,000 per annum per ship. In any event government assistance should not exceed a total sum of $3,000,000 for one year as against $25,000,000 suggested by the Shipping Federation.

(f) If such assistance is considered, it should be on the basis of one year only for the purpose of assisting owners to overcome temporary difficulties arising from devaluation.

Advantages

i) Security.   Criticism has been directed against the government on the grounds that we may have no deep-sea ships to face an emergency. The re-transfer aspects of this proposal would make ample tonnage available.

ii) Employment. The 30 or 40 ships retained under the Canadian flag would maintain employment of Canadian crews. There will be some protests from labour but the answer is that it is better to give employment to some men rather than having no men employed by reason of lay-up. The operation of 30 or 40 ships would maintain a nucleus of trained sea-going personnel of about 1,600 men regularly employed.

iii) Investment.   This proposal would prevent the possibility of capital loss to owners of $40,000,000 and would enable the eventual collection of $32,000,000 to the government.

iv) Government aid by way of a lump sum payment of $75,000 per ship would not be sufficient to pay present operating losses, but would afford Canadian owners an incentive to reduce operating costs.

v) If owners are not willing to operate a minimum number of ships on this basis, or if labour is not prepared to make a realistic approach to the problem, the government cannot be accused of not endeavouring to maintain a Canadian merchant marine.

Disadvantages

i) The proposal involves the granting of a temporary subsidy of $3,000,000 payable out of public funds.

(Between 1930 and 1940 the government paid subsidies averaging $1,500,000 per annum to foreign flag vessels for deep-sea operation, but no such subsidies have been paid since the war.)

(Coastal and inland subsidies paid by the government during the fiscal year 1948-49 amounted to $2,035,140.)

ii) The sum of $75,000 is not sufficient to cover operating losses and some owners will be forced to lay up vessels in any event as they lack the financial resources to contribute to payment of deficits, but on the other hand the inefficient operator should be eliminated in any event.

J. V. Clyne, Chairman, Canadian Maritime Commission

Of this proposal, Transport Minister Chevrier said when recommending its adoption to the Cabinet, its advantages

> are superior to the advantages of the other proposals and outweigh the disadvantages of a temporary government subsidy by way of assistance for one year. Viewing the payment of $3,000,000 in the nature of a defence contribution it is not a large sum compared to other outlays for the same purpose and is only for one year to meet the emergency created by devaluation. It is apparent that the Canadian flag vessels must be either laid up or transferred to other registries. I would hesitate to recommend any plan whereby all our ships should be transferred to other flags. Not only from the aspect of defence, but from the point of view of organized labour, Proposal No. 5 appears advantageous in that it affords for at least some employment to Canadian seamen.

With this green light from Cabinet, Clyne proceeded to negotiate with the British for the transfer of Canadian ships to the British registry while retaining Canadian ownership. At one stage of the negotiations it appeared that they might fail because Sir Stafford Cripps, the Chancellor of the Exchequer, was adamantly opposed. His advice to Clyne: mothball the ships. Somewhat ironically, Clyne "reminded Sir Stafford of the excellent job the Canadian shipping and shipbuilding industries had done during the war and said that I was going to see that the shipowners who had done their part were not damaged and that I was going to see that my government recovered its investment in the ships."[4] Sir Stafford was, however, overridden by the British Cabinet, who were fearful that if the Canadian ships were not transferred to the British registry, they would go to Greek registrations.

And so arrangements were concluded to transfer the majority of the 173 ships then still on the Canadian registry to Britain, while retaining a nucleus of 30 or 40 under the Canadian flag. This remnant of the wartime fleet hardly fitted the image projected by Government statements in 1947 that a Merchant Navy was "a definite part of the nation's defensive armour."

That ardent statement notwithstanding, Prime Minister Louis St. Laurent told Commons on 9 December 1949 that

> we have concluded that we are not justified from an economic viewpoint in maintaining a Canadian flag by artificial means. It is not the intention of the Government to maintain an industry at the expense of the taxpayer, and of other export industries, by the unhealthy method of subsidies, unless these countervailing considerations are very strong indeed.

Insofar as the national defence aspect of a Merchant Navy was concerned, the Government reckoned that by transferring the Canadian ships to British registry, "arrangements can be made to treat such ships as part of the Canadian contribution to any allied shipping pool in the event of war."[5]

For those with hopes for a Canadian flag Merchant Navy, that was that. Within a few years even the thirty or forty ships had dwindled away to a handful. As for J. V. Clyne, his job done, he resigned as Maritime Commission Chairman on 31 March 1950, to return to his first love, the law, in a new, challenging role as a judge of the B.C. Supreme Court. Several decades after he left the Maritime Commission and had served as MacMillan Bloedel Chairman and CEO, Clyne was honoured by having a ship named after him. The 28,000 ton *J. V. Clyne* was owned by Canadian Pacific, built in Japan, registered in Bermuda, and under long-term charter to MacMillan Bloedel. The world according to Adam Smith had unfolded as it should.

Chapter Thirteen

ST. MARGARET'S SCHOOL DAYS

It is mid-October 1943 and I am wondering what I am doing sitting on this Toonerville Trolley train out of Halifax, meandering along the eastern shore of Nova Scotia. I know it is headed for Hubbards Cove where the Canadian Government has established St. Margaret's Sea Training School to turn out embryonic seamen for Canada's wartime Merchant Navy, but I'm not sure that is where I should be going. A few months ago I wasn't aware that Canada had a Merchant Navy, yet here I am about to be moulded into a man of the sea, an improbable prospect, given my youthful yearnings. I don't really want to be a sailor; I want to be a pilot, flying Spitfires in the Battle of Britain. Well, too late for the Battle of Britain, but there are other air battles to be fought and I had willingly offered myself to the Air Force. What I really want is to fly airplanes, if not Spitfires then I'll gladly settle for Ansons.

When, on reaching the threshold age of eighteen, I present myself at the Air Force recruiting centre in Winnipeg, their medical assessors are not impressed by the physical attributes I have to offer, though the ones considered most essential for pilots are all present and accounted for. I see with the 20/20 perception required, directly ahead and peripherally and I distinguish red from blue more than adequately. I produce a urine sample of utmost purity with disdainful ease, while half a dozen other much better-endowed physical specimens crowd in the same tiny lavatory with me, straining nervously, sample containers at the ready to catch each reluctant drop. Not even with the compelling sound of the flowing washbasin tap are my fellow recruits able to produce the quick results that I do.

The medical examiner, an RAF doctor, pokes and prods me, voicing aloud his none-too-flattering critique. He places his hand on my chest. "Flat chested," he says. He moves behind me, places his hand on the small of my back. "Swaybacked," he says. He thumps my chest and listens while I breathe deeply. He thumps my back and in his well-rounded English accent commands: "Say noinety-noine."

"Noinety-noine," I respond nervously, anxious to please.

Still, the doctor does not want to be too critical because by this year, 1941, the RCAF's aircrew standards have been eased somewhat in the face of an increasingly acute manpower shortage. So, apparently, this less-than-perfect physical specimen might be acceptable to them in some aircrew role . . . except, there are those scars, ineradicable evidence of childhood ailment. Well, you know, it is not so many years ago you had that surgery; it seems fully cured but one never knows. If we took you in and it recurred, we might have to pay you a pension. Can't risk that.

A pension, for Pete's sake! There is a world war to be won and the Canadian Government is so desperate for bodies to fill uniforms that the we-promise-it-will-never-happen conscription pledge will eventually be broken. And these guys are concerned they might have to pay me a pension! The just-covering-my-ass syndrome is alive and well among the medical examiners. My disappointment is extreme. No Anson, never mind a Spitfire.

And yet, I don't want to miss out on the excitement I imagine is being enjoyed by my pals who have joined the services, so I offer my body to the Navy. They see the scars and decline. The Army is similarly unimpressed; the Army doctor not only notes the scars but is critical of the functioning of my sinuses. Thus the Army, too, declares me unsuitable stuffing material for a uniform. About this rejection I am not unhappy because as part of the day-long enlistment routine at Winnipeg's Osborne Barracks, we recruits are provided with a noonday meal. Huge soggy chunks of boiled cabbage, whole boiled potatoes, a wan meat serving cooked to remove all traces of flavour and colour that might provide a clue to its original identity. Plainly, the Army believes in exposing its recruits to the horrors of war from the moment they offer themselves for service. Canada's Army, unlike Napoleon's, surely has some other means of locomotion than its stomach.

And so I am rejected. Not just once, not just twice, but three times. I go back to my job as a test stand operator in Canadian Airways' engine overhaul plant at Winnipeg's Stevenson Field. Next best thing to flying airplanes is working on them. Even so, the feeling is deep and inescapable that I am missing out on the great adventure, about as far removed in central Canada from the action as it is possible to get. One day a small news report appears in the local press. Mr. Arthur Randles, Director of Merchant Seamen, is seeking volunteers. Contact your local branch of the Navy League of Canada.

And that is how I come to be on this Halifax-to-Hubbards local, nervously scratching at the bites that are a legacy of the YMCA hostel in Halifax where I stayed overnight, my mother's admonition to "sleep tight, don't let the bed bugs bite," being to no avail. The travel warrant supplied to me by the Department of Transport provides me with the luxury of berth and meals for the Winnipeg-to-Halifax train journey, but a hotel room for the overnight in Halifax is assessed as too effete for this hesitant not-quite-yet merchant seaman. So my travel warrant entitlement is for a YMCA bunk, where my occupation is resisted by its resident territorial creatures, defending their turf in the only way they know. Scratch, scratch.

The train slows and halts at the tiny Hubbards village station. Awaiting on the platform are maybe a dozen youths dressed in variegated combinations of sailorlike garb, bell-bottomed trousers, navy blue pullovers emblazoned with the school name, Navy blouses, what have you. They are there to see what odd specimen has been delivered this day to be added to the roster of St. Margaret's Sea Training School. They examine the lone new package curiously, not quite yielding to the urge to pinch and prod to determine the substance of the newcomer. One thing is apparent, he is, at twenty, the old man among this group of teenagers.

Somebody picks up my bag and my escort and I move off down a narrow path to the St. Margaret's complex a short walk away. As we head for the administration building, it is necessary to pass the two-storeyed dormitory. Some of my escorts hurry ahead while others lag, so there is free space in front of and behind me. I hear a rustling from above, followed by a cascade of water which splatters on the boardwalk just behind me. Ha, missed me! It is not too trying an initiation for this new arrival, given that the intended dousing was unsuccessful.

I go through the enrolment routine in the administration building, a large rambling white three-storeyed structure that I later learn was formerly the Gainsborough, a hotel for summer visitors to this very beautiful area of hilly coastland. It serves not only as the school's administrative headquarters, but also accommodates the messes for the trainees and for the instructional and other staff. It has as well a number of rooms for instruction, study and off-hours relaxation. The instructional staff, all retired Merchant Navy officers headed by the commandant, Capt. T. P. Wilson, also have their living quarters in this building, which fronts on the coast highway and overlooks St. Margaret's Bay and the school's wharf.

To the rear of the administration building and its attached powerhouse is the dormitory for the trainees and beyond that is a third building of similar size. This building, which has an open interior, is used for assembly, instruction, and as a gymnasium. Located elsewhere on the school grounds are structures that simulate basic ship sections. One of these is a section of deck with a cargo hatch, complete with winch and cargo-handling derrick. Another section offers a mast with typical rigging.

During the enrolment process, I am informed that being unmarried, I will be paid the princely sum of $21 per month while attending St. Margaret's. Were I married, and could prove I have dependents, the stipend would be an even more royal $50 per month. Room and board included, of course, my room being the lower bunk in one of the fourteen or fifteen two-tiered cots in the upper west dormitory. The board is simple and plentiful, prepared expertly by three ample local ladies.

Alongside my bunk is a locker for my private possessions, including what is in effect the basic school garb with which I am issued. This includes an ensemble of dungarees and a navy blue turtleneck topped by a pom-pommed knitted seaman's cap. I also acquire a set of bright yellow oilskins, of which I find myself inexplicably proud. Perhaps I am thinking in terms of clothes making the man, in this case, making the seaman. Didn't Lionel Barrymore wear a set just like this in *Captains Courageous*? As I am for the first time seeing even the fringe of the sea, in the form of St. Margaret's Bay, my feeling that a set of yellow oilskins makes me a seaman is pure illusion, but I indulge my fantasy anyway.

The school operates a slop chest-cum-canteen where the trainees can purchase consumable or wearable extras, such as pullover cotton tops emblazoned with the legend "Merchant Navy" and the Merchant Navy logo. The logo is an adaption of the British version, but with the name "Canada" added. Many of us also acquire Navy-type bell-bottoms, all part of an underlying desire to establish some sort of a distinctive image of role players in the sea war. A kind of semi-uniform has evolved, with minor variations, and because its composition usually involves at least the bell-bottoms, problems sometimes arise with the Navy shore patrol when St. Margaret's trainees occasionally visit Halifax. Technically, it is illegal for anybody but enlisted Navy personnel to wear the uniform items, but the Director of Merchant Seamen, Arthur Randles, who is very proud of "his" boys at "his" school, convinces the Naval establishment in Halifax that as long as nobody wears anything resembling the complete Navy uniform, the bell-bottoms are okay. Interestingly, it is an affectation most of the trainees soon drop once they are sent on their way to one of the seamen's manning pools in Halifax, Montreal, Vancouver or Saint John, New Brunswick. Probably because some of the other manning pool guests view the St. Margaret's graduates as pretenders, though many of them are themselves only one-voyage veterans.

Hubbards village itself is not much more than a scattering of houses along the coast highway, with the handsome school administration building being the most prominent structure. This imposing white three-storeyed wooden building faces the sea. Spacious open porches span the full width of the first two storeys and the ridged roof is centred by a very large gable which is flanked by two much smaller dormers of the same design. An addition to the rear of the original structure boasts conically-roofed round towers and several roof dormers.

Right next door to the south of St. Margaret's headquarters is a smaller, but still large building housing the local general store, where there is an extraordinary selection of dry goods offered as well as a full range of groceries and staples. Farther south along the paved two-lane coast highway is the village hall, which once a week becomes a movie theatre. It is, as they say, the only show in town, so we usually take advantage of it whenever open. One of the movies we see is *In Which We Serve*. We are very impressed by Captain Noel Coward and his noble, suffering, but uncomplaining British sailors. In our imaginations we credit these same qualities to ourselves.

A hundred yards beyond the village hall is a tiny snack bar known as Scotty's. Apart from the once-a-week movie shows, Scotty's is the only place of nightly entertainment in metropolitan Hubbards. There is a standing-room-only crowd of St. Margaret's boys every evening, ogling Scotty's staff of two pretty girls, (one of whom I see as a clone of the beauteous Hedy Lamarr) and recklessly spending their nickels on the snack bar's stock-in-trade of candy bars and soft drinks. Any money left over is fed into the mighty Wurlitzer juke box and the night becomes full of the Ink Spots mournfully rendering "I'm Going to Buy a Paper Doll (to call my own)," and other pop tunes of the times.

It seems safe to assume that in the tiny village of Hubbards, with its very low complement of single girls, Scotty's two girls, along with the two young secretaries who staff the school's administration office, are centres of attraction for St. Margaret's humming swarm of 130 or so mostly teenage youths, all recent graduates of Puberty U. Understandably, the girls love the attention. Wouldn't we if the ratio were reversed? Clearly, there is not much opportunity for sin or even minor misdemeanour in Hubbards and the closest town where the opportunity for path-straying might be offered is Chester, some ten miles down the road. Occasionally, somebody smuggles a bottle of beer into the dorm but for the most part, with the lack of public transportation and few opportunities to hitchhike in these times of rationed gas, those thirsty for some diversion more exciting than another night at Scotty's, are reduced in desperation to the two-aspirins-in-a-coke cocktail that high school myth has it will produce a synthetic buzz. It is thirteen weeks of clean living and early to rise to the drone of an instructor's cry of "Wakey, wakey. Rise and stow."

The atmosphere of St. Margaret's, I soon come to realize, is that of a boys' school. The student body, which appears to average about 130 in number at any one time, is made up mostly of sixteen-to-eighteen-year-olds. Not surprisingly, they are a prankish lot, much given to good-natured horseplay. An irrepressible pair of Montrealers, Seguin and Rainville, give our dormitory an extemperaneous demonstration of the energy-generating potential of the human body. One of them, Seguin, drops his pants, bends over and moons his fascinated audience. Rainville lights a match and holds it close to Seguin's bottom who then breaks wind. There is a bloop of blue flame, which brings a round of applause from the spectators. Demands for an encore are, however, refused, one of the staff instructors having been spotted coming up the stairs and Seguin not wishing to be caught with his pants down, or perhaps he is out of gas, so to speak. It is a never-to-be-forgotten demonstration of . . . what—biology? physiology? physics? chemistry? Whatever it is, it is not an experiment that our two demonstrators learned in any school classroom. Regrettably, memorable though it is, it does not advance our training as seamen-to-be.

For that purpose, all the instructional staff are seamen of long experience, some of whom, we are told, are survivors of torpedoings. The chief instructor, it is said, has not only been torpedoed, but while in the water suffered internal injuries caused by underwater shock waves from exploding depth charges. Our commandant, Capt. T. P. Wilson, is the quintessential old salt. He must be all of seventy, suitably crusty in appearance with a manner befitting my image of the master of an ocean-going ship. Though of stern demeanour, his underlying nature is kindly. His sea service embraces the 1914-18 war and despite his, to us, advanced age, he has also been an active participant in this war, sailing in hostile waters. Among these is the English Channel where his role in the evacuation of the British Army from Dunkirk earned him a British Government commendation.

Captain Wilson personally takes on some of the instructional chores at St. Margaret's and from him some of us learn to box the compass. Soon we can reel off the compass points backwards and forwards with ease. He is the ancient mariner who has sailed before the mast and enjoys quoting to us from his extensive lexicon of sailors' aphorisms (e.g., "Red sky at night, sailor's delight; red sky in morning, sailor's warning"). He adjures us to, when we spend long days at sea in the heat of the tropics, drink Rose's Lime Juice, and explains that water can be kept relatively cool in the hot latitudes by storing it in a canvas bag with a small quantity of oatmeal, the bag being hung in a shady place where it sweats, thereby cooling the contents. He tells us the true test of a seaman's eyesight is the ability to locate the seven daughters of Atlas and Pelione that make up the Plieades, a cluster of faintly visible stars in the constellation Taurus. To distinguish these tiny pinpoints of light with the naked eye is a test of visual acuity indeed. I picture a young Captain Wilson gazing past the topmast of his sailing vessel, searching the night sky for the Plieades to assure himself that his vision is up to the sailors' standard.

The St. Margaret's curriculum covers a broad range of subjects, and later, after I have actually served at sea for several months, I come to suspect some were included to pad out the course. Perhaps when a committee was struck to concoct a training plan that would produce ready-to-work Ordinary Seamen, some committee member suggested thirteen weeks as a nice period of time in which to introduce the trainee to the rudimentary skills necessary to turn him into a semblance of the lowest order of deckhand. Then followed the opportunity for each committee member to propose his favourite essential seaman's skill. One such proposal is that no trainee should emerge from St. Margaret's at the end of thirteen weeks without the ability to scull.

And so I learn to scull, sort of. This is the ancient form of sculling, not the modern version in which the sculler has the luxury of two oars. Sculling, as taught as an essential skill at St. Margaret's, permits the use of only a single oar. The sculler stands near the stern of the boat, in this case a dinghy, and with the oar seated in a notch in the transom, works it to and fro, simultaneously imparting a twisting motion. By means of this awkward manipulation, the boat is, through some mystery of hydrodynamics, propelled forward.

My first attempt at sculling brings a look of despair to my instructor's face. I have difficulty standing because as soon as I begin to-ing and fro-ing the oar, the dinghy rocks vigorously. Eventually I gain my sea legs and even manage to keep the oar in the stern notch. But something is still wrong. The oar blade seems to stay in more or less the same position in the water while the stern of the dinghy weaves from side to side as I manipulate the oar shaft. The dinghy does not move forward. The instructor looks distressed. Finally, it all comes together for me and the dinghy advances at barely measurable speed for about ten yards. My instructor signals the results are satisfactory and, with the aid of a second oar, which is fortunately at hand, we row back to the wharf where another trainee replaces me in the dinghy for his introduction to this ancient and esoteric method of watercraft propulsion. Three years later after service on three different ships, I still have not encountered anybody, apart from other St. Margaret's graduates, who knows what sculling is, much less how to scull. But there it is, right on my certificate of graduation from St. Margaret's, listed as one of the eighteen skills I have mastered.

But most of the course subjects are of a more practical nature, and of these none ever proves more useful than ropework—tying knots, hitches and bends, as well as rope and wire splicing. At one session we are taught the backsplice, in which the rope end is spliced back into itself, effectively preventing the strands of the rope from unravelling. Its disadvantage is that the backsplice doubles the thickness of the rope end. "Whenever you see a rope lying about on the deck, with ends fraying," our instructor says, "pick it up and put in a backsplice." I store his words of wisdom in my memory for future reference should I some day stumble across a rope end in an advance state of unravel.

We are also introduced to the idea that should we some day find ourselves on a ship under attack, we will be expected to be something more than passive bystanders. Behind the headquarters building are mounted a 12-pounder Naval LA gun and a 20-mm Oerlikon anti-aircraft weapon. Inside the instructional building is a .50 Browning machine gun twin mounting. They are on loan from the RCN so that we trainees can familiarize ourselves with the mechanical features of the guns, counterparts of those we will be expected to help man when we finally ship out on one of Canada's DEMS-equipped ships. However, no formal gunnery training is part of the school curriculum, this being provided in the form of a two-day post-St. Margaret's course at one of several RCN DEMS training establishments, staffed and equipped for that purpose.

As it happens during my stay at St. Margaret's, an RCN Petty Officer by the name of Cody has been temporarily seconded to the school, reluctantly, one senses. The bemused PO Cody, who is on hand to answer questions about the military hardware, is uncertain as to his authority over the quasi-military trainees. The all-powerful Naval line of command with which he is deeply ingrained is a bit frayed here. Are we enlisted military personnel? Well, military, no. Enlisted? Well, sort of. Are we civilians? Well, yes and no. It is all very stressful for Cody. In the manner instilled by his Navy NCO training, he barks commands at us, while attempting to temper the harsh tone that he would normally use when directing orders at Navy matelots. In spite of operating under the disadvantage of not having any real authority over us, he succeeds in drilling us on the 12-pounder gun positions. He even takes us on route marches, forming us up in a militarylike column, maintaining good order and mostly keeping us in step.

Most of us are destined to be posted out as Ordinary Seamen, but a few will be assigned to ships as Cadet Officers, though the training these candidates for future command receive at St. Margaret's seems to be the same as that for those of us who are headed for berths in the forecastle. One of these potential Cadet Officers is a young Canadian who already has spent enough sea time on a British ship to acquire a slight English accent. He quickly becomes known as Limey. What is he doing at this institute for learning the fundamentals of seamanship, something in which he must already be well grounded? Naturally, by our meagre standards he is most knowledgeable on matters nautical, and so, no surprise, he is the top student.

Limey's superior practical knowledge proves invaluable one day when a few of us, sans instructor, venture forth for a sail on the broad reaches of St. Margaret's Bay in one of the school's lifeboats. There is an offshore breeze, so with the aid of this following wind, our decidedly limited sailing know-how is not strained as we rapidly move out a considerable distance offshore. Eventually we realize that, pleasant as it is to run before the wind, if we continue on this course we will soon be out on the open ocean. We are not yet ready for this prospect. There is a group discussion on our next course of action. How do we stop this boat, turn it around and make it return to the rapidly diminishing shoreline? The discussion soon reveals the fact that of all the souls aboard, only Limey has had any prior sailing experience, limited though that has apparently been. Still, he knows you have to tack to make headway against the wind, and even more importantly, he knows enough of the required technique to execute this fundamental sailing manoeuvre. Naturally, Limey assumes command. Nonetheless, there is much confusion among the crew not only as to what it is he wants us to do, but which one of us does he want to do it? After some cranky sorting out, a semblance of order is reached by consensus and we begin inching our way back toward our beacon, the big white St. Margaret's headquarters building, now dimly seen in the distance. It seems like hours later that we tie up at the school's wharf, vowing never again voluntarily to venture so far offshore in such a demanding vessel. Our crew had been close to mutiny, but stayed from that most desperate crime of the nautical world because were it not for Captain Limey we would by now be out in the open Atlantic.

The weeks go by quickly as we absorb the basics of rope work, lifeboat handling, signalling, cargo work and navigation. These are all fundamental components of the seamanship that it is essential we learn if we are to be of any help at all the first time we set foot aboard a ship. But of course, it is entirely imparted to us while we are securely footed on dry land, apart from the time spent in lifeboat training and even that takes place on the more or less sheltered and placid waters of inner St. Margaret's Bay. Not until we go to work on the heaving deck of a ship at sea will our school-taught skills be truly tested.

None of the skills required of a deckhand are particularly demanding of either manual or mental dexterity, but there is a multitude of them, many more than the basic few taught at St. Margaret's. The Hubbards school is our seaman's kindergarten and our finishing school will be aboard some ship. Before the war brought on severe shortages of deep-sea personnel, a young landsman aspiring to a seagoing berth likely first spent some time as a lowly seamen's messboy, or "Peggy," while awaiting an opening for an Ordinary Seaman. An OS could not expect to earn an Able Seaman rating until he had several years[*] of seagoing experience, but by 1943, one short voyage is considered enough to transform an inept OS into a veteran AB. Most of us will make this magical metamorphosis within months of leaving Hubbards behind us.

The day finally arrives in mid-January 1944 when I am called to the school office to be told I am a finished product and handed my Certificate of Training attesting that I have undergone intensive training in the listed subjects and have reached the approved standard of proficiency for ability. I am also presented with Department of Transport Certificate of Efficiency as Lifeboatman, No. 9014. Is it significant that the mighty C. D. Howe has declined to endorse this assessment, two red lines having been drawn through his imprinted signature, and that of the lesser J. E. Michaud substituted?

I am one of four taking leave of St. Margaret's at the same time, all of us destined for the Vancouver Seamen's Manning Pool. Three of us, myself, Martin and Nordal, are Winnipeggers, while the fourth, Bill Mundie, calls Vancouver his home. He is

[*] According to statute, three years of foreign-going service were required to qualify as an Able Seaman, as quoted by Arthur Randles, Director of Merchant Seaman, in a memo 4 September 1942 to C. P. Edwards, Deputy Minister of Transport.

to be assigned as a Cadet Officer but the rest of us will ship out as very Ordinary Seamen. The fact that we are all westerners being posted to the west coast is a happy coincidence, or perhaps a thoughtful consideration in Captain Wilson's selection process. In any event, it means that en route to Vancouver, three of us are able to stop off for a few days at home where we swagger about like old seadogs, while Billy Mundie will have access to his family home until the ship to which he is eventually assigned actually sails.

The Seamen's Manning Pool is an elderly building at 500 Dunsmuir St. in downtown Vancouver, a former hotel—the Dunsmuir—that could not have rated four-star status even in its best years, and in its current manifestation would qualify for no more than a minus rating. The ancient lobby is furnished with tired chairs and lounges of matching antiquity. There is an elevator but this does not seem to be for the benefit of the resident seamen awaiting assignment. Access to the rooms, which are for sleeping only, is by the stairs, many flights of them. The rooms are sparsely furnished, indeed, all they contain are cots, several to a room. There is a large mess hall for the several hundred seamen awaiting ships. It is shelter and sustenance of the most basic kind. Little wonder that local relatives or acquaintances of the manning pool seamen find themselves being coerced into extending invitations to offer their spare bedrooms for a few days.

One day I am told that a medical examiner is on hand and I am to report for assessment as to my fitness for sea duty. I present myself to the doctor, who is seated at his desk. He waves me to a facing chair and while I am still in the act of lowering myself into this seat, he politely asks me how I am feeling today?

"Fine, thank you," I reply to his courteous inquiry. As I speak, he is writing something on a form. It is difficult to read a doctor's writing at any time, and even more difficult when trying to read it upside down, but unmistakably, his pen scribes "F-i-t."

"Okay," he says, dismissing me. "Would you send in the next man on your way out?" No concern about future pensions here. Maybe I should try the Air Force again.

My stay in the dismal atmosphere of the manning pool is thankfully abbreviated. Just twelve days after my unceremonious graduation from St. Margaret's ("Here's your Certificate of Training and here's your travel warrant to Vancouver. Go."), I am told I have been assigned to the *SS Green Hill Park*. My life as a sailor is, at last, about to begin.

Chapter Fourteen   FIRST TRIPPER

I *am* impressed. The sheer gray wall of riveted steel before me seems to soar several storeys above CPR Pier B, where I'm standing at the foot of the *Green Hill Park*'s gangway. I know she's but a middling size ship, yet to this prairie boy she is positively monstrous. How could anything this large be movable? But this is no time for awe-struck contemplation. It is a dull, damp and cold morning, 27 January 1944, 9 a.m.—more correctly, 0900—and this Ordinary Seaman in name only, just twelve days out of St. Margaret's Sea Training School, is about to join his first ship.

Lugging my heavy suitcase, I struggle up the steep gangway to deck level where I get directions to the crew accommodation at the stern of the ship. I pick my way along the littered deck past hissing, clattering cargo winches. The ship, moored portside to, is already loading timber from lighters secured alongside starboard, in preparation for her maiden voyage. I enter the aft deckhouse where the seamen's and firemen's messes are located, and proceed down the accommodation ladder to the quarters below deck that are to be my home for over a year. I already know two of my cabin mates—Martin and Nordal—both Winnipeggers and like myself, fresh out of St. Margaret's. I hope the rest of the crew members about to take this monster to sea have somewhat more experience than we three first-trip amateurs. It helps to learn that the fourth for our cabin, Art Bourgeois, is an Able Seaman, though in these wartimes of fast promotion that could mean he may have completed no more than one deep-sea voyage. Poor Bourgeois. To us he represents the security of experience, but to him, a volatile French Manitoban from St. Boniface, it must be depressing to find himself sharing quarters with three neophytes who, bad enough that they are first-trippers, have never before set foot on a ship. Furthermore, two of us are unilingual Anglo-Saxons; the other is possibly bilingual, but in English and Icelandic. No matter, Bourgeois accepts us with good-natured sufferance.

We are still changing into working gear when the Bosun summons us on deck to begin tidying up the clutter left behind by the shipyard workers. The Bosun, it is plain, is an old hand. I have often read the word *grizzled* in print but this is the first time I have seen it walking and talking. The Bosun, or more familiarly "Boz" (pronounced as in *hose;* I never *do* know him by name)is a heavy set man, a maybe forty Maritimer or Newfie, I think, from the slight lilt in his voice. His working clothes are well-worn but clean coveralls and a frayed tweed cap. A pipe is a fixture, so permanent that the teeth clamping it in place are bent outwards in accommodation. He comes with a sidekick, Jimmy. A veteran AB, Jimmy is the Bosun's longtime shipmate, but certainly no sycophant. The *Green Hill Park* is just the most recent of ships on which they have sailed together. They are a team who, it is soon evident, would be capable of shaping up this ship even were the entire deck crew as fresh from St. Margaret's as Martin, Nordal and I. The Bosun's appearance may not be prepossessing but there is no doubt that he is our authority figure. We are at the bottom of the shipboard chain of command and the Bosun is our link with the top. He speaks to the Chief Officer who speaks to the Captain who, in prewar shiplore at least, speaks only to God.

Martin and I are assigned to help Bourgeois, assistance it is soon obvious he would sooner not have. He picks up one end of a piece of scrap dunnage. No matter that it is only four feet in length, Martin and I vie to pick up the other end. Bourgeois curses quietly. He finds a tangle of rope, seeks out a free end and begins to coil. Martin and I eagerly search out the other end and together we hold it steady for Bourgeois. In this way, we subconsciously reason, he will know when there is no more rope left to coil. Bourgeois curses not so quietly. Our anxious, limpetlike attachment annoys him but we persist until in exasperation he invents jobs for each of us that we can do on our own. Separately. Away from him. And so we are launched inauspiciously on our introduction to practical shipboard seamanship. So far, not much of it seems to relate to the lessons of St. Margaret's.

Well, occasionally something does. One day I pick up a length of rope and notice that at one end, lacking any whipping, the strands are unravelling. I recall the words of wisdom of an instructor at St. Margaret's—at least I took them to be words of wisdom at the time—that the tidy seaman, on sighting an unravelling rope end, should put a stop to it by administering a backsplice. So, mindful of this sage advice, I execute a backsplice. Very neat. The trouble is, backsplicing entails tucking the loose strands back into the rope two or three times, which results in a lumpy rope end. That's a nuisance if, for example, it becomes necessary to reeve the rope through a block. Won't go. As it happens, I am alone and unseen when I perform this act of neatness. Fortunately. Some short time later, as the deck crew is being assembled to cast off, the bosun spots my handiwork. His jaw muscles tighten and he comes close to biting off the stem of his pipe. "Jayzuz H. Christ," he hisses through clenched teeth. Something in his reaction tells me not to claim credit for this demonstration of rope-splicing skill. He obviously does not approve.

The Bosun doesn't initiate a search for the culprit but he instinctively knows it is highly probable that responsibility lies with one of the three St. Margaret's graduates in his deck gang. He is aware that the demands of wartime manning have seen more than one untrained landsman metamorphose from factory worker to messman to Ordinary Seaman to Able Seaman in one or two voyages, without necessarily acquiring all the usual seaman-associated skills, rope splicing among them. Such wartime ABs are getting by because the Park ships are all new, delivered ready to put to sea and complete in every essential, including all required rope splicing. And of course there's usually enough of a leavening of genuine old hands, like the Bosun and his shipmate Jimmy, to handle any splice work that comes up sooner or later. That, in the Bosun's reasoning, brings him back to the St. Margaret's graduates, rapidly becoming ubiquitous on ships of the expanding Park fleet and eager to demonstrate their ropework knowledge. Who else could possibly have been responsible for that dumb backsplice?

* * *

The ship soon moves over to Vancouver Island to pick up ammunition and torpedo nets at Esquimalt, and to complete loading timber at Cowichan Bay and Port Alberni. I am on standby when, late at night we approach Esquimalt and prepare to take aboard a pilot. The order comes from the bridge: "Put out a boat rope." This ignorant Ordinary Seaman is all alone on the foredeck. What the hell is a boat rope? I don't remember such a thing being mentioned at St. Margaret's. Where is an AB when you need one? Mercifully, when it becomes clear to the bridge that nothing is being done forward to execute the boat rope order somebody is finally sent to bail me out of my confusion. A boat rope, I learn, is simply a rope fastened at points fore and aft so that it hangs in a bight down the ship's side, close enough to the sea surface for the pilot boat to secure temporarily while the pilot boards. Of course.

During one of these between island ports movements there is some modest rolling and pitching. My worst fear is realized: I'm seasick though we've yet to leave sheltered waters. The degree of queasiness I feel is in inverse proportion to the gentleness of the rolling of the ship. "It's all in your mind," an AB tells me. My gut reaction tells me otherwise. There is no escape, inside, outside, standing, sitting, lying down. Maybe the lying down is the worst because my bunk is positioned thwartships. That means as the ship rolls I am teeter-tottering, alternately sliding to the bottom of the bunk and then to the top. Pure misery.

Our last island port of call is Port Alberni, which we reach by entering Barkley Sound on the Island's west coast and steaming forty miles through stunning scenery along the fjordlike Alberni Inlet. During the final stages of taking on our deckload of timber at dockside in Port Alberni, the ship suddenly lists to port. Some time later it reverses, though the degree of starboard list at which it settles is somewhat lessened. Is this cause for alarm? Not to a credulous first tripper naively assuming those guys with the gold stripes on their sleeves know what they are doing.

When the closed hatches and all available deck space are piled high with sweet/sour smelling fresh sawn timber the deckload's neat stacks are cinched securely in place by turnbuckle-tautened heavy chains. Only the spectre of fire at sea is more frightening than that of shifting cargo. The last act of cargo loading is to spraypaint the deckload with a coat of gray to meld with the ship's suit of Admiralty gray camouflage. We're ready to sail when it's discovered a couple of messboys have deserted, so we have to wait for replacements from the Manning Pool. At last, still listing slightly, we cast off and set out to the open sea, southward bound for San Pedro, the port for Los Angeles, to take on a full supply of bunker oil for the long voyage ahead.

We travel coastwise in blustery but sparkling weather that gives a cold hard edge to the celebrated blue of the blue Pacific. The *Green Hill Park* is now doing some serious pitching and rolling and I'm seasick once more. But seasickness has never been identified as fatal so no sympathy is forthcoming from the Bosun. His prescription is the distraction of work. At his forepeak locker—a storeroom packed with every conceivable item required for running maintenance—he supplies me with scrubbing broom, bucket, measures of soft soap and caustic soda, directs me to mix same with water and take the powerful brew to the Captain's bridge, where I am to scrub the wooden deck. This assignment works quite well because as I periodically toss up on the Captain's deck, I am able to scrub up the mess promptly. Not that I am actually regurgitating much, having eaten nothing since reaching the open sea. But by the time we anchor in San Pedro harbour four days out from Port Alberni, the nausea is retreating. Although it returns after we depart San Pedro a day and a half later following bunkering, I get my sea legs within a few days and resume taking nourishment. The cure turns out to be permanent and I never suffer again.

The firemen's Peggy is not so fortunate, although it appears his problem is not so much seasickness as just plain fear. As a messboy, his job requires him to pick up containers of food from the galley midships and deliver them to the firemen's mess aft. While toting the heavy containers, he has to traverse a meandering catwalk that the carpenter has built across the deckload. On a heavily rolling and pitching ship this can be perilous trip. One day I see him making his way along the catwalk on his hands and knees, pushing the food containers before him. A sailor's life is plainly not for him and a replacement boards at San Pedro.

* * *

None of my past contacts with nature has been on such familiar terms. In its tireless, constant motion the sea is hypnotic, whether lighting up the churning wake with glowing phosphorescence or hissing in annoyance as it tries unsuccessfully to cling to the sides of our invading hull. With nary a wingbeat, albatrosses knap-soar at barely inches altitude, closely following the hills and valleys of the ocean's itinerant swell. Schools of dolphins mock the ship's 11 knots and just to show how easy it is, simultaneously perform acrobatically as they outrace us. One day flying fish make an appearance. A graceful white bird with a long pointed tail pays a visit. "That's a Bosun Bird," I'm informed. "See the marlin spike he's carrying in his back pocket?" On squally days, brief storms intermittently engulf us; other times they pass off beam, mini weather systems, their little rain clouds dumping their moisture back into the sea, sometimes wetting us down in the process. In my off hours I pass time simply watching the unpredictable sea and its environment. Mostly its relationship with us is friendly though occasionally and capriciously, just to keep us from complacency, it becomes confrontational.

At 11 knots, 264 nautical miles every twenty-four hours, seven days a week, the voyage across the Pacific is a long one. Unlike ships on the North Atlantic, those on the Pacific travel independently. With enormous armies and naval forces to be supported and Australia and New Zealand to be supplied, there must be hundreds of cargo ships like us plying this same route at this same time, but in the twenty-three days that eventually pass before we anchor at Brisbane roads, we sight only one other vessel, on an eastbound course.

We are in a time capsule. The four on, eight off watches cycle seamlessly and endlessly, twenty-four hours a day, day in, day out. The routine for the deck crew of ten is that six are assigned to watchkeeping, two per watch. On each watch, the two alternate, an hour on the wheel, an hour on standby. The other four members of the deck gang have an eight-hour work day which follows the curious British pattern of turning out for an 07:00 start, followed by a one-hour break for breakfast at 08:00. For the rest of the day, the schedule is a routine one ending at 17:00, and including morning and afternoon mug-up breaks. During that ten-hour span the standby watchkeeper is required to join the deck gang dayworkers for his off-wheel periods. While the two cadets also sometimes turn out for work with the dayworkers, most often they are assigned tasks considered more in keeping with their status as officers-in-the-making.

Early in my introduction to shipboard life, it becomes apparent that there is little that is romantic about a seaman's job. Our working day is mostly taken up in waging war on rust. Muscle-powered chipping hammers, scrapers and four-inch paint brushes are the pitifully inadequate weapons with which we engage in hand-to-hand combat against corrosion. The battleground covers what seems like several acres of steel, much of it often awash in salt water and what isn't awash is constantly exposed to salt air. It is a ludicrously uneven battle made the more difficult by the fact that these wartime-built ships have very often received their initial applications of red lead primer and Admiralty gray paint under less-than-ideal weather conditions. Even before the first crew boards a new ship, the rust is off to a head start beneath these supposedly protective shipyard-applied first coats.

I soon learn that at least while at sea, I can keep my participation in the tedious chores of chipping, scraping and painting to a minimum by becoming a watchkeeper on the 4:00-to-8:00 watch. This is not a problem because there is not much competition for the 4:00-to-8:00, with its decidedly unpopular 03:40 wake-up call for the start of the morning watch. My watchmate and I switch first wheel for the start of each watch, so only on every second day do I find myself on standby between 4:00 and 5:00 p.m., when I am required to join the day crew for the final hour of their workshift. That forced labour for the standby can also be avoided during the last hour of the morning 4:00 to 8:00 if he pads his duties in rousing the 8:00-to-12:00 watch. In tropical ports, however, where the weather is almost always permitting and there are no watches to keep, there is no escaping the inevitable paint brush. Except for one or two hands on deck to keep the paint buckets replenished, it's everyone over the side on stages or in bosun's chairs to freshen up the hull.

Going over the side to paint can be dangerous. We are maybe seventy miles up the mighty Congo river, moored alongside in the steamy port of Boma, taking on a load of palm kernels. I am painting along the waterline, working alone in the square-ended punt that Chips has built just for that purpose. I am close to finishing up at the bow when I hear a noise above me. I look up. There, protruding from the bulwarks is what is unmistakably a pair of naked Congolese buttocks. Just as unmistakably it is the moment of bombs away. With reaction speed and strength previously unimagined I seize an oar, and in a frenzy of paddling propel my blunt craft ahead with such force that it raises a white water bow wave. Safely clear of the drop zone, I look up again. The buttocks have been replaced by a laughing face. After decades of white Belgian colonial rule, the owner has by chance achieved his dream of a lifetime. As for me, I am the captain of the fastest punt on seven seas.

* * *

Steering a large 11-knot ship is like an aerialist trying to walk an elephant along a swaying slackwire. My introduction to the wheel consists only of being advised the course to steer by the helmsman I am about to relieve. What's to learn? Must be just like steering a car. Easier said than done and not particularly applicable considering that I have never driven a car. My instrument of guidance is the gyro repeater; the actual Sperry gyrocompass that the repeater is copycatting is in the chartroom behind me, a spinning top humming away at several thousand rpm. I am expected to keep the compass card steady on the mark. Even in light seas it is a frustrating learning experience. The card swings slowly, almost imperceptibly, indicating a starboard change. I turn the wheel a couple of spokes to port. With tell-tale ticks the card keeps moving. I look up at the bow, which seems to be in a mad race across the horizon. More port helm. There, I've stopped the turn; it's moving back. I'll check the swing when we're back on course. Oops. Too late. The repeater's ticking becomes a blur of sound as I try to overtake and restrain the swinging card. More wheel, less wheel, over compensate, under compensate. Anticipation is the key. Eventually I begin to cope with the ship's ponderous reaction to my movements of the helm. The Chief Mate, who has pretended not to notice my frantic wheel-spinning, wanders out to the wing of the bridge, returning a moment later. "You forgot to dot the *i*," he says in an allusion to the damning wake pattern that I have traced in my first trick at the wheel. It is an ancient cliché often employed by know-it-all officers to embarrass wandering helmsmen.

Compared with a magnetic compass, the gyro compass is positively a precision instrument that makes course-keeping a piece of cake. Gyro compasses are in heavy demand for warships so many cargo ships, particularly older ones, do not have them, but even on ships fortunate enough to be provided with the most modern navigational devices, the magnetic compass is standard backup. Occasionally we have to turn to it for guidance. It sits directly in front of the helmsman, housed in the traditional binnacle which, with its flanking soft iron compensating bars, in appearance would probably not look out of place on a ship of the early nineteenth century.[*] In anything but a calm sea, steering by the dipsy-doodling magnetic compass proves to be a skill—more accurately, an art—this helmsman never really masters.

Even in the South Pacific there are areas where submarine attack is considered a possibility. So we steer a zigzag course to put off the submariner's aim. The zigs and zags are of unequal length and are executed at varied time intervals. To signal the helmsman that it is time for a predetermined course change, the wheelhouse clock is fitted with a brass ring to which a series of adjustable markers are set at the required unequal intervals. When a fine spring extension on the moving minute hand makes contact with each marker, an electrical circuit is completed and a buzzer sounds. The course is then altered to the new preplanned heading. The zigzag pattern is so plotted that the ship's primary course averages out, though the overall effect is to reduce the distance made good. It also keeps the helmsman's mind from wandering.

* * *

---

[*] Matthew Flinders, British naval officer, navigator and explorer (1774-1814), developed the system of compensating bars that offset the deviating effects on the magnetic compass of a ship's iron components. The vertical bar affixed to the front of a binnacle is still known as the Flinders' Bar. The perfecting of these compensating devices became particularly important with the introduction of iron and steel ships. According to Peter Kemp's *The Oxford Companion to Ships and the Sea*, "The magnetism inherent in the iron ship's structure caused considerable difficulty in the early days, to such an extent that it was suggested seriously that such ships would never be successful for they would be quite unsafe in the absence of well-behaved compasses."

It is not only because I can dodge a great deal of deck work that I like the 4:00-to-8:00 watch. I particularly enjoy the solitude of the early morning 4:00-to-8:00 when all are abed except for the Chief Mate, me and my fellow watchkeeper, the Sparks, the cook and his assistant and, below deck, the engine room watch. If I'm on first standby, my only specific duty is to provide hot coffee to the Chief Mate on the bridge. I brew it in the saloon pantry where there are often goodies that we rarely see in the seamen's pantry aft. Naturally, I sample them.

Outside, it's a typical South Pacific night, air clear, sky cloudless. As the ship rolls gently, the cold light of the moon combines with the ship's all pervading gray paintwork to produce an eerie photographic negative effect of black and white tones and halftones. Sharply etched shadows cast by masts and booms and stays snake across hatch covers, down over the coamings, across the deck and over the railings, reaching out to everything in their paths. Then, as the ship rolls back, they make a slithering retreat. There's still time before I have to relieve the man on the wheel, so I flop on No. 3 hatch and stare up at the sky, swarming with stars of startling brilliance. We're south of the equator and the Southern Cross has taken over from the Big Dipper and Polaris. I notice that, strangely, the tip of the radio mast seems motionless against this backdrop. There is the illusion that the sky is moving; sometimes sweeping back and forth across the masthead, sometimes doing quick little twirls around it. Our ship is the centre of the universe. Maybe the Inquisition was right to condemn Galileo.

But such reveries are only for when I have first standby. Today I am first wheel. It is 03:58. Sleepy-eyed, I climb to the flying bridge and grope my way into the darkened wheelhouse. The Chief Mate and the Second are dimly silhouetted against the three tiny wheelhouse windows. Their official watch-relieving duties completed, they are in a gossip-exchanging huddle. As my eyes adjust to the blackness, I am able to make out the figure of the helmsman. The coconut matting on the deck deadens my footsteps as I pick my way over to him. Not until I am right alongside can I make out his face in the dim reflected glow from the compass repeater. We exchange places on the helmsman's platform. "Steering two six eight," he says, and even as he is saying it I watch the heading swinging past 275. "Steering two six eight," I repeat drily. "And thanks." I turn the wheel three spokes to port, hoping to ease her back on course without the mate noticing the shadows telltaling their way across the deck. Fortunately, he and the second are still absorbed in comparing social notes from the last port of call.

The 4:00-to-8:00 has begun.

Chapter Fifteen # ON CONVOY

Rare was the wartime merchant seaman who at some point did not find himself aboard a ship in convoy. An escorted convoy could be as small as two ships or it could number in the hundreds. The larger ones, multi-columned, stretched out over tens of miles of ocean surface, never failed to impress. This herding of ships under Naval escort, while providing a measure of protection from submarine attack, also introduced another element of danger. With so many ships travelling in relatively close formation, sometimes zigzagging, sometimes in dense fog, sometimes in stormy seas, the possibility of collisions among the slow manoeuvring elephantine hulls was ever present. For the men aboard the ships convoy travel could be many things, sometimes boring, sometimes exciting, sometimes frightening. Above all, it was a never-to-be-forgotten experience.

George Auby was not a merchant seamen but spent the first couple of years of the war masquerading as one while serving aboard merchant ships as a convoy signalman, one of the more offbeat jobs to which Naval persons sometimes found themselves assigned. A telegraphist with the Halifax RCNVR in 1938, he was one of about one hundred or more in that trade from across Canada called up for service in August 1939 when war seemed imminent. Because of their knowledge of Morse code, George and some of the other drafted telegraphists were attached to the Naval Control Service Office (NCSO) as convoy signalmen.

Each convoy would have a retired Admiral or other person of high rank aboard the centre ship of the front line of the convoy to act as convoy Commodore, and as convoy signalman, George Auby was a member of Admiral's staff. Although an enlisted Naval person, he was not allowed to wear uniform dress and was signed on ship's register as a member of the crew, sometimes on the same ship as the Admiral, sometimes on a corner ship to pass signals down the line of convoy.

The war was not many hours old when Auby was caught up into the thick of it.

> On September 10, 1939 the NCSO sent me to the Gordon B. Isnor clothing store in Halifax for an outfit of civilian clothes. My Navy gear was stowed in a locker at HMCS *Stadacona* and under complete secrecy. I was not allowed to use a phone and was given no indication of where I was being sent. I was escorted to the Polish liner *Batory*, where I signed ship's papers

as a communications civilian person. The Canadian Naval Auxiliary Vessels Signal Book was handed to me in a lead weighted bag, to be thrown over the side if we got in trouble with the enemy. The purpose of this book was to interpret messages from Naval escort and convert to International Code for the convoy.

Aboard the *Batory* was a retired English Admiral with all his important papers wrapped in a waterproof package. He spent the entire trip to England in the boardroom on A deck, sitting and sleeping in a chair at a table wearing his life jacket.

The voyage was not like anything Auby would encounter when he eventually returned to more regular Navy duties. On the *Batory*, women were still part of the crew complement and he remembers being served caviar, and beer in small stoneware bottles. It was a fast ship, taking only four or five days to complete the crossing to Liverpool, where Mr. Shaw, a resident Canadian government official, had him put up at a hotel.

The next morning he was issued a gas mask, helmet, identity card and pay book. He was asked how much money he wanted and, having neither Canadian funds nor any idea how much the English pound was worth, he suggested £150. They gave him £100, equivalent to $450, which was a handsome sum in those days. There was no ship immediately available to return to Canada so Mr. Shaw gave George a rail pass to London and told him he didn't have to report back for two weeks. At the end of the two weeks, which he spent visiting all of London's popular tourist attractions, he reported back to Liverpool, where Mr. Shaw had obtained passage for an uneventful trip back to Canada for him on the 10,000 ton passenger/cargo *Manchester Merchant*.

It was now about mid-October 1939 and, the Naval Control Service Office in Halifax temporarily having more communication men than ships, gave him a few days leave to visit his parents who, at that point had no idea what had happened to him since early in September. "My mother had me listed as lost until the RCMP came up with, 'Somewhere at sea'."

The next ship to which Auby was assigned by NCSO Halifax was the *Manchester Commerce*, similar in size to the *Manchester Merchant*. Sailing date was 20 October 1939, with the *Manchester Commerce* as lead ship in a forty-six-ship convoy. On board was a full Admiral's staff complement of Admiral, RN Signal Chief Petty Officer, Petty Officer, Leading Signalman and Ordinary Signalman George Auby. The DEMS gun crew, British Army, practiced daily on a 4-inch gun mounted astern on a roughly built platform. "The captain was not in favour of them firing this gun as it shook hell out of the ship."

South of Iceland they ran into severe storms and lost the convoy. Carrying on independently, their route took them south of Ireland where they came under attack by land-based Luftwaffe aircraft. Because their original destination, London, would have taken them into the English Channel, which was now considered too dangerous, the *Manchester Commerce* was diverted to Liverpool. After only a few days there, Auby was shipped back to Canada as a passenger on the *Manchester Guardian*. Once back in Canada, he returned to more typical Navy routine for several months, being drafted to an RCN minesweeper and other patrol vessels to relieve signalmen for courses.

George Auby's next assignment to signalling duties aboard a merchant ship proved to be the most stressful and dangerous he faced, though the danger came not from the external threat posed by the known German enemy, but from the recalcitrant French merchant crew whose wavering loyalties intermittently changed course. The ship was the *P.L.M. 17*, one of two Paris-Lyon-Marseille Railway coal boats that had been captured by British Commandos after France capitulated to Germany.

On 21 September 1940, Auby's orders were to stow his Navy gear, don civvies again and travel to Sydney, Nova Scotia, to be picked up there by *P.L.M. 17* after it had taken on a load of iron ore at Wabana, Newfoundland.

"The ship," Auby recalls,

> was totally French, even to the sabot footwear worn by many of the crew. The RCN drafting office must have decided my name looked Frenchy enough to converse with the officers and crew, and also maintain signals with the convoy in English. But I couldn't speak French and none of the crew, English. We were well out of Sydney harbour before this was determined. How does an ordinary seaman run an 8000 ton ship when there is a language barrier? Fortunately, the skipper, Captain Chadwick, an old sailing ship master from Cardiff, Wales, who had boarded the ship in Newfoundland, came to my rescue. By the way, he couldn't speak French either.

As if the problem of the language barrier were not trying enough, it quickly became evident to the English-speaking pair that the unspeakably bad sanitary conditions aboard the ship posed a danger to their health.

> We quickly sized up this impossible situation and went to work. We picked a small head and went to work with soap, water and scrubbers, cleaning the walls, floor, toilets and even the ceiling. There is no way to describe the filth of this one small room. In fact, the whole ship was like the filth of the toilet. The crew excreted everywhere—the decks, the bridge, the wings of the bridge; it was really hard to walk without stepping into a pile.
>
> We put a padlock on our clean bathroom, only to have to go through the same procedure a few hours later, the French crew having broken into and messed up our head again. This time after cleaning we put on double locks and Captain Chadwick managed to convey a warning to the French

officers without having to speak French. He also decided that I should share his cabin and meals and we should take turns standing watch.

We weren't out from port more than twelve hours when the crew revolted and refused to work. The Captain ordered better food for them and they went back to work. About three days out, after we joined the convoy from Newfoundland, the whole crew—officers and all—expressed the desire to leave the convoy and go back to France. We knew at that time we had the makings of a mutiny on our hands. Captain Chadwick made it clear through gestures that what they wanted was impossible. He pointed to a destroyer close by and indicated that we would be blown out of the water. This seemed to deter them and they went back to their duties.

On watch, the Captain and I had a most difficult time when trying to keep the *P.L.M. 17* on zigzag convoy courses. We used a large chalkboard with the compass degrees and the time to change plainly marked. The French expressed hostility to this type of sailing and, as the deployment of the zigzag changed every few hours, we were kept on our toes to make sure we were on the right course. We rubbed several ships and a number of times came close to collision.

About mid-Atlantic, there being no Naval escort in sight, the French crew decided to stop the ship's engines. As the average speed of the convoy was about 6 knots, it didn't take long before the last of the convoy was out of sight. Captain Chadwick strapped a revolver about my waist, armed himself with an old World War One Ross rifle, and we confronted the crew. He left no doubt in their minds that he meant business: either get the ship under way or face a German torpedo as a sitting duck. It took them about an hour to make a decision before we got under way in a vain attempt to catch the convoy. We sailed alone for the rest of the journey, this time going to the north of Ireland and into Glasgow. We were glad to be rid of this ship.

For his feat in bringing the mutinous *P.L.M. 17*[*] safely to port, Captain Chadwick was honoured with a dinner hosted by many high-ranking persons in Glasgow. To them, he described the trip as the most sinister and menacing he'd ever sailed, and, fine person that he was, he passed on much praise to me.

I was given passage back to Halifax on the 5500 ton *Glen Park*, a new built ship just fresh from the Glasgow shipyards on the Clyde. Our trials were to begin on crossing the ocean. Once again we sailed without escort and just about

---

[*] It was only about a year after the P.L.M. 17 crossing that George Auby found out there had been another similar ship, the P.L.M. 28 carrying iron ore, sunk off Grand Bay, Newfoundland. No survivors. The people of that small settlement tried to get the crew out of the water but, too late. There is a small cemetery close by with about twenty headstones of the French people who perished.

two hundred miles north of the Azores our engine bearings seized up. As usual we were in the midst of a howling Atlantic northerly storm. We had no ballast and came dangerously close to rolling over. All forms of anchor were used, kedge, sail, etc. I was told we drifted extremely close to the Azores. The chief engineer managed to effect makeshift repairs which allowed us to proceed toward Canada at a maximum speed of 5 knots. This was in 1941 and it took us nineteen days to cross. Why we were not spotted by some submarine and sunk is still a mystery to me. This is when Germany had its largest concentration of sea wolves in the area to intercept the convoys when the eastern escorts left the convoy and before they were met by western air and sea protection.

* * *

Fresh from St. Margaret's Sea Training School at Hubbards, Nova Scotia, sixteen-year-old Cadet Officer Edward Bain, now of Calgary, Alberta, joined the Westmount Park in September 1943 for her maiden voyage. After loading in Montreal, where the 10,000-ton ship had been built by United Shipyards, and Quebec City, it made for Halifax in a four-ship convoy. Bain's cryptic diary entries reflect the reaction of an impressionable sixteen-year-old from central Ontario to the scene in wartime Halifax Harbour.

Bedford Basin. What a sight! All around us were ships of all sizes and flags. Small boats everywhere. Ship's captains going and coming. Last minute stores coming aboard.

13 October: Today is the day. The Captain went ashore early and returned an hour or so ago and at 1230 hours we steered out of Halifax Harbour in a thirteen-ship convoy.

On 14 October I came upon a sight I know I will never forget for the rest of my life. Early in the morning we joined the main convoy from New York. Altogether we made a convoy of sixty-five ships and an escort of thirteen warships. As far as the eye could see there were ships. It took most of the day and many signals before we were in position, first column port side. We were one of the few ships with torpedo nets. This great sight lasted only for that day; on the fifteenth, off the Banks of Newfoundland we ran into a very heavy fog and lost the convoy.

* * *

John Covan of Markdale, Ontario, and Alex White of Regina, Saskatchewan, were shipmates aboard the Green Gables Park, which they both joined at the same time in 1943, Covan as a Cadet Officer after graduation from St. Margaret's Sea Training School and Alex White as a Radio Officer following training at the Radio College of Canada. Half a century later, when they met at the 1990 convention of the Canadian Merchant Navy Association, they reminisced about their days at sea, and particularly their recollections of convoy travel on the North Atlantic.

For Alex White, it was the sense of security the presence of RCN corvettes gave him.

I remember the feeling we used to have when we went into convoy with the Canadian corvettes. I guess we were biased but we seemed to think they did a better job than anybody else. I always remember whenever they gave that signal that they definitely had contact with a submarine, our feeling was that our guys had seen the whites of the sub commander's eyes, and knew his name and his mother-in-law and everything else about him. It was a funny feeling but I've never forgotten that because we seemed to think they could do a better job. Whether they did or not, who knows? It's nice to be biased.

And, John Covan added:

I felt sorry for those corvette crews. I think of leaving Halifax in convoy in January and merging with the convoy coming up from New York, and seeing the corvettes, oh, blowing like hell! The seas! And those corvettes just standing on their ears; I almost got seasick just watching them. I did all the visual signalling from daylight till noon, so I would be flashing back and forth, which meant I had to keep an eye on the escorts, and I thought, oh my God, those poor so and so's."

* * *

Brock Cummings, who now makes his home in Prescott, Ontario, was barely sixteen when he began his sailing career on a British-American oil tanker, travelling the Great Lakes and to Newfoundland and Canadian coastal points. In 1943 he went deep-sea, joining the Riverdale Park at Saint John, New Brunswick, as an AB, to make a series of voyages to the U.K.

I made about nine trips across there. We saw quite a bit of action, but I was very fortunate, didn't get into any trouble. There were a lot of ships I saw blown to pieces, tankers burning; picked up a few people from out of the water, here and there. Travelling in convoy, you weren't supposed to stop even for rescues because it would make you an easy target, but we just did. Our skipper, Captain Osborne, we used to call him Flight Lieutenant—his name was F. L. Osborne—was a good man. He didn't give a damn for anything, he would stop anyway. We'd see a bunch of guys in the water, we'd pick them up. Then we were fast enough—able to do 10 knots but in a convoy doing maybe only 6 or 7 knots because that was the speed of the slowest ship—that we could run back and get into our position again.

The HMS *Duke of York*, the battleship, used to do convoy duty. She'd be maybe twenty miles ahead of us, back and forth, and then between us and her would be the HMCS *Prince David*, a small liner that the Canadian Navy had converted into an armed merchant cruiser. We had them quite often.

* * *

George Devonshire, today a resident of Picton, Ontario, was twenty in February 1942 when he left his Toronto home for Montreal to join the Merchant Navy, but it was April before he received a call from CN Steamships offering him a job, which he accepted, as galley boy on the MV Asbjorn, a Danish-owned vessel which was being operated under charter to the Canadian government because Denmark was under Nazi occupation. During his single trans-Atlantic trip on the Asbjorn (he later joined the RCN) he kept a diary, two August 1942 entries of which provide a vivid picture of a convoy under U-boat assault.

Sunday, August 2: Past two days rainy weather and very rough. Sub alarms on and off and depth bombs heard quite frequently. Yesterday had lifeboat drill. Today, we hear from reliable source that escort actually sighted two subs on the surface. Escorts attacked and subs submerged. Was probably during the time I was having tea in the gunners quarters, because we heard a number of charges banging against the hull.

Monday, August 3: Last night was hell let loose. I turned in about 8:00 p.m. only to be wakened about 10:00 p.m. and told to dress for lifeboats. When I stepped out on deck I was amazed at the sight. It looked like a real expensive 24th of May exhibition. Snowflake and star shells littered the sky. The convoy was already under attack. It was an eerie sight to see the black forms of the ships when there was a rocket in the sky and quite impressive to see the gunners scurry past you in the dark, going about their job calmly and efficiently. Our part of the convoy was still organized, although there is a rumour the Commodore's ship was hit.

Gunfire could be heard on both the port and starboard horizon and depth charges kept up their infernal booming on our hull. The "lifeboat ready" sounded about 10:30 p.m., but we stayed down on deck. The Chief Steward was worrying about all the cigarette and beer money that was owing to him. It is hard to describe one's feelings at a time like that. You are too excited to be frightened. The only thing that troubled me is that I would have liked to have been doing something to help. Things quietened down about 12:00 a.m. so I turned in again, sleeping in a life belt. However, it was hard to sleep due to the excitement and also every half hour or so a pattern of charges would play hell. It was very foggy in the morning. I couldn't see more than twenty feet outboard. However, we are still holding some sort of convoy judging from the signal whistles of the ships. There are twelve ships not in the convoy.

* * *

Bob Downing, then a fifteen-year-old from Vancouver, began his deep-sea career in January 1943 as a messman aboard the ancient Imperial Oil tanker, Albertolite, which serviced west coast North American ports. He later signed on as an AB on IOL's more modern Ontariolite (an ex-German war prize), which was soon transferred from the west to the east coast to carry oil from Caribbean ports to Portland, Maine, where it was discharged into the Portland-Montreal pipeline. Convoy travel was mostly uneventful as a norm, but Downing, who is retired in Yuma, Arizona, remembers a couple of scares.

There was the time in Coffin Corner in a northbound convoy. It was a misty night with a lookout on the bow as we were timed, zigzagging, and had to keep an eye on the ship ahead. We were just off watch again when we felt the ship pulling over hard to port. We made a complete circle and headed back to the convoy going like hell. Next morning we were told we had nearly been torpedoed. It seems we were to make a starboard zig when the forewatch claimed he saw two wakes heading for our bow. He yelled to the bridge loud enough to be understood and the mate turned hard to port, into the convoy. The subject torpedoes were reputed to have crossed our bow. There was no bang but the ship to our port was zigging to starboard and we were damned close as we made the 360. The question was, did we zig to port, when it should have been a zag to starboard?

I was, as was my watchmate, sure we had been torpedoed one night. There was a hell of a bang. I came out of my bunk ballix. Would you believe I grabbed my wallet and leather jacket, that's all, and headed up to the mess deck, to be greeted by laughing shipmates. Yes, there had been a hell of an explosion; a corvette had raced by and dropped two depth charges. That was a little close. They inspected the aft plates at the end of that run.

* * *

After completing a one-year Radio Operating course at Toronto's Central Technical School, Alan Erson was licensed by the Department of Transport as a Radio Operator and subsequently joined the first of three Park ships on which he served as a Sparks in 1944 and 1945, before returning to resume life in Toronto. While on one of these, the Bridgeland Park, he learned that in convoy travel, your ostensibly friendly traveling companions could be as dangerous as the underwater enemy.

The *Bridgeland Park* left Vancouver in late February 1945 bound for London. At Chemainus, British Columbia, all her holds were loaded with lumber, as well as a deck cargo of lumber as high as the galley smoke stack. She proceeded through the Panama Canal and up to New York where she joined a convoy of several hundred ships. Practically unsinkable due to all the lumber on board, she was therefore assigned to Coffin Corner of the convoy. After leaving New York, the captain opened his sealed orders and announced we were to have gunnery practice on a certain day. As Second Radio Officer, I was put in charge of a group of seven seamen. Our mission was to rush to No. 4 gun station and fire a few volleys with the Oerlikon gun mounted on a metal turret. The equipment was covered with a tarpaulin which was secured with a long metal cable fed through eyelets in the tarp. When the alarm sounded, our group rushed to the gun station, but we were unable to remove the tarpaulin due to about a foot of ice which covered everything. We chopped at it with a fire axe for about twenty minutes but got nowhere.

Suddenly, there was a hail of bullets splattering all over the deck and the senior officers screamed for everyone to get below. Apparently, the ships on the far side of the convoy had not aimed high enough. The next morning, the ship beside us (a

Greek ship) signalled that one of their crew had been killed by the same fusillade. Both ships slowed to a crawl and we all stood at the rail and saluted as the body was slid from under a flag into the sea.

Two days later, the ship ahead of us, another Greek ship, signalled that her steering gear had broken and she wanted to change position with us, so that they could stop and make repairs. We did this, and almost immediately, a pack of U-boats appeared. Six ships in our vicinity were torpedoed, including the Greek ship that had taken our place in Coffin Corner. We were all ordered to put on our life jackets and stand outside the rail, and to jump if a torpedo came our way. Luckily, none did.

* * *

For most, the intricate task of assembling sometimes one hundred and more ships into convoy formation seemed an achievement of mind-boggling proportions, but for Victor Holt of Ladysmith, British Columbia, a fireman on the Elm Park, the breaking up of the convoy at the end of a crossing was even more impressive, a process having all the ingredients for the making of a major marine disaster.

A short time before reaching England no one knew where they were going, that is, to which port. At a certain time, all captains opened sealed orders to learn which port they were to go to. Some to the north, some to the south, etc. There was always mayhem as each vessel tried to get into position; ships crossing each others' bows and so on as they took up new courses for their designated port. I came off watch at 8:00 p.m.; it was pitch dark and I was standing by the deck railing amidships when I heard the roar of Diesel engines being put suddenly astern. I looked up and there was this large dark bow coming toward me. I took off just in time before the collision. Fortunately, the damage to our ship wasn't too great so we were able to continue into our port, Glasgow.

[Later] we were in the last convoy to cross the Atlantic. About midway across heading for Canada, the war was declared finished and the blackout was ended. All deadlights on portholes were opened, deck lights and navigation lights were turned on. The convoy looked like a floating city at night!

* * *

Bill Hutcherson, now living in Richmond, British Columbia, was Third Radio Officer on the Crystal Park for her, and his, first voyage early in the summer of 1944. The sights and sounds impressed on this young man from Ladner, British Columbia, while his ship sailed out of New York as part of what he believes was the largest convoy of the war, remain with him to this day.

It was in the afternoon . . . that we turned at the Ambrose lightship to head into New York harbour and as we entered the Hudson River we were amazed to see the congestion of shipping in the harbour. Ships of every Allied nation, big liners, Liberties, Forts, Parks, old single skinny stack veterans and even some ocean-going yachts. We were all crammed into an area much too small to hold us, so when the tide changed we'd all swing around on our anchors and one or two banged into each other. One night we came so close to a big Dutchman that we wiped the welded letters of his name right off the stern. Gee, the air was sure filled with Dutch curses (I guess that's what they were).

Several of us went ashore that first night . . . and then the following day the Captain, the Chief Engineer and the three Radio Officers were all taken by water taxi to dockside and then to a convoy conference. We were ushered into a huge hall with what seemed like a thousand or so of our brother officers, to be given instructions relative to the upcoming convoy forming up for the trip to England. Very little was said other than strict radio silence was to be maintained. All communication to be by Aldis lamp or foghorn and instructions relative to the new codebooks we would be supplied with. We were dismissed but told to be at dockside within two hours and not to reveal to a living soul that the convoy was about to leave or anything we had heard.

That night we left New York and a whole pile of Canadian corvettes showed up to usher us into various columns and assign us a position within one column. *Crystal Park*, being fully loaded with lumber and equipped with torpedo nets, was put at an outside column. That, I guess, was so we could catch the torpedoes and let the other important ships go by. Anyway, Captain Barry seemed pretty calm and he was a veteran of the sea war, having earned his MBE as master of the *Princess Kathleen*, which rescued many of the complement of the *Princess Marguerite* when it was torpedoed and sunk in the Mediterranean. We went up near Halifax and merged with ships waiting there, ending up with 176 merchant ships, which I believe was the biggest convoy of the war. Up ahead were several destroyers and frigates. Corvettes came prowling up our flanks; everything was just a mass of armed escorts wherever you looked.

Then off Newfoundland we hit into fog banks, real thick peasoupers, blotting out the ships in front, beside and astern of you—176 vessels all travelling at 11 knots and no one able to see anyone else, unless they were rubbing their flanks. Collisions, not submarines, now became the enemy, and in order to maintain station each ship would take turns blowing its column and position in Morse code on its siren or fog horn. For instance, our column was No. 23 and our position in the column was thirteenth ship. So every fifteen minutes out we would blast: BLAH, BLAAAH, BLAAAH, BLAAAH, BLAAAH—and that's just for the figure one, but it will give you the idea of the noise that went on day and night. Sleep at first was just impossible but you either got used to it, or you got so darned tired that within days you hardly noticed the continual roar of the whistle and those of the ships around you.

Through the dense fog off Newfoundland, one of our DEMS gunners, fellow by the name of Zimmerman, Zimmy we called him, was on stern lookout. All of these ships trailed a fog buoy which gave a bit of a wake behind it so that the ship astern, if it came up on a fog buoy, would know that there was another ship just ahead. Well, one morning as the fog was commencing to clear a bit, Zimmerman spotted something astern of us and started running for the bridge from the stern position instead of using the telephone. He missed the ladder, fell off the gun platform onto the deck below, bounced up, kept running, came up on the bridge, but he couldn't talk; all he could do was point. Finally he got the words out: "Periscope! Periscope!" At which point the Captain had the alarm bells going and Aldis lamps were flashing, warning the nearest escort of this periscope. The mate, who was scouring the sea astern of us for some sign of the sub, suddenly started scowling. "God dammit man," he roared, "that's our fog buoy back there!" It was indeed. For eight days it had faithfully followed us, sending up its feather of a wake, and this was the first time it had been sighted by any of our eagle-eyed lookouts.

* * *

Bill Hutcherson's last convoy crossing was, he says, uneventful insofar as the wolf packs were concerned, yet still full of the incidents that were commonplace in wartime.

Our convoy sailing on this winter crossing was one of the more uneventful trips in that the fog stayed away and the weather remained fairly mild-mannered. We had a Jeep carrier with us which sent up a couple of patrol planes each day and one of these returning old [Fairey Swordfish] biplanes came lumbering along our column, waggling its wings as he passed over each ship. We were the lead ship of the column and as he gave us his wave he banked in front of us and dipped right down into the drink. Through the glasses we were able to observe a corvette picking up the three-man crew.

The next night a more serious incident took place as one of the patrollers must have lost his way and by the time he picked up the convoy it was already pitch dark. He flew over us several times hunting for his carrier and finally settled into his approach. Unfortunately, in the darkness, he picked the wrong ship and smacked into the bridge of the big tanker, setting it on fire and lighting up the whole group of ships. We felt both sorrow and anger for the young men on the plane and on the ship, who surely died that night. And that was the last convoy excitement we would ever experience during the war as only days later we again entered the St. Lawrence and made our way up to Montreal.

* * *

William Liddell of Niagara-on-the-Lake, Ontario, a 1943 graduate of St. Margaret's Sea Training School from southern Ontario who eventually earned a Master's Certificate, was an AB on the 10,000 ton Dentonia Park for seven convoy crossings of the North Atlantic between August 1944 and the end of WW II. By that time, he reflects, the escort system had been much improved and subs were a reduced threat, but even so, a convoy crossing was not without incident and alarms.

I think subs were being lost faster than they could be replaced, at least in the Atlantic and the Caribbean. I was never torpedoed; I was in convoys that lost a ship or two but this could have been floating mines. The escorts sometimes dropped depth charges, which could have been a sub or some unfortunate whale, who knows? There were submarine attacks and ships lost on the East coast almost to the end of the war, but they were isolated incidents as I remember it.

[Our] cargoes were general: munitions, flour, grain and various other things. On one voyage we lowered the torpedo nets, but with the nets in the water we lost two or three knots and fell astern of the convoy, so the nets were never used again. We also tried out the paravanes, and the guns, dropping astern of the convoy to do so, also a one-time operation.

On one of these voyages I had a scare that I imagine many seamen had during the war. We were in convoy west of Ireland, in Gulf Stream waters. It was a dark but clear night and I was on lookout on the fo'c'sle head. I suddenly noticed a phosphorescent wake streaking directly for the bow. It was too close for me to do anything, so I grabbed the rail and waited. Nothing happened. When I looked again, there were several wakes criss-crossing the bow. Porpoises. So I breathed again, my vision of being blown mast high vanishing as quickly as it had arrived.

On VE Day we were in Hull, on the east coast of Britain. All I can remember of that day is not being able to get into a pub; they were all jammed to the doors. I believe that this was the last voyage in convoy, about fifty ships. At nightfall, all ships put their running lights on. This was quite a sight, especially for me, as I had never seen a ship at sea showing her running lights. The convoy gradually broke up, ships going their various ways at various speeds.

* * *

Arthur Lockerbie, now residing in Sydney, Nova Scotia, was a Radio Officer who served on several vessels, including salvage tugs, but his most intense convoy memories are those from his time on the Point Pelee Park.

There were some marvelous sights in the convoys, to see those columns of ships plunging along in the big swells, or to see all those flags going up and down at noon when the positions were compared, especially on a bright sunny day. Then when the convoy formed one long line to enter port, it was a sight to behold to look astern and see them coming, ships and more ships to the horizon.

* * *

Calgary-born David Martin-Smith, who eventually earned his Master's Certificate (Foreign Going), began his sea career in 1937 sailing on the British-registered King Gruffydd out of New Westminster, British Columbia, as a fourteen-year-old "workaway dogsbody," (i.e., a deck boy paid a nominal one shilling a month —which he says he is still waiting to receive). He worked his way through all the deck jobs on a variety of British and Canadian ships, qualifying first for his license as Second Mate and then, according to the Vancouver Manning Pool, as Canada's youngest Chief

Officer at age twenty-one or twenty-two. Of many convoy incidents remembered by the present-day Victoria, British Columbia, resident, one that occurred shortly after the outbreak of hostilities stands out in his mind.

In a slow convoy out of Halifax from 16 November to 5 December 1939, the benzine tanker *Arletta*, escorted by the battleship, *HMS Warspite*, smack in the middle of the formation, and us placed off her port quarter, one morning a few days after departure *Warspite* sounded her whistle and an internal siren or klaxon, ran up two black balls or shapes, which mean "my vessel is not under command," and slowed down, letting those astern of her pass by. She then took off to starboard at a great rate of knots. We felt alone and deserted, and our captain and officers were incredulous that they would desert the convoy without so much as an informational or warning. We plowed on and made it across to St. George's Channel where RN escorts picked us up and escorted us to Liverpool.

Years later I was reading one of Churchill's books on the war and noted that he reluctantly ordered *Warspite* to abandon her convoy to join other RN forces searching for two German pocket battleships thought to be on the loose in the Atlantic. As it turned out, they had been but had returned to their base by the time *Warspite* arrived in the dangerous area. However, it wasn't really known just where the two threats were, perhaps nearer our convoy and a gamble with the lives of about forty ship's crews. At age seventeen, one is of positive thought anyway, so the import of it only reached me in my sixties. All's well that ends well.

* * *

Born in 1920, Captain Hugh Halkett spent his early years in Victoria and Vancouver, British Columbia. In both places, he haunted the waterfront, watching the ships come and go, nurturing a growing interest in a sea career and dreaming of journeying to unknown ports. By 1941 he was Quartermaster in CP's Princess Mary, a job in which he was "frozen" under wartime essential service rules; nevertheless, he was successful in obtaining a leave of absence from the CP service in order to make one voyage as a seaman under sail on the five-mast schooner City of Alberni. When he rejoined CP, he qualified for his Mate's Certificate, beginning a progression up to Master Mariner status. In 1969 he joined the B.C. Ferry fleet as a Master, remaining there until his retirement in 1985 when he married and, "like the seaman who came inland with an oar until asked what it was, came to St. Albert {Alberta}, where we make our home."

In April of 1944 I was advised that I would be transferred to Canadian Pacific Ocean Service and would join the new vessel *Crystal Park* when she was commissioned out of the builders' yard in North Vancouver. On 5 May she completed trials and I signed on as Third Officer. The captain, deck officers and engineer officers were Canadian Pacific employees; the majority of the rest of the crew were from the manning pool. We proceeded to New Westminster to load ingots in the lower holds and part cargo of lumber after which we sailed for Port Alberni to complete loading lumber, topped off with a deck load. After the deck load was sprayed with gray paint we were ready for sea and under a B.C. coast pilot steamed down Alberni Inlet for Cape Beale where the pilot disembarked.

Our Captain was L. C. Barry, OBE, formerly of the Empress liners, and he did not appear happy with the proximity of land on the coast and when under pilotage the officer of the watch was required to fix the ship's position every fifteen minutes. Captain Barry had been Master of CP's *Princess Kathleen* when she was serving as a troopship in the Mediterranean.

We cleared Cape Flattery and headed southward for San Pedro, where we topped up with bunker oil, then on for Panama. At Balboa we loaded a small parcel of balsa wood on top of No. 3 hatch and covered it well against the weather. We understood that balsa wood was used in connection with aircraft construction in Britain. From Panama, we were part of a small convoy bound for Havana, Cuba, to join a slightly larger convoy bound for New York. At Havana, the American naval commodore chose our ship to be his Commodore's ship and it was an interesting experience to have him and his staff, including navigator and signals party, on board.

Anchored at New York, we waited quite some time while ships accumulated for the Atlantic convoy to the United Kingdom. For security reasons there was no shore leave granted in New York, but I managed a visit ashore to accompany a seaman with a toothache to the marine hospital and return. We sailed in a convoy of some 140 ships and, after a successful crossing, detached off the north of Scotland with eight other ships to proceed to Loch Ewe for orders. After another fairly long wait in the rains and mists of the Loch, we were advised to proceed independently to Cardiff for discharge. From Cardiff we sailed independently, light ship, for Swansea to load coal for Montreal. Coal from Wales to Canada! Seemed rather like the proverbial "taking coals to Newcastle." While at the Welsh ports, I managed leave to visit my aunt who lived in London and while there experienced the nightly attacks by V2s, known to Londoners as doodlebugs, that created devastating damage and casualties. When one heard the engine noise stop, one knew the thing was on its way down.

Laden with coal, we sailed from Swansea for Bangor Bay, Ireland, to join convoy for Canada. Again a safe crossing but there was one unfortunate and tragic accident. At the convoy conference, the ships' masters had been advised that about two days after sailing a Free French submarine would join the convoy and sail on the surface, in station, destined for a refit in the United States. It came about that the submarine joined at night, in moonlight, communications went wrong and she was sunk by gunfire from the Armed Guard of a Liberty ship. Our DEMS gunners had been well appraised that a friendly submarine would be joining.

* * *

Hugh Halkett also recalls a third and final convoy crossing he made in the Crystal Park before returning to the West Coast to resume service with CP's Coast fleet.

For the next voyage we loaded a grain cargo destined for a Mediterranean port, as yet not named. We were part of a coastal convoy to Cape Cod then, under pilotage, sailed down Long Island Sound to New York. The pilot, an old chap brought out of retirement, was a most interesting character who regaled us with yarns as we steamed down the beautiful sound. At New York we were anchored amongst a large assembly of ships and there was a tanker, riding light, close to us. At the turn of a tide and due to a wind the tanker swung to her anchor before we did and ended up broadside across our bow causing no appreciable damage to either vessel, but it took tugs to sort the situation out and we wondered why an empty tanker was among the laden ships.

Our convoy sailed for the Mediterranean and on the way across the war in Europe came to an end. On the night that the news was received a scattering of lights appeared throughout the convoy as celebrations took place. The following morning a bevy of flag hoists, originated by an irate Commodore who stressed that all convoy regulations still existed. He was right, of course, for submarines were known to be still on the loose and possibly trigger happy.

* * *

Not all convoy travel was in the Atlantic, nor was the submarine threat confined entirely to that hostile ocean. Marvin Park, a twenty-year-old graduate of the Marine Engineering Instructional School at Prescott, Ontario, remembers a 1944 voyage from Saint John, New Brunswick, to Calcutta, as a fireman on the Banff Park.* That voyage for Park, now living in Dunnville, Ontario, began in convoy but was completed as an independent (i.e., steaming alone through the Indian Ocean).

We had some exciting moments off the coast of Morocco when a sub got into our convoy. We got rid of it by the crew manning the anti-aircraft guns. Then the trip from Aden to Bombay was unforgettable. Although we did not run into any Jap subs in the Indian Ocean and the Arabian Sea, we had to travel without naval escort. The most exciting part was when the wireless operator reported that the

---

* The bombing report picked up by the *Banff Park* Sparks evidently referred to the massive blowup of the Canadian-built but British-manned, explosive-laden *Fort Stikine*, 14 April 1944, which was triggered not by a collision or Japanese bombing, but by a fire of unknown origin which started during dockside unloading and was allowed to smoulder for several hours before any action was taken—too late as it turned out. The ship blew up in two devastating stages, the second blast of 784 tons of high explosive stowed in the stern-most holds being more horrendous than the first. In the aftermath, ten other ships in crowded Bombay Harbour were destroyed and the radius of the following fire area reached a mile from the centre of the blast, penetrating deep into the city centre, causing heavy property damage. Casualties from the initial explosions and fires were severe. So powerful was the subsequent tidal wave that it lifted the 4000 gross ton *Jalapadma* over a dock shed, leaving it stranded there, high and dry and broken-backed. One hundred and twenty-four bars of gold valued at nearly one million pounds sterling that were part of the *Fort Stikine* cargo, simply disintegrated. Despite the wartime urgency with which repair work was proceeded, it was six months before the Bombay dockyards were returned to normal operation.

Japanese had bombed Bombay, our destination. He was not permitted to send out for confirmation. Pending definite information, the officers had to decide whether to continue or turn back. Captain David Jenkins, a tough old Welshman who had been recalled from retirement for wartime duty—and who was affectionately dubbed "Captain Bligh" by us—made it clear that turning back wasn't a consideration: "We are going to Bombay even if every tree is a Japanese!"

As it turned out, the explosion we heard about was caused by the collision in the channel leading to the docks between two vessels loaded with ammunition.[*] The explosion that occurred must have been as bad as the one in Halifax in 1916.

* * *

An August 1943 graduate from St. Margaret's Sea Training School, Donald F. Patterson of Hamilton, Ontario, joined his first ship, the Mount Revelstoke Park, *as an Ordinary Seaman after spending a month in Montreal's Place Viger Manning Pool. It was toward the end of an eight-month voyage to the Far East, in convoy westbound out of Gibraltar, when a "Man Overboard" signal was passed along.*

A few days out, there was quite a commotion. An American soldier sitting on the rail of a Liberty ship fell backwards into the sea. His ship was near the head of our column. As he floated past I saw him in a life ring with about seven or eight other life rings floating around him. We had a life ring ready to throw but of course didn't. As he floated by, some joker yelled, "Is the water cold?" Then we relayed the message that he would be picked up by one of the escort ships, which we saw happen.

* * *

American-born, but Maritimer-by-choice Frank Seems of Dalhousie, New Brunswick, first went to sea on the British-registered Corner Brook *in 1937, later joining International Paper's* R. J. Cullen *in 1940 as an AB. The last voyage of the* R. J. Cullen, *which ended in shipwreck in the Scottish Hebrides, was a convoy crossing that began with a German raider scare.*

It was the last trip of the *R. J. Cullen*, the last voyage. We loaded paper in Dalhousie, went to Halifax for convoy, and then we headed for London. The convoy got caught out there, just south of Newfoundland. We got word that the *Gneisenau* or some German battlewagon was out there and they put us through the Belle Isle Straits. And boy, we were many, many ships, about a hundred it was said but I can't confirm that . . . and icebergs, oh! It was thick fog; you couldn't see each other. There were two or three ships had collisions. The steam whistles were going twenty-four hours a day. It was "Slow," "Stop," "Slow," "Stop." Got on your nerves after a while.

* * *

Roy Spry of Cobourg, Ontario, a past president of the Canadian Merchant Navy Association, had just turned sixteen when he left his home at Leskard, Ontario, in July 1944 to go to sea. Without realizing how young he was, the union office in Halifax accepted his claim that he was a trimmer, though he had no idea what a trimmer was, and sent him to the 4700 ton Mayfair Park, which was signing on crew. When the ship's captain rejected him as being too young to work below deck, the chief mate said there was an opening for a firemen's Peggy, Spry exclaimed, "I'll take it!" He didn't know what a Peggy was either. It was December 1944 and he was soon to get a first taste of the brutal reality of the sea war.

The ships of our convoy were only three miles from Sambro Light when we were attacked by a wolf pack, at least that was the word we were given. I was just coming out of the crew's quarters aft when the minesweeper, HMCS *Clayoquot*, was hit by a torpedo (from *U 806* I learned much later in reading about the sea war). She was off our port side and had just overtaken us and was steaming past. If she hadn't got the torpedo it would surely have struck our ship . . . a sobering thought!

The DEMS gunlayer, Johnson I believe, came running aft and told me and two other crew members to follow him. We did and ended up on the after gun deck as his gun crew. We were all eager but it's a good thing we weren't needed in a big hurry. Although we had the gun loaded and ready to fire fairly quickly, there was little we could do against an unseen enemy.

The *Clayoquot* sank quickly. We watched her go down seeing only one life raft of survivors . . . the graphic photograph that is used so often to portray the war at sea. Thankfully we learned later that she lost only eight crew members.

The convoy was ordered back into Halifax Harbour, a mad scramble for every ship to reach safe haven. We were anchored out that night and could see the lights of Halifax shining. That was a cold and lonely Christmas Eve. We sailed for the West Indies, alone, early in the morning of Christmas Day, my first away from home.

* * *

Arthur Lockerbie, Sydney, Nova Scotia, Radio Officer, Liscomb Park.
Malcolm Naismith was the Second Mate of the *Point Pelee* and later Mate. He told us about an incident aboard another tanker, I believe it was the *Reginolite*. They had a commodore crew aboard led by a large fat USN officer who liked to take sun baths in his birthday suit, on a blanket on the monkey island. A bunch of flags went up one morning just as the 8:00-to-12:00 watch was coming on. A little DEMS gunner climbed onto the upper bridge to be met by the vision of the naked rear end of the Commodore staring him in the face while the Commodore was busy leaning over the ammunition locker reading the flags through his binoculars. "Well," says the gunner, "I see we have a new face up here this morning."

* * *

Jack Stewart was a locomotive fireman before he went to sea so it is no surprise that today's Burlington, Ontario, retiree's first stop on the way to the Vancouver Manning Pool was the six-week black gang course at the Marine Engineering Instructional School in Prescott, Ontario. After one trip on the Kensington Park, he joined the Crystal Park, an oil burner about to embark from Vancouver on her maiden voyage.

From Panama to Cuba we were in a six- or seven-ship convoy and from Cuba to New York it was about ten with a couple of Lakers, one of which buried their Second Engineer on the way. He apparently died from a stroke due to the heat and was a little old, too. They were standing at the rail . . . I suppose a short prayer was offered . . . and then they stopped the screws and he was deposited in to the sea. We of course kept on going and we could just see them in the distance.

I assume because we had torpedo nets they put us on the corner of the convoy. That was a very noisy spot to be. We wondered if they dropped depth charges just for fun or what. The noise was deafening in the engine room. You would look up at the condensation line inside on the ship's side, twenty feet over your head, and wonder why you were there. Then you hear the steel door over the fiddley grates above the boilers clang shut, and the chief engineer drops a marlin spike to lock it shut . . . just in case anyone decides to leave by the back door.

Then when the fog set in it really got noisy. As you know, they zigzagged, changed course every seven or eight minutes, and every time a ship in column changed course it blew its whistle. You can imagine what sleep was like. And down below it was crazy trying to keep steam pressure steady because they were always changing speed due to the ships being so close to each other . . . up 50 rpms, up 10 rpms, down 30 rpms . . . on and on it went. This was a 7-knot convoy needing about three weeks to get to Loch Ewe in Scotland.

* * *

Art Tarry, a British seaman who now lives in Mississauga, Ontario, spent most of the war serving on vessels of British registry as a deckhand, though his last ship was the Elk Island Park. The war was in its early stages when his then current ship, the Denpark (not part of the Canadian Park fleet, despite its name), crossed paths with a German submarine, an encounter which, he speculates, probably frightened the U-boat as much as it did the Denpark.

We sailed from Liverpool in early February 1941 with a cargo of coal, bound for St. Vincent in the Cape Verde Islands. The ship, the *Denpark*, net 2158 tons, registered in Glasgow and belonging to Denholme Shipping Co. of that city. She had been a tramp all of her life and just prior to the war had been sold to the Greeks for scrap. At the outbreak of war, however, some wise guy decided she should remain in service as the many coats of paint were still holding her together.

After joining the main convoy westbound from Greenock, we proceeded at a leisurely 7 knots out north of Ireland. Our escort consisted of an old RN destroyer and an armed trawler fitted out with a 4-inch artillery gun. The convoy was made up of approximately thirty-five ships and we were No. 2.3, meaning that we were the third ship in the second line from the port side of the convoy.

The second night out we lost two ships, one an empty tanker that just blew up when hit, and the second a Norwegian, which did not sink right away; I believe many were saved from her. On the third night, I was on the 8:00-to-12:00 watch and had the lookout from 11:00 to 12:00 midnight. As I came up to the bridge to start the lookout, I could hear a rumbling noise ahead of us and reported this to the Third Mate, who was on the other wing of the bridge. As I was talking to him, we both could see something between us and the ship ahead, with seas breaking around it. We knew at once it was a U-boat surfacing, laying at a 45-degree angle across our bow. "Call the gunner out," the Third ordered. Now, we had only one RN gunner on board and he was hopeless to wake, nevertheless I gave it a try.

I ran down the alley between the accommodation doors and banged them all (we didn't have alarms on the ship). When I reached our quarters aft I managed to rouse a couple of ABs and an Arab fireman and, after relating to them what was up, we climbed up to our 3-inch surface gun and started to take the tarp off. I did not realize at the time, however, that the Third Mate had given orders to the man at the wheel to go hard aport, thereby taking us down the outside line of the convoy, just missing a couple of ships in that line. There was nothing we could do at the gun so I ran back to the bridge where I found the Third Mate and the First Mate in the chartroom going through the books trying to find what signal to give in such an emergency. They never did find it, and I'm sure the skipper of that sub considered himself very lucky. We figured that he was in trouble and had to surface because he did not make any effort to attack us that night. Looking back the next day, we realized that if we had held our course and rammed the sub, we would have come off second best.

* * *

Ontario-born and -educated, Kelso Whyte joined the Canadian Merchant Navy in November of 1943 and after graduation from St. Margaret's Sea Training School he was assigned to the Runnymede Park as an Ordinary Seaman, sailing out of Montreal. He now lives in Charlottetown, Prince Edward Island.

Some of my memories of those days at sea are of the satisfaction that was present when you were at the wheel in the middle of a convoy, steering a zigzag course under black-out conditions, and when daybreak came all the ships were in the same relative positions as they were the evening before. It still makes me wonder why we didn't go bump in the night, given the rough seas, fog and all.

* * *

Murray Sommerville of Toronto, where he still makes his home, had trained as a radio operator at the Canadian Electronic Institute prior to enlisting in the RCN with the understanding that he would be entered into an advanced radio artificer's course. When, after donning a Navy uniform the service began to place previously unmentioned conditions on admission to the promised course, Murray Sommerville managed to get mustered out, thereupon promptly enrolling in the Montreal Manning Pool as a Sparks-in-waiting. By April 1944 he was assigned to the Whiteshell Park, on which he spent the balance of the war on the Atlantic convoy routes.

A happy event was when the occasional Catalina flying boat came around the convoy. I don't think any of us were too uptight about the risks or dangers we may or may not have been in, though subconsciously perhaps we were, because I know when I'd see these aircraft I'd always think, God, there's somebody on our side and it used to give me a kind of a warm feeling. After a few trips I began getting a bit seasick so I began taking a bucket on watch. This brought on a twinge of doubt. If being on watch was so important I couldn't leave to puke, what would I do if we took one and my life jacket was down in the cabin? So I start carrying both bucket and jacket back and forth. So obviously risk was not completely out of our minds.

The last eastbound convoy of the war! We left Bedford Basin on the night of 5 May and pretty soon we were in fog and on our own, nobody else with us. On the night of the seventh I got the message that Germany had surrendered and the subs were to come to the surface with a black flag, or fly the regular ensign upside down. Next morning we were still in fog, the good news had been spread and everybody's in a joyous spirit. I went out on deck for my morning fresh air and the fog began to thin. The next thing, there was a westbound convoy directly in front of us. We had no idea it was there. It was coming toward us so we went straight ahead . . . we couldn't avoid it. Went right down the centre of the thing, passing right next to the commodore's ship. He had all the flags flying and whistles were tooting. It was one hell of an experience, I'll tell you.

On the eleventh we caught up to our convoy and a day later the *U 190* surrendered on the port side and the day after that the *U 805* on the starboard side. By the nineteenth we were in Manchester; by the twenty-eighth we were saying good-bye to our girlfriends. On the way home we stopped at Eccles, Easton, etc. Into Vickers drydock in Montreal. I signed off and headed for T.O. [Toronto].

Chapter Sixteen

WINTER NORTH ATLANTIC

Ninety researchers from Canada, Japan and the United States are participating in the project {a $3 million federally funded study of Atlantic storms} to improve the ability to forecast when and how hard wintry blasts will hit. The fierce storms take an average of 50 lives in the North Atlantic every year, most of them on fishing boats. A winter storm killed 84 people aboard the oil drilling rig Ocean Ranger in February 1982 . . . Dr. {Peter} Smith and other researchers are becoming well acquainted with the wild winds of the North Atlantic. On a research ship in December, he encountered 16-meter waves. Twice in the period of October to December, the ship encountered waves of that magnitude, which are believed to appear only every 100 years.

The Globe and Mail, 3 February 1982

The fury that can be winter on the North Atlantic has for centuries been the *ne plus ultra* of stormy seas for sailors of many nations. In the days of sail, that reputation was challenged by the notorious westward passage around the Horn of South America through Drake Strait, where the prevailing winds, mostly from between SSW and NNW, not uncommonly blow at gale force for days and weeks at a time. Those from SSW sweep up from Antarctica at Force 9 and more, loaded with frigid projectiles of snow, sleet and ice. Many a tall ship venturing into this elemental battlefield of raging seas became a Lloyd's bell-ringer.

Then, six thousand miles east of Cape Horn, there are the waters of the Southern Ocean off the Cape of Good Hope (originally named Cape Tormentoto by the Portugese mariners who first experienced those dangerous seas). Even in periods of surface calm, they are characterized by enormous swells, known as Cape rollers, which winter gales can transform into enormous waves, markedly higher than even those encountered under winter North Atlantic conditions. So large are the troughs of such waves that they are called holes in the sea.[*]

---

[*] The 83,000 ton *Queen Elizabeth* was almost overwhelmed when she fell into such a hole in the sea in the North Atlantic off Greenland during a WW II troop crossing. In that incident, as described by Noël Mostert in his book *Supership*, the huge ship was moving through a bad storm when "her bows dropped into the trough below a gigantic wave that fell upon them, burying them deep. A second wave piled atop the first, shoving the bows even deeper, so that the ship seemed to be set virtually upon its nose. The officer of the watch staring from the bridge toward where the bows should have been, found himself staring past the crow's nest, normally well above his head, obliquely down toward the bed of the ocean." In the bridge, ninety feet above the waterline, thick plate glass windows were smashed by the water and the helmsmen was washed

Oceanographic records suggest that the power of the Southern Ocean, which is interrupted by no land barrier in its encirclement of the globe, exceeds that of the North Atlantic. Nonetheless, even before the Battle of the Atlantic's long dominance of wartime news had enhanced the North Atlantic's already legendary status, that stormy ocean's place in history was well established through its being the well-travelled link between the New and the Old worlds. From the fifteenth century and earlier it has been sailed by daring explorers of the unknown, the scene of countless historic sea battles, and crossed by millions in everything from primitive sailing vessels to mighty passenger liners and troopships. It should not be surprising that in the consciousness of both the seafaring and the public minds, though not necessarily in reality, the North Atlantic eclipses all other oceans.

There are those who will offer the ferocity of a Pacific typhoon as the equal in strength to a North Atlantic storm; some may also claim that the high latitudes of the North Pacific dispense the same trying winter conditions in various combinations of tempestuous seas, winds at the top of the Beaufort scale, and snow, fog and ice. But the Cape Horn passage is no longer a trade route and the high North Pacific latitudes never were, whereas since the beginning of the eighteenth century, the North Atlantic has been the world's most heavily travelled sea. More of humankind has suffered its indignities and its miseries (and enjoyed its pleasures), than any other body of water, the equal or greater furies of the Southern Ocean notwithstanding. Little wonder that for most merchant seamen, the North Atlantic is the criterion against which other oceans are measured.

* * *

With that assessment Frank Seems of Dalhousie, New Brunswick, would wholeheartedly agree. He was an AB on the last voyage of the R. J. Cullen in the winter of 1942, a never-to-be-forgotten experience in which the North Atlantic reached deep into its bag of tricks to test his ship and its crew. The Cullen was a newsprint carrier operated by International Paper, and Seems was aboard her as she prepared to join a wartime eastbound convoy.

We were four days getting through there. When we got through, we ran into heavy headwinds, which was unusual, going to England. We had about three or four thousand tons of steel in the bottom, and the rest newsprint. She rolled so much we had to take the lifeboats inboard, couldn't leave them out, started to lose them. So anyway, we got up, went through the Pentland Firth, which is between the northernmost tip of Scotland and the Orkney Islands, down the east coast of Scotland and England and up the Thames to London.

---

from the wheel. It was reckoned the height of the wave must have been not less than one hundred feet. The foredeck was displaced six inches downward, the anchors were jammed and equipment and machinery smashed. It took nine weeks in dock to repair the structural damage.

We discharged the cargo in London, then loaded some sand in Liverpool, fine sand for the Sydney steel mill. We were the Commodore ship when we left Liverpool, and we had heavy weather coming out. We were going to be home for Christmas but we thought we'd never make it.

We were supposed to be leading the convoy, but this ship, the *Cullen*, was an old Japanese ship built in 1919 in Yokohama, a very strong ship. About seventeen days out we were just off Cape Farewell, Greenland, and this morning the Captain, Stanley Gooch, comes up on the bridge and he says to the mate, "We've got to take the ship in position before the Commodore gets up." We were supposed to be leading [the convoy]. He says to the mate, "Call the Second Engineer and tell him to put her 'Full Ahead'." Called down and the Second says, "You're not getting one rev out of me. You better see the Chief Engineer." So they send for the Chief Engineer. The Chief Engineer comes up on the bridge, and the Captain says, "Chief, I have to put the ship full ahead to get her in position." The Chief says, "Impossible, Captain." The Captain says, "That's an order. This is wartime, so I want this ship full ahead." The Chief shook his head and says, "Look, Captain, five minutes and you'll have no propeller, that's for sure."

So they argued and talked for about ten minutes. Finally the Captain insisted that the Chief go down [to the engine room] himself and put her full ahead. So he went down. The first thing I know, I was up in the corner of the wheelhouse; the lights had gone out. We'd lost the propeller. So there we were, adrift . . . in heavy seas, real heavy.

They sent a four-funnel destroyer to try to put a line aboard us. We floated a line on a barrel, down to him. We put it over the lee side but we were drifting so fast that the rope went around the forefoot,* cut it off. So we tried a sail made out of a tarp fastened to No. 1 derricks. We lost that overboard, too, when the wind blew it to hell away. So anyway, we sent for a tugboat. We were about four or five days and they sent out a tug called the *Zuider Zee*, Dutch. In the meantime what we had to do was take the anchor off the chain, put it on the fo'c'sle head. That anchor was a new one we had got in Mobile; there was a brass pin in it, usually a wooden pin. Had to put an engineer over the bow with an electric drill and try to drill out that brass pin.

It was a very dangerous situation. It took two engineers relieving each other. They were hung out over the bow in a bosun's chair with the drill, and when she dipped her snout in, boy, I tell you, if they didn't get washed. It was pretty close. Oh, the weather was terrible. Anyway, they managed to do it but it took a whole day. We got that anchor up on the fo'c'sle head and lashed it. Then we

---

* The forefoot is the point in a ship where the stem is joined to the forward end of the keel.

had to pay out the anchor chain about, I think it was sixty fathoms, and flake it on deck, so when the tugboat came we'd be able to shackle his wire into the anchor cable.

The tug had a gun. They shot this steel rod over with a small line attached to it that was maybe a few hundred feet long; then they had another heavier line attached to that and we managed to get it on the winch, the windlass, and were able to heave the end of the wire up on board so we could shackle it onto the anchor chain. Then we had to lash the anchor chain to the bitts, make it fast, so they could tow us.

When the *Zuider Zee* shot that line, I remember, it went over the main aerial and we had a hell of a time getting enough slack to get it down on the other side of the aerial, get it aboard. With that gale out there we had quite a time to get that fast. Well, that went okay. Once he got us in tow we were okay, doing about 7 knots. We were doing real well; the sea would be behind us then. And the anchor chain very seldom became taut when we were under tow, only when she came up on a high sea, she'd get taut and then she'd slack off, you see, didn't break it, that was the idea. He managed to tow us back to Liverpool in seven or eight days, and it had taken us seventeen to get where we were.

So we were in Liverpool, and to Birkenhead where the blitz was on at the time . . . they put us in drydock there. They told us there was about eight feet of the tailshaft gone with the propeller. [But it] didn't leak any water. That's what we were scared of. We were taking soundings. In fact, we opened the hatches and went down; we were scared that the soundings weren't good, with that sand. They had sent for a new propeller from Mobile but before it arrived they decided to put on a propeller off an old Greek ship, so they put that on her. The new propeller arrived, a bronze propeller; we put it on deck and lashed it there.

[About the missing piece of shaft], they said they had a piece of shaft they put in as well. They had all kinds of junk there. But nobody went down in the drydock to look so I don't actually know if we had lost some of the shaft.

We spent Christmas there, then it was time to get her ready for sea. We still had that ballast aboard and they said we would sail. They made up a convoy in Liverpool and got in really bad weather. By then it was late in January or early February 1942. We were about one day out when we got word there were subs off Northern Ireland, so the Commodore ship, the *Empire Homer*, decided they would take us through the Minch,[*] the passage between the northwest coast of Scotland and the Outer Hebrides.

---

[*] The Minch is the stretch of water between the Scottish mainland and the outer Hebrides and is easy enough to navigate in good visibility provided due allowance is made for the strong tides that prevail. Usually the Atlantic convoys passed between the North of Ireland and Barra Head, which is the most Southerly point of the outer Hebrides. *Captain Roddy MacDougall*

We started up there in single file; it's a narrow place. The weather got worse. The Second Mate said to me, "When you go back aft, tell everybody that by midnight, we'll be on the rocks." And it was snowing, blowing, real winter's night. So I went back and told the boys. That was in the afternoon. That night, around midnight, I was in my bunk as I had to go on watch at four in the morning. First thing, there was one hell of a crash. She hit on top of a rock and she bounced over it and then she hit the one that stopped us. We all took our life jackets and went up to the boat deck to stand by the lifeboats. When she hit the rock that finally stopped us, it put the cylinder heads of the engine right up on the main deck. We were standing on the boat deck and all the steam was escaping from the boilers. You couldn't see the guy standing next to you for steam. And one lifeboat went over the side, then the derricks went over the side and oh, my God, all hell broke loose. Then she broke in half at No. 3. When she settled down, all you could do was stay on board. You couldn't launch a boat; we had only one left anyway. So we stayed there for four days. After we ran aground, the mate told the carpenter, "You take a man and go up and drop both anchors." The forepart was afloat but she was, from the engine room aft, well, under water, except that at low water you could see the guns sticking up.

After three days aboard they sent a trawler out to try and rescue us. No way. Couldn't get near us, couldn't get within a quarter of a mile. Terrible seas. That afternoon it looked to be a little better. The Captain called us all up on the boat deck and he walked along the line of us there. He looked us all in the eye and he said, "If you'll stay another twenty-four hours I think we'll get off safely." Nobody had been killed or anything, no accidents of any kind, just lucky, but some of them were getting pretty anxious to get off there. Anyway, they all said yes.

We had a little bit of food. In the midships it was still good. There wasn't heat or anything but it was out of the weather. We had water, but we couldn't use the galley. She broke in half right behind No. 3 by the galley. You could have jumped from one part to the other except it was too dangerous. And she would grind steadily. Jeeze, it would just about get you crazy, just listening to that.

They had a lifeboat station on that island, that they call Barra, a place they call Castlebay. They came out in this big lifeboat and we all got into it. The fellow that was captain of it, I said to him, "What are our chances of making it ashore here?" And he said, "Son, I've been here all my life and even I have to come out at dead low water to make sure I get through those reefs, those rocks. You'd never have made it." He said it was fifteen miles from where we were on the rock to a place where you could land on the shore. There were reefs everywhere and they only showed up at low water.

We were told there were thirteen [ships lost that night in the Minch] but we had no way of confirming that. I don't really know how many ships actually went through the Minch because before we got there, a lot decided they weren't going to go up through. We were in a blinding snowstorm so we could see only the couple of ships ahead of us. The first one was the Commodore; he hit a sandy reef. He broke in pieces in about half an hour, but they saved all their crew. The next fellow hit a straight cliff and all we seen was a puff of smoke. He went down, all hands were lost there but we happened to be lucky enough that we just broke up.

Getting off the ship into the lifeboat was quite an operation in itself. We had a seaman from Cape Breton, name of McIsaac as I recall, we were taking back to Canada. He had been down in Swansea or someplace and he got caught in an air raid and he'd lost his leg. So they decided they'd ship him back to Canada with us and there he went through all that, with one leg.

We had to go down a rope ladder to get off the ship into the lifeboat, but we put him in a sling and a life jacket and lowered him down. Fortunately, the part of the ship we were on, the forepart, was solid on the rocks, but the seas were terrific. Just happened we got a lull in the weather to get off her.

After being safely landed by the lifeboat, when we were out of there, you know, there was a bunch of young fellows standing on the beach . . . eight, nine, ten years old . . . so we were talking to them. About forty years later, when I was working for International Paper as a foreman on their dock at Dalhousie, the manager wanted me to go to England, to Avonmouth, have a look at this RO-RO [Roll On-Roll Off] ship, the *Avon Forest*, built in St. Catharines, Ontario.

When I got there, the Captain and some of the crew invited us to a restaurant for a meal. I was sitting alongside the Captain, Roddy MacDougall. When I noticed his manner of speaking, I said to him, "You must belong in those islands up there around the Hebrides." He said, "How the hell do you know?"

"Well," I said, "I was wrecked up there." He said, "What ship?" I told him. He said, "What year was that?" I said, "Forty-two." This was the late seventies then, nearly forty years later. When I told him the name of the ship, by gosh, he said, "You were wrecked on that ship? I was standing on the beach when you walked ashore!" He was a boy then, when we were wrecked on the islands. We didn't know each other of course. He and I became great friends. I still write to him.

About a year before we were wrecked on the *Cullen*, there was a ship called the *Politician* with a load of whiskey, wrecked in the same area. I don't know if you've seen the film *Tight Little Island*, or *Whiskey Galore*, inspired by that incident, but we survivors drank some of the whiskey, so they tell me, salvaged from the *Politician.*[*]

* * *

Edward Bain, Calgary, Alberta, Cadet Officer, Westmount Park

For the next two days the sun shone and the sea was very calm. On the eighteenth we ran into a hurricane and for the next five days it was very bad. Unless you have ever been in such a storm it is hard to describe. For four days no one could approach the port side. The night of 20/21 October '43 was the worst. During the 12:00-to-4:00 watch we lost our two port lifeboats. The boat davits were torn out of the boat deck and the main deck. The half-inch steel boat deck plating was torn as if it was a piece of paper. The force of the water also ripped out a one-quarter inch "life" line strung between the bridge housing and the after deck housing. After the storm the rest of the trip was uneventful except for the sighting of a ship's lifeboat floating on the sea. It was empty.

On the twenty-sixth we entered the mouth of the Mersey River and proceeded to Liverpool. On this day I saw my first results of German bombing. There were quite a few ships sunk in the entrance way but all that could be seen were some lifeboat davits and a few wreck buoys. Also on the way to Manchester could be seen large bomb craters from near misses to the ship canal.

The next two weeks in port unloading. I couldn't believe how much there was on the ship. Tons and tons of shells, copper bars, steel ingots, four large tanks and five hundred tons of dried cabbage. I bet we got a lot of thanks for that!

The twenty-seventh of November found us on the way back to Canada. The only eventful part of the return voyage was the breakdown of our steering gear. The first time was at 1950 hours 29 November. I remember the total darkness and quiet. The convoy had left us, also the escort. Nobody spoke very loud and you could hear the banging of the engineers as they repaired the gear. We were down for two hours. The gear broke down again two days later at 1430 hours and was repaired by 1600. That was a long one and a half hours floating dead in the water and not a ship in sight. December 4 found us again with the convoy.

---

[*] Comment by Captain Roddy MacDougall: "I . . . recall those far-off days of 1942 when I was approaching my ninth birthday. The *R. J. Cullen* ran aground on the East Coast of Barra. There was a Coast Guard Lookout Post on the Point close to where she ran aground and, to the best of my knowledge, they informed the Royal National Lifeboat Station at Castlebay of the grounding. The *Empire Homer* also ran aground that night on the small uninhabited Island of Sandry, which is south of Castlebay, maybe about ten miles from where the *R. J. Cullen* grounded. The Royal National Lifeboat Institution, which is supported by voluntary contributions (no Government funding), set up a Lifeboat Station at Castlebay in 1931 which has saved many lives over the years and is still very active in this field. I doubt if thirteen ships were lost that night, maybe that number lost by the time the U-boats finished with the convoy. I have no recollection of a ship being lost with all hands."

* * *

Brock R. Cummings, Prescott, Ontario, Able Seaman, Riverdale Park

I was on the North Atlantic in the wintertime, which was an awful thing to be doing. We had tank destroyers and railway engines on deck. I mind one evening we ran into a hurricane off Halifax and one of the tank destroyers broke loose where we had tied them down with turnbuckles.

When they loaded the tank destroyers—I think we put them on in Saint John—they had welded angle irons onto the deck and they had these heavy turnbuckles and they turnbuckled the tank destroyers down. We got out of Halifax after loading Picrite and ran right into a hell of a big hurricane. My God, it was fierce. This one tank destroyer on the port side abreast of No. 4 hatch broke loose. It was swinging around and tore the hatch cover all up and everything else. Smashed everything to pieces. It was the middle of the night. The bosun—he was a brave bird, that fellow—he jumped on it. We had cables and stuff there. He got cables on her somewhere and we tied her down enough that she wasn't going far.

The skipper came on the PA system and said he was going to turn her around and to hang on! Well, we turned around in that hurricane and she pretty near turned upside down. Oh my! But we got back into Saint John and they welded her up. Our decks were cracked!

* * *

Robert F. Downing, Yuma, Arizona, Able Seaman, Ontariolite

The sea can be wild for a tanker in heavy weather. Each run north and south we had to pass Cape Hatteras. Most often it was rough as hell; running light was the worst. She'd ride up on those big waves and pitch forward into the trough. If you let her get away she'd come back up and then down on the next sea about midships. She'd shudder as she hit and screws would come out of the water. There was hell to pay when that happened. The engine room would scream like hell. One night it was really bad. She got away from the helmsman and came down with such a whack we were afraid she had broken her back, but we survived. We found out what we had done to her on the return trip. A convoy escort started giving us you know what for spilling oil. What oil? There it was astern, a steady stream. When we unloaded it was found we had blown over 850 rivets.

* * *

Bill Hutcherson, Richmond, British Columbia, Radio Operator, Crystal Park

The convoy formed outside Halifax, a much smaller group than the monster of our last crossing. Included was the usual gaggle of frigates, freighters, corvettes, plus three small tugs which were being sailed over to the war zone and would have fared better as someone's deck cargo.

Only two days out into the Atlantic we ran into the full brunt of a hurricane. Gee, this was something. The barometer went whizzing down and when the wind arrived, at first gusty, it then developed into a steady force of Force 12 winds of over 100 miles an hour. The convoy . . . disappeared as the spume from the sea obscured everything. The underpowered ships had very little steerage way and spent most of their energy in attempting to avoid their neighbours. The whistle of our ship and many others blew a steady roaring blast as the ferocious wind held the whistle lanyard so taut that it was as if it was being pulled by hand. The mate on watch finally cut the lanyard in order to allow for some thinking and hearing ability. The sea, though, was fairly flat. The wind just kept the sea right down so any wave that tried to form was just blasted away immediately. Then, when the wind went down, the seas came up, and boy, did they come up. As anyone who has sailed would know, eating a meal in a rolling, pitching ship is an experience in itself. Soup plates have to be tilted to compensate for the roll, often plates have to be more or less caught as they're sliding by unless you've got your baffles up on the table.*

After the storm, those little tugs that were sailing with us, they were still there! They were like chips in a bathtub, I guess. They were just tossed about in a terrible manner. There were no windows left in them, the railings were smashed and I can imagine what the crews of those little things went through. It must have been terrible.

* * *

Peter Kelly of Scarborough, Ontario, was seventeen when he left his family home in Toronto to travel to Hubbards, Nova Scotia, and St. Margaret's Sea Training School, to fulfill a longstanding ambition to be a sailor. His first posting out of the Montreal Manning Pool was as an Ordinary Seaman on the Gatineau Park, which he joined at Saint John, New Brunswick, in February 1943. He followed the sea until 1947, serving on several other Park ships and latterly, on CN's Canadian Conquerer. One of his postwar ships was the Fort Boise, on which he was bosun at the time it was shipwrecked on rocks off the French island of St. Pierre.

It was fourteen degrees below zero Fahrenheit when we sailed from Saint John on a February morning 1943, bound for Halifax to join up with a convoy for the Atlantic crossing to Liverpool. To my shame, disappointment and disgust I had been given the duties of messboy for the first week aboard {the Gatineau Park}. In those preunion days the newest of the new Ordinary Seamen was assigned to bring seamen's meals from the galley, keep the coffee urn filled, wash the dishes and keep the seamen's mess reasonably clean. I wanted to be a sailor. I'd always wanted to be a sailor. And here I was a bloody messboy.

---

* Another common practice was to spread a dampened sheet over the table, making it difficult for the tableware to slide.

It was during one of these sessions of doing the messboy's chores that I nearly got washed overboard. We had a deck cargo piled high on the decks, huge wooden crates containing trucks and parts for the war in Europe. They were lashed down securely and you climbed steps at the forward and after ends of the crates, then walked along their tops hanging on to ropes rigged across them to get from one end of the ship to the other. In rough weather you hung on for dear life. On that, my first trip to sea, the weather was typical of the North Atlantic in wintertime. We'd already lost our convoy. Fierce winds whipped the waves as high as houses. The ship rode the waves like a cowboy on a bucking bronco and you risked your life every time you stepped out on deck.

On one of my trips from the galley with containers of food for the seamen's dinner I was hit by a ton of water that came crashing over the ship's rail. The food went flying, gobbled up by the sea. I was swept across the deck between the crates of cargo like a scrap of paper under a broom and crashed up against a section of closed-in railing. In blind panic I jumped to my feet when the water subsided and ran for the nearest doorway. In a few seconds I pulled myself together and realized with frightening clarity that I'd nearly been washed overboard and lost at sea with no one even knowing what had happened to me. But the worst was yet to come. I picked up the empty food containers, floating in the scuppers. Now I had to go back to the galley, soaking wet, still shaking, and tell the overworked cook, who was irritably trying to keep his pots and pans on the heaving stove through the storm, that I needed more food. He gave it to me, with a string of curses for dessert.

* * *

Jack K. Stewart, Burlington, Ontario, Fireman/Oiler, Crystal Park

I nearly stepped off the deck load in the North Atlantic one night. I had been back calling the watch. All we had was a lifeline from midships aft. It was cold and I did not wait for my eyes to adjust. I came up on the wrong side of the lifeline and just saw a whitecap in time, got on my hands and knees and crawled back along a chain. Very thrilling!

* * *

H. R. (Reg) Redmond of Manotick, Ontario, began his war in the Canadian Army but after being invalided out of the service was returned from England. Early in 1944, he tired of sitting out the war and applied to join the Merchant Navy which, despite his being a qualified Army signals instructor, persuaded him to train for membership in the black gang at the Prescott Marine Engineering School. Seems they already "had Sparks up to their gunwales" by that time. The first of his two ships was the Riverview Park.

After my first trip to the U.K., during which I was burned at sea and spent nineteen days in a hospital at Windegate, Fife, Scotland, we went to Lauzon,

Quebec, for a complete refit that lasted six weeks. Then came a trip to Manchester (Salford, actually) when we saw waves 45 to 60 feet high.

It was about mid-November 1944 and I was making my second voyage in the *Riverview Park* when we had two and one-half days of very high seas. Eating, pouring, walking and shovelling are difficult in a 10,000 tonner when waves are 45 feet high. Engineers and oilers had to throttle the engine constantly or, when the screw came out of the water, it would have shaken the vessel apart (not to mention losing much steam). No one was hurt or lost on that trip, however, and we didn't worry about being fished.

* * *

When Captain Sidney G. Williamson joined the Mount Maxwell Park in 1943, it was just the latest in a long string of deep-sea and lakes vessels on which he had already served. Born in Gaspé in 1899, he first went to sea in 1914, earning his Master's Certificate in 1924. Following WW I he sailed as Third, Second and Chief Officer with the Canadian Government Merchant Marine until 1925, when he began sixteen years as Master, initially on Keystone Canallers. In 1939 he switched to Shell Oil tankers travelling the canals, coastwise and the Arctic. After thirty-nine years as Master, Captain Williamson retired in 1962 and now lives in St. Catharines, Ontario. The battering taken by the Mount Maxwell Park in a humdinger of a Caribbean hurricane rates high in his memories of a lifetime at sea.

On a voyage during the war from Portland, Maine, to Caripito, Venezuela, to load crude oil, as I remember we had an uneventful trip. There were no calls of distress, and it was just like a peacetime voyage until we headed into the Caribbean.

The date was 19 August, my birthday. The steward told me at noon that the cook was baking a cake, and there would be wine for dinner. It was looking like a nice party. We were abeam of Navassar Isle at 1500 hours, and set course for Trinidad. I had turned in for a bit of shut-eye, and at 1600 the Chief Officer came on watch. He sent for me to come back to the bridge.

"Look at this!" he exclaimed. And there was certainly something to look at. To the east, the sky was black and purple with rose streaks, and the barometer was trying to tell us something. It read 29.50 and it was going down so fast it was ticking like a clock. The Chief Officer, Mr. Mitchell, was an older man who had served several years on the Indian coast and had weathered several hurricanes and typhoons.

One advantage to being a tanker was that there were no hatches to worry about. Our ship was named *Mount Maxwell Park*, and it was of the three-island type, built with a midship engine. This was to fool the German submarines which at this time of the war were concentrating on ships with the flush decks of the conventional oil tanker. My tanker was really an armed merchantman. We had a heavy stern gun and an anti-aircraft gun on the bow. Strung on the mainmast were torpedo nets ready to lower if we were attacked.

There were six rapid fire Oerlikons mounted port and starboard, on the bridge and elsewhere. We carried twelve DEMS, one a gun layer. There was also Paravane mine-sweeping gear, and we had very good speed. Because of that speed, we were called in for convoy only twice in thirty-five trips on the Portland route.

By the mate's estimation, it would be at least six to seven hours by the glass reading before the eye of the hurricane would reach us. So I called up the crew, doubled the watch, and had extra provisions brought to the bridge. At 1900 hours the glass reading was 27.60. At 2015, a sound like an express train came from the east, and I figure that in just a few minutes the wind went from dead calm to 170 mph. Anything that wasn't lashed down was gone. It was a real humdinger.

After the first half hour there was nothing we could do. We developed about a 15-degree list, and the ship wouldn't steer, so I stopped the engine. Our drift was away from the island of Santo Domingo with its reefs, so we didn't have to worry about that. We just waited.

About 0130 the wind stopped. The pouring rain continued, but the crew opened up and surveyed the damage. The port lifeboat was upside down on the engine room skylight. The davits, made of one-inch steel with a diameter of eight inches, were bent and twisted like hairpins. The life raft which had been cradled by the mainmast was gone. The men just had time for a quick survey when the wind roared in again, but this time from a westerly direction. I managed to keep the ship to her port side to weather. During the lull, the air was compressed; it was difficult to breathe and the clouds were so low they looked like a canopy.

Mr. Mitchell figured about two hours would see the last of the heavy wind, and we estimated we were about twenty miles south of Haiti. Some of the crew were getting scared, and one ordinary seaman named O'Hagan just about wore out his prayer beads. The waves were crashing over the stern, and in desperation because I didn't know how fast our drift was, I put the engine full astern, and she came up in the wind. Then I eased the engine back to half speed and was able to hold 30 degrees into the wind which was enough to hold us off the land.

At 0500 hours the wind started to ease up, but the sea became rougher. When daylight came, the wind calmed, but what a sight we saw. We came back to our course for Trinidad, and as far as we could see, the gulf was covered with palm trees, orange trees, roofs of houses, outhouses and sections of topsoil half an acre across which had been stripped from Santo Domingo.

I can remember when the wind subsided, we went back aft to the crew's quarters, and what a sad looking bunch of boys they were, especially the naval ratings. They had been penned up in cramped quarters during this long night.

We were lucky we were clear of the islands because there is nothing one can do—the wind just takes over. We were in ballast, which was lucky. During my two and one-half years on this route, we rode out some very heavy weather, and never at any time did I feel there was any weakness with a ship like this—no hatches to worry about.

One hurricane in a lifetime is enough, and I have always thought about hurricanes on 19 August ever since. But I never did get the birthday cake the cook was making; it got lost and was never found.

* * *

Born and raised in Markham, Ontario, Gordon R. Underwood was steered into the Merchant Navy by two brothers who were in the Army and suggested he try for some other service. The RCN proved not immediately receptive so he responded to an ad by the Director of Merchant Seamen for candidates for the merchant service's training program. After a term at St. Margaret's Sea Training School beginning in March 1943, he was posted to the Montreal Manning Pool and thence to the Kildonan Park as an Ordinary Seaman. He paid off his last ship, the Mount Maxwell Park, in July 1946. Still a smalltown boy at heart, he now lives in Sundridge, Ontario.

When I tell anyone of the number of missing men overboard, I'm sure they feel I am going overboard myself. In the North Atlantic we ran into all kinds of storms when you could be held in one place for two or three days. One Christmas day we lost ten men in our convoy; it was a bright day but rough and the flags were going up all over the convoy. None was ever recovered that I know of because you couldn't lower a boat.

We never did lose anyone from the ships I was on, although I came close to going over one night while going up to relieve the man at the wheel. We used to stay behind a mesh bulwark until three waves hit then go to the next shelter and wait for the next three. I got as far as the petty officers' quarters, or nearly, when the fourth wave came and hit. I threw my arms out to see if they would catch the rail and I hooked my toe on an angle iron welded to the deck for cargo. After floating for I don't know how long, I realized I was up against a ladder so I grabbed it. I was outside the PO's door so I opened it and went in. One of the engineers asked where I had been or where I was going. I said I had gone back to Halifax but changed my mind. He said I was white as a sheet and shaking, so he gave me a toddy. He phoned the wheelhouse to say I wouldn't be up and I stayed a day and a half with the POs.

It was years after the war when talking to a sailboat sailor that he informed me that there are rogue waves which come after the third and that he had nearly lost his boat during a storm when one had hit.

* * *

Kelso S. Whyte, Charlottetown, Prince Edward Island, Able Seaman, Belwoods Park

When we were returning from Casablanca with a minimum amount of ballast, and planning to be in Halifax about a week before Christmas, we got hit with a hurricane off Sable Island. After a day or two we had been driven back to point where even if the storm ended we didn't have enough coal to steam into any port.

At this point the Captain made a decision to move everyone amidships and shut down the engine. I recall we were all over the dining hall floor with our backs to the wall for support. I don't remember how long it took but at some point we lost some superstructure off the stern deck, including our fresh water tank, vent pipes, life raft, etc., but still didn't take any amount of water as the hatch covers held up. I remember one of the mates coming up and telling me we were going to be fine because he had seen some atheist he knew praying. When the storm cleared we managed to steam into St. Georges, Bermuda. After some emergency repairs we got some coal and ballast and got to Saint John, New Brunswick, for New Year's.

* * *

Peter T. Kelly, Scarborough, Ontario, Ordinary Seaman, Gatineau Park

During World War II the worst fate that could befall a seaman on the North Atlantic was having his ship blown out from under him on a dark, cold night by a German torpedo. The next worst thing was having his ship pounded and smashed by angry, mountainous waves for days and nights on end. That's what happened on my first ship, the *Gatineau Park*, a 10,000 ton cargo vessel built for wartime service.

We sailed from Saint John, New Brunswick, on a bone-chilling February morning in 1943 with the temperature minus fourteen degrees Fahrenheit, and the 3-inch mooring ropes, as we hauled them in from the dock, were frozen stiff. Instead of coiling them in neat piles as seamen always do, we could only string them out along the deck until they thawed. In addition to a full cargo in our holds, our decks were piled high with huge wooden crates containing vehicle parts and other supplies to support the war in Europe. To walk from one end of the ship to the other we had to clamber up and down wooden ladders and along ramps constructed on the tops of the crates.

We headed for Halifax, a thirty-six-hour trip by sea, to join up with a convoy for Britain. Sailing on our own we kept a sharp lookout for German submarines that might be waiting to pick off loners like us along the coast. Offshore, the air was warmer, the sea was fairly calm and we reached Halifax with only one minor incident. On our first night out darkness had just fallen when a Canadian corvette loomed close alongside. Its skipper, shouting through a bullhorn, warned that if whoever was smoking on our deck didn't put out that lighted cigarette, he'd shoot it out himself before the Germans did.

We reached Halifax, anchored in the outer harbour, and sailed a few days later with a convoy of other merchant ships and their naval escorts for Europe. The *Gatineau Park*'s position in the convoy of perhaps eighty ships was on Coffin Corner. That meant we were the last ship in the outermost column on the port side of the convoy, easy pickings for marauding U-boats.

On the second night out of Halifax our convoy was attacked. The alarm bells rang. Our naval gunners raced to their positions, a 4-inch gun mounted on the stern and four Oerlikons, two on the port side and two on the starboard. We merchant navy men, inexperienced with guns, were assigned to "help" them. We waited in the dark. The boom of the depth charges, dropped by our escorts, shook the ship below the waterline. Twice the sky lit up with fiery explosions as tankers on the far side of the convoy blew skywards. The chilling "breep-breep-breep" of naval sirens reaching a shrieking crescendo as they sounded the attack and the escorts whirled in phosphorescent curves to chase the subs, told us the Battle of the Atlantic was still being fought. But the fight remained where it was, on the far side of the convoy, three or four miles away. The following night we had a repeat performance. Three more ships were lost, again a distance from us.

The next day, our own battle began, waged not against German submarines, but against the mighty forces of the wintry North Atlantic. The skies darkened. Gale force winds whipped the seas, and the waves rose like rolling mountains. The ship's bow pointed skyward as it mounted one side of a wave, then tilted like a dive bomber beginning an attack as it slid down the other side, only to plunge its nose into the raging water at the bottom and begin the next climb. That night we lost touch with the convoy. The order had been given by the convoy's Commodore to string out and leave more space between each ship to avoid the danger of collision in the heavy seas. At night, you couldn't see another ship.

In the gray light of the next dawn there was nothing around us but vast stretches of angry, white-capped waves, as wind-swept and desolate as only the North Atlantic can be in midwinter. Not a ship was in sight. The convoy, broken up in the bad weather, would probably re-assemble when the weather moderated.

But the weather didn't moderate. For ten days we were buffeted by high seas and almost hurricane force winds. There was one consolation, however. It would be unusual for a submarine to attempt an attack in such rough weather. It would be difficult for him to sight us and difficult for the enemy to get a bearing on us. The zigging and zagging and fighting the heavy seas made for a long, slow voyage. On one course, the ship would throw its bow into the waves head-on, fight its way up like an exhausted mountain climber, then literally fall down the other side. With the stern lifted completely out of the water the propeller would suddenly spin wildly out of control. The vibration of its shaft would cause the ship to shudder violently, as if an unseen giant was trying to shake it to pieces. When we zigzagged to another course we rolled in the troughs of the waves until we thought the tops of the masts would strike the water and we'd capsize.

One night was particularly bad. Tons of water cascaded over us from stem to stern every time the bow plunged into a wave. The Old Man gave the order to reduce speed, fearing the propeller, as it lifted out of the water at the top of each wave, might fly off the shaft and leave us at the mercy of the seas. With only enough speed on the ship to keep her head into the seas, we plunged on, but the helmsman couldn't always keep her into the wind. As he fought with the wheel the ship would veer off, exposing its side to the crashing waves and the tearing wind. No one slept that night. Veteran sailors, used to the roughness of the North Atlantic for many years, sat in the messroom when they were off watch. Fully dressed and with life jackets on, they joked and laughed with first trippers like myself to cover the tension. When the watch changed at 4:00 a.m., the men going on watch had to leave the crew's quarters at the after end of the ship and clamber forward over the deck cargo and up to the bridge. They tied ropes around their waists and clipped them to a wire cable that had been strung fore and aft so they couldn't be washed overboard.

At 5:00 a.m. came the crash. The ship must have veered as the helmsman fought the wheel. Tons of water, lifted through the air in the storm around us, crashed onto our port side like tons of steel being dropped from above. The ship shook from end to end as if it had been struck a mortal blow. It shuddered downwards into a sea trough, heading for the ocean floor, every rivet in its steel plates strained to the limit. In the messroom, clutching the tables, we held our collective breaths and waited. Slowly, like a beaten dog coming to its feet, the ship rose gallantly, her bow pointing defiantly toward the night sky, her propeller steadily churning the heavy waters, pushing us ahead. We relaxed. The joking and the laughing began again until the bosun poked his head through the blackout curtains in the doorway and ordered everyone on deck.

Both lifeboats on the port side had been stove in, and their shattered remains, hanging uselessly from slackened pulleys, were thrashing about the upper decks. A cargo derrick on number two hatch in front of the bridge had been torn loose. The size of a telephone pole, it was hanging over the ship's side, threatening to punch a hole in the steel plates. The cook's galley was in a shambles. As the ship rolled sideways, sea water sloshed across the galley deck from port to starboard and back again, carrying with it a thin soup of pots, pans and food supplies. Much of the deck cargo on the port side had been crushed in by pounding waves, and was damaged beyond repair. One crate, six feet square and a couple of tons in weight, had been torn from its strappings and had simply disappeared, washed overboard through the twisted steel of the ship's railings. Under the bosun's direction, in the early morning darkness and cold we fought the flying spray and wind, dodged the crashing waves and watched each other carefully, fearful that the hungry seas might grab one of us and wash us into the night as it had the heavy crate. Everything that was loose we tied down with ropes and cables. The cargo derrick still hung over the side like a broken arm, but lashed to the railing so it could do no damage.

By eight o'clock, as gray clouds scudded across the barely lightening sky, our work was done. There was no breakfast, but the cook did manage to supply us with hot coffee. The watch changed. The weather, too, began to change. The winds died down. The seas, as if exhausted, gave up their fight and settled into long rolling swells. Our lonely, zigzag course continued. In two more days we'd be in Liverpool.

Battered, but not beaten, the *Gatineau Park* steamed up the Mersey River in mid-morning that gray February day. We limped into Liverpool without the convoy, and without our naval escort. We were just another ship that had fought the battle of the North Atlantic and won. But we did get a bit of a surprise welcome from the stevedores on the dock who were waiting to come aboard to handle our cargo. As the tugboats eased us into our berth and we passed our lines ashore the stevedores gave us the victory sign, two fingers held up in a *V* and gave us three cheers. Looking at the damaged cargo on our decks, the smashed-in crates, the twisted steel of our railings, the fallen cargo boom hanging over the side, and the two wrecked lifeboats, they thought we must have just come through a battle with the Führer's U-boats. We hadn't, but the cheers were welcome just the same.

Chapter Seventeen

NO DOCTOR
ON BOARD

At sea or dockside, a ship is a dangerous workplace. Abroad in its element, it is, after all, a very large steel object with many sharp edges, moving in what seems like even more than the standard three dimensions, sometimes violently, rolling, pitching, surging dizzily to the tops of mighty ocean waves, falling precipitously into cavernous troughs. Add a winter's glaze of ice to all that to make shipboard life even more interesting. A trip up a vertical steel ladder to the crow's nest in even a modest sea could be one not for the faint of heart. Similarly, the steeply descending open steel mesh stairs down into the gaping vastness of the engine room/stokehold might be a vertiginous challenge for some. And in the engine room/stokehold of those wartime-built cargo ships there was that big, pounding engine with its thrashing connecting rods, spinning crankshaft and whirling gears, all exposed and all kept in motion by superheated, barely contained, high-pressure steam generated in adjacent hell-fired boilers. The possibility of physical injury aside, heat prostration was a not uncommon coal firemen's malady in tropic seas. Down below could be an unpleasant place to work.

For deckhands, too, then as now, there is much exposure to operating heavy machinery, powerful winches capable of handling multi-ton loads of cargo, windlasses for weighing anchors and for mooring operations in which wire rope spring lines are drawn to the rigid tautness of solid steel bars, seemingly near breaking point as they haul ship forward or backward to its desired position dockside. To hear them singing with tension was to make believable the stories, told by old hands to first tripper prairie boys, of suddenly unleashed, wildly thrashing broken wire rope ends whipping in a deadly path across the deck.

A ship, as can be seen, is a place rife with possibilities for injury, and injuries do happen even with the most stringent safety measures. At least dockside medical attention is quickly available for injury or illness, but the story at sea in wartime was somewhat different. Naval ships carried either a doctor or a trained medical aide, so a merchant ship in convoy might be able to obtain assistance if the sea state permitted a ship-to-ship transfer of either the injured party or of the Navy medico. At the very least, professional advice could be relayed. Such solutions were not available to ships travelling independently, and on voyages commonly extending weeks between ports, particularly in the long reaches of the Pacific, medical situations could become critical. The designated "doctor" aboard a wartime merchantman was commonly the second mate or the chief steward, armed with a first-aid manual and a medical dictionary. In prewar peacetime, a ship at sea could call on an International Marine Radio Medical Service, but this was suspended for the duration because of restrictions on radio transmissions. And so, a lone ship at sea with an injured or sick crewman was very much on its own.

* * *

Peter Kelly of Scarborough, Ontario, an AB on the Cypress Hills Park (one of Park Steamship Company's hybrid tankers) as the war in Europe was nearing its end, did not take ill and he suffered only scrapes and bruises in a dockside episode at a Caribbean oil port. But he did come frighteningly close to meeting his demise as either the filling in a steel sandwich or as shark meat. The memory of the nightmarish incident still was with the Acton, Ontario, native with an it-seems-like-only-yesterday clarity when many years later he sat down at his typewriter to record it.

When a sailor says he's "between ships" he usually means he's left one ship and hasn't yet picked up a job on another. For me the expression will always conjure up a picture of me physically caught between the hulls of two ships, the *Cypress Hills Park* and another whose name I never knew.

In April 1945, just before the war in Europe had ended, the *Cypress Hills Park*, a 10,000 ton tanker, left Halifax and headed south for Cartagena, Colombia. There, she took on a part cargo of some kind of petroleum. We deck sailors seldom knew the exact details of our cargoes. We then sailed for the Dutch island of Curaçao off the coast of Venezuela to pick up further cargo. Curaçao refines and exports vast quantities of petroleum products and it has a large harbour that can accommodate a great many tankers. When we arrived we had to tie up alongside another tanker and await our turn at the loading docks. Naturally, when one ship ties up alongside another, the one tying up has to make its lines fast on the deck of the other. I was one of the crew on our forward deck working under our Chief Officer as we prepared to handle the mooring lines and cables.

The tugboats nosed us in carefully until we were sitting within a few feet of the tanker we were tying up to. We dropped cork fenders over the side to cushion the impact of the two ships coming together. From the foredeck we could hear the clang of the engine room telegraph on the bridge as the skipper ordered "Slow Ahead," "Stop," or "Slow Astern." The huge length of steel that was the *Cypress Hills Park* eased forward, the engines stopped, then the ship shuddered a little as the propeller reversed to make it go slow astern. The man at the wheel, we knew, was swinging her hard astarboard as she moved forward, to bring her closer to the other ship.

Then, as we began the swing toward the other tanker he'd spin the wheel amidships and then hard aport to slow the swing. Now we were within a couple of yards of the other hull and the gap between the two ships was closing inch by inch. With a gentle crunch the two mountains of steel hull, like the walls of two moving buildings, squashed the cork fenders between them. Dancing like clumsy giants the ships moved apart on the gentle harbour swell.

The Chief Officer signalled me and I knew what I had to do. I had already tied the end of a light heaving line to the eye of a 3-inch mooring rope and I was standing by the rail waiting for his word. I flung the heaving line across the gap between the two ships so that it landed on the deck of the other ship. I climbed over our rail and stood on the outside, balanced on the gunwale, the upper edge of the ship's side. With one hand on the rail I gauged the distance between the two ships for a second, then stepped across the gap to the other ship's gunwale and grabbed its rail. Once over the rail and on the other ship's deck I could grab the heaving line I'd thrown over and begin hauling in our mooring rope. Quickly I untied the heaving line and made the 3-inch rope fast on one of the thick steel bollards on the other ship's foredeck. I tossed the heaving line back aboard our ship, scrambled over to the outside of the rail and once again stood poised, with one hand on the rail, judging the distance of my jump across the open gap to get back aboard the *Cypress Hills Park*.

The men on our foredeck were busy taking up the slack on the mooring rope. No one was watching me. The two ships gently came together on the swells, squished the cork fenders flat and parted like lovers after a kiss. They began their dance again, coming together slowly, and I began my jump, letting go my grip on the one railing and reaching out for ours. The heel of my boot caught the edge of the steel plate I'd been standing on. I missed my step and fell. Desperately I reached out to nothing and plummeted straight down into the gap between the two ships.

The ships had been coming together when I jumped and they caught me halfway through my fall. With a wrench that scraped my back from waist to shoulders I came to a sudden stop. The gap was too narrow to let me fall farther. I looked up in panic. In front of me and behind me, stretching upwards for fifteen feet were gray steel walls. I looked down. Below me was water. Sharks! I knew there were sharks. We'd talked about them as we came into the harbour.

The two ships were still moving apart in slow motion, like movement in a dream. I couldn't let myself fall and be eaten alive by sharks. The bows of the two ships began to curve away from each other at the point where I was trapped, so as the hulls parted an inch at a time, riding on the swell, I was in danger of falling again. I shifted sideways, turning so that my left arm and leg were pressing against one hull and my right arm and leg against the other. Crablike, I scrambled away from the bow, farther into the narrow gap so I could hold myself up between the hulls. I felt them shifting. The walls were coming together and I knew I was going to be squashed like a cork fender. Pushing my arms and legs against the hulls as if vainly trying to push two buildings apart, I scrambled forward again to where the bows began their outward curve so I wouldn't be crushed. I yelled at the top of my voice in blind panic. "HELP! HELP!" I fought to save myself, afraid to drop into the water with the sharks, afraid to stay where I was for fear of being crushed. I heard shouts from above. Someone on the bridge had seen me fall. A rope came down, hitting me on the head with a thump. I grabbed it and hung on. In a moment I was hauled up and over the rail like a giant tuna on a fishing boat. I got more cuts, scratches and bruises being hauled up than I'd sustained in falling down. As I realized what a narrow escape I'd had, shock set in and I began to shake. The Chief Officer ordered me to rest for the remainder of the day. But I was awfully glad to be alive.

From then on, if any of my sea-going friends told me they were between ships, I'd laugh and ask them if they wanted to know what it was really like to be between ships.

* * *

H. R. (Reg) Redmond, Manotick, Ontario, Fireman, Riverview Park

I was burned at sea on my very first trip in the *Riverview Park*, July 1944. Following seven weeks at the Marine Engineering School, Prescott, Ontario, (a low-cost holding tank for merchant sailors destined for the "black gang") and about ten days in the Merchant Seamen's Manning Pool at Place Viger, a once glorious, then faded hotel in Montreal's southeast central area, I shipped out as a trimmer (the MN taught "engineering" the hard way).

Late in the 4:00-to-8:00 watch, as we were approaching Methil, Scotland, the firemen were "burning down" one of the three fires in each boiler. I asked one fireman if I could help, and he agreed.

The fuel we were using was "Sydney slack," a Nova Scotian coal with mineral content that turns to incandescent treacle and with a high proportion of volatile hydrocarbon. It was from the bottom of the bunker and almost pure dust. The fireman I was helping had not turned off his top check with the result that a jet of heated air was streaming over the burndown.

Being inexperienced, I threw a shovelful of Sydney slack dust in such a way that a cloud of it entered the fiery chamber. It exploded like black powder. The blowback mushroomed on the stokehold bulkhead eight feet away, and my left arm was caught in the flame. My face would have been hit, too, had I not instinctively bent my head, so that the peak of the cap I was wearing acted as a shield.

My arm below my short sleeve was all black, except where the skin split. I had two small areas of third degree burns and severe second degree burns on the rest. The hand and wrist were okay, protected by heavy leather gloves.

The next day, we anchored in stream off Methil and I went ashore in a small motor vessel and ended up in a hospital at Windegate, Fife, Scotland. There I underwent a scraping operation to clean the wound and spent the next nineteen days until the *Riverview* returned (fortunately for me) and picked me up. The hospital had wanted to hold me three days longer, but by releasing me to my own ship, avoided the process of sending me home as a Distressed British Seaman (DBS) in a Canada-bound ship.

* * *

M. J. (Mort) MacRostie, Rockland, Ontario, was just seventeen when he left his Ottawa home in 1944 to train at St. Margaret's Sea Training School. His first ship as an Ordinary Seaman was the Riverview Park, on which, sailing out of Saint John and Halifax, he made two trips to the U.K. Eager to see other parts of the world, he transferred to the Quetico Park, a tanker, a breed of ship that offers its own unique brand of hazard.

I signed on the *Quetico Park* at Dartmouth, sailed to South America and brought back a load of gas. I recall very well an episode after we emptied our tanks back in Dartmouth. They have to flush out the holds with water as well as vent them for fumes. They have a two-way nozzle attached to a good size hose that slowly rotates when lowered into the holds. This nozzle got stuck in one of the tanks and we sent a seaman down to correct it. A few minutes later this seaman didn't come up. The fumes got him. The bosun told us to go to the fo'c'sle and get a mask. He put it on and went below and got the seaman close enough to the ladder so we could pull him up with a rope. After the seaman got a bellyful of fresh air he was all right, scared but all right.

* * *

Vancouver-born George Byrnell's first shipboard job was aboard Canadian Pacific's coastwise Princess Charlotte as a porter, "or in plain English, as a dishwasher." After further coastal service on other vessels, including that of deckhand on Shell Oil's Shellco, he joined the Vancouver Manning Pool as an Ordinary Seaman. Now living in Victoria, Byrnell served on several ships during and after the war, but it was on his second, the Winona Park, that the crew was ravaged by an outbreak of the dreaded cholera.

On our way back to Colombo, Ceylon, after discharging part of our cargo in Calcutta, some of the crew started feeling ill and as it progressively got worse we realized we had a very serious condition. It was cholera and a total of twenty-one of the crew would have it. Two of them died, the donkeyman, Tom Mullins, and the second cook. I can't recall the second cook by name but he was in his sixties, came from Port Mellon in Howe Sound, British Columbia, and was one of the nicest guys aboard the ship. He died ashore in Madras.

Tom died aboard the ship and we buried him ten miles out of the harbour. With the remaining gunners in full uniform and the crew as such, a ceremony was held and Tom's body was transferred to the deep. We wrapped his body with the Canadian flag after sewing him up using the canvas wind funnel to the galley. The *Winona* was what was known as a convertible, being so constructed as to be able to be converted to coal, so Tom's wrappings were weighed down with shake irons from the stokehold, so to speak, and homage as best as possible was paid.

The second cook was put ashore in Madras with twenty other crew members. He died in the makeshift hospital and was buried in a plot back of the hospital. Conditions were grim in that hospital and not much attention was given to the men. I was union secretary at that time and with the agreement of the unlicensed personnel I drafted a letter to the Canadian Seamen's Union head office in Toronto. As a result of action taken by the Union and the Canadian Red Cross, conditions were improved considerably for anyone who might be a patient there at a future date. We continued on to Colombo and then up to Bombay, running short-crewed by twenty-one people. Some of the gunners assisted in watchkeeping; in the engine room it was more of a problem. However, we reached Bombay without further incident and shortly after we arrived, the remaining nineteen men arrived by train from Madras. We were an angry crew by this time but after many years I realized that probably as much as possible was done by the powers that be, including the crew.

* * *

Ted Clark of Brighton, Ontario, must have wondered what he was getting into when he joined his first ship, the Rocky Mountain Park, in Montreal, as Second Radio Operator. The English skipper, who had a drinking problem, habitually wandered around his bridge firing his revolver in the air. Fortunately for the safety of all those standing watches, the bibulous ship's master was replaced at first stop in New York and peace returned to the bridge. Clark remembers serious incidents of injury and illness, and particularly the episode when his Captain designated him ship's surgeon, a role that he in the end did not have to play out, to the great relief of the candidate for surgery.

While under way all by ourselves across the Atlantic (it was actually the Sargasso Sea), we had two shipboard casualties. It was the spring of the year, the sea was calm and it was very warm. While on watch the stokers, or firemen, would come up on deck for a little relief from the hellhole below. One fireman, sitting on the edge of an open hatch for the bunker fuel hold was calling to his comrades way down below tending the fires in the boilers. He lost his balance and fell backwards down some forty or fifty feet into the bottom of the hold. He was hauled out and put in the ship's hospital. He was sore all over and couldn't move. Normally, the bunker hold would have held a good quantity of fuel coal, but because we had been so long at sea our coal supply was so low that there was some doubt we would be able to reach New York without stopping in Bermuda for refueling.

Also, a young seaman developed abdominal pains which he and everyone else diagnosed as appendix. In a convoy, there was always a doctor, but we were in no convoy! Nor could radio silence be broken. Whereupon, Captain Edwards came to me saying he would need my help (a radio operator) to operate on the young seaman. He presented me with his small medical handbook which had about two paragraphs describing symptoms and the location of the appendix, etc. He said naturally he must assume all responsibility but would the operator be good enough to help him? Both fully understood the two paragraphs about appendix in the ship's medical book. Maybe it was thought the operator's best qualifications were that when he went through high school, he worked after school and on Saturdays as a butcher. Maybe he mentioned in the saloon one day that his great-grandfather, grandfather, father, uncle and two brothers had all been butchers. The Captain may have thought blood would have little effect on the operator. To slice the skin, search out an appendix, remove it and then sew the skin up, maybe the cook or steward would assist? All this could have been overheard by others and reported back to the sick seaman.

In the meantime, seamen who had had their appendix removed were checked because the exact location for the incision had to be known. All this organization and planning was reported back to the seamen's mess from two general sources. The seaman at the wheel was adjacent to the chart room and the radio shack where he could overhear the officers' discussions; similarly, the steward serving meals in the officers' mess. They, the helmsmen and the stewards, were always listening and reporting anything of interest back to their own messes. So the young seaman, who wasn't feeling so well, was wishing he was feeling a lot better!

Approaching Bermuda, the Captain had to make a decision to either remain on course or head into Bermuda. If there wasn't enough fuel to take us to the U.S. coast, or enough food to feed the crew, or the young seaman had to be operated on, he could change course and go into Bermuda. So for three or four days, right up to the last, the Captain was consulting with the Chief Engineer about fuel and the Chief Steward about food supplies. They were both low but meanwhile the young seaman seemed to be feeling a bit better. He was taking soup and crackers. On the final day of reckoning, he informed the Captain that he was good for another three or four days, and that he would prefer good medical treatment ashore.

Our vessel sailed merrily along at a fast 5 or 6 knots (its hull was encrusted with barnacles and other marine growth accumulated during some twelve months in warm waters). We had to take the protected route into Long Island Sound where we changed course through the Cape Cod Canal. The U.S. Coast Guard took the two sick and injured seamen off, and the vessel proceeded up the coast to Saint John and drydock.

* * *

Frank Seems, Dalhousie, New Brunswick, Able Seaman, Makedonia

I had malaria in Freetown. The *Makedonia*, the Greek ship I was on, stopped there for convoy; we were there for three weeks. While we were anchored in the bay, we went out for lifeboat drill, which we had to do at least once a month. There were three of us on the *Makedonia* caught malaria. And on the convoy going from Freetown to Liverpool, in England, twenty-one died. The Navy had so much of a problem themselves, they couldn't afford to give us any medical assistance.

When I had malaria they gave me Atabrine. That was a new drug that was out [as a substitute for quinine, which was in very short supply during WW II].

* * *

Jack K. Stewart, Burlington, Ontario, Fireman/Oiler, Temagami Park

We clowned around India for about three months, visiting Cochin, Cocanada, Calcutta and Colombo again. It seems due to a famine we could not pick up stores and many of us came down with scurvy. The food we had was rotten. My teeth came loose, my gums were bleeding, I had running sores. And Hungry! I ate a lot of worms that trip. Before our bread ran out, if you held a slice to the light it was alive with weevils. Needless to say, we made toast. I tried to kill the pain [in my gums] by chewing tobacco; it was mildly successful but only a temporary stopgap.

On the return journey I was put into the dental hospital in Melbourne. I was lucky not to loose my teeth, so I'm told.

* * *

James L. Boughner, who now lives in Guelph, Ontario, graduated from St. Margaret's Sea Training School in July 1943 and joined the Stanley Park as an Ordinary Seaman. He sailed on several other Parks as well, and latterly, before leaving the sea in February 1948, on CN's Canadian Constructor. He was an AB on his second ship, the Mayfair Park, when he witnessed the fall of another deckhand.

We were tied to dock in Venezuela after unloading a powdered red clay from Nova Scotia. I was just coming on deck to get ready to embark. Some of the fellows were lowering the booms and one of them fell through the hatch. I ran forward to tell the Chief Officer of the accident. The Chief yelled to the bridge to hold the ship at dock, which the Captain did as there was no anchoring in the river. It was daylight when we brought him out of the hold on a steel stretcher with four heaving lines attached. He had glanced off the [propeller shaft] tunnel and would be okay later—broken teeth, arm and hip. There was an investigation. They asked me if he was drinking and about the hatch planks not all being used. But never using all the hatch planks in the Islands was standard practice.

* * *

Gilbert O. L. Tate's first assignment to a ship was from Montreal's Place Viger Manning Pool as a Peggy (messman) on the British-registered Guerdin Gates, but by the time he got to the ship at Port Colborne, Ontario, he was "either promoted or demoted to a coal passer." This job ended, happily for his overstrained muscles, in Sarnia, Ontario, when the ship broke down. The Manning Pool then sent him to St. Margaret's Sea Training School, from whence he graduated as a Cadet Officer. It was while serving on the Stanley Park in the apprentice capacity that today's retired Halifax, Nova Scotia, resident learned to expect no sympathy from a ship's master.

At anchor in Port of Spain, I kicked a catfish that the galley boy had just caught; the fin bone broke off in my foot and I ended up in the hospital. I was in the operating room twice before they got it out. Needless to say, it was pretty sore. I had to hop from the operating room to my bed, stayed overnight.

The next morning I hopped downstairs to a waiting car that took me to the agent's office where I went up a long flight of stairs. When I got to the top they sent me right back down to the same car. The agent took me down to the dock where the Captain met me and took me back to the ship. We sailed the next day. Thirty days later we arrived in Cape Town; my foot was still bleeding so I went with the agent to the doctor. He gave me bandages, etc. When the Captain found out, he stopped my shore leave. Incidentally, I stood my watch during the voyage.

We had sailed from Port of Spain with a sick DBS South African on board. The Captain made him go to work down below. That night he came up on deck and sat on No. 4 hatch and died. We dropped out of convoy the next day and buried him at sea. We had no Bible on board so the Mate borrowed my Prayer Book that I had received in a ditty bag.

* * *

George Byrnell, Victoria, British Columbia, Ordinary Seaman, Winona Park

In Beira, Mozambique, the *Beaton Park* was in port bound for Matadi in the Belgian Congo. We—the *Winona Park*—gave them most of our supply of quinine as we were bound for Cape Town and on to New York. This later almost cost me my life as well as that of eleven other of my shipmates. A few days out of Beira I was on the 4:00-to-8:00 and had just finished an hour on the wheel; the Mate had me go to the galley and light the stove before calling the cook and the galley boy. I felt rotten, something like having the flu, and I sat in the galley for about five minutes before heading back to the bridge to tell the Mate I was ill. I went aft and asked my friend the gunner from New Westminster if he could finish my watch, and headed for the sack. The next clear recollection I have, it was three days later; I was the first of twelve of us to come down with malaria.

I lost twenty-three pounds in thirteen days and it was three weeks before I resumed watchkeeping. We had given most if not all our quinine to the *Beaton Park*, so the Chief Steward, so I'm told, gave me and the others hot wine to help break the fever. Once in Cape Town we received a small amount of quinine, but it wasn't until we got to Trinidad that we received Atabrine, which we were kept on for three weeks. Between the tanning of the sun and the yellow pigmentation caused by Atabrine, we were quite a colourful lot. One tugboat skipper who came alongside the bow in New York asked me what in hell I'd been up to. Fortunately, it didn't take long to clear your system when discontinued and we resumed our normal colour.

* * *

Joe Wood was, literally, the son of a sea cook, and not yet fifteen in the late summer of 1943 when he joined the Belwoods Park in Montreal. There was an opening for a galley boy so his father, the ship's chief cook, reasoned that his son was an ideal candidate for the job. Tall and skinny as he was, Joe was easily passed off on the Skipper as sixteen and a half going on seventeen, when in fact he was only fourteen going on fifteen. Moments of hazard and drama that were common in Atlantic crossings left a deep impression on the Montreal boy, who now, half a century later, is retired and living in St. Thomas, Ontario.

During one of the convoys across the Atlantic, one of the oilers had slipped and somehow his right hand got caught in the gears of the engine; his fingers were ripped, literally ripped right off. And he came up on deck and I remember my father getting the oiler's hand and putting it into a bag of salt and then, between my father and the chief steward, they managed to bandage up his hand. The idea of the salt was to stop the bleeding; it congealed, and they put his hand up, raised it up in the air, and bandaged it all over as best they could to stop the blood.

An American destroyer came alongside so the oiler could be transferred for emergency operation. They fired a rocket over trailing a line, which was used to pull over a cable on which the injured man, seated in a bosun's chair, was pulled across between the two heaving ships. It was quite a sight to see him going across in the bosun's chair, with the ships weaving and bobbing, and him hitting the cold Atlantic waters and then coming up again. Anyway, he made it across though I never heard what finally happened to him.

Another time, the water was just as calm as a sheet of ice; again, this was going across in a convoy in the North Atlantic. There were Canadian merchant ships as well as American Liberty ships, and it was an American Liberty that I saw conducting a burial at sea. It seemed the good Lord had just made that setting that particular day for that particular incident. Like I say, the water was calm, it was warm, and the sun was just going down on the horizon. All the ships had slowed down. You could actually hear "The Last Post" being played and you could distinguish the body slipping into the ocean. It was touching yet beautiful. And after that all the ships speeded up to normal convoy speed, I believe about 8 knots. I don't think there's too many have seen a burial at sea, or even a transfer of a person from one ship to another. Oh, I'd seen it in the movies, but I'd never actually seen it until I experienced it there during the war.

Chapter Eighteen   # TORPEDOES, MINES AND OTHER HAZARDS OF WAR

The submarine, to do it justice, has never made any claim to be a blessing, or even a convenience. I well remember, when it became an accomplished military fact of peculiar significance to the British Isles and the British Navy, there was a general belief even in the Admiralty, where I presided, that no nation would ever be so wicked as to use these underwater vessels to sink merchantmen at sea. How could a submarine, it was asked, provide for the safety of the crews of the merchant ships it sank? Public opinion was shocked when old Admiral Fisher bluntly declared that this would be no bar to their being used by the new and growing German Navy in the most ruthless manner. His prediction was certainly not stultified by what was soon to happen.

Winston S. Churchill, Boston, 1949 [*]

Even in times of peace, the seafaring life can be a dangerous one. But in wartime, as if the hazards of fog, winter storms and tropical hurricanes weren't enough, there were the added threats of sudden violent explosions, often in the dark of night, from the silently streaking torpedo or the lurking mine. If a ship managed to elude both of these hazards of the sea war, there still remained the possibility of attack from the air with bombs, rockets and automatic weapons fire, and, at least in the early years of the war, by mighty surface raiders like the battle cruisers *Scharnhorst* and *Gneisenau*.

* * *

For Captain Angus Campbell of Halifax, Nova Scotia, who was Second Officer on the James McGee, one of fourteen Panamanian-registered Standard Oil tankers being operated by Imperial Oil with Canadian or British crews to bypass U.S. neutrality laws, his rude introduction to the reality of the war at sea was by a magnetic mine. He has no trouble remembering what followed that sudden unexpected encounter on 20 June 1940 as his ship proceeded up what seemed to be the friendly waters of the Bristol Channel.

Having the 12:00-to-4:00 watch, I was on the bridge as was the Captain when we passed Swansea. Our Captain, being a Welshman, was telling me about Wales as

---

[*] Excerpt from an address delivered at the Mid-Century Convocation of the Massachusetts Institute of Technology by Winston S. Churchill on 31 March l949. Churchill, at that time, was Leader of the Opposition in the British House of Commons.

I conned the ship, and passed comment on having seen Welsh girls, I'd never look at a Canadian girl again. He remarked that we were safe in Wales and that Jerry would not get us here. The Mate came up to relieve me at 1600 and the Master made the same remark to him. At the same instant, the ship was lifted up on a 45-degree angle by a magnetic mine that had exploded about six feet under our bottom.

I gripped the bridge rail that I was leaning my arms on and was lifted horizontal like a sheet in a gale force wind. Pulling myself forward to look over the canvas dodger to check ahead, everything was black. Glancing toward the wheelhouse I saw the Captain disappearing under the oil that was flooding in the wheelhouse windows. I then let go of the bridge rail and turned to face aft. The ladder up to the top of the chart room and wheelhouse was at a 45-degree angle. The next whip of the ship threw me halfway up this stairway. Then the oil hit me, but the visor of my cap kept it out of my eyes. When the weight of the oil lessened I continued up the ladder to look for the torpedo track. The lookout on top of the wheelhouse was apparently leaning on the tripod that held the gyro repeat, and by gripping it was not thrown clear. I then looked for the main deck and found it had departed, except the stringer plate on the starboard side from the bridge to the foremast; the two anchors were running out, claws were off, as we were running up the channel. I ran down to the ladder and slid down on the rails to the main deck and then ran forward on the only deckplate left. Arriving at the windlass I found both brake bands parted and the casting of the windlass shattered. There was no way of stopping the anchor chains. I left the windlass and ran back to the foremast rigging where I stopped to see if the chains would part.

While there I looked up for the lookout man in the crow's nest on the foremast. I saw him climbing down and he informed me he was not hurt. He was ordered to his lifeboat station. The anchor chains did not part, although the ship with flooding tide was making 10 knots over the ground, the pressure of the chains pulled her head down. When I returned to the bridge, the starboard after boat was in the water with most of the crew in it. The only crew left were the Master, the Mate, the wheelman, the lookouts who had been in the crow's nest and on monkey island, the Steward, the Third Mate, and me.

The lookout man in the crow's nest 40 feet above the deck, had been blown a further 40 feet up from the crow's nest but landed back in it when he came down in free fall. His only injury was some broken bones in his foot. The standby seaman, who was about ten feet away from me on the bridge wing, was lifted over the awning spars 8 feet above the deck he was standing on. Judging by his trajectory, he must have been blown 50 feet above where he was standing and landed abaft the pump room. This was over 100 feet aft of where he had been standing. His injuries: a dislocated shoulder, when he was brought up against a pipe lip. The AB who was at the wheel got his kneecap fractured when it came in contact with the wheel stand. The Master had his nose broken and was suffering a concussion after hitting the wheelhouse bulkhead head first.

We lowered the forward starboard boat with the two lookout men and the wheelman in it. When the boat was in the water, it sheered off as it was on a boat rope and the ship was anchored with a 4-knot tide flowing by her. The rudder had not been shipped and the Mate ordered the AB in the boat to ship the rudder and steer her alongside so we could get the injured Captain onboard. He picked up the rudder, rested his knee on the transom thwart to ship it, opened his hands and the rudder went overboard. The Mate then ordered the crutches shipped, and an oar to steer the boat alongside. They could not think of that, but shipped an oar on the outboard bow and after some rowing brought her alongside. The Mate grabbed the lifeline and slid down it quite rapidly, there being no knots tied in it. Fortunately, he did not hurt himself, and shipped a steering oar to keep her alongside.

Our next problem was to get our injured Captain onboard. I had the Steward, who was in the forward end of the boat, swing the boat falls so I could catch them, as they had a canvas cover and were not greased by crude oil. The Master objected, but was forced to go down at the dry forward boat falls. That left the Third Mate and myself on deck. Looking aft, we noted the port afterboat was hanging vertically in the afterfall and only three men by the boat. In boat drill, this was the Third Mate's boat, and he volunteered to go and complete the launching, which he did successfully.

I then went to the bridge to collect the signal books and to try and find my sextant. The weighted bag of signal books I found hanging on the whistle pull lever on the bridge, but the sextant shelf had collapsed into the stairwell from the chartroom. This room was flooded with oil and the sextant could not be found. I returned to the boat deck and threw the bag of books into the boat and was going to get my bag that was already packed in my cabin. I was turning away to get it when the Captain shouted to get away from the ship as she was going to explode. I then noticed the Steward fumbling with the toggle that secured the boat rope. He pulled it, releasing the boat. Running to the after falls, I got into the bow of the boat as it passed beneath me. I was quite disgusted with myself for panicking, for the forward port boat was still swung out, and I could have lowered myself before the ship went down. I was relieved to meet the Third Mate's boat with his crew of one fireman, an ordinary seaman and boatswain Carl Shaw (who was later lost on a ship bound for Murmansk, Russia).

The RN destroyer HMS *Wolverine* came back and picked us up. Twenty minutes later, the SS *James McGee*'s forefoot rested on the sea floor of the channel with her stern afloat, where she remained for four days. Later, a tug took the Chief Engineer and the Mate and me back to her to get a load of stores from her fridge to supply the Seamen's Mission, which had taken us in when the destroyer landed us at Barry, Wales. We were also able to get some of the crew's personal gear that had been left by the salvage men.

That ended my days in the Merchant Navy for the duration of the war. When we returned to Halifax 13 July 1940 on the Polish liner *Batory*, the Imperial Oil Company had no berth for me as the U.S. took back surviving ships of the fourteen that were manned by Imperial Oil employees. And seeing that the expanding RCN was short of navigators, I joined up.

* * *

For Alex White, of Regina, Saskatchewan, and John Covan of Markdale, Ontario, Radio Officer and Cadet Officer respectively of the Green Gables Park, there is the strong feeling that only an unauthorized course diversion for their ship saved them from being the victims of a Japanese torpedo. They recalled the incident in a 1990 taping.

Alex White: One of the things they used to do in wartime was that they tried to keep the routes very, very secret . . . how you got from Vancouver to Australia. We didn't travel in convoy, except sometimes when you'd get near the coast you'd pick up a convoy, but most of the time you travelled on your own. I've never forgotten one night I was on watch in the wireless shack, [Second Officer] Walker coming into the cabin and he really did have a strange look. He said, "Sparks, I know this is against Navy rules and everything. If I was a Japanese submarine, I'd sit right there, right in our path. I'm going to go wide. This is going to be between you and me. You don't say anything, I don't say anything, and we're going to go around this point." It was called the Friendly Islands [now Tonga] on the old maps.

Well, we changed course, be it ever so slightly when you're only travelling at 10 knots. Whatever it was it apparently worked because that night, within about an hour after that, I got three separate signals by the three Liberty ships that had been following us of having been torpedoed somewhere along the trail. You know, you hear of people getting hunches, and now when I hear somebody's got a hunch, I can believe them.

John Covan: I was on the Mate's watch and I can remember the Captain coming up because when you'd received the messages of the ships being sunk . . . the First Mate asked him if we should go back to look for survivors. I forget the expression the Captain used, but he didn't say, "You've gotta be kidding!" He reminded the Mate of the cargo we were carrying. I remember bombs coming on board; also we had maybe a couple of hundred tons of magnesium bars and these things would go up like a flash if exposed to any flame. So we never did go back and if we had I'm sure we wouldn't be here now.

You never really know whether you avoided it, or if the submarine came into position after we passed. Of course Walker had been sunk in the North Atlantic prior to this . . . I don't think the Third Mate had, but the First Mate, the Captain, the engineers.

Alex White: They'd all been off ships that had been sunk. Sheil [the Chief Sparks] certainly had. He was twenty-four days in a lifeboat, I remember.

* * *

George Foote, who latterly lived in Hamilton, Ontario, until his death in 1992, left Newfoundland in 1938 to join a fishing schooner working out of Sydney, Nova Scotia. With the outbreak of war in 1939 he began his deep-sea sailing career as an Ordinary Seaman on the Philip T. Dodge. Surviving the torpedoing and sinking of the Kitty's Brook in May 1942, he continued to sail until after the war ended.

I was sent down to New York by the manning pool to join a Belgian ship called the SS Mercier, which was registered in London under Lloyd's Shipping. We took a load of grain and general cargo in our holds, and six fighter planes and four motor torpedo boats as deck cargo, plus twenty passengers. After a convoy crossing, we docked at Alexandria Docks in Liverpool where we spent three months discharging because the Germans were bombing day and night at that particular time.

I paid off the *Mercier* on return to Halifax and ten days later she was sunk by a German U-boat. After completing a navigation course, I sailed as First Mate on the tug, *Preventor*, later signing on the SS *Kitty's Brook* as Third Mate. The *Kitty's Brook* was torpedoed and sunk in the North Atlantic, ten of the crew going down with her. I was one of twenty-two survivors who got away in two lifeboats, later to be picked up and taken into Lockeport, Nova Scotia. After a short time in hospital, I returned to Halifax and went back to sea.

* * *

John Harris of Dalhousie, New Brunswick, joined the Merchant Navy at Saint John, early in 1943, his first ship being the High Park. He continued at sea as a fireman on a variety of ships until 1949 when the seamen's strike ended his seafaring days.

I joined the *Prince Albert Park* in Saint John, 22 February 1945. On the *Point Pleasant Park*, which left a month ahead of us bound for Cape Town, I had a new friend by the name of Singer Breen. When we were about two or three hundred miles from Cape Town, our wireless operator got a message that a Canadian ship named the *Point Pleasant Park* had been sunk. We all felt scared as we knew it could happen to us and we took precautions. Some of the survivors were staying at the Seamen's Club in Cape Town. We took three survivors and a lifeboat they were picked up in, brought them back to Montreal. My good friend Singer Breen was one of the guys lost.

* * *

George Auby, Yarmouth, Nova Scotia, RCN, Convoy Signalman, SS Batory

Liverpool, Lime Street, the noon hour rush: Two Canadian convoy sailors wearing long coats to their ankles. Made me feel good to see someone from home. They were torpedoed on the *Empress of Britain*, left money, etc., and ran in their birthday suits for the lifeboats. Landed in the water and picked up by a Norwegian ship. They opened their coats to prove they had nothing on. It seemed the traffic, people and time stopped to see their point. The names of these two were Soulis from Winnipeg and Rogers from Montreal. Their biggest regret was that they didn't grab the bottle of rum on the dresser on their flight to safety.

* * *

W. (Bill) Hutcherson, Richmond, British Columbia, Radio Officer, Crystal Park

We cleared Liverpool on a cool drizzly day and Zimmerman (our DEMS gunner who had earlier caused a flap when he mistook our trailing fog buoy for a periscope) pulled another of his specialities. After his periscope sighting, he was relieved of the after lookout and placed on the bridge to observe things in front and around us, and where he could be watched. We had barely dropped the pilot when Zimmy again started his mute pointing and gesticulating. He was somewhat more articulate this time, however, as he was pointing to an object in the water—a mine! Very carefully the Captain headed away from the rusty but scary-looking thing. As we passed it, it drifted about twenty feet away from our side with many of our crew leaning on the rails looking it over. If it had decided to slide toward us and explode, I'm sure we would have had a complete complement of over thirty headless sailors. The DEMS of course clamoured to be allowed to shoot and explode the floating bomb, but as it was now between us and the already damaged city, the Old Man wisely elected to signal the shoreside naval station to have them take care of this menace to navigation.

* * *

Arthur Lockerbie, Sydney, Nova Scotia, Radio Operator, Point Pelee Park

I remember an article in the old *Toronto Star Weekly* about the subs in the Gulf. It claimed that what it called the Battle of the St. Lawrence was won by the Germans, but that nobody knew about it at the time and that no Allied ships went up the River after '42. Everybody in the Maritimes and Newfoundland knew what had happened and heard of a lot that never happened. I was up to Quebec with the *Ocean Eagle* in '43, and to Montreal with the *Point Pelee Park* in '43, '44 and '45. We saw the frigate HMCS *Magog* get hit by an acoustic torpedo up in the St. Lawrence estuary in the fall of '44. We were in convoy then and we made one more trip up the river that fall on our own.

We met a British ship, the *Fort Thompson*, coming down on her own. A few minutes later I copied a distress message and passed it on to the Chief Mate. When he looked at the position he said, "Holy Jesus, it's the fellow we just met!" Those were the last two torpedoed in the area but neither was sunk.

* * *

When Angus MacIsaac of Halifax, Nova Scotia, couldn't get into the RCAF, he turned to the Merchant Navy in the summer of 1944, signing on as a deckhand on his first ship, the Victoria Park, sailing out of Halifax to the West Indies and New York.

Between Christmas and New Year's 1944-45, news was that twenty-eight ships were fished in convoys leaving Halifax and so it was that when another seaman, Raymond Verge, and I tried to get into the pool in Halifax, we were told that it was full to capacity. So on 21 January 1945 we headed for Saint John, New Brunswick, by train. As we were walking up Dock Street we passed Elder Dempster Lines office so we decided to see if there were any job openings. We were told that there were several jobs open on both the *Point Pleasant Park* and the *Rocky Mountain Park*. We decided to take the latter. Both ships had trouble with the water pipes freezing and it ended up that *Point Pleasant Park* was in shape before us, so they sailed a day ahead of us. Then we had union problems on board with the delegates saying that we were not properly stored for our voyage, an event which was labelled a mutiny as the ship was under sailing orders.

We eventually arrived in New York City to pick up an American Navy officer and his staff as we were designated Commodore ship of the convoy to Trinidad, where we took on coal bunkers; the next day we were underway. About a day out of Cape Town we received word that the *Point Pleasant Park* was fished just off an old German port in southwest Africa. When we reached Cape Town we met the survivors and they told us their experience. They said it was a brand-new sub, the *U 510*, which fired the torpedo into the stern of the *Point Pleasant* and as the ship was sinking stern-first, the sub surfaced and let everyone get off into the lifeboats. Then they shelled the Park boat and she sank. There were nine casualties, all from the engine room.

* * *

A lifelong sailor who was born in Port Aux Basques, Newfoundland, J. Stanley McKenzie has made Yarmouth, Nova Scotia, his home port for some forty-five years. He began his career under sail and served on many ships initially as an Able Seaman and later as an Engineer. His adventurous seagoing life included many high points, not the least of which was as a member of the crew of the RCMP vessel St. Roch, commanded by Henry Larsen, for its 1944 east-to-west navigation of the famed North West Passage. He became the Engineer of the MV Bluenose in 1955 and held that position until he retired in 1975 following heart surgery.

I started going to sea at the age of eighteen and I was on an old sailing ship called the *Audrey Bartlett* registered in St. John's, Newfoundland. There, after serving on several other ships as an Able Seaman, I joined the SS *Kitty's Brook*, which was owned by the Bowaters Company, England, but registered in Newfoundland. This is the ship I was torpedoed in, 9 May 1942, spent three days in an open lifeboat, lost nine men.

At the time of the torpedo attack the weather was flat calm and the visibility was a very black night and spitting snow. We were not in convoy and had no warning whatsoever. I was in my bunk at the time so I was wearing only my underwear shorts when I escaped into one of the two lifeboats. The Captain and the Third Mate were in the same lifeboat while the Second Mate was in the other one. The Chief Officer drowned. We were torpedoed Friday night and rowed eighty-three miles into Lockeport, Nova Scotia, arriving there around ten o'clock Sunday morning.

It must have been a submerged attack as most of us didn't see anything. A few said they thought they had, but in my opinion no one did. It took the ship seven minutes to go down. There was no communication between the submarine and the survivors. One of our chaps had the top of his foot blown off. Many of us were badly bruised. I had a rupture operation in the summer of 1943 which I believe stemmed from this attack. Thirteen of us were sent to Camp Hill Hospital, Halifax, for exposure, and two were kept in Lockeport Hospital.

I had a foster brother, Dick Feltham, in the other lifeboat, who came back and joined the Nova Scotia-Newfoundland ferry *Caribou* out of Port-Aux-Basques, and was torpedoed and lost in the Gulf. I was supposed to go with him but changed my mind at the last minute.

* * *

Scarborough, Ontario, resident Gerard F. (Jerry) McTague, left home in August 1943 to begin sailing as a sixteen-year-old deckhand on the Great Lakes, but after nearly a year on inland waters, he went deep-sea, initially as a trimmer, later as a fireman, serving on the Whiteshell Park and several other Park ships plying the Atlantic in supply convoys. For "the black gang," the engine room environment was a fearful place to be even when you knew the thunderous sounds assaulting your ears were being made by "we're doing this for your own good," friendly escorts.

It was scary in the coal bunkers when depth charges were dropped. You got out fast. There was much vibration on the boiler and engine room floor, and dust would come off the rivet heads on the side of the ship if depth charges went off near you. When I joined the *Beresford Park* in Halifax on 2 February 1945 it was carrying a load of salt to St. Pierre and Miquelon Islands. We had convoy part way only. When the cargo was discharged we left St. Pierre and Miquelon around midnight, light ship for St. John's, Newfoundland. About 2 a.m. we sighted a sub on the surface a couple of miles away. The Captain ordered the rear hold flooded to get the screw all the way down in the water.

We had a DEMS gun crew aboard and were well armed. The sub could not catch us underwater and did not come near us on the surface but stayed a couple of miles away until dawn, then disappeared. If he had come near us on the surface, our DEMS gunnery crew would have blown him out of the sea.

* * *

W. (Bill) Hutcherson, Richmond, British Columbia, Radio Officer, Tuxedo Park

Aside from the heat, the sight of flying fish dashing out from our bow waves, the happy dolphins keeping pace with us for mile after mile, and the perpetual brace of albatross gliding down the wave troughs and over the next crest, all combine to make the Pacific trip to Australia peaceful and enjoyable.

But that all changed shortly after crossing the equator. The first indication that a war still existed occurred when our afternoon suntanning was interrupted by a spasmodic coughing sound. The next noise heard was the sound of airplane engines and then over the horizon came two planes flying low. The first was an American fighter, followed closely by a Japanese Zero who every so often burped off a few rounds at the Yank. They flew right over us and both waggled their wings before they went on their way over the next horizon. No general alarm had been sounded so we resumed our suntanning.

The same night the mate on watch noticed a brilliant streak heading our way from quite a distance. The captain was on the bridge and in his booming voice let everyone on board know that a torpedo attack was heading our way. We had ample time to turn away and to watch it stream by hundreds of yards away as it continued on. It was really easy to see as its route was lit up by the phosphorescent wake. We commenced zigzagging to confuse the Jap submarine commander and felt quite successful when no more tracks were observed. Years after the war ended, I read that Japanese submariners were allowed only one shot at merchant ships, two at naval escorts, more at capital ships and everything at aircraft carriers. It would have been helpful if we'd had that sort of information at the time, far less worrisome.

* * *

Arthur Lockerbie, Sydney, Nova Scotia, Radio Operator, Point Pelee Park

Besides the tankers built like freighters, Park Steamship Company had some small properly built tankers built in Collingwood, Ontario. The first out was the *Nipawin Park* and she was torpedoed off Halifax a few days after Christmas 1944. The Mate, whose name was Carroll, was lost, and the Captain had a bad cut about the face. The bow broke off but the rest of her from the bridge aft was salvaged by

Captain John Lahey with the tug *Security*. She sailed to a ripe old age for Irving Oil with a new bow and renamed the *Irvinglake*.

* * *

Gordon Noseworthy was a ship's carpenter, Chips, who served on three ships during wartime when his native Newfoundland, though then still officially a British colony, had a strong Canadian connection in the shape of a large RCN contingent based in St. John's, where Canadian escorts and merchant ships, as well as those of many other nations, regularly found safe haven. Now retired in Fortune, Newfoundland, Noseworthy survived many convoy crossings..

I served in the Merchant Navy on three different ships, the *Humber Arm*, the *Corner Brook* and the *Sexton*. It was no picnic, I can tell you, with very little protection and often times none. I served a lot of time on the *Corner Brook*, and we were usually the Commodore ship; the others took orders from us. We always formed convoy in Bedford Basin, Halifax. There would be around sixty ships in convoy and often times only thirty arrived on the other side. Subs and planes did a lot of damage but we were not allowed to stop and pick up survivors in the water. But thank God, never a torpedo or bomb touched the ship I was on. Our First Mate and Third Mate left us to join the ship their father was captain of, the *Caribou*. She was hit in the Gulf and the two sons and their father were drowned. A fellow living next door to me was in the water quite a few hours before he got picked up. He had a little baby in his arms all night but they both lived okay.

I can tell you it was no fun on the North Atlantic run from over here to the other side. We had an old fellow for gunner who had been a gunner in the Navy for twenty-eight years, and you can say that what he pointed at he always hit. In the Irish sea a German sub came to the surface and he lined up the gun we had at it and put a shell right through the conning tower so it could not go down. An old American destroyer arrived and took it into Liverpool. There were times it was exciting!

* * *

H. R. (Reg) Redmond, Manotick, Ontario, Fireman, Riverview Park

A character I remember was a huge French Canadian from Gaspé who had sailed most of his thirty-odd years. He told of being "fished" twice in one hour earlier in the war. He was in a Greek vessel, on the after deck, when a torpedo hit amidships. He was thrown into the water.

"All 'roun' me I hear 'chuque chuque chuque' like in barnyard," he said. "Dere's chicken in water." The vessel had carried live fowl, in lieu of refrigeration, and the birds had been blown into the sea.

The Gaspesian and others were quickly rescued by a Norwegian ship. Minutes later, that ship, too, was struck. Twice.

He said that, after the first hit, the steward said, "Let's go to the officer's quarters and see what we can find." While they were scrounging, the second torpedo hit and the cabin door wedged tight. The old matelot said, "Dat young steward, he lay on deck and say, 'we're dead.' Me, I'm not dead. I run against dat door and she come open. Den you should see dat young fellow come alive."

He was picked up by a British warship after two days in a boat. After his frozen toes had healed, he went back to sea.

* * *

Clarence C. Richard of River Bourgeois, Nova Scotia, left the sea after spending seven and one-half years as an Imperial Oil tankerman. It must have been a proud moment when he was promoted to Third Mate, but with the promotion came his appointment to the strangest ship in the Park fleet, the ancient Riding Mountain Park. Prior to being placed under the management of Imperial Oil, the gloriously named vessel had enjoyed a previous life more mundanely as PWD-1 (later W. S. Fielding), having been built in 1905 as a dredge, a role in which it served until being converted into a 2000 DWT tanker in 1943.

On 25 November 1943, I was promoted to Third Mate from the Halifax office of Imperial Oil and had to leave at once with seventeen men to join the *Riding Mountain Park*, a converted misfit, or should I call it a tanker. We departed Saint John, New Brunswick, on Christmas day for New York and while on our way there we received word we were too slow for convoy so we were on our own from there on.

Our destination was Brazil, then Africa, the Gold Coast and the Ivory Coast also. Our cargo was to be palm oil for Lever Bros. in Montreal. We arrived in Nigeria, Lagos, on 8 May 1944 and departed on 27 May 1944 for our cargo in Takoradi, where we loaded our $7 million cargo and headed for Trinidad, which we never reached. We were three days out of Takoradi when we hit a submerged object. We had no escort. We were at the mercy of the sea, had to be towed back to Takoradi, and divers had to come from England to inspect the damage. They discovered we had lost seventeen plates and our cargo was a total loss; it went sour with salt water.

A four-month trip that ended up being eleven months. They repaired the ship enough to get us back to New York sans cargo. We were in drydock for two months and then they had the nerve to ask us if we would go back on the same trip. You have an idea what kind of an answer they got from the crew. We paid off in New York and came back to Halifax.

* * *

T. E. (Tom) Rockburne, Calgary, Alberta, Ordinary Seaman, Kildonan Park

We did not stop in Madras, why I don't know. On to Calcutta. However, on the way, off of Visagapatam, the Blue Funnel ship right next to us in the convoy was torpedoed. The escorts went into action and the convoy took off out of there as quick as merchant ships could. We found out after that the ship in question made its way to the inland harbour of Visagapatam.

* * *

Frank Seems, Dalhousie, New Brunswick, Able Seaman, R. J. Cullen

In 1942 I joined a Greek, the *Makedonia*, in Saint John, made about a nine-month trip. After that, I came back, was supposed to join a ship called the *Bic Island*. Couple of my friends went up a few days before us, but I got caught in a snowstorm, back in the country, and when I came to town another friend of mine was waiting for me, said that Charlie and Scotty had gone to Montreal, told me to meet them up there. But we were too late. They'd shipped out on this *Bic Island*. She was torpedoed.

* * *

Murray Sommerville, Toronto, Ontario, Radio Operator, Whiteshell Park

A bit of excitement, coming away from Manchester, just got out of the Manchester ship canal and I had the headset on at the time. There was a great blast came out of the wireless, just about broke my eardrums. I think the message was in plain language. It said that there's a drifting mine at such and such a location, longitude and latitude, so I nipped out with the message to the bridge and spoke to the Second and he went to the chartroom to see where he was. While he was there I looked out the side of the ship and there's the damn mine about 50 feet off the starboard side, maybe 100 yards ahead of us.

We were just nicely past it when we noticed a small vessel coming upstream, a little thing about 30 feet long, probably a crew of two on it, heading directly for the mine. We thought, he doesn't have a radio on board, does he know anything about this? We thought we'd better try to give him a message. We got the Aldis lamp out and started flashing at him but that didn't do anything. And I think I got a bullhorn and started at it. Anyhow, we figured we had the guy so distracted that he was liable not even to see the damn mine, so we shut up and let him go. There was no explosion so she made it all right.

At the mouth of the Mersey River we often used to see floating mines. I remember on one occasion seeing a submarine trying to explode a mine with rifle fire.

* * *

Duncan Wilson of Vernon Bridge, Prince Edward Island, was a stripling of only fifteen in 1942 when he lied about his age to sign on the tanker Emperor Oil. He travelled the world as a fireman on several Park and Fort ships, continuing into the postwar period. His last ship was the Lake Chilco (ex-Dunlop Park) and when it was sold to Greek interests he returned to home life on Prince Edward Island.

The closest I ever came to a German sub was on the *Lady Laurier*, a Newfoundland buoy boat, when we were approaching Argentia, Newfoundland. The sub was lying on the surface, presumably charging her batteries and when we spotted it we immediately went in the opposite direction, while I went up on deck to the lifeboat. The Chief Engineer asked me who was on watch in the stoke hole. I informed him Newfie and I were supposed to be. He told me to get below. I told him only if he came with me. He didn't come and I stayed on deck until we got away from the sub. We heard that the sub was sunk the next day.

* * *

Brock R. Cummings, Prescott, Ontario, Able Seaman, Riverdale Park

I went in the pool in 1943 and they sent us to get the *Riverdale Park*. This time we first went to London; we were one of the first, I think we were the second ship up the Thames. There were a lot of ships sunk there at that time. You could see their masts sticking up. There had been so many sunk in the Thames that nothing could get up there for a long time. You know, they had to blow them out of there first and that took about three months.

We were in the Charles II, West India Docks. We had a lot of ammunition on us, Picrite dynamite that we had picked up in Dartmouth, Nova Scotia, in Bedford Basin. Had about two thousand tons of that on, and of course at that time the Germans were bombing practically every night. Pretty well every evening we would move before dark, shift the ships around the docks. Of course we had fire watches on the ships; every night there were four to six men had to stay on fire watch and they had the hoses hooked up, fire extinguishers. A lot of good that did us.

* * *

George Devonshire, Picton, Ontario, Galley Boy, MV Asbjorn

Picked up pilot at pilot station about six miles from Liverpool at 3:00 p.m. Our top mast will have to come down to go up the Manchester Ship Canal. Moved into Liverpool at 5:00 p.m. What a sight. *George V* battleship there and half the RN. Went up MSC and had our mast down and by nightfall found us in a lovely little town on the Mersey. Was good to see cattle, sheep and even rabbits running along the canal bank and everything so green. What a sight for sore eyes. Even the sun came out for our trip up the canal. It's nice to look out a porthole and see green banks and lovely countryside instead of the very boring sea. Anti-aircraft balloons dot the countryside and also many pillboxes line the river and canal. Have seen evidence of bombing, quite a bit at Liverpool docks. There are quite a few wrecks—about twenty in the outside channel and harbour, due to heavy blitz in May 1941. Jerry dropped many mines in the Mersey during the blitz and they floated down the river and played hell with the ships, even outside the harbour.

* * *

W. (Bill) Hutcherson, Richmond, British Columbia, Radio Officer, Crystal Park

When I got back to Montreal, *Crystal Park* was well along in her loading. The forward holds were already solid with small arms, ammunition, tanks and various weapons. More of the same in Number 3 hold, but the sealed 'tween decks lockers were crammed with cartons of Sweet Caporal cigarettes and cases of Scotch whiskey destined for the Army's use overseas. Four and five holds held much general cargo but a large space remained and it was evident that this was being reserved for something yet to come. We left Montreal in September '44 and headed again for Three Rivers. There we stayed out in the stream while several barges were towed into position and they began to load into those empty spaces in four and five, cases of a new explosive, RDX-3, very powerful stuff evidently. Interestingly, they loaded them by putting spiral chutes down into the hold; they were waxed and the boxed cases were put on the chutes and they went whizzing down . . . to the bottom of the hold. Every once in a while a box would jump the track and go crashing down, smash and scatter its contents on the deck of the hold way down below.

Some of our DEMS people got hold of some of this stuff and wondered what it was all about. They had it back in their quarters and they were gawking at this yellow, soapy junk, cigarettes dangling from their mouths, when the DEMS lieutenant arrived on the scene. He took one look and went white as a sheet, saying that it was entirely safe to handle but the slightest spark could set it off! That one handful was enough to blow the entire stern off our ship, let alone what it would set off in the two holds. The lieutenant, by the way, was a one-trip observer whose nerves had been frazzled by too many close calls.

An American Liberty ship pulled in astern of us and commenced taking on some of the same cargo as our own. No name was visible. Its battleship gray lines were relieved by an excellent painting of Mickey Mouse on its forward gun turret. She sailed with us and was placed next ship astern of us. Every morning, fog permitting, we'd come off watch and automatically we'd check to see if Mickey was still back there. He was still with us until the Irish coast, and then one night there was a terrific explosion and Mickey disappeared. He was torpedoed and the RDX-3 went off. There was nothing left, nothing came down and there was only some oil burning on the water to mark where he had been.

* * *

Alan J. Erson, Islington, Ontario, Radio Operator, Wellington Park

The *Wellington Park* left Montreal in November 1944, loaded with 10,000 tons of RDX, an explosive ten times more powerful than dynamite. Before reaching Liverpool, the radio operators took down the antennas to facilitate unloading. The harbour at that time had several concrete islands which supported towers that carried power lines from one shore to the other.

The Captain suddenly commanded the radio operators to send an SOS as the ship's steering gear had broken and the ship was drifting aimlessly. There was a good chance she would collide with one of the concrete abutments. The sparks from such a collision could have exploded the cargo of RDX and blown Liverpool off the map. All three radio operators worked feverishly to get the antennas back up, but there was just not enough time. We were drifting closer to the concrete island so we got the Aldis lamp, but due to fog the land officers could not read us. Luckily, the pilot came on board just at that time, and was able to contact shore on his ship-to-shore telephone and three tug boats took hold of the ship when she was less than ten feet from collision.

* * *

George Devonshire, Picton, Ontario, Galley Boy, MV Asbjorn

The *Asbjorn* was a general cargo ship, built in Copenhagen in 1935. She was owned by a Danish company but in 1942 she was operated by Canadian National Steamships to haul munitions and war material to the U.K. During my time aboard we were loaded with 500-pound of aircraft bombs and explosives.

I was very surprised at the depth of the holds when looking down from above. The bombs had lifting rings in the noses and were without tailfins. They were hooked, four at a time, from the dock and dropped through the hatches to four stevedores with hand carts who wheeled each bomb into position and set them down on their ends. There was a gang of carpenters who laid plank floors between the many layers of bombs. The planks were laid somehow to pass between the rings, which projected above the floors. As soon as a floor was completed, a new level of bombs would be placed and the whole process of building another floor would begin again. I don't know how many thousands of bombs we had. I seem to recall it took about two weeks to complete the loading.

Later, we sailed to Sorel and anchored in the river, well out from shore. Barges secured alongside and we hoisted aboard 500 tons of TNT and 250 tons of Picrite. These explosives were in small wooded boxes and I remember the TNT ones were stencilled, "TNT, Grade No. 1, Flaked."

The next stop was at Quebec City where we docked in Lower Town over by the grain elevators. In retrospect, it seems odd that a ship full of explosives would be allowed to dock so close to the city. I can't recall any guards or security in the dock area at all. I suppose a fire aboard and subsequent explosion could have caused enormous damage to the city.

* * *

Earle Wagner was a seventeen year old from West La Have, Nova Scotia, in February 1941 when he joined Imperial Oil's Reginolite as a deckhand. After twenty-six months at sea, including one year as OS and a second year as AB, he received his Mate Home Trade Certificate in September 1943, permitting him to sail up to chief officer on coastal vessels and with a permit also in the same rank in Foreign Trade. After twenty years at sea he moved on to a number of senior shore positions, latterly that of marine superintendent of a fleet of Government ships. Since retiring in 1989 he has been active in the Canadian Merchant Navy Association and was the driving force in the creation of the Merchant Navy Memorial, in Halifax, where he now lives.

My wartime experiences on the *Reginolite* in 1942-43 involved sailing singly or by convoy in sub-infested waters. At age eighteen I was a trainer on a 4-inch breech-loading poop deck gun. Yes, we fired it. Accuracy was good enough that at three-quarter mile we blew up a smoke float. I have impaired hearing because of this experience. My most notable recollection, which is indelibly impacted on my mind, was sailing along the U.S. coast in sight of the land in the spring of 1942 and counting eighteen merchant ships during the daylight hours which had been destroyed by German U-boats.

Most of the sunken ships had part of their hull, masts, bridge, funnel or top structures exposed. One vessel was on fire, listing and abandoned. U.S. planes were overhead, no subs visible. I was painting my cabin, below decks, observing the havoc wrought by the enemy. At age eighteen I felt that it wouldn't be us, but the other fellow who would get fished. On another occasion just north of "Mona Passage" in 1942, we steamed for an hour through oil. There was no vessel in sight but we knew a tanker had been sunk. I was lucky and was never torpedoed.

* * *

M. Buchanan, Master, *Jasper Park*.
To: Naval Control Service Officer, Durban, South Africa

The following is my account of the torpedoing of the SS *Jasper Park*, which sailed from Cochin [India] 4 p.m. 22 June and was torpedoed at 8:10 G.T. 6 July 1943, position 35:52S, 42:15E.

Two torpedoes were fired by the submarine [*U 177*] striking one in the way of the boiler room, and the other apparently at number two hold on the starboard side.

Crew immediately at stations, lifeboats on the starboard side found useless. Port lifeboats ordered lowered and crew ordered into them, as it was apparent vessel would not remain afloat long.

Code books dumped overboard and Chief W/T Operator ordered to send W/T message by emergency set, reporting torpedoing, also ship's position.

Chief Engineer reported impossible to get down Engine Room owing to steam, and water had risen to twelve feet, also impossible to see anything in the Boiler room, owing to steam and water. He also reported engines had stopped immediately on vessel being struck by torpedoes, condition existing below in the Engine Room and stokehold were such that it would be impossible for anyone below to be alive.[*]

Lifeboats ordered away, when it was found that all hands that were alive were aboard them.

Submarine did not surface till after vessel went down, which took about three-quarters of an hour. I then ordered lifeboats to make for the rafts of which there were several floating around, transferred provisions and equipment from rafts to lifeboats; while lifeboats were occupied on this, submarine came along, and commenced questioning the crew of the other boat, then came alongside the lifeboat in my charge, questions such as "Where from?" and "Where bound? Port of registry? Tonnage? and Cargo?", etc. Replies varied and misleading. He also asked if we had the torpedo nets down the night previous as he had fired his [two] torpedoes. From what the Sub commander said (this latter part gathered from my own crew) he had been following us from the day previous, which was 5 July.

On the later part of the 8:00-to-12:00 watch on that date, the Third Officer had reported the streak of something crossing the bow. On the Third Officer's report, course was altered 90 degrees for one hour, then altered to original line of advance; on different previous occasions such reports had been received.

Submarine departed after picking up several cases of tea, which were floating around, also that he would send W/T message on shore for us. All answers to his questions were given by crew.

As we had received instructions on 4 July changing our port of call and route, before replying to our instructions, I had enquired of our W/T operator if it was possible for a submarine to get bearings when wireless was being used, it appears not from his information. He used HF 8290 Kc/s.

We were sighted and picked up at 11:25 G.T. approx. by HMS *Quiberon*.

Gunners had reported guns not usable, starboard Oerlikon in pieces and 12-pounder training gear jammed, which with the list made firing impossible if the submarine had surfaced. The Second Engineer reports he saw torpedo strike opposite stokehold.

W/T Operator reports he saw conning tower of submarine some time after torpedoing and before leaving ship.

(1) He agrees that he received one position of a vessel being torpedoed on 15 June and one of her lifeboats being picked up on 21 June.

* Four engine room crew were lost: Fourth Engineer Nicolson, and three firemen, J. D. Wilkinshaw, N. J. Wood, and G. W. Taylor.

(2) And of a U-Boat operating in the Persian Gulf.

(3) Also that he received a message from Jacobs Radio, also the same message from Rugby on 3 July, which we were unable to decode, which was replied to 2130 G.T. 3 June.

(4) Received repetition of message on different code, time approx. 6 G.T. and replied to 2000 G.T. on 4 July.

Chief Officer reports submarine asked name of vessel, name given; What cargo? Told Tea, crew told not to joke; Q. Where were we going? A. America; Q. Asked if we had W/T Operator in the boat. A. Yes. Q. If we had nets down when torpedoed, A. No; Sub crew seemed astonished.

Description of Submarine: Large type 4-inch gun forward, also aircraft gun, smaller gun aft, three anti-aircraft guns on conning tower.

Nets: Crew had overhauled forward blocks and after blocks were being overhauled, and winches were being overhauled, as our experience on previous occasions had proved winch brakes would not hold nets, had used 4-by-8 inch wood blocks through winch drums in place of brakes.

My recollections of any message being received about submarines contacting vessels was on the early part of the passage, as such messages are left on the Chart room table for office use.

* * *

Frank Seems, Dalhousie, New Brunswick, Able Seaman, R. J. Cullen

The *R. J. Cullen* was in Dalhousie one time and Captain Gooch's wife came up on the bridge and said, "Stanley, what do you do when you see a torpedo?" Stanley says, "I generally run down and change underwear right away." He was a comical one.

EPILOGUE

Almost as quickly as plans had been laid to create a Canadian Merchant Navy as a weapon of war, arrangements were being made to dismantle it. Long before the last shot was fired in WW II, the decision had been taken. Underlying the Government's logic was the premise that the Park ships were essentially just another form of "munitions." It followed that when the war ended in what now appeared to be certain victory, there would be a rush to disarm, and the Merchant Navy was nothing more nor less than a weapon of war. It was not to survive the peace, at least not as a branch of Government.

True, C. D. Howe, the Minister of Munitions and Supply, in a spring 1943 report to the Commons had envisaged a postwar merchant fleet of more than two hundred ships, which he saw as a "substantial source of employment in the postwar years [that would] be a real benefit to Canadian postwar commerce."[1] What he did not have in mind was that those two hundred ships would be flying the flag of a Canadian Crown corporation. By way of confirmation, in a December 1943 speech Transport Minister J. E. Michaud stated that nobody should plan on a Canadian Merchant Marine beyond the duration of hostilities.[2]

With the memory of the failed Canadian Government Merchant Marine still fresh in mind—the last of that post-World War I fleet having been sold off in 1936 by none other than then Transport Minister Howe—it was simply inconceivable that in 1945, less than ten years later, the Government would choose to become the guarantor of a two-hundred-ship fleet. The decision was to sell the Park ships at bargain prices to Canadian shipping companies, the sales carrying the proviso that the ships be operated under the Canadian flag and therefore with Canadian crews. Predictions that the North Sands type vessels would have no place in postwar shipping because of their inefficiencies proved completely inaccurate, at least in the near term. More modern ships might be on the way, but the need was immediate for sea transport to help rebuild the war-shattered European and Russian economies. Little wonder that there was a rush by the shipping companies to buy the Park and Fort ships when they were offered for sale by the Government at bargain prices on easy terms.[3] By the end of February 1946, sales of 87 Park/Fort ships had been closed while a further 49 had been chartered out. By year's end, the sales total had reached 162[4] with a further 20 being added by April 1947. It was a period when

Canadian crews who had sailed away from their home port on a Park ship found on their return that not only had their ship acquired a new owner but it was about to acquire a new name.

For both owners and crews, there were several good postwar years. Profitable cargoes aplenty meant profits for the shipping companies and steady employment for over 4,500 seamen. It was not to last.

To some, blame for the eventual failure of the postwar Canadian flag fleet to survive more than a few years could be attributed to the militant activities of the Canadian Seamen's Union. In fact, these headline-attracting activities were a defensive reaction to the economic-driven scenario that was being written, but not co-authored by the CSU, for the fleet of Canadian ships and their future place in the international shipping industry.

The uneasy truce between the CSU and management during WW II had ended in August 1945. By then the Union was engaged on two fronts. It was now confronting not only the inland waterways shipping interests of the Great Lakes system, but also the substantial war-created deep-sea industry operating from the east and west coasts as well as St. Lawrence River ports. The combination of the worldwide postwar shipping boom and the Canadian flag proviso brought the Union its best years which, as events unfolded, ended almost before they could be relished. Within four years of war's end, the demand for shipping slumped, the little business available going to low-cost (i.e., low wage and low safety standard, flags-of-convenience ships). A compliant Canadian Government, faced with the possibility of subsidizing the Canadian merchant ship operations, responded to the shipowners' pleas by allowing the ships to be sold off for transfer to foreign registries. The CSU, confronted with this threat to the livelihood of its membership, attempted to stop the erosion of its power base by calling a strike in 1949.

At first, the action was highly effective. Ships were tied up in ports around the world when the crews refused to sail. When shore-based trade unionists in foreign lands threw their support behind the CSU, the effect of the strike was out of all proportion to the size of the Canadian Union or the number of ships involved. Most particularly, this support came from British dockworkers, backed by tugboatmen and British seamen. For nearly four months beginning in the spring of 1949, there was labour turmoil in British ports as the dockworkers refused to handle Canadian ships. Eventually, the situation escalated to complete paralysis of the Port of London. The British Labour government proclaimed a state of emergency and invoked the Emergency Powers Act to force the British workers back on the job. For the rank-and-file dockers, who were defying their own union executive by staying out, the issue had become one of principle, and that was simply that they did not work "disputed" ships and the Canadian ships were clearly disputed.

By this time it was apparent that the CSU had lost the fight in Canada. As if the virulent anti-unionism of the shipping companies was not enough, the forces arrayed against it included the Canadian Government, which in violation of its own immigration laws had imported a convicted felon, Harold (Hal) Banks, as a strong-arm union buster who brought firearms, clubs and strikebreakers into the government/industry-sponsored campaign to destroy the CSU. Then there was the U.S.-based American Federation of Labor, which saw the CSU as a threat to its control of its Canadian affiliates and made certain that the sort of union support provided in Britain was not duplicated on the American seaboard. The final straw was that the Trades and Labour Congress of Canada (TLC), whose president, Percy Bengough, had been the staunchest of supporters of the seamen's organization, caved in to AFL pressure and suspended the CSU.

Overlaying all this was the issue of Communism. From the earliest beginnings of the CSU, its movers and shakers had been admitted members of the Communist party. For most of them their affiliation was a byproduct of the fact that when in the depression years the first attempts were being made to improve conditions and wages on the lake boats, a Communist-backed organization was the only one to extend a helping hand. Though the particular brand of politics of the CSU leadership undoubtedly heightened their sense of what constituted social injustice, their first order of business was always to do what unions are supposed to do (i.e., try to get the best deal for their membership). But in 1949, McCarthyism was in flood tide and to be accused of being a socialist, much less a Communist, could be devastating. In Canada the hysteria reading on the anti-Communist scale was but a few degrees lower than it was south of the border. The CSU was accused of not only being Communist directed, but of taking its orders directly from Moscow. It did not help that from its earliest days the Union had taken an "anti-fascist" activist stance in international political matters. In 1938, the CSU had backed the efforts of longshoremen and seamen to prevent shipments of scrap iron to Japan on the grounds that it would be returned in the form of armaments, a highly accurate assessment as was soon to be proven by the events of December 1941. More damning, in the minds of those seeking proof of Communist domination, was the CSU's postwar front and centre role in attempts to stop Canadian shipments of aircraft and munitions to the Nationalist regime of General Chiang Kai-Shek, then locked in combat for control of China with Communist forces lead by Mao Tse-tung.

To those determined to torpedo the CSU, the issue of Communist influence was seen as a principal weapon. It mattered not that the Labour-Progressive Party, the

Canadian Communist Party by another name, had actually opposed the 1949 deep-sea strike because, according to CSU historian Jim Green, "the issue of 'communist domination' would be used to defeat the strike and destroy the union."[5] In the end, the combined forces brought to bear on what was by any measure, a very small union, proved too much for its human and financial resources and the CSU effectively breathed its last when its national executive was left with no choice but to thank its British supporters and declare on 15 October 1949 an end to the worldwide deep-sea strike.

The CSU members may have been seen in the role of villains by the Mackenzie King and St. Laurent governments, and, of course, the shipping interests, but to an on-the-scene observer from the vantage point of the bridge, the seamen were victims of miscasting. Captain David G. Martin-Smith of Victoria, remembers from his postwar service as Chief Mate of the *Lake Chilco* (ex-*Dunlop Park*):

> I . . . recall good relations with the so-called Commie Canadian Seamen's Union and most of the members who sailed under me, and I . . . [remember] . . . the many good shipmates and fine seamen they provided. They do not deserve the brand that was placed upon them to provide the image the big shipping [money] interests devised for the public's consumption in plotting their demise—in favour of a union run by gangsters brought in and nurtured by two successive Canadian governments [the infamous Hal Banks era], almost unreal were it not indeed a fact and permanent blot upon the character of Canadian politics and the still ongoing[6] deceit and spitefulness toward its wartime and postwar merchant mariners of all ranks.

* * *

How much did all this union turmoil influence the Government in its eventual decision that once and for all the concept of a Canadian flag fleet should be consigned to a watery grave? Not very much, it would appear. Just a month after the CSU had conceded defeat, neither strike nor Union was mentioned in a Canadian Maritime Commission memorandum[7] to the Minister of Transport outlining possible courses of action open to the Government.

The memorandum made clear that the Commission saw the overriding factor in the conclusions reached to be economic. It cited studies to show that the cost of operating a Canadian flag vessel was approximately double that of a comparable one flying the U.K. flag. At the same time, the charter rates available were insufficient to cover the expenses of ship operation, and were indeed lower than had been offered in 1939. The actual operating deficit of Canadian flag ships was stated as averaging about $300 per day. The memorandum noted that due to these unfavourable conditions twenty-three ships had already been laid up and "by the beginning of the year [1950] fully half the fleet will be immobilized for lack of employment."

In March 1948, the Government had modified its position on the Canadian flag covenant by introducing a plan that allowed ships to be sold to foreign purchasers on the condition that the funds received be set aside "to be used for the modernization of Canadian flag shipping." At the time of the CMC memorandum, thirty-nine ships had been sold under this plan. CSU historian Jim Green[8] records that by the end of 1952, seventy-four Canadian vessels had been sold to foreign interests for $41 million, but only two new Canadian deep-sea ships had resulted from the program. The balance of the funds was said to have been used to build lake ships, not foreign-going vessels as had been the original intention.

The alternatives available to the Government, as outlined by the Canadian Maritime Commission, ranged from doing nothing and allowing the fleet to become idle, to full subsidization. One of the disadvantages of the first of these choices, it was noted, would be that with the ships earning no revenue, their owners would not be able to keep up on their payments to War Assets Corporation, which was still owed a total of $32 million on the ships it had sold at such favourable prices and on such favourable terms less than five years earlier. CMC said the Government could also expect public criticism in view of its 1947 statements that a merchant navy "is a definite part of the nation's defensive armour."

The full subsidization scheme was based on a proposal from the Shipping Federation of Canada, the shipowners organization. As proposed, the subsidy would be in the form of a reduction in the price that the owners had agreed to pay War Assets for the ships and would make possible the continued operation of a 176-ship fleet. CMC dismissed this proposal as impractical, effectively amounting to an annual subsidy to the ship owners of some $25 million.

The compromise solution offered by CMC, and the one Transport Minister Lionel Chevrier recommended to the Cabinet, was that a maximum of $3 million be provided for one year to subsidize the operation of up to forty Canadian flag vessels, with the individual vessel payment being limited to $75,000. This fell far short of the amounts the shipowners had campaigned for, but no matter, they got what they really wanted, release from what CMC had described as "this disability," the Canadian flag covenant. In his recommendations, the Transport Minister had rationalized to his Cabinet colleagues that: "The covenant under which Canadian owners must operate under Canadian flag has been in force for about four years and it may not have been intended to maintain such restriction indefinitely." In this choice of words, Mr. Chevrier had written the final epitaph for the idea of a Canadian flag fleet. Half a century after World War II, effectively all Canadian exports are carried abroad in foreign bottoms crewed by foreign nationals. Just as they were in 1939, before and after the Park ships.

And as a corollary to the death of the Canadian Merchant Navy, there was the withering of the Canadian shipbuilding industry to a frail spectre of its wartime embodiment. In a metaphor of the fate of the industry that had flourished under the wartime merchant shipbuilding program, there is the little-noticed 1990s disposition of one of the showpieces of the industry. Gone to distant shores is the marine railway built at Sorel, Quebec, by Marine Industries Limited to launch the thirty Park/Fort 10,000 ton freighters the company constructed on adjacent parallel slipways. The marine railway still has a useful life, but it is no longer in Sorel. In 1992, it was sold to a New Zealand firm, which planned to reassemble it by 1994 at the South Island seaport of Port Nelson. The buyers expect the acquisition will "pump between $12 million [N.Z.] and $15 million into the Nelson economy each year in contractor wages, ship repair materials and through increased Nelson visitors."[9]

* * *

And what of the merchant seamen, the captains, the mates and the engineers, the deckhands and the black gang, the stewards and the Peggies? In the soaring hyperbole of wartime government ministers, they were the heroes of the 1939-45 war, the fourth arm of the Services. By 1948 they had undergone a quick image change, transformed from heroes to anonymous "Labour," troublemakers who were preventing the shipping industry from maintaining a true course. The same Transport Minister who had denied them training benefits akin to those for service veterans, on the ground that such benefits might encourage them to leave the sea, now emasculated the fleet that was to have supplied the jobs from which he had said the seamen couldn't be spared.

Once the fleet was gone, the wartime merchant sailors vanished from the public consciousness. The hostility generated in Government circles toward the CSU strikers doubtless meant that even if the subject of veteran-type benefits had been raised, it would have met a decidedly cool reception. In Government eyes, the seamen had blotted their copy book. It was of significance, too, that as a group the wartime seamen had no voice, no veterans' organization to represent their interests and would not have one until 1982. So it was that successive Governments over nearly five decades simply forgot or ignored the issue, and it was only in 1992 that an obligation was begrudgingly acknowledged with the passage of legislation granting a kind of Veteran status. But the Government chose to do this not by amending the War Veterans Act, as should have been done, but by passage of the omnibus Bill C-84, which included amendments to the Civilian War Pensions and Allowances Act. The surviving merchant seamen, by now numbering as few as thirty-two hundred by some estimates, are finding that Bill C-84, complex catchall legislation rushed through just before the House recessed in June 1992, is seriously flawed in both content and application.

Though Veterans Affairs continues to insist that Merchant Navy veterans now have the same access and same benefits as service veterans, groups representing the merchant seamen point out that there are at least forty areas from which the Merchant Navy veterans are denied equal access, equal benefits. A typical example is that merchant seamen who were prisoners of war are not compensated in the same way as their service counterparts. Though most Merchant Navy POWs spent an average of fifty months in captivity, they qualify for only thirty months of compensation.

Despite the fanfare that greeted the passage of C-84, what is being delivered by Veterans Affairs is not as advertised, and furthermore the department appears reluctant to exercise even the limited mandate provided by the legislation. When then Veterans Affairs Minister Gerald Merrithew announced the Merchant Navy program in 1992, he said it would have a budget of $100 million over five years. Though this was later reduced to $88 million for an average of $17.6 million per year, it is plain that lack of funding should not be a problem. Yet, in 1993 less than $1 million was expended on the program and in 1994 only about $2 million, representing a shortfall in promised spending over the first two years of some $32 million. Such a lead-footed response hardly seems to fulfill the promise made that, in recognition of the rapid aging of the surviving Merchant Navy population, applications from merchant seamen would be fast-tracked. Claims by Veterans Affairs that there are ongoing discussions with Merchant Navy representatives to resolve problems are denied by Merchant Navy groups.

To add insult to injury, the Royal Canadian Legion mean-spiritedly tried to block equal-status inclusion of Merchant Navy veterans in the 1994 Remembrance Day ceremony in the national capital. The Legion, which has become increasingly Colonel Blimpish with the passing of years, reluctantly relented only under the prodding of the Secretary of State for Veterans Affairs, Lawrence MacAulay, who argued that the Merchant Navy should be allowed to participate at least in 1994 because the Merchant Navy Book of Remembrance was being officially dedicated on that same day. The Legion insisted, however, that this was a 1994 concession only, saying that it gets so many requests from such "groups" and "associations" that it can't accommodate them all. Clearly, in the eyes of both the Government and the Legion, a wartime Merchant Navy veteran is still not the equal of an Armed Services veteran. So much for the "Fourth Arm of the Services."

And so full and unequivocal recognition for service in Canada's WW II Merchant Navy remains wanting. Perhaps the reason is because for the more than fifteen hundred Canadian and Newfoundland merchant seamen who did not survive the war at sea, there are no crosses row on row to remind the nation of their contribution.

* * *

The Battle of the Atlantic was not won by any Navy or Air Force. It was won by the courage, fortitude and determination of the British and Allied Merchant Navy.

RAdm. Leonard W. Murray

Commander-in-Chief, Canadian Northwest Atlantic 1943-1945

APPENDIX 1

COMPARATIVE SCALE OF WAGES ON ROYAL CANADIAN NAVAL VESSELS AND PARK STEAMSHIP VESSELS (10,000-TON)

RANK	Wages Monthly Tax Free	Equivalent Rank in Merchant Navy	Wages Monthly Gross	Income Tax Married 1 Dep.	Net Wages
Commander	$415.50	Master	$330.92	$68.30	$262.62
LCdr	331.50	Chief Officer	212.92	25.90	187.02
Lieutenant	250.50	2nd Officer	192.92	17.55	175.37
Lieutenant	250.50	3rd Officer	167.92	7.70	160.22
Chief PO	121.50	Carpenter	133.02	-	133.02
Engineer, LCdr	331.50	Chief Engineer	268.42	45.75	222.67
Lieutenant	250.50	2nd Engineer	212.92	25.90	187.02
Lieutenant	250.50	3rd Engineer	192.92	17.55	175.37
Lieutenant	250.50	4th & Other Engs.	167.92	7.70	160.22
Chief Stoker	121.50	Donkeyman	125.82	-	125.82
Lieutenant	250.50	Chf. Steward	162.92	5.80	157.12
Warrant Stew.	93.00	2nd Steward	115.82	-	115.82
Off. Steward	93.00	Mess Room	112.42	-	112.42
Off. Steward	93.00	Pantry Boy	90.17	-	90.17
Chf. PO Cook	124.50	1st Cook	149.92	3.15	146.77
PO Cook	93.00	2nd Cook	112.42	-	112.42
Chief PO	121.50	Bosun	127.42	-	127.42
Ldg. Seaman	102.00	Quartermaster	121.42	-	121.42
Able Seaman	90.00	Able Seaman	119.12	-	119.12
Ord. Seaman	78.00	Ord. Seaman	104.62	-	104.62
Boy	-	Deck Boy	75.42	-	75.42
Ldg. Stoker	102.00	Greaser (Oiler)	123.57	-	123.57
Stoker 1	94.50	Fireman	121.42	-	121.42
Stoker 2	94.50	Trimmer	119.12	-	119.12

Naval Pay includes Command Money, Senior Officers Allowance (Marriage Allowance), Entertaining for Commander Allowance. In addition issues of free clothing and travelling allowances are granted to Naval Personnel.

Park Steamship Company gross wages are the combined total of basic wage, plus $44.50 War Risk Bonus, plus $18.42 Cost-of-Living Bonus.

Income Tax: The only deduction from income so far permitted by the Canadian law is that effected by the recent amendment which added paragraph (w) to section 4 of said Act and which in effect permits a deduction from income of the amounts received by an officer or man of the Merchant Marine paid as a bona fide war risk bonus in accordance with the usage of the Merchant Marine in respect of service in zone recognized by the Governor-in-Council as a war risk zone together with the value of board or lodging on ship board received by an officer or man while performing services in respect of which war risk bonus is payable.

Source: Canadian Shipping Board, 15 July 1943

APPENDIX 2

WAGE SCALE COMPARISON

RANK OR RATING	UNITED KINGDOM	PARK STEAMSHIP CO. 10,000 ton	4700 ton	AMERICAN (Average)	NORWEGIAN
	See (a)	See (b)		See (c)	See (d)
Captain (Master)	Subj. to Agreement	$330.92	$299.67	$803.50	Subj. to Agreement
Chief Officer	$183.56	212.92	197.92	490.00	$218.25
2nd Officer	149.07	192.92	177.92	420.00	178.50
3rd Officer	122.37	167.92	152.92	390.00	151.00
Bosun	115.70	127.42	127.42	245.00	131.00
Able Seaman	106.80	119.12	119.12	217.50	126.50
Ordinary Smn.	82.32	104.62	104.62	182.50	105.25
Chief Engineer	219.72	268.42	243.42	812.50	237.50
2nd Engineer	183.56	212.92	197.92	528.50	185.50
3rd Engineer	149.07	192.92	177.92	459.75	166.25
4th Engineer	122.37	167.92	152.92	417.50	-
Wireless Oper.	-	152.92	152.92	465.00 (Approx.)	150.00
Donkeyman	114.03	125.82	125.82	255.00	131.00
Oiler	111.25	123.57	123.57	237.50	106.75
Fireman	109.02	121.42	121.42	220.00	128.25
Trimmers	109.02	119.12	119.12	197.50	-
Chief Steward	131.27	162.92	162.92	312.50	183.50
Cook	122.37	149.92	149.92	282.50	137.75

APPENDIX

(a) UNITED KINGDOM: United Kingdom rates given in £ and converted at $4.45 to the £. Rates include basic wage, plus £10 ($44.50) War Risk Bonus.

(b) PARK STEAMSHIP COMPANY: Park Steamship Company rates include basic wage, plus $44.50 War Risk Bonus, plus $18.42 Cost of Living Bonus. Scale for ratings on 4700 ton vessels effective 5 May 1943.

(c) AMERICAN: American rates include basic wage, plus 100% Voyage bonus, plus $25.00 per month Port Attack and Area Bonus. In addition $125.00 is paid each crew member each individual occasion a ship experiences enemy action, as well as an additional danger area bonus of $5.00 per day.

(Average earnings of an Able Seaman, with all bonuses, would be about $300.00 per month).

(d) NORWEGIAN: Norwegian rates given in Kroner and converted at 4 Kroner to the $1.00.

Rates include basic wage, plus War Risk Bonus of 250 Kroner ($62.50).
Extra Bonuses to:

Chief Officer	60 Kroner ($15.00)	Included in
Chf. Eng.-Steam	60 Kroner ($15.00)	rates used in
Stewards	30 Kroner ($ 7.50)	comparison.

Source: Canadian Shipping Board, 15 July 1943

CANADIAN REGISTERED MERCHANT SHIPS LOST BY ENEMY ACTION, 1939-45

The following list is based on one compiled in 1993 by Robert C. Fisher of the Department of National Defence, History Division, supplemented by information from other sources. It includes only Canadian-registered ships actually lost to enemy action. It does not include those damaged by enemy action but not sunk, nor does it include accidental losses unrelated to enemy action.

Newfoundland ships are not listed because Newfoundland was still a British colony during the period covered. Thus, among others, the Nova Scotia-Newfoundland ferry *Caribou*, sunk in the Gulf of St. Lawrence with the loss of 137 lives, does not appear.

No Fort ships are listed because though Canadian-built and owned, they were operated under British registry by the British Ministry of War Transport. *Collingdoc* is included as a loss because though salvaged it was only to be sunk as a blockship. *Taber Park* and *Avondale Park* have been included, but it is believed that at the time of their loss, their Park names notwithstanding, they were on British registry being operated by the Ministry of War Transport with British crews, which may explain why British historians describe *Avondale Park* as the last "British" merchant ship to be sunk during WW II. German records do not show *Taber Park* as being torpedoed by a U-boat, midget or otherwise; it was probably the victim of a mine. *Soreldoc*, which some historians list as a Canadian loss, was, according to National Defence historian Robert Fisher, registered in Panama when sunk on 28 February 1945. She had been Canadian owned, but in 1944 was acquired by the U.S. War Shipping Administration and transferred to the Panamanian flag.

1940

Erik Boye	Torpedoed by *U 38* , 15 June
Magog	Torpedoed and shelled by *U 99*, 5 July
Waterloo	Bombed by German aircraft, 10 July
Thorold	Bombed by German aircraft, 22 August
Kenordoc	Torpedoed and shelled by *U 48*, 15 September
St. Malo	Torpedoed by *U 101,* 12 October
Trevisa	Torpedoed by *U 124* , 16 October

1941

Maplecourt	Torpedoed by *U 107*, 6 February
Canadian Cruiser	Sunk by raider (*Admiral Scheer*), 21 February
A. D. Huff	Sunk by raider(*Gneisenau*), 22 February

J. B. White	Torpedoed by *U 99* , 17 March
Canadolite	Captured by raider (*Kormoran*), 25 March; Sunk by RAF in 1944
Portadoc	Torpedoed by *U 124* 7 April
Europa	Bombed by German aircraft, 3 May
Collingdoc	Mined, 13 July
Vancouver Island	Torpedoed by *U 558*, 15 October
Proteus	Cause unknown, sabotage suspected, 25 November
Nereus	Cause unknown, sabotage suspected, 12 December
Shinai	Seized by Japanese forces , 12 December

1942

Lady Hawkins	Torpedoed by *U 66*, 19 January
Montrolite	Torpedoed by *U 109*, 5 February
Empress of Asia	Bombed by Japanese aircraft, 5 February
Victolite	Torpedoed and shelled by *U 564*, 11 February
George L. Torian	Torpedoed by *U 129* , 22 February
Lennox	Torpedoed by *U 129* , 23 February
Sarniadoc	Torpedoed by *U 161* , 15 March
Robert W. Pomeroy	Mined 1 April
Vineland	Torpedoed and shelled by *U 154*, 20 April
James E. Newsom	Shelled by *U 69* , 1 May
Lady Drake	Torpedoed by *U 106*, 5 May
Mildred Pauline	Shelled by *U 136*, 7 May
Mont Louis	Torpedoed by *U 162*, 9 May
Calgarolite	Torpedoed and shelled by *U 125*, 9 May
Torondoc	Torpedoed by *U 69* , 21 May
Troisdoc	Torpedoed by *U 558* , 21 May
Frank B. Baird	Shelled by *U 158*, 22 May
Liverpool Packet	Torpedoed by *U 432*, 31 May
Mona Marie	Shelled by *U 126* , 28 June
Lucille M.	Shelled by *U 89* , 25 July
Prescodoc	Torpedoed by *U 160*, 29 July
Princess Marguerite	Torpedoed by *U 83* , 17 August
Donald Stewart	Torpedoed by *U 517,* 3 September
Lord Strathcona	Torpedoed by *U 513*, 5 September

John A. Holloway	Torpedoed by *U 164*, 6 September
Oakton	Torpedoed by *U 517* , 7 September
Norfolk	Torpedoed by *U 175* , 18 September
Carolus	Torpedoed by *U 69* , 9 October
Bic Island	Torpedoed by *U 624* , 29 October
Rose Castle	Torpedoed by *U 518* , 2 November
Chr. J. Kampmann	Torpedoed by *U 160* , 3 November

1943

Angelus	Shelled by *U 161*, 19 May
Jasper Park	Torpedoed by *U 177*, 6 July

1944

Watuka	Torpedoed by *U 802*, 22 March
Albert C. Field	Torpedoed by German aircraft, 18 June
Cornwallis	Torpedoed by *U 1230,* 3 December

1945

Point Pleasant Park	Torpedoed by *U 510,* 23 February
Soreldoc	Torpedoed by *U 1302,* 28 February
Taber Park	Probably the victim of a mine, 13 March
Avondale Park	Torpedoed by *U 2336* , 7 May

NOTES

■ INTRODUCTION

1. After the U.S.A. and Britain. The U.S.S.R. flag fleet is also assumed to have been larger than Canada's, though actual wartime numbers are undetermined. The Norwegian and Dutch governments-in-exile also continued to operate large fleets after their home lands were occupied.

2. At wartime peak, the aircraft industry employed 116,000, the shipbuilding industry 126,000.
    Expenditures were $900,000,000 and $1,185,000,000 respectively.

3. Measured on a population ratio basis, the Canadian record for standard ship production compares favorably with that for the U.S.
    By 1945, when Liberty ship production was terminated at 2,770, the U.S. had a population of 139,928,000. At the same time, Canada with a population of 12,072,000, less than one-eleventh that of the U.S., had wound up 10,000 DWT ship production at 354.   On such a population/ship ratio basis, the Canadian output of what were directly comparable types of ships, was close to one and a half times that of the United States.
    In addition to the Liberty ships, however, the U.S. wartime industry was simultaneously producing substantial numbers of larger, more complex merchant ships suitable for postwar service.

4. It was not until recent years that the Canadian Legion opened up its membership to Canadian merchant seamen with wartime service. Many ex-seamen tell of having applications rejected by Legion branches because only "Service" personnel qualified.
    The Legion did, however eventually broaden its membership criteria to include merchant seamen and others, a move some cynics attribute to the rapid dwindling of its potential membership stock due to the ever-growing number of ex-servicemen appearing in newspaper death notices. To the Legion's credit, once having made the commitment, it did support and play an important role in the campaign instigated and driven by the Canadian Merchant Seamen's Association, to gain "Veteran" status for merchant seamen.

5. The Canadian Merchant Navy Association was formed in 1982 at Niagara Falls, Ontario, through the efforts of its founding president, the late Merv Hartley of Niagara Falls. Growth was at first slow, news of the existence of the Association spreading primarily through word of mouth and assisted by affiliation with the Royal Canadian Naval Association. Membership was still less than 300 as late as September 1989 when the applications began to flood in as awareness spread not only of CMNA's existence but of the work its executive and other members were doing to promote the cause of "Veteran" recognition. By mid-1992, when Parliament passed enabling legislation granting the long sought recognition, membership exceeded the 1,200 mark, representing about one in three of surviving WW II merchant seamen.

6. Total comprised 321 merchant ships plus 12 stores ships and 21 maintenance ships ordered by the Royal Navy; these latter vessels were all conversions of the standard 10,000 DWT hulls. Most of the 21 maintenance ships were delivered postwar, but five were sold while still under construction and completed as merchant ships.

■ CHAPTER ONE

1. 1978 study by Alcan Shipping Services Ltd., Montreal, for the Federal Government, as reported by columnist Ronald Anderson, "A Deep-Sea Fleet," *The Globe and Mail*, Toronto, 19 January 1979.

2. Deadweight, customarily abbreviated DWT, represents the cargo carrying capacity of a merchant ship expressed as weight in tons. The most common measure of ship size, it represents the difference in the weight of water displaced when a ship is unladen (but fully ready for sea with all necessary fuel and stores aboard), and the weight of water displaced when fully loaded with cargo. As more simply defined in Peter Kemp's *The Oxford Companion to Ships and the Sea*, "Deadweight tonnage . . . is a measurement of the number of tons of cargo [a ship] can carry to trim her hull down to her allotted Plimsoll marks." The Plimsoll mark, of course, comprises the series of lines painted on the side of a ship "to indicate the draught levels to which the ship may be loaded with cargo for varying conditions of season and location." Another common designator of size is gross tonnage, which is the figure entered on a ship's certificate of registration and which is arrived at by calculating the ship's enclosed capacity below the upper deck in terms of cubic feet, and dividing the result by 100, 100 cubic feet being considered as equal to one ton. Passenger liner size is usually expressed as gross tons, warship size as displacement tons.

3. The *Royal William*, listed at 363 tons, was under the command of Captain John McDougall. As described in the National Archives of Canada's *The Archivist*, she carried seven passengers, thirty-six crew, a box of stuffed birds, six spars "produced of this province," one box and one trunk, household furniture and a harp. Fuel for the voyage comprised 253 chaldrons of coal, a chaldron in the nineteenth century being equal to 32, 36 or more bushels.

4. The *Royal William*, while not the first to cross the Atlantic under steam power, was probably the first to do so from west to east. In 1819, the *Savannah* made a crossing in twenty-nine days, but used steam propulsion only at the beginning and end of the voyage. In 1827, the *Calpe*, built in Bristol, and sold to the Netherlands to be converted into a warship, completed a steam crossing to South America. In 1838, the *Sirius*, under charter to Cunard rival British and American Steam Navigation Company, steamed all the way from Cork, Ireland, to New York in eighteen days ten hours to inaugurate the first regular scheduled trans-Atlantic passenger steamship service.

5. The annual subsidies, which were regularly stepped up, reached £173,340 sterling by 1852, making it difficult if not impossible for other lines to compete and effectively gave Cunard a virtual monopoly on the Atlantic service.

6. *The Preparedness of Canada's Merchant Marine for Two World Wars, 1913-1947*, K. S. Mackenzie, CD, Ph.D., Corporate Archivist, Canadian National. Paper presented to The Canadian Navy in the Modern World Conference, Halifax, October 1985.

7. Canadian Government Merchant Marine, Limited, Third Annual Report, year ended 31 December 1921.

8. CGMM was born with its incorporation by Dominion Letters Patent on 30 December 1918, with an authorized capital stock of $1,000,000 in shares of $100 each (*Annual Report*, year ended 31 December 1935, Canadian Government Merchant Marine, Limited). An Order In Council passed 16 March 1920 provided

for all vessels on completion being turned over to the Canadian Government Merchant Marine, Limited for operation. Previously they had been turned over to the CNR, of which CGMM now became a subsidiary.

9. PC 530, 29 January 1923, Report of the Committee of the Privy Council.

10. Canadian Government Merchant Marine, Limited, Third Annual Report, year ended 31 December 1921.

11. Peter Evans, *Ari: The Life and Times of Aristotle Onassis*, (New York: Summit Books), and by the *London Times* team of Nicholas Fraser, Philip Jacobson, Mark Ottaway, Lewis Chester, *Aristotle Onassis*, (New York: J. B. Lippincott Co). *Onassis Socrates* and *Onassis Penelope* were initially registered as Greek but in 1938 registration was transferred to Panama. In 1940 Onassis sold two of the six Canadian freighters he had purchased in 1932-33 to a Japanese shipping firm. Both were sunk by the USN during WW II. Onassis had other Canadian dealings. His pride and joy, the luxurious yacht *Christina* (sold by the Greek government in February 1994 to an unidentified Greek-American for $2.1 million), was a much modified ex-RCN WW II frigate, HMCS *Stormont*. In 1946 he acquired ten other ex-RCN frigates and converted them to passenger liners intended for an Aegean inter-island service he had proposed to the Greek government which, however, ignored the proposal. An Onassis-controlled company was also believed (but never proven) to be the owner of the notorious Liberian-registered 11,000 ton tanker *Arrow* which, while under charter to Imperial Oil, ran aground in Nova Scotia's Chedabucto Bay and befouled the coastline with its spilled cargo of crude.

12. Peter Evans, *Ari: The Life and Times of Aristotle Socrates Onassis*, (New York: Summit Books, New York).

13. A. H. Allan, to A. J. Hills, Assist to Vice-President i/c Operation, CNS.

14. Minutes of Meeting of Executive Committee of Directors of Canadian Government Merchant Marine Limited, 25 April 1933.

15. Letter 22 May 1933, A. H. Allan, General Manager, Canadian National Steamships, to V. I. Smart, Deputy Minister, Department of Railways and Canals.

16. Between 1923 and 1935, CGMM's annual results, with one exception, showed operating deficits (before interest and depreciation) ranging from a high of $1,873,695 in 1923 to a low of $17,938 in 1933. The one exception was 1935, the year before the sale of the last ten ships was negotiated, when an operating profit of $311,822 was reported.

17. *Reports of the Canada Select Committee on Railways and Shipping Proceedings*, 24 April 1928, p. 133.

18. Letter 5 November 1934, A. H. Allan, CNS General Manager, as quoted in *Reports of the Canada Select Committee on Railways and Shipping Proceedings*, 9 April 1935.

■ CHAPTER TWO

1. The *Erik Boye* was actually Danish owned but had been taken over by the Canadian Government, transferred to the Canadian flag and placed under the management of the Canadian National Steamships company for the duration. There were no casualties reported as a result of its sinking.

2. The *Bic Island* had been the Italian *Capo Noli* when she was seized by the armed trawler HMCS *Bras d'Or* on 10 June 1940, becoming Canada's first WW II prize

of war. A short time later, *Bras d'Or* herself became the first Canadian naval vessel to be sunk, in October of the same year.

3. Only 9 of the first contingent of 25 lakers survived the war, 15 of the 16 lost being to enemy action.

4. One of the names appearing on the DND/DEMS list is ex-CGMM *Canadian Cruiser*, reported sunk in the Indian Ocean by the pocket battleship *Admiral Scheer* 22 February 1941. By the time of its sinking, in fact, the 10,000 DWT *Canadian Cruiser* would have been transferred to British registry, being one of the last ten CGMM ships sold, all going to British interests when the Crown company was being wound up in 1936 (C. D. Howe, Minister of Railways and Marine, 30 April 1936, "Reports of Canada Select Committee on Railways and Shipping Proceedings"). The name was, however, revived in 1946 by Canadian National Steamships for application to a modern 16 knot Diesel-powered cargo/passenger 7500 DWT vessel. Completed postwar by Canadian Vickers at Montreal, she was one of three sister ships operated by CNS on West Indies routes. The other two were *Canadian Challenger* and *Canadian Constructor*, built respectively by Davie Shipbuilding of Lauzon, Quebec, and Burrard Dry Dock of Vancouver. Both were also namesakes of long-gone CGMM vessels. All three were sold to Cuban interests in 1958 following the shutdown of Canadian National Steamships.

5. More recent research into the records of the Registry of Shipping and Seamen, Cardiff, Wales, by Captain Paul Brick and Gordon Olmstead of the Canadian Merchant Navy Association, found names of additional Canadian casualties which, when added to others discovered since the compilation of the Government's official list, bring the total number of Canadian merchant seamen lost in World War II to 1,578 (*CMNA Newsletter*, August 1993).

6. *Stüreholm* was part of the thirty-seven-ship convoy attacked 5 November 1940 in the North Atlantic by the German pocket battleship *Admiral Scheer*. In the naval action which ensued, the convoy's lone escort, the armed merchant cruiser HMS *Jervis Bay* (7 x 6-inch guns) held off the *Admiral Scheer* (6 x 11-inch guns) long enough before succumbing to allow the convoy to scatter. The *Stüreholm* returned later to the scene to pick up survivors of the *Jervis Bay*. These did not include Captain E. S. Fogarty Fegen, RN, who was awarded the Victoria Cross posthumously for his leadership role in the brave action.

7. Later information revealed that the *Eugenie Livanos* was sunk by the raider *Michel*. Nineteen of her crew were picked up but unfortunately they were put ashore in Japan.

8. "It's Almost Too Late," Report of the Subcommittee on Veterans Affairs of the Standing Senate Committee on Social Affairs, Science and Technology, January 1991.

■ CHAPTER THREE

1. So-called Slow Convoys were assembled in Sydney, Nova Scotia, and usually comprised older ships capable of only between 7.5 and 8.9 knots. Fast convoys, made up of ships capable of between 9.0 and 14.8 knots, were assembled in Halifax. Faster ships were allow to proceed independently.

2. Acronym for Allied Submarine Detection Committee, which in 1918 developed the system of tracking submerged submarines by sound detection. In their book, *Night*

of the U-Boats, authors Paul Lund and Harry Ludlam describe how, at the outset of war, the Royal Navy believed that in ASDIC it had the ideal weapon to contain the threat of submerged U-boat attack, providing its escorts with the essential detection and tracking capability. It believed these underwater attacks would be confined mainly to daylight because, it was assumed, poor visibility at periscope depth would make night attacks unlikely. RN anti-submarine defence planners were unaware that Admiral Karl Dönitz had already conceived and planned to implement wolf-pack tactics involving night surface attacks by groups of U-boats. ASDIC was of little value against surfaced submarines and at night they could be detected only by radar, which in the early stages of the sea war was not standard equipment on escort vessels. Admiral Dönitz had actually outlined his innovative plan of attack in detail in his book *Die U-bootwaffe*, published in January 1939. The book, unfortunately, was apparently not on the RN's prewar reading list.

3. As outlined in Chapter 1, Backgrounder, CGMM operations continued until the mid-1930s, while gradual disposition of its ships was taking place. The last ten were sold in 1936. It seems, however, that CGMM lived on well into WW II, at least as a paper company under the umbrella of CNS. Eleven foreign-registered ships that had been seized or requisitioned following the outbreak of war, were assigned to CGMM, which was by then being operated as a division of CNS.

4. The two exceptions were the *Taronga Park* and the *Fawkner Park*, 4700 tonners that took the name of Australian parks in Sydney and Melbourne respectively. Both ships were so named because they were tagged to be Mutual-Aided to Australia. In the event, only the *Fawkner Park* went Down Under; the *Taronga Park* was diverted to the U.K. as one of fourteen Park 4700 tonners sent there in response to a request by the Allied Shipping Pool.

5. Defensively Equipped Merchant Ships: DEMS ratings were responsible for maintaining and manning the ships' defensive armament. In the manning of the guns, they were assisted by designated members of the merchant crew. The number of DEMS ratings varied with each ship and at different times of the war, but on the 10,000 DWT Park ships usually numbered from eight to ten.

6. The *Fort Camosun* was one of ninety North Sands 10,000-ton ships ordered from Canada by the U.S. for delivery to the U.K. under Lend-Lease. Built by Victoria Machinery Depot, Victoria, British Columbia, it had been handed over to its British crew on 1 June 1942. After sea trials and cargo loading it had cleared the Strait of Juan de Fuca and was not far south of Cape Flattery on its maiden voyage on 20 June when it was attacked by a Japanese submarine at 47:22N/125:30W.

7. Forty-three Gray ships were built by Canadian yards. At one point plans called for the delivery of six to the British, to be named after Canadian military establishments. In the event, ever-shifting war requirements resulted in a change in this program and only one, named the *Camp Debert*, was taken on by the British Ministry of War Transport. In 1944, while still retaining their Park names, an additional fourteen were transferred to the British.

8. Canadian Shipping Board submission to Hon. James A. MacKinnon, Minister of Trade and Commerce, 15 July 1943, lists the official manning scale for a 10,000 ton Park coal burner as: 1 captain, 3 navigating officers, 2 apprentices (aka cadet officers), 3 wireless operators, 1 bosun, 1 carpenter, 9 seamen, 1 chief engineer, 3 engineer officers, 1 donkeyman, 3 greasers, 12 firemen, 1 chief steward, 4 stewards,

1 cook, for a total of 46. In practice, the number varied; some ships did not carry a donkeyman, for example, and an oil burner would require fewer firemen. In addition, each ship had a complement of DEMS gunners which varied with the level of threat in the area in which the ship was expected to operate, but was commonly eight to ten.

9. *The Oceans, The Forts and The Parks*, by W. H. Mitchell and L. A. Sawyer, records the *Taber Park* sinking as having occurred 13 March 1945, "Sunk by midget submarine 52:22N/01:53E (South East of Yarmouth)." *Die U-Boot-Erfolge der Achsenmächte 1939-1945*, by Jürgen Rohwer, an exhaustive compilation of all Axis submarine operational records of sinkings, does not list the *Taber Park*. It was probably the victim of a mine.

10. Transport Minister Lionel Chevrier, in a Department of Transport pamphlet issued in 1945.

11. Six of the 104 Canadian-built Fort ships Mutual-Aided to the U.K. were lost to enemy action. Of the ninety Forts sold by Canada to the U.S., which had Lend-Leased them to the U.K., twenty-nine were lost. The postwar survivors were returned to the U.S. Maritime Commission for disposal.

12. The deck officers and the engineering officers were also organized, in the Canadian Merchant Service Guild and the National Association of Marine Engineers respectively, but it was the Canadian Seamen's Union which took the role of "point man" in the general postwar drive for better pay and improvements in shipboard working conditions.

■ CHAPTER FOUR

1. Interdepartmental Committee on Merchant Seamen, Memorandum, 3 November 1943.
   The Memorandum was signed by Arthur Randles, Director of Merchant Seamen and Committee Chairman. Other Committee members were: Captain E. S. Brand, RCN, Naval Services; Brigadier R. J. Orde, Judge Advocate General; A. L. Jolliffe, Director of Immigration; J. Scott Macdonald, Department of External Affairs; Captain J. W. Kerr, Department of Transport; Dr. C. P. Brown, MD, Department of Health; D. W. Mundell, Department of Justice; Inspector F. A. Regan, RCMP; W. J. van Allen, Committee Secretary.

2. Chapter 32, "Park Steamship Company Limited," *History of the Department of Munitions and Supply*, by J. deN. Kennedy.

3. The Place Viger Manning Pool was being operated by the British Ministry of War Transport to house British crews awaiting delivery of new Canadian-built Fort ships, which were the same as the Park 10,000 tonners, and also American-built Oceans, which were of the same basic North Sands design as the Parks and the Forts. Under the takeover agreement, the Canadian Director of Merchant Seamen had to maintain accommodation for nine hundred British seamen in the Montreal Manning Pool.

4. *The Lady Boats: The Life and Times of Canada's West Indies Merchant Fleet*, by Felicity Hanington and Captain Percy A. Kelly, MBE.

5. Approximately 1,200 were graduated from Prescott and 800 from St. Margaret's. The St. Margaret's graduates included nearly 200 cadet officers who then became indentured to Park Steamship Company for a period of four years, which qualified

them to sit for examination for the Second Mate's Certificate. Although Arthur Randles, Director of Merchant Seamen, recommended before his retirement (Memo, "Government Policy re Shipowning," 13 December 1945) that the two schools be continued to serve postwar shipping, they were officially closed 31 August 1946.

6. The Naval Boarding Service's original function was to board the merchant ships to search for sabotage and to determine that they were ready to sail in convoy. Considered especially vulnerable to sabotage during the period prior to the U.S. entry into the war, were ships loaded in American ports before coming to Halifax to join a convoy. The resolution of crew complaints was often a major factor in determining a ship's state of readiness, so the roles of conciliator and morale booster were soon added to the boarding party's duties and eventually became its central raison d'être. The full story of the Service is told by Commander Frederick B. Watt, RCN(R), in his book, *In All Respects Ready*. Commander Watt was awarded the MBE for his work in the development of the Naval Boarding Service and in particular its contribution to the improvement in general morale among merchant seamen.

7. All three of the Canadian Services had to fight continuously to maintain their national identity.
   The preferred British colonial scenario was that Canada and the other Commonwealth countries would train personnel and send them to Britain for assimilation into the British Services. The RAF, for example, resisted the formation of separate RCAF fighter and bomber squadrons and larger formations, and only under strong Canadian Government political pressure did it accept the formation of 6 Bomber Group as a distinct all-Canadian unit within Bomber Command.

■ CHAPTER FIVE

1. The more practical Americans, faced with a similar problem, made it easier for green hands, and for the peace of mind of ships' officers, by resorting to such simple solutions as sticking with left and right, and avoiding skill-demanding and time-consuming wire rope splicing as much as possible, utilizing instead quick and easy "Yankee" splices (i.e., U-clamps).

2. Parachute and Cable Device, a 2-inch rocket which "carried some 400 feet of piano wire into the air, then floated down on two parachutes in front of the attacking aircraft. The idea was that the aircraft wing would snag the wire thereby causing the aircraft to become unairworthy." *DEMS At War,* by Max Reid, Commoners' Publishing Society Inc., Ottawa.

3. Superintendent Naval Armament Depot, Halifax.

4. Letter 30 October 1990, H. R. (Reg) Redmond, Manotick, Ontario, fireman, *Riverview Park, Point Pelee Park, Rockcliffe Park.*

5. The job of the lone trimmer on each four-hour watch was to keep three firemen supplied with coal for three boilers. Working right in the bunkers he kept the coal flowing down to outlets in the stokehold. In the stokehold it was his additional job to maintain a supply of stoking coal for the fireman of the centre boiler (the firemen for the two flank boilers were within easy reach of the outlets feeding coal from the bunkers). For this the trimmer used a wheelbarrow, a task that even in modest seas could be "fun at times," as described in obvious understatement by ex-*Riverview Park* fireman Reg Redmond (Interview, 5 October 1993). In high seas, a wheelbarrow was impossible, so it became a labourious shovelful-by-shovelful task.

Ash disposal was also the trimmer's responsibility. Reg Redmond estimates that in the course of a trimmer's two four-hour daily watches, he would push, lift, shovel or otherwise move a total of twenty-four tons of coal and a ton of ashes. This was the introduction to seafaring faced by graduates of the Marine Engineering Instructional School. "The MN taught 'engineering' the hard way," says Redmond.

■ **CHAPTER SIX**

1. Lieutenant Commander Jeff Agnew, as quoted by Campbell Morrison in an Ottawa datelined report headed "Feds Consider Benefits for Merchant Marine Vets," published in the 5 February 1991 edition of *The Daily News*, Dartmouth, Nova Scotia. According to the report, merchant seamen were described as "mercenaries" in the Battle of the Atlantic by Lieutenant Commander Agnew, who was identified as a Defence Department spokesman. He was further quoted as stating that merchant seamen earned far more than their navy counterparts, and that they could work as they pleased.

2. *The Toronto Star*, 2 June 1993, "You Asked Us" column. Once signed on ship's articles, seamen were certainly subject to discipline, less rigid than military discipline it is true (and did not extend to behavior ashore), but nevertheless strongly enforced through a well-established body of maritime law which was wielded very effectively by ship masters, shipping companies and Government agencies, backed up worldwide with the threat of force when necessary, by armed units of whatever Allied Navy happened to have local jurisdiction. The Government's wartime manpower controls, conscription, the Two-Year Manning Pool Agreement and the draconian Merchant Seaman Order 1941, all combined to make it difficult and often impossible for seamen to "quit whenever they liked." In practice, for their own personal reasons, most of them just kept going back to sea because that was their job.

3. Letter, Captain E. S. Brand, Director of Trade, RCN, to J. S. Thomson, Marine Superintendent, Park Steamship Company, 25 September 1944. Such sentences were levied not by a judicial court but by a Merchant Seamen Order Board (MSOB) made up of representatives of the Navy, the Transport Department and the Immigration Branch, appointed by the Minister of Justice under the authority of the Merchant Seaman Order 1941. The Boards enjoyed sweeping arbitrary powers and there could be "no appeal to any court or tribunal from an order of the board, which order shall be final."

4. At the time the Canadian Shipping Board comparison was made, the War Risk Bonus for a Master was $62.50, and for a Chief Engineer, $50.00. Beginning 15 November 1943 these were increased to $75.00 and $62.50 respectively.

5. Under the terms of a collective agreement between the Canadian Seamen's Union and Park Steamship Company Limited, signed 19 September 1943, unlicensed personnel received wage increases. Under the new scale, which prevailed for the balance of the war, an AB received a base wage of $70.00, plus War Risk Bonus of $44.50 and Cost-of-Living bonus of $18.42 for a total of $132.92. In November 1943, the Cost-of-Living bonus was increased to $19.93. That same month the pay rates for licensed personnel were also increased (e.g., Master's gross went up to $394.93, Chief Mate's to $234.43). Even at these higher rates, the MN officers were still well below the rates prevailing in July 1943 for their Naval counterparts.

6. National Archives, File, "Randles, Director of Merchant Seamen."

7. This average figure of $300.00 per month for an American AB appears in the text of the Canadian Shipping Board submission of 15 July 1943. In Appendix 2 the CSB supplies an average figure for an American AB of $217.50. In addition, the American rates listed include what appear to be anomalies; in particular, a Chief Engineer is shown as being paid at a higher rate than a Captain. Indeed, under the American rates listed, all the engineering officers were paid at higher rates than their deck officer counterparts. The usual practice on the ships of other nations would see the Chief Engineer paid at a lower rate than the Captain. For lower ranked deck officers and engineering officers, should there be a discrepancy, it would favour the deck officers.

■ CHAPTER SEVEN

1. Personnel numbered only 1,700, all ranks, and the Navy was then operating on a skimpy annual budget of $8 million. When Brand joined NSHQ, it essentially comprised only eleven officers, including himself, plus two civilians who were in charge of stores. Rear Admiral, later Vice-Admiral, Nelles was CNS and Captain L. W. Murray (later Rear Admiral Murray, C-in-C, Canadian Northwest Atlantic) was Deputy CNS. Commander Brand, as he then was, in effect became 3 IC. Everybody had secretaries and there was a small clerical staff.
    The imposingly named Naval Service Headquarters had offices on the third and fourth floors of the old Robinson building. On the ground floor there was an Italian delicatessan, second and third floors Department of Agriculture, fifth floor the Government's Radio Licensing Branch. Brand puckishly called NSHQ as he found it at the time, "eleven men over a grocer's shop." Interview, 22 February 1967, Captain E. S. Brand, OBE, RN (Ret'd.), with E. C. Russell, Executive Officer, Directorate of History, CFHQ.

2. Cdr. F. B. Watt, RCN(R), Ret'd., author of *In All Respects Ready*, the story of the Naval Boarding Service. The Service was a function of the Naval Control Service, which was a responsibility of Captain Brand's Trade Division.

3. Interview, 22 February 1967, Capt. Eric S. Brand, OBE, RN (Rtd.), with E. C. Russell, Executive Officer, Directorate of History, Canadian Forces Headquarters.

4. Captain Brand credited Cdr. Richard H. Oland, OBE, with this quick start-up of convoy operations. Commander Oland, a veteran of WW I and postwar RCN service, had come out of retirement to become Naval Control Service Officer at Halifax, rapidly laying the groundwork for convoy assembly. According to Brand, it was entirely due to Oland's preparations that Convoy HX.1 could be assembled ready to sail by 17 September. Commander Oland died suddenly in September 1940, but not before, Captain Brand noted, "he got Halifax running as a model convoy port."

5. Cdr F. B. Watt, RCN(R), Rtd., *In All Respects Ready*, (Scarborough: Prentice-Hall Canada Inc.), p. 210.

6. Order In Council P.C. 2385, 4 April 1941.

7. Members included Norman Robertson, Under-Secretary of State for External Affairs (Chairman); P. M. Anderson, Department of Justice; H. L. Keenlyside and Saul E. Rae, External Affairs; Captain J. W. Kerr, Department of Transport; A. L. W. McCallum, Canadian Shipping Board; Inspector A. Drysdale, RCMP; Immigration

Commissioner A. J. Joliffe; Capt. E. S. Brand, Director of Intelligence and Trade, RCN.

8. Leslie Roberts, *Canada and the War at Sea*, (Montreal: A.M. Beatty Publishing, 1944), p.91.

9. Letter, Capt. E. S. Brand to Chief of Naval Staff, RCN, April 1941.

10. Internal departmental Memo, C. P. Edwards, Deputy Minister of Transport, to Ernest Dufour, Private Secretary to Transport Minister, 10 January 1942: "This is a Great Lakes Union and does not touch deep sea operations." Letter, 20 January 1942, Arthur Randles, DMS, to R. B. Teakle, General Manager, CN Steamships: "I do not know what the Canadian Seamen's Union is going to do in Halifax considering there are few members of that Union who are foreign-going seamen." Letter, 12 February 1942, Randles to J. W. Sutherland, Regional DMS, Manning Pool, Halifax: "The CSU have never had any stake or interest in men sailing on foreign articles and there is no particular service they can render the Canadian Government."

11. Memo, 23 December 1942.

12. Cdr. F. B. Watt, RCN(R), (Ret'd.), *In All Respects Ready*, (Scarborough: Prentice-Hall Canada Inc.), p.199.

13. It was calculated that sixty pairs of socks per lifeboat would be required to meet the manning scale, including DEMS gunners, of a 10,000 DWT Park ship, each of which was equipped with four lifeboats.

14. Jim Green, *Against The Tide: The Story of the Canadian Seamen's Union*, (Toronto: Progress Books, 1986).

■ **CHAPTER EIGHT**

1. Jim Green, *Against the Tide, The Story of the Canadian Seamen's Union* (Toronto: Progress Books, 1986), p. 6.

2. Jim Green, *Against the Tide: The Story of the Canadian Seamen's Union*, (Toronto: Progress Books, 1986), p. 27.

3. Jim Green, *Against the Tide: The Story of the Canadian Seamen's Union*, (Toronto: Progress Books, 1986), p. 19.

4. A CSU agent was charged with inciting seamen to desert when he boarded a ship to advise the crew of the pending walkout. He was sentenced to nine months in prison. Jim Green, *Against the Tide: The Story of the Canadian Seamen's Union*, (Toronto: Progress Books, 1986), p. 88.

5. The CSU internees were released in March 1942, nine months after the German Army swept across the eastern frontier of the U.S.S.R. on 22 June 1941 to signal the start of Operation Barbarossa. The invasion of its erstwhile partner in crime by Germany brought about an abrupt change in the Allied Nations' attitude toward the U.S.S.R. The Red Menace was expediently no longer menacing, though even without this excuse for holding the Communist Party sympathizers, the Canadian Government, still suspicious of their loyalties, proved in no hurry to release the CSU executive.

6. R. B. Teakle was appointed President of Park Steamship Company 23 April 1942, and served in that capacity until 27 October 1943.

7. Correspondence, J. W. Sutherland to Sam Pryor, CSU Business Agent, Halifax, and Arthur Randles to Sutherland, 12 February 1942.

8. Memorandum, 4 September 1942, Arthur Randles, Director of Merchant Seamen, to C. P. Edwards, Deputy Minister of Transport.

9. Memorandum, 12 January 1943, C. P. Edwards to Arthur Randles, advises that the letter was never sent and requests an updated review. Attached to the memo is an aide's note saying, "We were doing some cleaning up in the deputy minister's [C. P. Edwards] office, and he told me to send you the attached." Implied is that Randles' draft letter for C. D. Howe's signature got buried in a pile.

10. Dated 8 August 1942, Montreal.

11. E. F. Riddle became President of Park Steamship Company 27 October 1943, serving until 13 July 1946.

12. Jim Green, *Against the Tide: The Story of the Canadian Seamen's Union*, (Toronto: Progress Books, 1986), p. 97.

13. The figure of 7,705 appears in "It's Almost Too Late," the January 1991 report of the Subcommittee on Veterans Affairs, which concluded that veterans benefits should be extended to Canadian wartime merchant seamen. The same report also uses the figures of 12,000 and 10,000 for the total number of Canadian seaman who served on merchant ships during WW II. Transport Canada is cited as the source of the number 7,705 who sailed in "dangerous waters," but the Department has been unable to provide the Author with information as to how this figure was calculated. A retired official of the Department who was closely involved with postwar merchant seaman affairs and claims stated to the Author that to his knowledge and recollection, no such number was ever established by the Department, there being too many unknown factors (e.g., Canadians who served on ships of foreign registry, and Newfoundland seamen who served on British, Newfoundland and Canadian ships, as well as on others of foreign registry, and of course became part of the Canadian family when Newfoundland joined the Confederation in 1950). The qualifying term "dangerous waters" is also highly suspect. Where were there waters that were completely safe from attacks by submarines, surface raiders or aircraft, whether of German, Japanese or Italian origin?

■ CHAPTER NINE

1. Letter, 27 January 1944, C. D. Howe, Minister of Munitions and Supply, to C. L. Dewar, President, Wartime Shipbuilding Limited.

2. Thomas C. Steven, "Canadian Shipyards Notably Increase Production in 1942," in *Canadian Shipping and Marine Engineering News*, January 1943.

3. It is not clear whether this particular folklore was an accounting assessment, or was based on the fact that a wartime standard ship was considered expendable and therefore it had to successfully deliver only one cargo to justify its having been built.

4. Marc Milner, *North Atlantic Run*, (Toronto: University of Toronto Press, 1985). A fast convoy ship had to be capable of not less than 9 knots and not more than 14.8 knots. Faster ships were expected to travel independently. Slow convoys were for ships capable of between 7.5 and 8.9 knots.

5. "Park Freighter Averages 12.6 Knots" in *Canadian Shipping and Marine Engineering News.*, January 1946.

6. In the nuclear age it is perhaps too often forgotten that nuclear energy is merely the successor to, or substitute for, coal or oil or gas as the source of heat to turn water into steam to do the same things that steam has been doing for over 150 years.

7. Peter Kemp, ed., *The Oxford Companion to Ships and the Sea*, (Oxford University Press). The triple-expansion engine was developed by adding a third intermediate cylinder to the then prevalent two-cylinder compound engine, a development made possible by the introduction of improved boilers capable of higher pressures.

8. Had all manufacturing capacity not been already fully utilized, the U.S. Maritime Commission would have preferred steam turbine power. In its absence, it was accepted that the triple-expansion engines were the only practical alternative to meet an urgent requirement.

9. In their basic physical layout, the Park ships were fully standardized. However, depending on the shipbuilder and the dictates of Wartime Merchant Shipping Limited, many variations were introduced over time in the subdivision of crew accommodation space for both licensed and unlicensed personnel, as well as in the location of stowage spaces for ship's stores. These and many other modifications and improvements reflected construction experience gains, as well as the practical lessons learned with the entry into service of more and more of the ships. Whether or not a ship was a coal burner or an oil burner also made a difference in the division of internal space.

10. All three Park variants were also equipped with four quick-release wooden life rafts, two forward and two aft, located port and starboard, usually just aft of the foremast and the mainmast respectively.

11. Removable air scoops were developed for fitting in the portholes. These were baffled internally to prevent light emission, so they could be used at night during blackout as well as throughout the day. To be most effective, they had to face forward, but this meant that if they did submerge when the ship rolled, a stream of high pressure water was propelled across the cabin, cold-soaking the startled occupants of the bunks closest to the hull, and, of course, flooding the cabin.

12. John deN. Kennedy, "Wartime Merchant Shipping Limited," in *History of the Department of Munitions and Supply*, Ch. 44.

13. Naval Boarding Service Report, *Kootenay Park* (I), 13 October 1944.

14. With one exception, all of the forty-three Canadian-built Gray ships were given the Park family name. The odd ship out was the *Camp Debert*, which was delivered to the British Ministry of War Transport. Later, under the Canadian Mutual Aid Program, a further fourteen were transferred to the British without changing their Park names. Similarly, two were earmarked for Australia and both were named after Australian parks. As it happened, only one of these proceeded Down Under, the other being included in the fourteen vessels transferred to Britain. As a result of these transfers, the number of 4700 tonners operated under the Canadian flag by Park Steamship Company in the last year of the war was reduced to twenty-seven.

15. Thomas C. Steven, "Canadian Shipyards Notably Increase Production in 1942," in *Canadian Shipping and Marine Engineering News*, January 1943.

16. The figure of 400,000 rivets in a single 10,000 DWT cargo vessel appears in "The Reborn Shipyards" (Ch. 1) in *Canada and the War at Sea*, Vol. II, Part III, by Wallace Ward and J. Alexander Morton. Other requirements listed include 3,000 tons of steel shapes and plates, 110 tons of piping and tubing, 25 tons of copper wire, 11 tons of bronze, 600 different types of valves and fittings, rigging and cargo handling gear requiring 13,000 feet of wire rope and more than 500 blocks of various sizes.

17. R. C. Thompson, CBE, MA, and Harry Hunter, OBE, BSc. "The British Shipbuilding Programme in North America 1940-42" in *Canadian Shipping and Marine Engineering News*, February 1943.

18. H. R. (Reg) Redmond of Manotick, Ontario, who spent several weeks in a British hospital after being burned in July 1944 while learning to be a fireman on the *Riverview Park*, recalls that one of his hospital mates was a young American merchant seaman who had once been a welder: "The Yankee told us that welders building the U.S. Liberty ships were paid piece rates. Sometimes, to improve their earnings, instead of welding plates together properly, they would lay a welding rod in the seam and simply melt it. That struck me as crass stupidity or criminal greed. If true, it could explain why Liberties broke in half at sea." Letter, 8 January 1991.

19. Among the solutions was the reinforcing of square hatch corners. Eventually, new grades of weldable steel were developed that resisted brittle fracture down to temperatures in the vicinity of -40C.

20. I. G. Stewart, *Liberty Ships in Peacetime*, (Rockingham Beach, Western Australia: Ian Stewart Marine Publications), 1992. The Army ruling followed a report that a Liberty ship loaded with troops had split open while moored alongside a wharf.

21. As quoted by Arthur Randles, Director of Merchant Seamen, Letter, 18 February 1944, in response to comment from a Naval Boarding Service officer who "considers conditions on Park ships to be very poor."

■ CHAPTER TEN

1. *Canadian Shipping and Marine Engineering News.*, January 1946.

2. Max Reid, *DEMS At War! Defensively Equipped Merchant Ships and the Battle of the Atlantic 1939-1945,* (Ottawa: Commoners' Publishing Society Inc., 1990).

3. Report of the Naval Service Committee on "Security of Canadian Merchant Vessels in War," 31 May 1938.

4. *Naval Service of Canada*, Vol. II, (Ottawa: King's Printer, 1952), p.11.

5. Max Reid, *DEMS At War! Defensively Equipped Merchant Ships and the Battle of the Atlantic 1939-1945,* (Ottawa: Commoners' Publishing Society Inc., 1990).

6. Secretary of State for External Affairs, Ottawa, to Secretary of State for Dominion Affairs, London, 20 November 1941.

7. The American counterpart of the DEMS service was the USN's Armed Guard, which was responsible for the manning of all of the weapons positions on U.S. merchant ships. The U.S. merchant crews did not participate as was the practice on Canadian and British ships, except as ammunition passers. The USN Armed Guard complement for a Liberty ship was approximately twenty-four, plus a commissioned officer in command, more than twice the number of RCN DEMS gunners (including a petty officer i/c) normally assigned to a Park ship.

8. Memo 27 September 1944, Captain E. S. Brand, Director of Trade Division, to Naval Staff.

9. Max Reid, *DEMS At War! Defensively Equipped Merchant Ships and the Battle of the Atlantic 1939-1945,* (Ottawa: Commoners' Publishing Society Inc., 1990).

10. So-called because of an imagined resemblance of the shielded cockpit in which the operator sat, to the familiar British pillar box mail drops.

11. Memo 27 September 1944, Captain E. S. Brand, Director of Trade Division, to Naval Staff.

12. The nets were also installed on the Canadian-built Fort ships, as well as on Liberty ships supplied to the British under Lend-Lease. Torpedo nets were not adopted for American operated Liberty ships. When the booms were stowed they reached over 75 ft. above deck level; when deployed, they extended over 50 ft. beyond the sides of the ship. The nets, which had a 5 ft. x 2.5 ft. diamond mesh, worked effectively only at speeds in excess of seven knots.
   They were manufactured in Canadian prisons.

■ CHAPTER ELEVEN

1. "Canada's Shipbuilding Effort a Remarkable Achievement," in *Canadian Shipbuilding and Marine Engineering News*, August 1943, p.78.

2. While 348 10,000 DWT ships is the total cited by *History of the Department of Munitions and Supply*, the Author's count of hull numbers listed in *The Oceans, The Forts and The Parks* by W. H. Mitchell and L. A. Sawyer, shows the following: 321 completed as Fort and Park merchant ships plus 12 RN stores ships plus 21 RN maintenance ships for a total of 354. The discrepancy in totals may be associated with the fact that of the Admiralty ordered ships, 1 stores ship and 13 maintenance ships were not completed until after war's end. Ultimately, 5 were not taken over by the Admiralty but were completed as merchant ships in 1946 and 1947. The stores ships, all bearing Fort names, were operated for the RN by shipping companies and carried merchant crews, plus a Naval contingent to manage the stores function. The maintenance ships were all HMS Naval vessels and as such, though based on the standard 10,000 DWT hulls, were classified by their displacement weight, which for all but one was 8580 tons.

3. John deN. Kennedy. *History of the Department of Munitions and Supply,* (Ottawa: King's Printer, 1950), Ch. 44.

4. Wallace Ward and J. Alexander Morton, "Of Ships and Shipbuilding," in *Canada and the War at Sea*, Vol. II, Part III., (Montreal: A. M. Beatty Publishing, 1944).

5. Jak P. Mallman Showell, *U-Boat Command and The Battle of the Atlantic*, (St Catharines: Vanwell Publishing Limited, 1989).

6. The other members were: William Bennett, Principal Surveyor of Lloyd's Register of Shipping for U.S.A. and Canada; J. S. Heck, Principal Engineer Surveyor of Lloyd's Register, New York, and R. R. Powell, an Assistant Secretary, Admiralty, who was the Mission Secretary. The Mission was joined in February 1941 by John Robson, Department of Merchant Shipbuilding, Admiralty.

7. R. C. Thompson, CBE, MA, and Harry Hunter, OBE, BSc, "The British Shipbuilding Programme in North America 1940-42, Part I," in *Canadian Shipping and Marine Engineering News*, February 1943, p.30.

8. Unknowingly, the German Navy almost caused a significant delay in implementation of the British North American program when on 14 December 1940 one of its submarines torpedoed and sank the passenger cargo vessel *Western Prince*, en route to the U.K. from New York. One of the passengers was R. C. Thompson, leader of the British Technical Merchant Shipbuilding Mission, who survived the sinking and salvaged the blueprints of the planned Ocean vessels, which he was carrying back to London. Another VIP survivor of the sinking was C. D. Howe, Canada's Minister of Munitions and Supply, and a key role player in setting up of production of the riveted version of the ships to be built in Canada.

9. John deN. Kennedy, *History of the Department of Munitions and Supply*, (Ottawa: King's Printer, 1950).

10. In January 1944 some functions of the Naval Shipbuilding Branch of the Department of Munitions and Supply were transferred to Wartime Merchant Shipping Limited. The company, renamed Wartime Shipbuilding Limited, assumed responsibility for the Escort Vessel component (frigates, single screw corvettes, etc.) of the Naval program in addition to the cargo ship program. Excluded were the destroyer and small craft programs, which remained with the Naval Shipbuilding Branch. At the same time, H. R. MacMillan returned to private industry and was succeeded as president by C. L. Dewar.

11. Wallace Ward and J. Alexander Morton, "Of Ships and Shipbuilding," in *Canada and the War at Sea*, Vol.II, Part III.

12. John deN. Kennedy, *History of the Department of Munitions and Supply*, (Ottawa: King's Printer, 1950), Ch. 44.

13. John deN. Kennedy, *History of the Department of Munitions and Supply*, Ch. 44.

14. Thomas C. Steven, ed., *Canadian Shipping and Marine Engineering News*, January 1943, p.25.

15. Only 2 vessels were completed and delivered under the original British "cash" order for 26. The balance of 24 ships was paid for and delivered under the Canadian Mutual Aid program, or under American Lend-Lease as part of the 90-ship U.S. Maritime Commission order.

16. The figure 38 for the number of days from keel-laying to launch for the *Fort Romaine* appears in "Of Ships and Shipbuilding" in *Canada and the War at Sea*, Vol. II, Part III, by Wallace Ward and J. Alexander Morton; the figure of 58 for the number of days from keel-laying to delivery appears in the *History of the Department of Munitions and Supply* by John deN. Kennedy, Ch. 44, p.496.

17. Thirty-eight is cited in the *History of the Department of Munitions and Supply* as the number of berths in use at 15 January 1944, the date on which the Naval and cargo programs were merged and Wartime Merchant Shipping Limited became Wartime Shipbuilding Limited. In addition, the *History* states, there was a yard with 6 berths being used for both 3600 ton tankers and corvettes. Yet another DMS compilation dated 29 May 1942 lists a total of 42 10,000 ton berths at ten shipyards, and 9 4700 DWT berths at three shipyards. *Canada and the War at Sea* reports 44 berths whereas *The Oceans, The Forts and The Parks* gives the number as 46. The differences may simply reflect the variations in the number of berths actually being employed at a given time.

18. "Canada's Shipyards Are Helping to Finish the Job," in *Canadian Shipping and Marine Engineering News*, August 1943, p.39. By the time a hull was ready to be slid onto the marine railway, its weight was probably at least 3000 tons, presenting what to a layman seemed an awesome moving task; to the shipbuilder it was simple routine. In 1992, the marine railway was sold to Nelson & Biddle Limited of Nelson, New Zealand, by GEC Alstrom, which had earlier acquired it from Marine Industries Limited. It has since been dismantled and shipped to Nelson where, pending completion of a site environmental assessment, it was to be re-assembled and put to work once more, probably in 1994. The new owners report that though the marine railway is some fifty years old, its original steel work is in excellent condition owing to never having been exposed to the corrosive effects of salt water.

19. Marine railway detail as described in *Histoire de Saint-Joseph-de-Sorel et de Tracy* by Olivar Gravel.

20. W. H. Mitchell and L. A. Sawyer, *The Oceans, The Forts and The Parks*, (Liverpool: Seabreezes, 1966). The two Escort Carriers manned by Canadian Navy crews were HMS *Puncher* and HMS *Nabob*.

21. Memo, 20 August 1945, to Hon. C. D. Howe, Minister of Munitions and Supply, from D. B. Carswell, Director General, Shipbuilding Branch.

22. News item, *Canadian Shipping and Marine Engineering News*, June 1946.

23. News items, "Firm Price Is Maintained in Sale of China Coasters," April 1946 in *Canadian Shipping and Marine Engineering News*, and "China Buys Seven Coasters, Canadian Price Holds Firm," July 1946.

24. As listed in *The Oceans, The Forts and The Parks* by W. H. Mitchell and L. A. Sawyer, (Liverpool: Seabreezes, 1966).

25. Charles M. Defieux, "War-Built Tankers Stand Up," in *The Vancouver Province*.

26. *Marine News, Journal of The World Ship Society*, November 1993, from listings in U.K. Defence White Paper of July 1993.

27. Letter, 3 April 1991, Naval Historical Branch, Ministry of Defence, London.

28. Thomas C. Steven, "Building Marine Engines for 'Manufactured' Ships," in *Canadian Shipping and Marine Engineering News*, November 1943, p.37.

29. John deN. Kennedy, "Wartime Merchant Shipping Limited," in *History of the Department of Munitions and Supply*, Ch. 44.

30. "Secret" letter to N. A. Robertson, Under-Secretary of State for External Affairs, 5 August 1942.

■ CHAPTER TWELVE

1. J. V. Clyne, *Jack of All Trades: Memories of a Busy Life*, (Toronto: McClelland and Stewart, 1985), p.128.

2. J. V. Clyne, *Jack of All Trades: Memories of a Busy Life,* (Toronto: McClelland and Stewart, 1985), p.135.

3. J. V. Clyne, Chairman, Canadian Maritime Commission, in a memorandum to the Minister of Transport re: State of the Canadian Shipping Industry, 24 November 1949.

4. J. V. Clyne, *Jack of All Trades: Memories of a Busy Life*, (Toronto: McClelland and Stewart, Toronto, 1985), p.137.

5. Hansard, 9 December 1949, as quoted in *Jack of All Trades: Memories of a Busy Life*, by J. V. Clyne, (Toronto: McClelland and Stewart, 1985), pp.137-138.

■ **EPILOGUE**

1. *Canadian Shipping and Marine Engineering News*, May, 1943.

2. Confidential memo, 17 February 1944, Captain E. S. Brand, Director of Trade Division, RCN, to Captain J. S. Thomson, Marine Superintendent, Park Steamship Company.

3. Domestic ownership was encouraged by offering Canadian-based companies first choice, and more favourable terms than available to foreign buyers. Among the first in line in December 1945 was Canada Shipping Company Limited, represented by E. F. Riddle (*Canadian Shipping and Marine Engineering News*, January 1946), an owner and director of the Vancouver-based company. At the time, Mr. Riddle was also president of Park Steamship Company Limited, a post he had held since 27 October 1943 and which he would not relinquish until 13 July 1946. He was also said to be one of the authors of a 1944 report to the Government recommending that the wartime fleet be sold off to private interests (*The Green Hill Park Disaster*, by John Stanton, published in *The Beaver*).

4. *Canadian Shipping and Marine Engineering News*, March, 1946, p.31.

5. Jim Green, *Against the Tide: The Story of the Canadian Seamen's Union*, (Toronto: Progress Books, 1985), p.217.

6. Letter written 7 January 1991, prior to passage in 1992 of Government legislation regarding "Veteran" status for merchant seamen.

7. Memorandum Canadian Maritime Commission to Minister of Transport, 24 November 1949, *State of the Canadian Shipping Industry*, signed by J. V. Clyne, Chairman. Mr. Clyne was concurrently President of Park Steamship Company Limited.

8. Jim Green, *Against the Tide: The Story of the Canadian Seamen's Union*, (Toronto: Progress Books, 1985), p.211.

9. *The Nelson Mail*, 7 August 1992, Nelson, New Zealand.

BIBLIOGRAPHY

Bassett, John M. *Samuel Cunard*. Toronto: Fitzhenry & Whiteside, 1976

Bothwell, Robert and William Kilbourn. *C. D. Howe: A Biography*. Toronto: McClelland & Stewart, 1979.

_____. *The Canadians at War 1939/45*. Montreal (Canada Ltd): Readers Digest Association, 1969.

_____. *Canadian Shipping and Marine Engineering News*. Toronto: Maclean-Hunter Publishing Co.

Clyne, J. V. *Jack Of All Trades: Memories of a Busy Life*. Toronto: McClelland and Stewart, 1985.

Edwards, Peter. *Waterfront Warlord: The Life and Violent Times of Hal C. Banks*. Toronto: Key Porter Books Ltd., 1987.

Evans, Peter. *Ari: The Life and Times of Aristotle Onassis*. New York: Summit Books, 1986.

Fraser, Nicholas, Philip Jacobson, Mark Ottaway and Lewis Chester. *Aristotle Onassis*. New York: J. B. Lippincott, 1977.

Green, Jim. *Against the Tide: The Story of the Canadian Seamen's Union*. Toronto: Progress Books, 1985.

Hadley, Michael L. *U-Boats Against Canada: German Submarines in Canadian Waters*. Kingston and Montreal: McGill-Queen's University Press, 1985.

Hanington, Felicity and Captain Percy A. Kelly. *The Lady Boats: The Life and Times of Canada's West Indies Merchant Fleet*. Halifax: Canadian Marine Transportation Centre, Dalhousie University, 1980.

Harbron, John D. *C. D. Howe*. Toronto: Fitzhenry & Whiteside, 1980.

_____. *It's Almost Too Late*. Report of the Subcommittee on Veterans Affairs of the Standing Senate Committee on Social Affairs, Science and Technology, 1991.

Kemp, Peter, ed. *The Oxford Companion to Ships and the Sea*. Oxford: Oxford University Press, 1976.

Kennedy, John deN. *History of the Department of Munitions and Supply*. Ottawa: King's Printer, 1950.

Lamb, James B. *On The Triangle Run*. Toronto: Macmillan of Canada, 1986.

McNally, Larry, Alan Poulin, Sheila Powell, M. Stephen Salmon and Bruce Weedmark. "Crossing the Atlantice by Steam. "*The Archivist*, July-August 1990. Ottawa: National Archives of Canada.

Milner, Marc. *North Atlantic Run: The RCN and the Battle of the Convoys*. Toronto: University of Toronto Press, 1985.

Mitchell, W. H. and L. A. Sawyer. *The Oceans, The Forts and The Parks*. Liverpool: Sea Breezes,1966.

Mostert, Noël. *Supership*. New York: Alfred Knopf, 1974.

Reid, Max. *DEMS At War!: Defensively Equipped Merchant Ships and the Battle of the Atlantic 1939-1945*. Ottawa: Commoners' Publishing Society, 1990.

————. *Reports of the Canada Select Committee on Railways and Shipping*, 1920, 1925, 1928-29, 1934-36.

Roberts, Leslie. "The Canadian Merchant Navy at War" in *Canada and the War at Sea, Part II*. Montreal: A. M. Beatty Publishing, 1944.

Rohmer, Richard. *E.P. Taylor: The Biography of Edgar Plunket Taylor*. Toronto: McClelland and Stewart, 1978.

Rohwer, Jürgen. *Die U-Boot-Erfolge der Achsenmächte 1939-1945*. Munich: J. F. Lehmanns.

Showell, Jak P. Mallman. *U-Boat Command and The Battle of the Atlantic*. St. Catharines, Ontario: Vanwell Publishing Ltd., 1989.

Stewart, I. G. *Liberty Ships in Peacetime*. Rockingham Beach, Western Australia: Ian Stewart Marine Publications, 1992.

Ward, Wallace and J. Alexander Morton. "Of Ships and Shipbuilding" in *Canada and the War at Sea, Part III*. Montreal: A. M. Beatty Publishing,1944.

Watt, Commander Frederick B., RCN(R) Retd. *In All Respects Ready: The Merchant Navy and the Battle of the Atlantic, 1940-1945*. Toronto: Prentice-Hall Canada Inc., 1985.

INDEX